Metternich's Europe

A volume
in
THE DOCUMENTARY HISTORY
of
WESTERN CIVILIZATION

METTERNICH'S EUROPE

edited by
MACK WALKER

WALKER AND COMPANY
New York

Contents

Introductory Essay

Pick up a newspaper, in 1815; booksellers in the larger towns have them. The news of Europe is news of high politics, diplomacy, and war. There is gossip about what the prominent figures of high politics have been saying and doing. That was the "Europe" of the people who read newspapers in 1815. Its most eminent political figure was the Austrian statesman Prince Metternich.

The workings and the aims of high politics make the headlines in the great cosmopolitan newspapers nowadays, too. But modern journalists include many other matters that were not part of the "Europe" of 1815. The newspaper reader of 1815 would find no mention of gross national product, for example, nor of what labor wants, nor of the effect on national economies of price rises instituted by a major industry, nor of the need to foster capital formation or technological progress so as to keep up with rival powers, nor even of the farm problem. For some of these questions he might find equivalents, usually in terms of the politics and goals of leading individuals; but for many others he would not. They were not Europe.

One must not conclude from this that there was no economic motion, no social tension in the Europe of that day. Of course there was. But circumstances varied so much from place to place that these were local matters, unconnected and out of phase with one another. They did not add up to a general picture that would interest the reader who wanted to know and talk about the world outside his own homely surroundings. They were not part of what the French called *le monde*—the world, society—and they entered into the political artistry of the statesmen and the literary artistry of the writers who made *le monde* only obscurely, intuitively, or anecdotally. That is one reason why the men trained to prominence in 1815 resisted the coming of a world that measurements, totals, and classified descriptions *could* portray, and that made their ways of understanding and of acting obsolete.

The analytical and statistical descriptions we should now think fundamental for understanding a country or a continent (the descriptions one finds today, say, in an almanac or an encyclopedia) were neither possible nor did they seem useful in 1815, apart from tax surveys and some very rough population counts. The beginnings of these descriptions would come together with the end of Metternich's Europe, in the 1840's. There was no fundamental economic entity, comparable to the modern steel industry, to affect everybody, unless it was land and climate, and they were in the hands of God. Economic resources on the European Continent were uncentralized, separate, and autonomous, and so were the populations that lived directly from them. They were not interdependent—except sometimes when it came to high politics and war. Nobody talked of the laboring class, not because there were no laborers, but because they were scattered and had little in common with one another. As for finance: of course there was banking, associated mainly with state finance, some commerce, and a modicum of industry in western Europe. But not one person in a thousand was materially affected by transactions among financiers, except where fiscal decisions affected the conduct of soldiers and statesmen.

The life of any individual, to be sure, was mainly made up then as now of questions surrounding his changing prosperity, the security of his personal relations with the people around him, and so on. But these were pretty much his private concerns, or shared within a small group. They did not provide the common denominators that connected him with large numbers of others and made him part of Europe. Europe in 1815 was too diversified and fragmented, and the changes within it were too uneven, to provide many common denominators—except for the high politics of war and peace.

Except for high politics: the Congress at Vienna, called to reestablish European order out of a quarter-century of revolution and war, was a common denominator of politics the like of which Europe had never seen, nor has it since. The Congress of Vienna *was* Europe in 1815. It was attended by nearly everybody who was anybody in "the world," even by representatives of the countries defeated; and news of the doings there would sell the same newspapers in Paris, St. Petersburg, Belgrade, Rome, or London—or Boston or Philadelphia for that matter. Here a number of men were going to settle that crisis of political arrangement and political consciousness that had mauled the Old Régime of stable leadership so badly.

At Vienna the politicians and aristocrats and kings and soldiers were in charge. Reforming enthusiasm, or the brooding doctrinaire passion and moralism of a Robespierre, were more than bad form among the Europe assembled at Vienna; they were a threat to the success of its deliberations. Levity and a studied absence of principled seriousness were in style, as they are in most restorations. The Congress did not talk of the need to get Europe moving again. Europe moving was just what had been giving them trouble. Europe moving was not the Europe at Vienna.

Yet serious work was done at Vienna: the political reconstitution of Europe, with a redrawing of nearly every frontier; the establishment of an equilibrium that was to bring peace among the states. There was indeed peace among the states for forty years, but whether this was a result of an equilibrium of powers planned at Vienna, as some historians have contended, is doubtful. The assumption at Vienna was that the kind of stability sought there required more than the redrawing of boundaries. Stability was associated with social peace and ethical peace, even with moral casualness, perhaps. For stability there had to be contentment, and quiet, however these might have to be safeguarded.

* * *

What brought the politicians of Europe together at Vienna, and what made them seem Europe itself, was their shared political experience of the preceding years. The French Revolution and the Napoleonic domination of Europe that followed it had been such pervasive events that they had provided nearly everyone with the same mental equipment for viewing the world and deciding how to proceed. That is what gives the thirty-year period of Metternich's Europe its particular character. Notions of what actions or events were likely to lead to what consequences were drawn from the lessons of the recent past. The sequence seen in past events was a progression from the fashion in the later eighteenth century for "enlightened," rational, and humane practices to a quest for progress and change, then to the overthrow of order and authority, the Reign of Terror, the guillotine, despotism, and decades of continental warfare. It was the *historical* logic imposed by this succes-

sion of events that made up the lesson, rather than any essentially
logical connections among them.

Before the Revolution, the principle of rational, humane progress
and movement had been associated less with individual rights than
with supreme state authority, a situation reflected by the label
"enlightened despotism." The state and its arms had been the
bearers of change and reform, and so they had been the enemies
of the established orders of aristocracy and clergy. Some of the reformist tradition survived into the Metternich era, but on the
whole the chief politicians, the rulers and their ministers, came out
of the revolutionary period firmly attached to conservative social
elements and to political principles opposed to change. Progressive
ideas formerly associated with strong monarchs were dreaded by
monarchs uncertain of their security, with the example of revolutionary France always in their minds. Statesmen regarded any kind
of daring with fear and suspicion.

Observers had come to believe, with the support of considerable
evidence and even classical political theory, that the sequence from
reform through chaos and terror to tyranny was normal, once
under way; it was natural. The formulation is still widely used in
describing revolutions, and we have many examples that can be
described that way. So had Aristotle. The British statesman Ed-
mund Burke had used the formula very early in the Revolution, in
his *Reflections on the Revolution in France* (1790), to argue
against reform theories that directly attacked existing traditions
and institutions. Once men are encouraged to believe their circumstances can be changed, he said, they cease to find pride and fulfillment in what they are; they try to be something else, they know
not what. Once the breach is there, however small, contentment
dissolves into chaos and then into terror and tyranny. The events
that followed Burke's polemical warning gave it considerable
prestige as a political axiom. For the men of Metternich's Europe,
even a minor dissent or disorder was really the starting point in a
process of overthrow that spread with the power of a law of history.

A later age has made the belief that progress is inevitable a hallmark of liberal political ideas. But in Metternich's Europe, conservatives and liberals alike believed that the process of change was
all of a piece and fed upon itself, so that it was in the long run inevitable. In this sense, the belief in the inevitability of progress was

grimly shared by conservatives, though they were unlikely to give it the name of progress; and that is why pessimism became—again, historically rather than logically—a feature of the conservative view. They saw the simple passage of time as a remorseless enemy of themselves and the values they cultivated; historical necessity was the enemy of good and beauty. What distinguished conservatives from liberals was not the question of whether progressive change was inevitable or not, but whether it was good or not; liberals expected much the same things to come with the future, but they did not dread them. They thought the future would bring wealth, freedom, and power to themselves and to the peoples of Europe.

History's propensity for progress and liberation seemed to lie partly in the popularity of these processes. To prevent or slow the process, then, called for unpopular restraint and suppression. But those who sought to speed it up believed they could count on popularity. Ideas advocating change and offering liberation were thought of as "enlightenment" by their proponents and "infection" by conservatives; both believed fervently in the historic power of such ideas. The case for the inevitability of change became all the more credible when processes other than purely political came to be interpreted in analogous ways: technological changes made inevitable by the profits they brought and the material goods they provided; population growth and movement, associated in turn with technological change but also caused apparently by inevitable thoughtless procreation and social irresponsibility. Revolution, technological advance, and population growth all seemed self-propelled and irresistible in the long run; dissent, materialism, and indulgence dissolved existing social ties, systems of obedience, and supernatural faiths. The coining of the terms liberal and conservative in the western European politics of that time tied freedom (or dissolution) with action and the future, and discipline (or autocracy) with immobility and the past. This may be something more than a historical accident. But to understand the time, many of us even now must inquire whether there is a logical reason why there cannot be radical changes, and advances in power and wealth, where there is no freedom; and whether there is a reason why there cannot be stagnation and poverty where men are free to think and do as they please.

A hallmark of the earlier nineteenth century in Europe was the common assumption that popular liberation, material gain, and the progressive direction of history when left to itself, all went together. Think of this not as an ideal, but as a way of interpreting or forecasting events and as a guide to action; it cut across the spectrum of ideologies. Its pervasiveness and force came from the profound common experience of revolution and war that began the era. The wave of revolutions in 1848 ended the era, because, while they were the era's direct offspring and its climax, their frustration and failure taught a new Europe that the connection between freedom and progress was not spontaneous and inevitable. That put matters in a new light, for liberals and conservatives alike, and so brought an end to the age of Metternich.

* * *

Metternich's domination of European politics, which began with the fall of Napoleon in 1814 and 1815, ended with those revolutions of 1848. During the first half of the period, from 1815 until the revolutionary wave of 1830, the arts of domestic politics were almost indistinguishable from the arts of diplomacy. Revolution and Napoleon had brought European politics together into one system, and the one Europe they had made was inherited by counterrevolution and Metternich. In Metternich's phase, as in Napoleon's, England thwarted the Continental statesmen by staying engaged in their affairs, yet out of their reach.

Insofar as Metternich dominated the Europe of his era, he did so as a skillful political practitioner who thought about politics as the Europe of his era did. It would be a sterile exercise to try to distinguish genuine (or hypocritical) ideals from the expedients and strategies of Austria's first minister. Not many successful men keep their principles and the practical demands of their careers in separate compartments.

Metternich had been born a Rhenish gentleman, and had no difficulty in the 1790's in choosing between his boorish fellow students (clamoring for a revolutionary politics of power and freedom) on the one hand and the gentlemanly French exiles he met at the better homes on the other. He wrote a bitter pamphlet about the execution of Marie Antoinette, queen of France and aunt to the Austrian emperor; and in 1795 he married the rich granddaughter of Austria's greatest eighteenth-century foreign minister,

Count Kaunitz. For his rapid rise in the Austrian diplomatic service
he owed less to the power of his ideas or the persuasiveness of his
purposes than to a subtle understanding of his associates, very considerable personal charm and social talents, and a gift for sensing
the direction of European affairs that rivaled and perhaps surpassed
Napoleon's own. By 1806 he had the prize ambassadorial post at
Paris. There he studied the politics of revolution and war; and in
1809 he was Austrian foreign minister, with the duty of preserving
the Habsburg state from the violence of Napoleonic Europe.

From these experiences Metternich drew the same conclusions as
many other Europeans: revolutionary France from the beginning
had needed foreign adventures to minimize the disunity its revolt
had caused at home. True to its moralizing principles, revolution
had clothed its foreign adventures as crusades for humanity, crusades against foreign tyrants like those dethroned at home, crowned
heads intent on re-establishing their royal brethren in France and
revoking what the Revolution had achieved. The many who had
gained power, prosperity, and freedom from the Revolution had
reason to defend and support it, and so had those who hoped for
similar gains from its spread. Revolutionary France had called for
revolution among the subjects of the European states against whom
it sent its armies. It had promised French aid to all peoples who
wished to "regain" their "natural" liberties. This was the mechanism of international subversion. There seemed to be a principle
here: that revolutionary upheaval and violence not only encouraged foreign wars and aggression, expanding on a military
front beyond the borders of the revolutionary country, but revolution itself also spread internationally by subverting the susceptible
populations of neighboring states. Revolution in one country
meant war and revolution in others.

Under Napoleon the same situation prevailed. Metternich, like
many others, admired the order Napoleon had brought to France,
and blamed the Bourbon governments of the old régime for bringing the Revolution about. But he came to believe (as did Napoleon
himself) that the Corsican soldier-autocrat must continually disturb the peace of Europe as long as there was anybody left for him
to fight. He could not become a quiet ruler of France, for he had
ridden to power on the hurricane and needed victories and dis-
plays of power to ensure his future and legitimize his rule—what
else could legitimize it?

But there was a terrible corollary to the principle that revolutionary régimes make international war, and that was that they were likely to win. As far back as the War of American Independence, and especially after the victories of the French Revolutionary armies in the early nineties, observers had tended to explain the astonishing success of armies that lacked dukes to command them with the theory that popular enthusiasm for the cause made the soldiery fight better, winning the battles because of their greater fervor. Just as revolution was likely to win at home because it seduced the people, so it was likely to win abroad because a state that fought in the name of the rights of the people was militarily stronger than other states. Here was a way to explain the failures of the soldiers and statesmen of the old régimes, an explanation even they would consider. The most notably successful resistance to Napoleonic domination came as a popular, nationalist movement in Spain. To rally popular patriotic enthusiasm against the invader might be the strongest resource a statesman had. The Prussian official Hardenberg wrote about it this way to his king, after the devastating defeat of Prussia by the armies of France in 1807:

> The French Revolution, of which the current wars are an extension, has brought the French people a wholly new vigor, despite all their turmoil and bloodshed. . . . All their sleeping energies have been awakened. . . . Those who stood in the path of the torrent . . . have been swept away. . . .
> It is an illusion to think that we can resist the Revolution effectively by clinging more closely to the old order, by proscribing the new principles without pity. This has been precisely the course which has favored the Revolution and facilitated its development. The force of these principles is such, their attraction and diffusion is so universal, that the state which refuses to acknowledge them will be condemned to submit or to perish. . . .

This perilous last resort might be contemplated while France was a greater threat to the European states than their own peoples were. But alliance with the apparent Spirit of the Age was riding the tiger. Where would it end? If peace could be maintained and assured, on the other hand, such alliance might not be necessary. In the Europe built at Vienna, the principle of peace seemed opposed to the Spirit of the Age and to the peoples.

The theory that international warfare went together with domestic upheaval and change, and that to enchain the one the other must be avoided, transformed the principle of international equilibrium and peace into political repression and fear of change. And it was a theory that could be used for cynical self-interest as easily as for disinterested statesmanship. The bargaining for spoils among the powers at Vienna, influenced by the strong Austrian and English interest in establishing international peace on the Continent, fed the doctrine of equilibrium. The experience of the Hundred Days, when France went over almost to a man to a Napoleon escaped from exile, so that it took all Europe to defeat him again, strengthened the corollary that only international cooperation could restrain revolutionary imperialism and uphold the tranquillity of equipoise. Such was the birth of the Concert of Europe—a diplomatic arrangement that never ignored the need for something more than diplomatic technology, if peace was to be maintained. The Holy Alliance is a name given to an agreement engineered in 1815 by the Czar Alexander I, binding the powers of Europe to conduct their affairs on Christian principles. And the cynicism with which statesmen contemplated this document should blind nobody to the very real international agreement that domestic affairs in any one state should be conducted along certain lines, for the safety of all the states.

Metternich's great achievement was the adaptation of this European axiom to Austrian state interests. The complex and multinational Austrian Empire had more to fear from internal disruptions, mass excitement, and foreign wars than any other European power. He promptly made use of the idea of "legitimacy"—a device applied by the French foreign minister Talleyrand to give standing to the restored monarchy of Louis XVIII—to support existing dynastic arrangements as the only legitimizing principle of states. Austria's existing dynastic arrangement was very nearly the only legitimizing principle it had within, just as its stabilizing role legitimized its influence in European affairs. In Italy, Austria's predominant influence was secured by Habsburg rulership over the provinces of Lombardy and Venetia and by the extension of Austrian protection to the "legitimate" lesser princes of the peninsula. As for Germany, Austria's influence there had been rivaled for generations by the energetic Prussian state. But now Prussia and thus Germany were made subservient to Austrian diplomacy by the Prussian king's fear of revolution—a fear that could be stimulated by minor acts of violence if one were convinced that they were only the exposed tip of an iceberg, symptoms of a European infection that would ravage the Continent if the régimes did not sacrifice their independence to the common cause. This was achieved by the time of the Carlsbad Decrees, in 1819, when, in the name of collective peace and safety, the German Bund, dominated by Austria, was empowered to intervene in the several German states to suppress disorders or the advocacy of political change.

With Germany secure, Metternich applied the same principle on a wider stage. Uprisings in Italy and Spain in 1820 showed that "European revolutionary conspiracy" was not dead. The affected monarchs scurried for cover when faced with what might otherwise have seemed minor mutinies—such was the belief that the disturbances were only the surface stirrings of a terrible tide. Metternich brought before the Concert of Europe the doctrine of "intervention" on a European scale to prevent changes in the system of government of any state. Accordingly, the basis and the work of Metternich's European Concert was the suppression of any change; the effectiveness of "Europe" as an international instrument depended on the proposition that internal disorders, since they had European ramifications, were too much for any one government to handle, and that if they were not suppressed they would in the natural course of events end by attacking the rest. This was the theme on which Austrian pre-eminence in Europe relied.

There is no doubt that the particular interests of states might conflict with Metternich's principle of intervention. The Czar Alexander's enthusiasm for intervening all over Europe was a constant threat to the interests of Austria itself. Successive events called for careful discrimination, not to say sophistry, in expounding the doctrine. But the real threat to "Europe" from the conflicting interests of states came when European statesmen saw that there was more to be gained in pursuit of their separate interests than there was to fear from change, disorder, or the disapproval of their European colleagues. The first open breach in the system came from England.

The 1820 revolt in Spain was connected with Latin-American wars of independence; and Great Britain by virtue of its maritime power could expect to dominate Latin America commercially and politically if the area could be made and kept independent of other European states. More specifically, an independent and unstable revolutionary government in Madrid suited England better than a conservative one based on the power of England's overseas rival France, which planned to do the intervening in Spain in 1820. Accordingly Foreign Minister Castlereagh, though an architect of the Concert of Europe, refused to support European sanction (the Troppau Protocol) for intervention in Spain. The Italian case was nearly analogous to the Spanish one, from the British point of view; where England's Mediterranean fleet dominated, Britain had reason for preferring small and weak independent states to the rule of the major European powers of the Concert. That same fleet and that same predominance of maritime over Continental European interests made Great Britain invulnerable to Continental retaliation. Relations between Britain and the conservative coalition worsened (the Monroe Doctrine was one outcome of this development) to the point where the new British foreign minister, Canning, could rejoice in the divergence between the "liberal" and the "conservative" forces in international affairs, and announce in 1822: "Things are getting back to a wholesome state again. Every nation for itself and God for us all! The time for Areopagus, and the like of that, is gone by."

Great Britain's state and commercial interests probably suffice to explain, without citing ideological or constitutional reasons, why it assumed a "liberal" foreign policy in defending revolutionary movements against conservative intervention. It is hard to see why there need be an essential connection between the domestic institutions of a country and the calculations of its diplomats. Yet that too is in the character of Metternich's Europe; it was probably no more accidental and no more hypocritical for England to be on the side of liberal international actions than for Austria to be on the conservative side. For England feared change far less, abroad and even at home (especially a popular figure like Canning), and England could hope to reach competitive gain from a condition of international flux. British statesmen and their constituents could imagine that time and the free flow of events into the future were on their side; Metternich and his associates never could. If Metternich's great achievement was to adapt fear—of what might come if changes were allowed—into an effective instrument of Austrian state interests, he had to pay the price of a negative attitude toward

nearly every political event. It was a serious disadvantage, which
he recognized very well, and gloomily. Canning, whom Metternich
called a "malevolent meteor hurled by an angry Providence against
Europe"; Canning, who spoke of "the union of public sentiment
with the public councils"; Canning, ally of Latin-American rebels
and the North American Republic (which Metternich labeled as
the source of a "flood of evil doctrines and pernicious examples")—
Canning and Great Britain seemed to have the advantage of history, for they feared less what might come from allowing nature
to take its course. "Every man for himself and God for us all" was
a motto they conceived to serve their interests, material and political; time and flux and freedom all worked for them. Metternich
believed that these things worked against him, and against the kind
of world he could live in. And the political, economic, and social
events that ensued confirmed his melancholy expectation.

* * *

British politics at the end of the twenties were dominated by
agitation for Catholic emancipation (passed in 1829) and the immense question of parliamentary reform to broaden and more
nearly equalize the suffrage (passed in 1832). And now a new
revolution occurred in France, apparently moving in harmony
with the reform wave in England.

The French Revolution of July, 1830, led by liberal publicists
and Paris radicals, was promptly identified as a breakthrough for
the liberal camp. It had been directed against the ultraconservative
Charles X, and installed Louis Philippe, Duke of Orleans, of the
notoriously liberal younger Bourbon line, as constitutional King
of the French. If more proof were needed of what the July Revolution signified in European politics, it was followed promptly by
risings in Belgium against the Dutch king, in Poland against
Russian rule, and by significant stirrings in Italy and Germany.
Metternich said the July days in Paris were the bursting of a dike.
The Vienna dynastic settlement in France had been a principal dam
against the wave of European revolution; now revolution was in
flood again, and it would not stay penned up in France! Indeed,
many of the Belgian Catholics and liberals in revolt did have close
connections with the French Left; Italian insurgents hoped for
support from the liberal French government against their rulers

and the Austrian overlords; and there was reason to believe that the strongly conservative Czar Nicholas I was prevented from taking action to suppress revolution in western Europe by the diversion in Poland.

Thus political change and revolution in many parts of Europe *were* all of a piece, and sustained one another. The defeated Poles were widely held to be martyrs of a European liberal cause, and the western liberal peoples had shirked a fraternal duty by not coming to their aid. "Noble heart! Warsaw! She has died for us!" begins a famous verse that appeared in Paris; and when the news of Warsaw's fall reached the city, crowds shouting "*Vive la ré-publique!* Vengeance! War with Russia!" smashed the windows of the royal palace.

To confirm further the international character of European political movements, the new revolutionary wave came at a time when the eastern conservative powers were divided, regarding one another with suspicion, over what to do about a Greek war for independence against the Turks. The revolt had persisted through the twenties and had led to war between Russia and the Turkish Empire. Sympathy for the Greek Revolution, and after 1830 for those in Belgium and Poland, offered a kind of surrogate liberalism, an enticement into the liberal international camp to many Englishmen and Frenchmen even of quite conservative domestic sentiments and interests. To favor the liberal nationalist revolts against rival powers was to adopt the liberal path in foreign policy, and this in the long run was bound to affect one's whole political stance. Foreign affairs offered an opening to the Left, and made it easier and more popular for statesmen to come down on what was thought the liberal side at home.

Very soon after the establishment of the Orleanist monarchy, certain concrete international events joined France with Great Britain in an overtly liberal diplomatic bloc, and widened the gulf dividing them from a distinctly conservative bloc composed of Austria, Russia, and Prussia. This happened despite Louis Philippe's efforts to present himself to the conservative powers as a man of moderation who would not unleash revolution and annexation beyond his borders, and despite his efforts at home to keep the movement of French politics from going further Left. Once more the diplomatic events are explicable in terms of the self-interest of states, and the diplomatic process took place without any neces-

sary reference to political ideals; but the outcome, in true early-
nineteenth-century style, firmly associated liberal régimes with
liberal foreign policies.

Belgian revolution threatened to bring British and French state
interests into conflict. The solution, satisfactory to both, was an
independent Belgium with the most liberal constitution in Europe,
formed and defended by Anglo-French cooperation in defiance of
the Vienna Settlement and the wishes and interests of the eastern
conservative powers. To be against the conservative powers meant
to be against the archconservative Russia of Nicholas I, oppressor
of the Poles; and soon enough, England and France, in pursuit of
their strategic and commercial interests, found themselves together
in opposition to Russian state interests in the eastern Mediterranean. In the First Egyptian Crisis (1832–33), British and French
fleets confronted a Russian effort to establish itself as a Mediterranean power, and perhaps to penetrate and control Turkish affairs.
Russia turned to Austria and Prussia for support against the enmity
of the British and French (whom diplomatic historians at this
stage begin to call "the maritime powers," when they do not call
them "the constitutional powers"). And the cement of the agreement binding Russia, Austria, and Prussia that emerged from their
consultations was a mutual guarantee of the slices each held of
Poland, against any change revolution might wreak there—Poland,
whose national martyrs were heroes of western liberal idealism.
That was the Treaty of Münchengrätz, in 1833; and when word
of it got to Paris and London there was dark talk about the iniquities of the Holy Alliance.

In the next year France and Britain replied to Münchengrätz
with an agreement of their own respecting Spanish dynastic
struggles, "of course taking," writes a British historian, "the constitutional side." In the arena of the Iberian Peninsula the diplomatic mechanism was even more complex than in the Turkish
Empire, but somehow England and France ended by backing little
liberal princesses for the thrones of both Spain and Portugal against
the wicked reactionary uncles with whom the conservative powers
saddled themselves. The outcome was a diplomatic defeat of the
Münchengrätz powers, who could not contest a France and
England of one mind on Iberian affairs. When the representatives
of the eastern powers at Madrid learned of the Anglo-French
alliance they simultaneously asked for their credentials and went

home, and the British foreign minister Palmerston wrote: "This treaty establishes between the constitutional states of the West a quadruple alliance [France, England, and the Spain and Portugal of the little princesses] which will serve as a counterbalance against the Holy Alliance of the East." French entry into the alliance, by the way, had been mainly the work of Talleyrand, who had served the diplomacy of Revolution, Empire, Bourbon Restoration, and July Monarchy, and who was the greatest cynic in Europe.

The liberal constitutionalism of the July Monarchy was an important reason why France was regarded with suspicion by the conservative powers, so that Louis Philippe was obliged to reconcile himself with the foreign policy of England. Liberal sentiment within France affected him too. It can be argued with considerable force that the development of two camps—one in which liberal foreign policy coincides with liberal domestic régimes, over against one made up of régimes conservative at home and abroad—resulted from the predominant social compositions of the several countries, and thus neither from diplomatic accident nor political ideals. What united home liberalism with foreign-policy liberalism, the explanation goes, was a strong infusion of commercial motives into state decisions, reflecting important political strength in the hands of a commercial or industrial middle class, a bourgeoisie. This kind of explanation dates, in fact, from the time of Metternich's Europe. In both Belgian and Egyptian matters, Britain and France each had interests that were in part economic. To call them "the maritime powers" implies such an explanation; it identifies them as commercial. To call them commercial suggests in turn why they were constitutionally liberal, on the grounds that a country with a large commercial, bourgeois class that is politically influential is likely to be liberal and parliamentary in its domestic political life and forms. This subject will be more fully developed a few pages farther on, when the discussion turns to the political import of economic change for Metternich's Europe. Britain and France had the most highly developed commercial and industrial economies among the five major powers, and it is not difficult to attribute their liberalism to this fact, and the conservatism of the east to economic backwardness and an agrarian character.

In the case of England, nobody doubted or doubts now that the strong commercial and industrial development of the country was a factor for constitutional liberalism at home and also for a foreign

policy of breaking the holds of conservative old régimes in pe-
ripheral and colonial areas, sometimes by supporting revolutionary
movements there. The case of France is more difficult. The July
Monarchy that entered the liberal (or constitutional, or maritime)
international camp was indeed called the "bourgeois monarchy"
from its inception, both at home and abroad. But "bourgeois" was
more nearly a cultural than an economic characterization. It was
an epithet like "philistine," and had more to do with Louis Philippe's black frock coat and umbrella than with the actual influence
of entrepreneurs on his government. It meant the absence of the
political drama and dash France had known so long from nobility
of blood, revolutionary leaders, and military heroes. As an epithet,
it was directed against the citizen-king's policy of studied moderation, the *juste-milieu;* the bourgeois materialism of which both
reactionaires and fervent liberals accused his régime largely meant
its unwillingness to take risks for dramatic nonmaterial goals and
ideals. This moderation of course provided security for financial
investment, and brought about a strong influence of the comfort-
ably wealthy on politics. But it did not mean high profits from
rapid industrial expansion or economic imperialism.

Rather early in Louis Philippe's reign, however, his government
took on that color of government in the interest of an economic
class that was caught and perpetuated in the socialist thought, especially the Marxian, taking shape during the years of the July
Monarchy. What turned the notion of dull bourgeois moderation
and the *juste-milieu* into the idea of bourgeois class oppression of
the laboring poor was mainly this: government efforts to enforce
social stability for political reasons, to avoid sliding off into the
revolutionary chaos presumed likely to follow any sharp political
upheaval, turned to economic repression when applied to insurrections of workers in places like Paris and Lyons. These events
progressively took on the character of a class struggle, between a
middle class in control of the monarchy and a proletariat. A specific marriage between political and economic radicalism, between
romantic intellectuals and the angry poor, came when the government seemed to lump secret political societies and workers' leagues
together as dangerous "associations," and the two movements
began to throw out feelers toward each other. The Chartist movement in England showed a comparable combination of political
radicals and the economically deprived. But the reason for con-

sidering France particularly in this connection is that there, more than anywhere else, the political tradition of the great Revolution was strong. Perhaps the most distinct and crucial feature of European history in the nineteenth century is the way in which the tremendous economic and technological changes of the century (and the demographic and social changes that accompanied them) were incorporated into the framework of political traditions and axioms left by the experience of the Revolution.

*   *   *

The growth of European industry, cities, and population in the nineteenth century constituted visible changes that seemed connected and seemed to be going somewhere. Historians agree with contemporaries that population growth and industrialization were related developments, though the exact connections are not certain. Probably the best place to study the connection is in the growth of cities, which grew by virtue of migration from the countryside, urged on by rural population growth or attracted by the higher wages and greater excitement of town life. The large town populations supplied the concentrated volume of labor that industrial technology and organization required, and industry provided productive employment for the crowds of migrants from the countryside.

The great cities of western Europe approximately doubled in size between 1815 and 1848, and the factory system grew up in such places. Often indeed a "factory" was not more mechanized to begin with than the old hand-tool trades had been; the advantages of organizing large numbers of workers in one place, with some rational division of labor, were often exploited before the technological advances we generally call industrialization. All the same, the pooling of labor in cities made the large, expensive machine and power plant feasible and economical. No part of Europe, to be sure, was heavily urbanized or industrialized by our modern standards in the early nineteenth century. But growth came at an increasing rate. Plotted graphs would have curved toward infinity: what mattered about economic growth in Metternich's Europe was less the effect already experienced than what it seemed to portend.

England led the way in economic development, so that England for the Continentals was an advance look at their own futures. England led partly because of good supplies of the coal and iron needed for this new kind of industry, but also because the highly developed English commercial system, and the profits it had accumulated, provided the high capital investment that heavy industry required. Moreover, the British political system at least since the end of the seventeenth century had accepted the idea that private profit for individuals was a legitimate aim of government action or inaction. Government sympathy for private economic interest might appear in the form of plain parliamentary corruption or favoritism. Or it might appear in economic theories of the harmony of interests, like those developed by Adam Smith, who argued that the pursuit by each of his own self-interest would result in benefits for the whole nation.

Most Continental governments had tried more or less methodically to create and control economic enterprises for the sake of the fiscal resources and self-sufficiency they might bring. But this had usually conflicted with the interests of individual entrepreneurs, and had rarely succeeded on a large scale. The English practice of leaving to private interests freedom of action, and influence on government through the House of Commons, seemed a better path to the entrepreneurial success and economic growth the future demanded. Accordingly, economic progress and industrialization were associated with constitutional government and individual freedom. Since the Middle Ages the town-dweller, the bourgeois, had been considered a freer individual than the members of the rural feudal régime that surrounded him. Now the bourgeoisie, the class of industrial and commercial entrepreneurs, became identified as the bearer of liberal doctrines and of the economic revolution that seemed to characterize the coming time.

Actually, the main spokesmen for liberal doctrines and even economic freedom were not bourgeois in a technically economic sense at all; they were more likely to be intellectuals or government officials. But such was the determination of the nineteenth century (and, more uneasily, of our own time) to believe that change and progress were all of a piece, that the bearers of the visible economic and social change were presumed to be the bearers of fundamental political change. Industrialization was lumped together with liberal revolution as the historical enemy of the political order.

As economic change took on the character of historical growth, not only the middle class assumed the role of bearers of change, but the working poor were soon assigned a historic part as well. Insofar as the working *class* was a result of urban industrialization, it was a new phenomenon. The city mob was no new thing in Europe, and neither was poverty. But Metternich's Europe knew revolution was made in cities, and cities were made by the accumulation of population and by industrialization. History transformed the crowd into the proletariat—a word increasingly common by the forties. It is not certain whether poverty was more serious or more wide-spread in the early nineteenth century than it had been before. In the past most cities, being small and stable enough to do so, had excluded most people who did not assume some stake in the existing social order by plying a secure skilled trade or profession. The rural poor were eternal, but too scattered to make much political mischief by themselves or to attract much notice. Poverty and insecurity invaded the cities now in a volume probably only Paris and London had known before. The social problem was quite unlike the old problem of poverty; it came from the changes of the century, it marked them, and it would have to be met by change. Concern for the poor had become more than common charity and humanity; it was part of an attitude toward the coming world.

No one doubted that the smoking chimney, the railroad track, and the sprawling workers' suburb were symbols of the future. They, too, were symptoms of an age in motion, linked with the irresistible force of political liberation—or dissolution. In such a time, phrases like "the spirit of the age" and "the progress of the century" could become commonplace. And like revolution, its new partner economic development was international in scope, connecting what went on in a country with Europe at large, for the movement of money, labor, goods, and techniques was at odds with state boundaries. The "natural" quest of capital for higher returns, of industry for markets, of the unemployed for work, and of railroads and canals for profitable location all attacked the integrity of administrative or political borders, and undermined the efforts of those who sought control and tranquillity within them. Some Europeans rejoiced to see it; others felt only gloom and anger, but they too saw it. To anyone who had a vision of the new economy and society that was coming inexorably into being—whether he liked it or not—what had been done at Vienna seemed a fossil remnant of another age.

* * *

What to do about this new age, and how to keep the forces for change from destroying men's places in their world, and then, having isolated them from what they knew, from crushing them—these were problems that troubled some of the most honorable minds of the time. There are better places than this introductory essay to look for a description of the advent of the isms, and for formal analyses of them. But the political ideologies of the early nineteenth century were significantly similar in their conscious striving for harmony of men with their environments and of men with other men. Conservatives sought harmony through quietude and habit, liberals through the "natural" free interaction of men and groups. Others (like the social revolutionary Marx, for example, or the messianic nationalist Mazzini) sought equilibrium and an end to conflict as the culmination of active and sometimes violent reform. All, I should say, believed that the disharmony they sought to overcome was a peculiarity of their own age and the changes it had wrought, for disharmony came from the incongruity of the traditions of the past with the vital forces of the present. The nineteenth century was something new, and it had to find new means to spiritual and social harmony.

A useful objection can be made here. The important cultural movement among young students and poets around the twenties—call it the romantic mood, or late romanticism—emphasized the clash of individuals with their environments. Young romantic admirers of Byron were very interested in themselves, and in differentiating themselves from the stuffiness and fussiness of the established world of their elders. Yet romanticism was a mood and not an ideology, and it grew in part from the conscious youth of its adherents; and the yearning of romantic youth for absorption of their selves into an ideal mission or goal is unmistakable. An earlier generation of romantics had blamed individualism and materialism, then attributed to the eighteenth century, for the terrors of revolution and war, and they often sought to immerse themselves in what they thought to be the mystic communion of the medieval Church. Admiration for medieval political forms brought many into the conservative camp. But the years when Restoration was in control changed all that. Victor Hugo, for example, turned from a devotion to cathedrals and kings to a devotion to common men, preferably ugly ones—but notice that in both stages the enemy was the bourgeois, the philistine, the comfortable Biedermeier.

Byron himself died in Greece, fighting in the name of human liberty to unite and to free from foreign domination that race presumed heir to the serene genius of classical antiquity. The strength of the Philhellenic movement throughout Europe showed that it stirred sentiments based on more than devotion to a dubious Mediterranean nationality. The political organization of Metternich's Europe divided peoples whose natural unity seemed apparent from language, history, or geography, and imposed foreign rule upon them. It frustrated discovery of their true identity, and corrupted development of their national genius. Young men turned to the ideal of nationality as a fulfillment of natural harmony within peoples and among peoples. The remarkable Napoleonic cult that arose in France dreamed of a fusion of people with heroic purpose, and its members believed that their Napoleonism was directed against the governments, not the peoples, of Metternich's Europe. Socialism attracted many of the Romantic-minded; and socialist doctrines especially in their early-nineteenth-century forms dwelt on association and love and spiritual harmony among men.

The ideological movements differed in what the participants thought the specific causes of present frustration and disharmony were. Liberal doctrine held that restraints on individual freedom caused the trouble, and that—a remarkable assumption—social harmony would be greatest where "artificial" restraints were fewest. But also those who denounced liberal individualism from the Left, on the grounds that it set man against man and replaced the values of the human spirit with crass materialism, had no thought of reducing freedom. Those who sought to overcome the fragmented Europe of the states, where petty princes ruled, with love for one's nation rarely thought of making hate among nations. Over against the great fact of an old Europe guided from Vienna and sustained by the armies of the Czar, the differences among the dissatisfied were merely sectarian. All seemed part of one historic force because they leaned together upon Metternich's bulwark against history. The differences among them, and features of young ideas less pleasant to contemplate, were not apparent until the bulwark of Metternich's Europe gave way and they had freedom to mature.

At the end of 1847, Metternich wrote that the year past had been the most confusing he had ever experienced. Europe was full of contradictions. He warned that matters would come out into the open in 1848. Purely political and administrative problems might be understood and controlled, as always; but social movements, wrote the old chancellor, went their own way, and were outside his grasp.

By that time men who had been young with the century were reaching maturity and influence. The generation that believed in the future, and believed that time was on its side and revolutionary change inevitable, was sure of victory for natural harmony and progress against the unnatural, archaic, unpopular, autocratic, oppressive, doomed old Europe of Metternich.

Then with victory the future would be allowed to happen, and they would lead, and the springtime of peoples would come.

I

War and Revolution

In about 1810, Napoleon Bonaparte, emperor of the French, appeared to have the affairs of Europe firmly under his control. Central and southern Europe, except for that area in Spain where guerrilla activity persisted, were in his hands; Russia, at the other end of the Continent, had been forced to come to terms; only England remained inaccessible behind its navy. Bonaparte the Corsican soldier had taken the daughter of the greatest house in Europe, the Archduchess Marie Louise of Austria, to be his empress.

What reasons could be found for his total defeat and exile five years later? Perhaps even the Habsburg marriage was as much a sign of parvenu insecurity as it was of imperial triumph; Napoleon had to pay the price of leaving the Austrian emperor on his throne. More directly, despite all his conquests and apparent military supremacy, Napoleon did not dare or could not dare to leave the Russia of Alexander I free to succumb to British diplomacy and subsidies and to turn against him. In 1812 he drove on into limitless Russia, in a campaign beyond even his capacity. His terrible failure and defeat were the beginning of the end. A European coalition against him revived; and in France itself, opposition compounded of war-weariness and distaste for constant innovation arose against a soldier-emperor who was no longer invincible. In 1814 the Allies were in Paris. The Vienna Congress began, but it completed its work of reconstituting Europe only after the alarming interruption of the Hundred Days, Waterloo, and the second abdication and exile of Napoleon.

Europeans could not be sure, even then, that peace and stability were secure. They had reason to believe (the reasons are more fully developed in the general introductory essay) that war and revolution were inseparable, and that any unrest, however feeble and diffuse, was continental in its implications. Now it is not surprising, in retrospect, that there were many symptoms of unrest throughout Europe after twenty-five years of upheaval. Nor is it suprising that contemporaries took such symptoms very seriously.

Germany was a critical area, for reasons that combined questions of interstate and domestic conduct; and interest soon centered there. The German Bund, or confederation of states, was the most disarrayed part of Europe in terms of political order and monarchic control, and also

of international relations. The two most important members of the
Bund, Prussia and Metternich's own Austria, were traditional rivals
for favor and influence in Germany; yet Austro-Prussian understanding was necessary for security against the unpredictable actions of the
Russia of Alexander I. Metternich's foreign policy required that he
impress the need for understanding, on his terms, upon the nervous
King Frederick William III of Prussia. The second section of readings
in this book (pp. 68–136) will treat this theme. But Germany was also
an arena for dramatic student agitation and for the publication of radical literature, the importance of which was hard to gauge, let alone
control, because of the dozens of mutually suspicious tiny states that
composed the federation. There was a danger that some German prince
—perhaps even the king of Prussia, tempted by ambitious ministers—
might try to exploit German political unrest and ride it to power over
his neighbors, in just the way that popular unrest and the politics of
expansion had fed each other in the recent past. In 1817, five hundred
students from all over Germany burned emblems of reaction and petty
despotism at Wartburg Castle, in a combined celebration of the Reformation and victory over France, calling for a united Germany. The
event aroused great excitement, for local disturbances and agitation
were a threat to the security of the states and the system of states.

Germany, in summary, was Europe writ small; and in Germany the
Metternich pattern for European politics had its beginning and its first
trial, and established the base from which it was extended into Europe.
The process began with the murder of Kotzebue—a czarist agent and
dramatist who made fun of students—by an unbalanced student in the
spring of 1819.

A CHRONOLOGY

1789	Onset of the French Revolution
1793	Execution of Louis XVI
1793–94	The Reign of Terror. War between France and a European coalition
1799	General Napoleon Bonaparte to power in France
1806–7	Napoleon defeats Austria and Prussia, and makes a settlement with Russia
1812	French invasion and retreat from Russia
1814	Allied armies invade France. Napoleon abdicates
1814–15	Congress of Vienna
March–June, 1815	The Hundred Days
September, 1815	The Holy Alliance
1816–17	Disturbances in many parts of Europe Wartburg Celebration, October, 1817
March, 1819	Murder of Kotzebue

BIBLIOGRAPHY
F. B. Artz, *Reaction and Revolution, 1814–1832* (New York, 1934).
C. Brinton, *A Decade of Revolution, 1789–1799* (New York, 1934).
G. Bruun, *Europe and the French Imperium, 1799–1814* (New York, 1938).
J. Lucas-Dubreton, *The Restoration and the July Monarchy* (New York, 1929).
F. M. H. Markham, *Napoleon and the Awakening of Europe* (London, 1954).
H. Nicolson, *The Congress of Vienna* (New York, 1929).

1. Metternich's Conversation with Napoleon, June 26, 1813

After Napoleon's failure in Russia in 1812, his control of central Europe began to crumble. Russian and Prussian armies, supported by English subsidies, entered the field against him there, and Austria made ready to do so. By attacking at Bautzen in Saxony in May, 1813, Napoleon stemmed the allied advance at great cost. During May and June, Metternich journeyed to visit first the allied leaders, then Napoleon, to determine whether Austrian entry would now be safe, timely, and profitable. Six weeks after the conversation reported below, Austria joined the war against France. Metternich's account was written in 1829, presumably from notes and dispatches of 1813. How much hindsight reasoning entered the account is impossible to say, but important to consider. [Clemens L. W. Metternich-Winneburg, *Memoirs*, I (London, 1880), 184–192.]

I TRAVELLED from Gitschin on June 24, arrived the next at Dresden, and went to Count Bubna. Napoleon was just then absent from Dresden, and returned in the evening of the day of my arrival. I therefore did not receive Napoleon's invitation to go to him till the next day, the 26th. His head-quarters were at the Marcolini Garden, near the Elster meadows. He had not the courage to live in the town; more than twenty thousand men of his troops were assembled in Friedrichstadt, and about this suburb.

The position of Napoleon with regard to the army and the French people was at that time a very critical one. The nation, formerly split up into several different parties, had now only two—the party of the Revolutionists and the party of the Bourbon Royalists. The first of these consisted of the immense number of individuals whose fate was bound up with the Government, or who relied on it for their positions, their professions, or their property, which was mostly derived from the nation. The first party lamented the precarious position in which Napoleon's love of conquest had placed their interests; the latter, not yet daring to raise their heads, waited with anxiety to see the result of the new campaign, for which the nation had just made new and enormous efforts.

The French army sighed for peace. The generals, without exception, had little confidence in the issue of a war which was more than unequal when the Russians and Prussians entered into the new alliance. The hatred of the German races could hardly be longer restrained by the efforts of the Governments of the Confederation of the Rhine, and when the attitude of this Government itself began to be somewhat equivocal, Europe looked all the more anxiously at Austria.

The appearance of the Austrian Minister of Foreign Affairs at Napoleon's head-quarters could, under such circumstances, only be regarded by the leaders of the French army as decisive in its results. I was received in Dresden with this feeling. It would be difficult to describe the expression of painful anxiety shown on the faces of the crowd of men in uniform, who were assembled in the waiting-rooms of the Emperor. The Prince of Neufchâtel (Berthier) said to me in a low voice, "Do not forget that Europe requires peace, and especially France, which will have nothing but peace." Not seeing myself called upon to answer this, I at once entered the Emperor's reception-room.

Napoleon waited for me, standing in the middle of the room with his sword at his side and his hat under his arm. He came up to me in a studied manner, and inquired after the health of the Emperor. His countenance then soon clouded over, and he spoke, standing in front of me, as follows:

"So you, *too*, want war; well, you shall have it. I have annihilated the Prussian army at Lützen; I have beaten the Russians at Bautzen; now you wish your turn to come. Be it so; the rendezvous shall be in Vienna. Men are incorrigible: experience is lost upon you. Three times have I replaced the Emperor Francis on his throne. I have promised always to live in peace with him; I have married his daughter. At the time I said to myself you are perpetrating a folly; but it was done, and to-day I repent of it!"

This introduction doubled my feeling of the strength of my

position. I felt myself, at this crisis, the representative of all European society. If I may say so—Napoleon seemed to me small!

"Peace and war," I answered, "lie in your Majesty's hands. The Emperor, my master, has duties to fulfil, before which all other considerations fall into the background. The fate of Europe, her future and yours, all lie in your hands. Between Europe and the aims you have hitherto pursued there is absolute contradiction. The world requires peace. In order to secure this peace, you must reduce your power within bounds compatible with the general tranquillity, or you will fall in the contest. To-day you can yet conclude peace; to-morrow it may be too late. The Emperor, my master, in these negotiations is only guided by the voice of conscience; it is for you, Sire, now to take counsel of yours."

"Well now, what do they want me to do?" said Napoleon, sharply; "do they want me to degrade myself? Never! I shall know how to die; but I shall not yield one handbreadth of soil. Your sovereigns, born to the throne, may be beaten twenty times, and still go back to their palaces; that cannot I—the child of fortune; my reign will not outlast the day when I have ceased to be strong, and therefore to be feared. I have committed one great fault in forgetting what this army has cost me—the most splendid army that ever existed. I may defy man, but not the elements; the cold has ruined me. In one night I lost thirty thousand horses. I have lost everything, except honour and the consciousness of what I owe to a brave people who, after such enormous misfortunes, have given me fresh proofs of their devotion and their conviction that I alone can rule them. I have made up for the losses of the past year; only look at the army, after the battles I have just won! I will hold a review before you!"

"And it is that very army," I answered, "which desires peace!"

"Not the army," interrupted Napoleon, hastily. "No! my generals wish for peace. I have no more generals. The cold of Moscow has demoralised them. I have seen the boldest cry like children. They were physically and morally broken. A fortnight ago I might have concluded peace; to-day I can do so no longer. I have won two fights, I shall not conclude peace."

"In all that your Majesty has just said to me," I remarked, "I see a fresh proof that Europe and your Majesty cannot come to an understanding. Your peace is never more than a truce. Misfortune, like success, hurries you to war. The moment has arrived when

you and Europe both throw down the gauntlet; you will take it
up—you and Europe; and it will not be Europe that will be defeated."

"You think to conquer me by a coalition, then," continued
Napoleon; "but how many are there of you Allies—four, five, six,
twenty? The more you are, so much the better for me. I take up
the challenge. But I can assure you," he continued, with a forced
laugh, "that in next October we shall meet in Vienna; then it will
be seen what has become of your good friends, the Russians and
Prussians. Do you count on Germany? See what it did in the year
1809! To hold the people there in check, my soldiers are sufficient;
and for the faith of the princes, my security is the fear they have
of you. Declare your neutrality, and hold to it, then I will consent
to the negotiations in Prague. Will you have an armed neutrality?
Be it so! Send three hundred thousand men to Bohemia; the word
of the Emperor is sufficient, that he will not make war against me,
before the negotiation is ended."

"The Emperor," answered I, "has offered the Powers his mediation, not his neutrality. Russia and Prussia have accepted the mediation: it is for you to declare yourself to-day. If you will accept
what I have just proposed, we will fix a time for the duration of
the negotiations. If you refuse it, the Emperor, my gracious master,
will consider himself free to make what decisions and take up what
attitude he chooses. The situation is critical: the army must live;
very soon there will be two hundred and fifty thousand men in
Bohemia; they may stay there a few weeks, but they cannot remain
for months in quarters."

Here Napoleon again interrupted me, to go into a long digres-
sion on the possible strength of our army. According to his calculation, we could at the most send seventy-five thousand men to take
the field in Bohemia. He based these calculations on the normal
condition of the population of the country, on the supposed losses
in the last wars, and on our rules for conscription. I expressed my
astonishment at the incorrectness of the information he had obtained, when it would have been so easy for him to obtain fuller
and more correct statistics.

"I will pledge myself," I declared to him, "to give you an exact
list of your battalions; and should your Majesty not be as well
informed on the strength of the Austrian army?"

"I am so;" said Napoleon, "I possess most minute information
respecting the army, and am certain I do not deceive myself as to

its effectiveness. M. de Narbonne," he continued, "sent a number of spies into the field, and his information includes the very drummers of your army—my head-quarters have done the same; but I know better than anyone the value to be placed on such information. My calculations rest on mathematical grounds, and are therefore reliable; in fact, no one *has* more than he *can* have."

Napoleon took me into his study, and showed me the lists of our forces as they were daily sent to him. We examined this with great particularity, and almost regiment for regiment. Our discussion on this subject lasted more than an hour.

On returning into the reception-room, he did not speak again on political subjects, and I might have thought that he wished to draw my attention away from the object of my mission, if a former experience had not taught me that such digressions were natural to him. He spoke of the whole of his operations in Russia, and expatiated at length and with the pettiest details about his last return to France. It was clear to me from all this that he was constantly endeavouring to show that his defeat of 1812 was entirely owing to the time of year, and that his moral position in France had never been firmer than it was in consequence of this same event. "It was a hard test," he said to me, "but I have stood it perfectly well."

After I had listened to him for more than half an hour, I interrupted him with the remark, that in what he had just told me I saw strong proof of the necessity of putting an end to so uncertain a fate. "Fortune," I said, "may play you false a second time, as it did in 1812. In ordinary times armies are formed of only a small part of the population, to-day it is the whole people that you have called to arms. Is not your present army anticipated by a generation? I have seen your soldiers: they are mere children. Your Majesty has the feeling that you are absolutely necessary to the nation: but is not the nation also necessary to you? And if this juvenile army that you levied but yesterday should be swept away, what then?"

When Napoleon heard these words he was overcome with rage, he turned pale, and his features were distorted. "You are no soldier," said he, "and you do not know what goes on in the mind of a soldier. I was brought up in the field, and a man such as I am does not concern himself much about the lives of a million of men."[1] With this exclamation he threw his hat, which he had held in his hand, into the corner of the room. I remained quite quiet,

[1] I do not dare to make use here of the much worse expressions employed by Napoleon—Metternich's note.

leaning against the edge of a console between the two windows, and said, deeply moved by what I had just heard, "Why have you chosen to say this to me within these four walls; open the doors, and let your words sound from one end of France to the other. The cause which I represent will not lose thereby."

Napoleon recovered himself, and with calmer tones said to me the following words, no less remarkable than the former: "The French cannot complain of me; to spare them, I have sacrificed the Germans and the Poles. I have lost in the campaign of Moscow three hundred thousand men, and there were not more than thirty thousand Frenchmen among them."

"You forget, sire," I exclaimed, "that you are speaking to a German."

Napoleon walked up and down the room, and at the second turn he picked up his hat from the floor. Then he began to speak of his marriage. "So I have perpetrated a very stupid piece of folly in marrying an Archduchess of Austria."

"Since your Majesty desires to know my opinion," I answered, "I will candidly say that Napoleon the conqueror made a mistake."

"The Emperor Francis will then dethrone his daughter?"

"The Emperor," I replied, "knows nothing but his duty, and he will fulfil it. Whatever the fate of his daughter may be, the Emperor Francis is in the first place a monarch, and the interests of his people will always take the first place in his calculations."

"Well," interrupted Napoleon, "what you say does not astonish me: everything confirms my idea that I have made an inexcusable mistake. When I married an Archduchess I tried to weld the new with the old, Gothic prejudices with the institutions of my century: I deceived myself, and I, this day, feel the whole extent of my error. It may cost me my throne, but I will bury the world beneath its ruins."

The conversation had lasted till half-past eight o'clock in the evening. It was already quite dark. No one had ventured to come into the room. Not one pause of silence interrupted this animated discussion, in which I can count no less than six moments in which my words had the weight of a formal declaration of war. I have no intention of reproducing here all that Napoleon said during this long interview. I have only dwelt upon the most striking points in it which bear directly on the object of my mission. We wandered far away from it twenty times; those who have known Napoleon, and transacted business with him, will not be surprised at that.

When Napoleon dismissed me, his tone had become calm and quiet. I could no longer distinguish his features. He accompanied me to the door of the reception-room. Holding the handle of the folding-door, he said to me, "We shall see one another again!"

"At your pleasure, Sire," was my answer, "but I have no hope of attaining the object of my mission."

"Well, now," said Napoleon, touching me on the shoulder, "do you know what will happen? You will not make war on me?"

"You are lost, Sire," I said, quickly; "I had the presentiment of it when I came; now, in going, I have the certainty."

In the anterooms I found the same generals whom I had seen on entering. They crowded round me to read in my face the impression of the nearly nine hours' conversation. I did not stop, and I do not think I satisfied their curiosity.

Berthier accompanied me to my carriage. He seized a moment when no one was near to ask me whether I had been satisfied with the Emperor. "Yes," I answered, "he has explained everything to me; it is all over with the man."

2. Benjamin Constant on the Spirit of Conquest and Usurpation, 1813

Benjamin Constant (1767–1830), a French writer and politician, studied in England and Germany and adopted moderate republican views. He was influential in literary circles and held posts in the French government from 1799 to 1802, when he was purged by Napoleon and went into exile in Germany, where he mixed with the Goethe-Schiller circle. After Napoleon's defeats in 1812 and 1813, Constant returned to politics, publishing his Spirit of Conquest and Usurpation, as They Affect the Civilization of Europe, in Hanover in 1813. Two chapters from this attack on the Napoleonic régime, taken from a Paris edition of 1814, appear below. It may be instructive to wonder whether the arguments he puts forward comport more logically with a conservative or a liberal political position. [Henri Benjamin Constant de Rebecque, De l'esprit de conquête et de l'usurpation, 4th edn. (Paris, 1814), pp. 27–30, 53–61. Translation by the editor.]

The influence of the military mind on the domestic condition of peoples

THE EFFECTS of a habitual system of conquest are not limited to the army itself and its relation with foreign countries. What a system based on conquest does to the relations between army and citizens must be considered as well.

An exclusive and hostile caste spirit always seizes organizations whose goals are separate from the goals of the rest of mankind. Despite the mildness and purity of Christianity, organizations of its priests have often formed separate states within the state. Men brought together in military bodies, too, always separate themselves from the nation. They develop a special respect for the use of force, that being their particular province. Their standards and ideas become subversive of those principles of lawfulness, and of peaceable and ordered liberty, that all governments have an interest in supporting as well as a duty to uphold.

So it is a serious thing to create within a country, by a system of prolonged or constantly renewed wars, a large body imbued exclusively with the military spirit. For the unpleasant effects cannot easily be held within established limits. The army, though its mentality is different from that of the people, becomes confused with the public will in practice and policy.

A conquering government has more reason than any other to reward its direct instruments with power and with honors. It cannot shut them up within an entrenched encampment. On the contrary, it must adorn them with pomp and with civil dignities.

But then, will these warriors, even when they lay aside their weapons of iron, also lay aside the mentality bred in them since childhood by habitual danger? When they put on the toga, will they also assume respect for the laws, and attention to legal safeguards, those deities of human association? The unarmed class will seem to them an ignoble herd, and laws only useless subtleties, and formalities nothing but insufferable delays. They admire speed of maneuver above all things, in civil affairs as well as war. They consider uniformity of opinion as necessary as a single uniform for soldiers. They conceive opposition to be sedition, argumentation to be revolt, civil tribunals to be councils of war, judges to be soldiers who have their orders from above, the accused to be enemies, and judgments to be battles.

This is in no way a fanciful exaggeration. Have we not seen, over the past twenty years, the introduction almost everywhere in Europe of military justice, whose first principle has been to abbreviate formalities—as if all abridgment of forms were not the most revolting sophistry. For if the forms are pointless any court must exclude them, but where they are necessary, all must respect them. And surely, the more serious the accusation, the less superfluous will be painstaking examination. Again and again, have we not seen seated as judges men whose costumes showed only that they were sworn to obedience, so that they could not be independent judges?

Our posterity will never believe, if they have any sense of human dignity, that there was a time when men, illustrious no doubt for immortal deeds, but reared under canvas and ignorant of civilian life, tried prisoners they were incapable of understanding, and condemned without appeal citizens they had no right to judge. Posterity will not believe, unless it is made up of the most degraded of peoples, that legislators, writers, and persons accused of political crimes have been forced to appear before military tribunals, so that ideas and thoughts were judged, in a terrible mockery, by courage without intelligence and obedience without enlightenment. Nor will they believe that warriors returning from victory, covered with laurels as yet unsullied, were burdened with the terrible task of turning themselves into hangmen, of hunting down, seizing, and butchering fellow citizens whose names, and whose crimes, were unknown to them. No, posterity will cry, such were never the rewards for great deeds and triumphal glory! No, that was never how the defenders of France returned to their country and greeted their native soil!

The fault, indeed, lies not with the defenders. I have seen them regret their dismal obedience a thousand times. I am glad to repeat it: they have the virtue to withstand, more than human nature would permit us to hope, the influence of the militarist system and the actions of a government that seeks to corrupt them. That government alone is guilty, and our armies should have credit, rather, for all the evil they do not do.

On uniformity

It is quite remarkable that uniformity has never found more favor than in a revolution made in the name of the rights and liberty of men. First, the systematic spirit was fascinated by symmetry. Soon love of power discovered what advantages this symmetry provided for it. Although patriotism can exist only through a living connection with local interests, traditions, and customs, our self-proclaimed patriots declared war on all those things. They ruined that natural source of patriotism, and tried to replace it with an artificial passion for an abstraction, a general idea, stripped of everything that might touch the imagination and of everything that might speak to the memory. To build their structure, they began by pounding and grinding to dust the materials they had to use. They barely missed designating cities and provinces by numbers, just as they designated army corps and legions by numbers, so much did they fear that some moral value might be attached to what they instituted!

The despotism that followed upon the demagoguery, and made itself heir to the fruits of all its labors, kept very adroitly to the path prepared. The two extremes agreed on that point, because behind both extremes lay tyrannical will. The concerns and the memories born of local traditions contain a seed of resistance that authority is reluctant to allow, and which it hastens to uproot. It can deal with individuals better; it can roll them flat with its enormous weight as easily as if they were grains of sand.

Nowadays, admiration for uniformity, an admiration that is real in some narrow minds and pretended by some servile minds, is received like a religious dogma, with a chorus of diligent echoes to all officially approved views.

Applied to the parts of an empire, this principle must rule in all the countries the empire can conquer. So, actually, it is the direct and inevitable consequence of the spirit of conquest.

But every generation, says one of the foreigners who has best foreseen our errors since the beginning [the German Rehberg], *every generation inherits from its forebears a treasure of moral riches, an invisible and precious treasure, which it bequeaths to its descendents.* The loss of this treasure does a people incalculable harm. Deprive them of this, and you take away all sense of their own value and self-respect. Even if what you substitute should be of higher value, what you deprive them of had their respect; and when you impose your improvement by force, the effect of the operation is simply to do them an evil deed, one which debases and demoralizes them.

The quality of laws as such, we venture to say, is a much less important thing than the spirit in which a nation submits to its laws, and obeys them. If it cherishes them, and observes them, because they seem to come from a sacred source, the gift of generations whose departed spirits the nation reveres, then the laws will be intimately tied up with the moral sense of the nation; they will ennoble its character; and even though they be imperfect laws, they will produce more virtue and thus more happiness than better ones based only on official decree.

I must say that I have much veneration for the past; and every day my veneration grows, as experience teaches or reflection enlightens me. And I shall say this, though it greatly shock our modern reformers who entitle themselves Lycurgus or Charlemagne, that when I see a people who have been offered institutions more perfect, metaphysically speaking, and who yet refuse them so as to remain faithful to those of their fathers, then I esteem that people, and I believe them happier in their hearts and souls, even with their defective institutions, than they could be under all the proposed improvements.

This doctrine, I take it, is not of the kind that will receive favor. Men like to make laws; they think laws they have made are excellent; and they take pride in the merits of them. But the past acts alone; nobody can claim glory from what it does.

Apart from these considerations, and distinguishing happiness from ethics, notice that man bows to the institutions he finds established just as he does to the physical laws of nature. He adjusts his interests, his thoughts, and his whole plan of life to the very faults of these institutions. The faults soften; for whenever an institution lasts for a long time, there is an interaction between it and the interests of man. His connections and his hopes are grouped around what exists. To change all that, even for the better, is to do him an injury.

Nothing is more absurd than to violate someone's habits on the pretext of serving his interests. The first interest of all is to be happy; and habits form an essential part of happiness.

Even in states long constituted, where the hatefulness of the violence and conquest surrounding their formation is forgotten, one sees how the patriotism born of local variations, the only true patriotism, rekindles from the ashes as soon as the hand of power relaxes its pressure for a moment. The magistrates of the tiniest communities take pride in adorning them. They carefully maintain the relics of their past. Almost every village has some erudite person who loves to recount its rustic annals, and who is respectfully listened to. The inhabitants take pleasure in everything that gives

them the appearance, however fictitious, of being bodily constituted as a people, held together by special connections. One
feels that if the development of that innocent and beneficent
tendency were not arrested, they would soon form among them
a sort of community honor, so to speak, a town honor, a provincial
honor, which would be a satisfaction and at the same time a virtue.
But jealous authority observes them, is alarmed, and crushes any
seed ready to sprout.

Attachment to local customs partakes of all unselfish, noble, and
pious sentiments. What a deplorable policy it is to make rebellion
out of that! What happens? In every state where all local varia-
tion is destroyed this way, a little state takes form in the center; all
interests focus in the capital; all ambitions rush and collect there;
outside, all is motionless. Individuals, lost in unnatural isolation,
strangers to the places of their birth, without contact with the past,
living only in a hurrying present, and thrown like atoms upon an
immense leveled plain, detach themselves from a fatherland of
which they can perceive no part, and to whose totality they become indifferent, because their affections can find no hold on any
of its parts.

Variety is organization; uniformity is mechanism. Variety is
life; uniformity is death.

Thus conquest in our times has an additional disadvantage,
which it did not have in antiquity. It pursues the vanquished into
the heart of their existence; it mutilates them so as to reduce them
to uniform proportions. Formerly, conquerors demanded that representatives of conquered nations kneel in their presence; now it is
the soul of man that must bow down.

There is constant talk of the great empire, of the whole nation—
abstract notions with no substance at all. The great empire is
nothing, conceived apart from its provinces; and the whole nation
is nothing, separated from the parts that compose it. It is by defending the rights of the parts that the whole nation is defended,
for it is portioned out among all of its parts. If they are successively
stripped of what they hold most dear, if each one, isolated as a
victim, becomes then by a strange metamorphosis a portion of a
grand whole, so as to serve as a pretext for the immolation of another portion, then real things are sacrificed to abstract things; to
"the people" as a mass one makes a burnt offering of the people in
particular.

It is wrong to hide the fact that great states have great disadvantages. Laws are sent out from a place so far from the places where they must be applied that serious and frequent errors must result from the remoteness. The government supposes the attitude of its immediate associates, or at most, of the place where it is situated, to be that of the whole empire. A local or temporary circumstance may become the basis for a general law. Inhabitants of the most remote provinces are suddenly surprised by unexpected innovations, by undeserved severity, and by trouble-making regulations, which undermine all the bases of their planning and all the safeguards of their interests, all because two hundred leagues away, some men of whom they know nothing whatever thought they foresaw danger, or prophesied some disturbance, or perceived some advantage.

3. The Act of the Holy Alliance, and Castlereagh on Unity among European States, 1815

The following two documents may be considered separately, or they may be compared as characteristic statements from the two wing powers of the victorious alliance, Russia and England, on the need for and the means toward a common political front among European states late in 1815. The Holy Alliance was pressed upon the European statesmen by Alexander I; the document was viewed with cynicism by those who knew Alexander, and astonishment by those who did not. It was affirmed by all European monarchs save the prince regent of England, the sultan of Turkey, and the pope. The dispatch from Viscount Castlereagh, British foreign secretary, to his ambassador in Prussia deals with his anxiety lest Prussia under the leadership of the cool reformer Hardenberg should come into conflict with Alexander's Russia. [Holy Alliance: James H. Robinson, ed., *Translations and Reprints*, I (Philadelphia, 1897), No. 3, pp. 9–10; Castlereagh to Rose: *Memoirs and Correspondence of Viscount Castlereagh*, XI (London, 1853), 104–107.]

IN THE Name of the very Holy and Indivisible Trinity.

Their majesties, the Emperor of Austria, the King of Prussia and the Emperor of Russia, in view of the great events which the last three years have brought to pass in Europe and in view especially of the benefits which it has pleased Divine Providence to confer upon those states whose governments have placed their confidence and their hope in Him alone, having reached the profound conviction that the policy of the powers, in their mutual relations, ought to be guided by the sublime truths taught by the eternal religion of God our Saviour, solemnly declare that the present act has no other aim than to manifest to the world their unchangeable determination to adopt no other rule of conduct, either in the government of their respective countries or in their holy religion, than the precepts of justice, charity and peace. These, far from being applicable exclusively to private life, ought on the contrary directly to control the resolutions of princes and to guide their steps as the sole means of establishing human institutions and of remedying their imperfections. Hence their majesties have agreed upon the following articles:

Article I. Conformably to the words of Holy Scripture which command all men to look upon each other as brothers, the three contracting monarchs will continue united by the bonds of a true and indissoluble fraternity, and regarding themselves as compatriots, they will lend aid and assistance to each other on all occasions and in all places; viewing themselves, in their relations to their subjects and to their armies, as fathers of families, they will direct them in that spirit of fraternity by which they are animated, for the protection of religion, peace and justice.

Article II. Hence the sole principle of conduct, be it between the said governments or their subjects, shall be that of rendering mutual service, and testifying by unceasing good-will, the mutual affection with which they should be animated. Considering themselves all as members of one great Christian nation, the three allied princes look upon themselves as delegates of Providence called upon to govern three branches of the same family, viz.: Austria, Russia and Prussia. They thus confess that the Christian nation, of which they and their people form a part, has in reality no other sovereign than He alone to whom belongs by right the power, for in Him alone are to be found all the treasures of love, of knowledge and of infinite wisdom, that is to say God, our Divine Saviour, Jesus Christ, the word of the most High, the word of life. Their majesties recommend, therefore, to their peoples, as the sole means of enjoying that peace which springs from a good conscience and is alone enduring, to fortify themselves each day in the principles and practice of those duties which the Divine Saviour has taught to men.

Article III. All those powers who wish solemnly to make avowal of the sacred principles which have dictated the present act, and who would recognize how important it is to the happiness of nations, too long agitated, that these truths should hereafter exercise upon human destiny all the influence belonging to them, shall be received into this Holy Alliance with as much cordiality as affection.

Engrossed in three copies and signed at Paris, year of grace 1815, September 14/26.

Signed:

FRANCIS

FREDERICK WILLIAM

ALEXANDER

Blickling, December 28, 1815

My dear Sir—I take advantage of a bad day to spare the pheasants and to send you a despatch, which I shall probably make circular to all our missions.

I perceive in more than one quarter a tendency to alarm as to the designs of particular Powers, but especially of Russia, for which I have no reason to suppose there is the smallest foundation, but of the prudence of which I should equally doubt, were I apprehensive (which I am not) that the Emperor of Russia, after making such stupendous sacrifices for a peace, which in its provisions has met his cordial concurrence, was stupid enough to meditate new convulsions to pull his own work to pieces. His language, his engagements, and his proceedings, as far as they are known to me, are in direct opposition to such a conclusion; and it must be my duty to discourage a line of conduct, which, although unauthorized, may produce distrust and alienation between two Courts, whose counsels being in unison is perhaps more essential than any other circumstance that can be stated to the preservation of that state of relations in Europe, which is best calculated to preclude any serious interruption of peace.

When I thus express myself with respect to the views of Russia, or indeed of any Court, I must be understood as not indulging that species of blind confidence which does not belong to the politics of any foreign State; but I wish to guard our missions abroad against the danger of accelerating, if not producing, a conflict for influence between the two States. The existing state of European relations may possibly not endure beyond the danger which originally gave them birth, and which has recently confirmed them; but it is our duty, as well as interest, to retard, if we cannot avert, the return of a more contentious order of things: and our insular situation places us sufficiently out of the reach of danger to admit of our pursuing a more generous and confiding policy.

In the present state of Europe, it is the province of Great Britain to turn the confidence she has inspired to the account of peace, by exercising a conciliatory influence between the Powers, rather than put herself at the head of any combinations of Courts to keep others in check. The necessity for such a system of connexion may recur, but this necessity should be no longer problematical when it is acted upon. The immediate object to be kept in view is to inspire the States of Europe, as long as we can, with a sense of the dangers which they have surmounted by their union, of the hazards they will incur by a relaxation of vigilance, to make them feel that the existing concert is their only perfect security against the revolutionary embers more or less existing in every State of Europe; and that their true wisdom is to keep down the petty contentions of ordinary times, and to stand together in support of the established principles of social order.

I have every reason to hope that the advantage of this course of policy is justly appreciated by the Allied Cabinets. The negotiations at Paris were terminated with the utmost cordiality—whatever differences of opinion had existed either at Vienna, or in the early stage of our discussions at Paris, had ceased to disturb the general harmony; and there appeared a general satisfaction in the results of our labours. I should say that the relations between Austria and Russia had become much more amicable, those of Russia with Prussia perhaps proportionably less intimate; but this I attribute not to any essential relaxation of friendly feeling, but to the manner in which the Prussian counsels were conducted at Paris being less congenial to the Emperor of Russia's feelings than the more moderate tone of the Austrian Cabinet. All, however, appeared to separate deeply impressed with the value of their common connexion to themselves and to the world; and I trust nothing may arise to shake this impression.

With respect to the particular Court to which you are accredited, every consideration of common interest must make me partial to the conservation of its preponderance as a great Power, inasmuch as Prussia must be the basis of every system in the north of Europe to preserve Holland as an independent State, and to keep France in check; but, with all that partiality and a grateful admiration of the conduct of that nation and its armies in the war, I fairly own that I look with considerable anxiety to the tendency of their politics. There certainly, at this moment, exists a great fermentation in all orders of the State; very free notions of Government, if not principles actually revolutionary, are prevalent, and the army is by no means subordinate to the civil authorities. It is impossible to say where these impulses may stop, when they find a representative system in which they may develop themselves.

I call your attention to these circumstances, not as any motive for interference on your part, but in order to impress your mind with the importance (and especially to Prussia herself) of keeping up a good understanding amongst the adjoining States, on which these disorganizing principles have made less impression, till the internal state both of France and of the north of Germany is more assured than it can now be considered to be. To this view of European policy, I can venture to assure you, the Sovereigns themselves and their immediate Ministers are not insensible.

Your safest course at present will be to *keep quiet;* to cultivate the good will of your colleagues; to inspire them, as far as possible, with confidence in your Court, by making them feel that it is equally the ally of all; and, in order to do so with effect, you will avoid evincing distrust of theirs. Consistently with these suggestions, you will not neglect to cultivate suitable channels of intelligence, and to keep me accurately informed. I shall not neglect to put you in motion, when I see occasion to do so; but, in general, it is not my wish to encourage, on the part of this country, an unnecessary interference in the ordinary affairs of the Continent. The interposition of Great Britain will always be most authoritative in proportion as it is not compromised by being unduly mixed in the daily concerns of these States.

I trust you have found Prince Hardenberg return in good health.

I regret his age does not present the prospect of his being long at
the head of affairs in Prussia. I have always found him, although
warm, alive to every honourable feeling, and incapable of long resisting an appeal to his reason upon any question. I beg to be remembered most cordially to him, and that you will believe me,
dear sir, with great truth and regard, very faithfully yours,

CASTLEREAGH

4. Metternich on the Sects in Central Europe, 1817

Emotional excitement did not have to be directly political to arouse the
concern of governing statesmen. Probably there was no more religious
radicalism in 1817 than in many other times in the history of Europe,
but these were not other times. And the religious mystic Madame de
Krüdener, who seemed to be stirring up religious and social unrest,
was intimately connected with Czar Alexander, and was believed to
represent the spirit that lay behind the Act of the Holy Alliance. This
made the problem all the more alarming, and the more ticklish to
handle as well. Metternich's dispatch is to his ambassador to Russia.
[Metternich, *Memoirs*, III (London, 1881), 58–61.]

June 28, 1817

THE PROGRESS of sects which are beginning to threaten the peace
of many countries, especially in Central Europe, is an object
worthy to occupy the attention of Cabinets.

The human mind generally revels in extremes. A period of irreli-
gion, a period in which pretended philosophers and their false doctrines have tried to overturn all which human wisdom has recognised
as intimately connected with the eternal principles of morality, has
been necessarily followed by an epoch of moral and religious reaction. Now, every kind of reaction is false and unjust, and it is only
given to wise and consequently strong men to be neither the dupes
of false philosophers nor the sport of false religions. If any one
doubted the intimate connection which exists between the moral
and material world, proofs would be found in the march and progress of certain maladies of the mind, which present all the symptoms of true epidemics. For some time the Methodists have made
great progress in England and America; and this sect, by following
the track of all the others, is now beginning to extend its proselyt-

ism to other parts of Europe. There are at the present moment, principally in Upper Germany and Switzerland, hundreds of thousands of individuals morally affected by mysticism. The kingdom of Wurtemberg, the Grand Duchy of Baden, contain an entire population, fanatical to the point of abandoning all the comforts of this world to seek existence and happiness in the holy places which they regard as the proper preparation for a future life. There are in Swabia whole families who practise the greatest self-denial, young men who will do nothing unless they are allowed to emigrate either to Palestine or to some desert place, where, withdrawing from all society, they can constitute among themselves a theocratic government more or less similar to that of the Jews after their departure from Egypt. Some of these sects have an exclusively moral and religious object. Others betray decided tendencies towards a political malady, and as Jacobinism, even extreme as it is, still admits of further extremes, many of these sects wish to found their new society on the principles of the agrarian law.

You will have heard, Sir, of the extraordinary errors into which the so-called *Poeschlianer* in Upper Austria have fallen. A ramification of this same sect has been discovered in the country of Wurzburg, and young men, and especially young women, have given themselves up to the most frightful torments, and even to death, in order to render themselves worthy of Paradise. In Swabia there are a number of Independents, a religious and political sect, who dream only of an agrarian law, theocrats who wish for the law of Moses, and many other associations, each one more fanatical than the other.

You have doubtless seen in the Swiss newspapers, and especially in that of Aarau, articles which the Governments have been forced to publish against the predications of Madame de Krüdener; the tendency of this woman is more dangerous than all the others, because her predications are all intended to excite the indigent classes against the proprietors. She invites the poor to put themselves in the place of the rich, and her fanaticism no doubt prevents her from perceiving that she thus establishes the most vicious circle possible, as she would, in fact, thus give to people formerly rich but now poor, the undoubted right of ameliorating their condition in their turn, by putting themselves again in the place of those who had dispossessed them.

It is, doubtless, worthy of the wisdom of the great Powers to take into consideration an evil which it is possible, and perhaps even easy, to stifle in its beginning, but which can only gain in intensity in proportion as it spreads. The Courts must not forget that there exist in Europe disturbers of the public repose, who are deceived in all their calculations by a firm and continued progress, and the just and liberal principles of the great monarchs who have saved Europe. These men, desperate, and forced from their last intrenchments, regard as their own property all questions of disorder whatever, and it is perhaps reserved for us to see the editors of the *"Nain jaune"* and the *"Vrai Libéral"* preach against the vanities of this world, and to see Carnot and Barère make themselves the apostles of the New Jerusalem. This subject deserves the most serious attention; it is connected with the well-being of society and the tranquillity of States more closely than is supposed, and the great Courts should not be slow to take into consideration the means of checking the designs of these fomenters of a new kind of revolution.

I beg you, Sir, to sound the Russian Cabinet on this subject, and to inform us of its ideas. The Courts will easily find means within their reach, whenever they come to an understanding with each other about the matter, and it belongs doubtless to the first Powers of Europe to confine their views to measures beyond the reach of the Governments of small States, who can only expel a dangerous individual from so small a territory, and who, if they endeavour to save their own people from the contagion, can only pass it on to their neighbours.

5. Heinrich von Gagern to his Father on the German Student Movement, 1818

Heinrich von Gagern (1799–1880) was a son of a fairly prominent Hessian liberal statesman. He had shared in the excitement of the "liberation war" against Napoleon's France, and had fought at Waterloo. Then he entered university studies, and helped form the *Burschenschaft* student fraternal movement, which he here tries to explain to a sympathetic but skeptical father. Note his concern to relate the special situation of German students to the life of the nation, and what he thinks the student spirit and organizations should foretell for the nation. The final section of this book will present (pp. 330–36) another

letter from Gagern to his father, written thirty years later in the last
days of Metternich's Europe, when the student of 1818 was becoming
one of Germany's most conspicuous and ambitious liberal politicians.
[P. Wentzcke and W. Klötzer, eds., *Deutscher Liberalismus im Vormärz* (Göttingen, 1959), pp. 57–61. Translation by the editor.]

Jena, June 17, 1818

IT IS very hard to explain the spirit of the student movement to
you, but I shall try, even though I can only give you a few characteristics. At first glance the prudent and experienced man will
find fault with the student spirit here, but with a closer view and
better understanding he will come to expect the best of the same
people when they reach a more mature age. It speaks to the better
youth, the man of heart and spirit and love for all that is good,
and gives him nourishment and being. For the average student
of the past, the university years were a time to enjoy life, and to
make a sharp break with his own background in defiance of the
philistine world, which seemed to him somehow to foreshadow
the tomb. Their pleasures, their organizations, and their talk were
determined by their *status* as students, and their university obligation was only to avoid failing the examination and scraping by
adequately—bread-and-butter learning. They were satisfied with
themselves if they thought they could pass the examination. There
are still many of those nowadays, indeed the majority over-all.
But at several universities, and especially here, another group—in
my eyes a better one—has managed to get the upper hand in the
sense that it sets the mood. I prefer really not to call it a mood;
rather, it is something that presses hard and tries to spread its
ideas—ideas in the spirit of the Wartburg, as you yourself said; but
in that case it was a bit exaggerated, perhaps through external
circumstances: collective feelings, thoughts of the holiness of the
festival, associated with that place and date, emotions raised by
individual events. All these things may have led to overexcitement.
But this much is sure, from all I have heard, that festival was
undertaken in a noble spirit.

This is going to be a long letter again, for I am already beginning to tell long stories.—Those who share in this spirit have then
quite another tendency in their student life, Love of Fatherland
is their guiding principle. Their purpose is to make a better future
for the Fatherland, each as best he can, to spread national con-

sciousness, or to use the much ridiculed and maligned Germanic expression, more folkishness, and to work for better constitutions. Their student organizations, their self-development, and their whole way of life are means to these ends. They hold no particular bias as students that would lapse when they cease to be students; rather, they want to bring the ideals they have grasped as students into civic life with them and adapt their civic careers to their student ideals as best they can. They are accused of trying to express their German sentiments in an absurd way by wearing old-fashioned Germanic cloaks. But to this they answer: "We are not trying to make something special out of wearing Germanic cloaks, we only want Germany to have its own fashion. Let anybody who likes invent a native form of cloak in Germany, and we shall wear them as German cloaks; but until that happens we shall wear the cloak our forefathers wore, rather than let other peoples impose their fashions upon us and have us copy them."—People say to them: "How high and mighty do you think you are? How can you take it upon yourselves to create something new in the world?"—They answer: "Do we want to create something new? We only want to sustain it and always sustain it, wherever civic circumstances give us the chance to do so. If we stay true to this principle, and if those who come after us at the universities behave as we do, and if there are more and more such, then in civic life too there will be larger numbers of like-minded, who will also show it by their cloaks. We are not trying to be high and mighty at all. We are young people who act according to their convictions, though we willingly accept better advice when we hear it. But until we hear it we must be true to our convictions still. The prejudice that the world in general has against students will cease little by little when we engage in more regular activities, and when we try to overcome the sharp contradiction between ordinary civic life and the special status of student life—which is of course our aim. We shall not always remain students, either; many of the chief servants of the state will emerge from among us. Let us see whether we hold to the same principles then. At most they will have been led from the boiling torrent of youthful imagination into the quiet, peaceful channel of cooler intelligence and of reality. But we hope that these ideas will not suffer the fate of champagne, whose spirit flees when the effervescence does; the spirit rather will have settled into the wine."

As an informed observer you will say now, my dear Father: "That is all well and good, but what is the aim in practical fact? What do you want Germany to be? What are your political views? What is your purpose?"—This I have only briefly suggested so far, and now I shall make some additions. We want more sense of community among the several states of Germany, greater unity in their policies and in their principles of government; no separate policy for each state, but the nearest possible relations with one another; above all, we want Germany to be considered *one* land and the German people *one* people. In the forms of our student comradeship we show how we want to approach this as nearly as possible in the real world. Regional fraternities are forbidden, and we live in a German comradeship, one people in spirit, as we want it for all Germany in reality. We give our selves the freest of constitutions, just as we should like Germany to have the freest possible one, insofar as that is suitable for the German people. We want a constitution for the people that fits in with the spirit of the times and with the people's own level of enlightenment, rather than what each prince gives his people according to what he likes and what serves his private interest. Above all, we want the princes to understand and to follow the principle that they exist for the country and not the country for them. In fact, the prevailing view is that the constitution should not come from the individual states at all. The main principles of the German constitution should apply to all states in common, and should be expressed by the German federal assembly. This constitution should deal not only with the absolute necessities, like fiscal administration and justice, general administration and church and military affairs and so on; this constitution ought to be extended to the education of the young, at least at the upper age levels, and to many other such things.

There is a learned society here made up entirely of young people, or I should say it is just now really getting started, in which the members come together just as they like and choose, to work out certain things bearing on all kinds of subjects. One group works on historical subjects, another on constitutional law, where constitutions are made and existing ones criticized and so on. There are drafts of church statutes, others on education, and so on. Drafts and proposals are submitted first within the groups working on each subject, and then laid before larger meetings of the whole. Ideas are developed there, discussed, criticized, praised, accepted or rejected. Because this is a very good system and there is no compulsion, we can learn a great deal that way. Sometime I shall send you work that comes from this for your inspection and criticism. The state constitutions are examined very closely there; and that certainly has the value of making us very well acquainted with them.

6. Josef Gorres, "Germany and the Revolution," 1819

Johann Josef von Görres (1776–1848), a German Catholic publicist and scholar, had in 1799 worked for the annexation to France of German provinces west of the Rhine; but by 1813 he had turned against the French and become a strong German patriot. His "Germany and the Revolution," published shortly after the murder of Kotzebue in 1819, led to his flight and exile to escape arrest. From the excerpt printed below you may wish to analyze what it was that the authorities found dangerous about his views in 1819, and also to consider how romanticizing the past might have revolutionary implications in Germany—and warlike implications. This translation (within months there were many, in several European languages) appeared in London in 1820; the opaque and rhetorical style faithfully reproduces Görres's German. [*The Pamphleteer*, XV (London, 1819–20), 546–560.]

THE IDEA of the possibility of a revolution now pervades all minds; and in the one party it excites a mortal terror, whilst the other treats it with culpable levity. A revolution is a catastrophe of such terrible importance in history, that none but senseless or desperate men can wish for it. A total overthrow of social order can only be the result of the passions: and as in fits of fever nature employs delirium, lest the vital powers should be weakened by useless fatigue, so a nation, in such paroxysms, must be seized with madness, should the disease come to a strong crisis. Thus at the commencement the thing appears easy; an unusual sentiment of life, and a newly-created enthusiasm, appear to promise the most favorable results. The greatest number of well-disposed men are to be found in the party that first rises up. But the axis which connected all the elements of the social union being broken, the dominion of the party attached to order cannot long prevail, and as intellectual power loses its influence, animal power gains ground, and seizes the reins of affairs. Thus each party exceeds that which pre-

ceded it in every species of extravagance. As was the case in Eng-
land, the Protesters and Resolvers will be succeeded by the
Millenians, who acknowledge no government; next will come the
Levellers, who require equal division of property; and finally the
Antinomians, who regard all ethical duties as tyrannical. Thus in
France, the Girondists were succeeded by the Jacobins, and in the
Low Countries the Iconoclastes followed the Geuses. This progres-
sion continues through every degree of human turpitude, until all
that once existed be overthrown; all that was lofty, levelled; and
all property transferred to new possessors.

When the nation is thus exhausted by anarchical phrenzy, a return takes place, by inevitable re-action, to individual authority.
This power gradually advances to the most revolting despotism,
commits a succession of crimes of an opposite nature to those of
the preceding period, and finally, when the whole circle is run
through, an internal or external catastrophe brings the two extremes to a just medium. Such has been the progress of the revolutions of England, of France, and of every other revolution. A
German revolution will not be an exception, for the war of the
peasantry has already proved that if our blood be less lively, it is
not the less easy to urge the people to any extremity. In Germany a
new idea is added to those which effected the change in France;—
the idea of unity, which will render the ferment stronger than
ever it has been elsewhere. A German revolution must terminate
with the expulsion of all the reigning families, the overthrow of
all ecclesiastical establishments, the extirpation of the nobles, and
the introduction of a republican constitution. And when Germany
shall find another and more fortunate Wallenstein, as every revolu-
tionized nation necessarily becomes a conquering nation, she will
advance from her boundaries, and overthrow, even to the confines
of Asia, the fragile system of the European state edifice. But she
must purchase this revolution with the blood of millions of her
people, the destruction of one half of the rising generation; and in
the end, she will gain nothing but what she might have obtained
by a far cheaper sacrifice.

Such a prospect can offer no attractions to the governments, or
to the people, or even to the foreigner who might hope to profit
by our disasters. All parties, therefore, should agree to pursue the
tranquil course. While reason exerts her sway, reform may be
effected without shock or tumult; but when we once reach the

brink of the abyss, exhortation and counsel are as vain as to attempt by words to arrest the ravages of an earthquake or a storm. The more the approaching tempest lowers, the greater the vertigo of governments, the more it behoves parties to agree, at least on this point, that by united efforts the uncertain and violent movement may be rendered gentle and regular, and that the inundation may be prevented by guarding against the breaking of the dykes.

Now of the parties in opposition, the one looks to historical consolidation, the other to spontaneous creations, for supplying deficiencies: a commencement must take place with the removal of this dispute; and as to the views of these parties, it may be observed, that the different ages of natural existence in succession, are as necessarily and inseparably the property of the people, as the different contemporaneous institutions and personalities, since these form the immanent state, and those the permanent: and as with regard to the latter, rights and duties are reciprocal, so in respect to the former, any rights an after-age may inherit are accompanied by previous established duties. Besides, if each age should happen to have the same proportion of formative powers to bestow, since an early age can only transfer to a later what itself possesses, the formations must be considered with regard to the powers employed; and if the latter times claim more enlarged and practical principles, the more early may be allowed the preference in every thing connected with the lofty and the ideal.

If all things are to be judged of by their results, history sufficiently proves the blessings diffused by the middle age, particularly in Germany. Out of the onyx rock on which the Church was founded, and round its cathedral—the Gothic, Byzantine, Imperial fortress, another Mons Salutis, was cut and built. Our institutions were so judiciously regulated, that they all united harmoniously in one powerful and florishing state-body. A legislation was established similar to which no other nation had formed an idea. Germany was distinguished for genius and morality, and had attained a degree of advancement in arts and literature, exceeded by no previous age. Finally, throughout her whole conduct and existence, she exhibited an animation and activity, of which we can scarcely form a notion. All this is shown by history, and the wrecks of her greatness that still remain sufficiently attest its truth.

Our age would be placed in a perplexing situation, should it, in one of those fits of arrogance with which it is often seized, attempt to inquire into the foundation of this past existence. Should Fame say:—Show what you have accomplished: tell what you have speculated, and what you have effected, that I may know what honor is due to you, and grant you the merited prize:— Should the age then expose its poverty, and display the theatrical wardrobe of its virtues to the sharp and penetrating eye of the judge, she would doubtless pronounce the following sentence:

"You have eloquently boasted of your achievements and glory; but I have examined your merit, and find that all is founded on vanity and nothingness. In no respect do you possess a truly creative power; the source of every formative impulse is obstructed: you have forsworn that inward tranquillity which tends to preservation. Your whole existence is confusion, and your strength consists only in subversion.

"I built a Church for you, whose foundation was washed by the waters of the earth, while its spires reached the clouds. But you have thrown a fire-brand into it, under pretence of divesting it of all that was earthly and combustible, and now only the naked walls and pillars remain.

"Germany I encircled with a mural crown like a strong coat of mail. But you have burst open the gates, the towers and walls are leveled with the dust; so that the empire has become an open village, guarded only by Custom-houses. The embroidered imperial mantle, which covered all, has been torn by the feudal tenants, who, decked out in the shreds, resemble Negro Princes strutting about in the foreign dresses for which they barter the liberties of their subjects.

"With the savings of ages I endowed both Church and State, so that they might become an organ and an earthly inheritance. I raised to independence the military, the lower classes, and even the trade corporations; but all has been destroyed in a few years. All the ideas of your real basis being dissipated, now, spectre-like, wander as orphan-shadows in society, driven here and there by the wind of opinion. And with all this, there is not, throughout the whole extent of the empire, a single monument of your founding, that will go down to posterity.

"Your rash spirit of inquisitiveness has carried you into the empire of Faith; and by measuring heavenly things by a human

standard, you have confounded them with what is earthly. The
pure, unvariegated ray of truth has been obscured by many colors,
and what was in its nature united, has been split into irreconcile-
able parts.

"By the allurements of the senses, you have perverted all philosophy, so that forgetting its heavenly origin, even philosophy
has occasionally sent unsubstantial schemes into the world of fancy
—like Gnomes, Salamanders, Sylphs, and other imaginary beings
which have mortal lives without immortal souls; and even your
intellectual occupations have become merely a coarse sensual enjoyment.

"The arts have been turned aside from their sacred destination;
without system, depth, or meaning, are become the children of this
world, devoid of reflection, and suited to empty frivolous impulses;
and the intricate extravagances into which they plunge, are, like
those in music, merely the resoundings of folly.

"Your diplomacy is the doctrine and practice of absolute nothingness, joined to the readiness of perverting historical events;
your art of government is merely vain bookish learning, which,
entirely foreign to nature, exists merely in artificial abstractions;
pursuing the phantoms of empty theories, and only occasionally
quitting the world of imagination, to grasp at any thing solid.

"Your policy has hitherto consisted merely in destroying. The
great discoveries you boast of having made in the affairs of life,
appear to me no great matter. Your liberty and equality is nothing
but the elective affinities of the elements of society, with which
all constitutions have had their commencement. The anxious separation of powers;—the formation of two chambers, in which national freedom is to take up its abode;—all these things seem to me
a small indemnification for the evils preparing for you. I regard
your liberty as an emancipated slave, who still feels the wounds
of his chains,—your power as a weak and feeble despotism wavering between arbitrary caprice and liberality. The history of your
public life is only a disgusting struggle between timid self-will and
frightful licentiousness, a fermenting movement without result,
a dishonorable system of concealment and deception, a disposition
to contention without struggle or dignity. All your conduct is
built on phrases; a silent concurrence in reciprocal falsehood and
deceit, which descends to the lowest affairs of life, is praised as

worldly prudence. In corrupting and leveling, however, no other age can with you dispute the palm."

Thus might the reprover easily arraign and put to shame that conceit, which the age in its folly refuses to recognise, and its presumption would be justly punished. What indignation has here with so much sincerity expressed, ought not however to be left without reply; and with a well-understood self-knowledge, and a satisfactory view of the world, it might not be difficult for the harshly-accused to offer a defence of this sort:

"It is true you built a strong edifice, but even the mountains which nature has erected on the firm foundations of the earth are thrown down and crumbled into ruins, when the internal sustaining life is departed. Besides you must also have founded your new work on the florishing past of an earlier antiquity. Is it my crime that there is a time for every thing on earth, and that States, when they have run through their phoenix period must renew their existence amidst devouring flames? The dome of your church did indeed ascend to heaven; the stones of which it was formed were not however dead masses, but rather free self-existing natures, which believing resigned their wills to the idea. Can I resist, if they resume their pledged freedom, and the elements hasten to unite under new forms? You consolidated Germany, but gunpowder has blown up the Cyclopean walls, and the invention of the monk was only the symbol of that awful intellectual power which about the same time began to unfold itself.

"Your constitution was founded on the subsisting peaceful possession; but lo! the flood of gold from a remote quarter of the globe has washed it away. When the life from above is departed, that which is yet growing green in the organic structure must, according to the eternal laws of nature, either be absorbed by death, or thrown off into the mass; as abandoned by the in-dwelling spirit, it becomes withered. Thus the idea of the Emperor was gone before his external representation had vanished. In the same manner as the Church became first benumbed in her spiritual organs, so is the whole feudal system dead in spirit; for the possessors being gone, the property has fairly fallen to the survivors. It has been chiefly taken possession of by the third estate. The spirits are fled—God has set them free—can I then prevent them from using their rights, and abandoning the mother's safe and warm nest to spread themselves abroad? That only faith walks in pure light, and reason, a fallen angel, wallows in darkness, is a heresy. All knowledge has become more comprehensive, more intelligible. Since the third estate has florished, it has, according to its custom, aimed chiefly at the practical, the substantial, and the useful; and science is made subservient to wants, the arts to relaxation. Freedom is as yet young, and knows not how to conduct itself; arbitrary power, grey and feeble with age, knows not how to choose between the *to be* and *not to be*.

"This situation of things then exhibits only a quieting and disputing, a forming and dissolving, a creating and destroying; the fire must ever be watched to see that the seething goes quickly on. The attraction and impulse of the internal focus being relaxed, old chaos has returned to society, and the old creator is followed by a destroyer. But life can only come from death. The formative power of the world, when the elements were first mixed in the cup of Hermes, and the influences, heaving, fermenting, hissing, and thundering, came together, made at first before the just proportion of the structure was discovered, many discordant formations, which the mountains still enclose. Require not, therefore, of me, that I should even in a first sketch, form a permanent structure; you can only interrogate the future respecting my work."

If the reproach be calculated to check overweening pride, this Defence may preserve us from an unnecessary dejection, and it will then be easy to find the just mean in which the past, which also had once been present, maintains its rights, and the present, which in its turn must as a past, fall into the rear of the coming time. Since history is composed of ages, he who denies one, must reject all that has gone before. What dismembers itself, is at all times injurious. As a general principle, whatever operates as it were instinctively, and with an efficacious effect on the whole, is historical, and as such ought to be honored and esteemed; and whoever, guided by a false theory, excludes it, may be certain that he is proceeding in an erroneous course.

The first relation however in which the opposition of times and views comes practically forward, and puts forth its interposition, is that of the State with the Church. According to the idea of antiquity the Church represents, in the great community of believers, the ideal side, while the European Republic in the imperial dignity, and particularly in the State, represents the real side. But the relation between the two spheres is such, that the ideal is free in its nature, self-powerful, reposing on itself, self-transparent, and enlightened by ideas which, like stars in the conflux of their light, intersect each other, and are bounded and encircled by that serpent, which ever returns on itself. The real, however, though embraced by the former, as the earth by the celestial sphere, is in its turn shut up in itself, and moves in an eternal circle, according to fixed laws of a natural necessity, and in so far as it is subject to necessity, freedom is removed from the former, and a peculiar law is obligatory. The one is therefore the symbol of the other, and the ideal takes precedence of the real as first in dignity; but in so far on the side of nature as the idea has actually embodied itself, it has stepped out of the jurisdiction of the ideal, and must resign itself to the natural laws of the real sphere.

Thus the ethic has the preference over the pathic, and does not acknowledge the jurisdiction of passion, or the dark side in Man; and at the same time assumes no direct rule in the dominion of the passions. All it does is to act upon them by the laws of beauty, so as to regulate as far as possible, the eruptions of natural impulses; the Church is therefore among the ruling powers, but yet not the exclusively ruling; on the contrary, the state, governed by many terrestrial relations, possesses the sole ruling power, which the Church may sanctify, but cannot usurp.

But when the dark spirit rises from the depth to attack and obscure the stars of the sky, then the attacked justly vindicate their dignity, and hurl the aggressor down again to his abyss. This happened in the time of Henry the Fourth, when the eternal order of things was revolted against; then was sent that great man, too much cavilled at in modern times, who powerfully saved the liberty of the Church. But during this hard contest, the other extreme was produced, and the Church, abusing her victory, now assumed, in the persons of some of the following Popes, a worldly power to which she had no right; and this deviation from the central path necessarily produced another reaction which developed itself in the reformation.

A political sect has since arisen, which maintains that the Church forming part of the state must necessarily be subjected to it. Such a doctrine, which raises necessity above liberty, which makes heavenly things subservient to the earthly, from which christian-

ity had freed them in her contest with old heathenism, which en-
slaves mind in the fetters of matter, although quite in unison with
the spirit of the age, is yet in itself so humbling and revolting,
that this spirit, which has now reached its extreme, will certainly
find here its climax, and give way to higher and more dignified
views. A Church going to court with the German sovereignties,
divided like the rest of the commonwealth into so many factions,
that would degrade herself by exposing her power over the
conscience, to the jests and frivolities of courtiers; giving up her
doctrines, to be blown to and fro by the wind of theories, would
soon become the most contemptible of institutions, and a Diet
would not be able to keep together, even in appearance, her frail
members.

As liberty formerly protected the ambition of Popes, she must
now stand by the oppressed Church, and defend her freedom and
independence against the state, and assist in emancipating spiritual
things from the trammels in which they are kept by a usurped
power. Therefore there can be no question, for the Catholic
Church in particular, respecting a *subordination*, but only as to
a *co-ordination* with a temporal power, and the Church must rise
again to that equal balance of right and privileges, when, in the
reciprocal relations of both, the principle of christian morality,
Do unto others, as you would that others should do unto you,
must be obligatory.

But to attain this point, the Church must concentrate herself
more strongly than ever upon her unity, and still firmly maintain the closed phalanx of her hierarchy, by which arbitrary
power has more than once been repulsed. When this is done,
and her moderate endowments secured, then will be the time to
oppose every kind of arbitrary authority, which she might attempt to display; for Catholic Germany is as little inclined to
ecclesiastical as to political despotism.

For the Protestant Church, however, which, without abolishing
itself, cannot take a retrograde course, nothing will remain but
to complete the reformation in discipline, and to carry it so far
that all power will be vested in the community, as Somer in his
work "On the Church in the Present Age," has ably shown. Her
relations are to be established on the principle of generality, as
those of the Catholic Church on that of unity. But the focus of
political power, though also of a collective nature, by no means

corresponds with that of the ecclesiastical. All other diverging directions proceeding from preconceived opinions, partial views, or confused notions, being of no value, and reducing each other by their friction, are not adopted by history, which only acknowledges what composes the great stream of existing movement.

These reflections naturally lead us to the second great point of discussion in the present age, namely, the difficulty of uniting the interest of the *governors* and the *governed*. Antiquity, guided in all its notions by a just natural instinct, had almost unconsciously given to society the form of organic life, and, passing from the particular to the general, still reproduced the type of individual organisation. But there are two sorts of life, the *automatous* and the *discretionary*. The former, possessed of all the faculties of inferior life, contains its laws within itself, having its own in-dwelling natural soul, which sends the necessary instincts to each independent organ, and has its individual and independent ideas, but which are subject to the general laws of nature as in a dream. The other, the motions of which are discretionary, is notwithstanding subject to a higher power; instead of the dark instinct, all its actions are regulated by a free deliberating will; its motions have not eternal sameness, they are only mediately connected with external nature; they therefore submit to that superior will, which uniting all parts into a whole, has still access to each individually. Connected by intermediate organs, and animating and preserving each other, both form that perfect free-acting whole which is the finest work of creation.

The former, however, possesses more of that real essence of which we have spoken, and is therefore properly the governing element of the state; the second approaching more to the ideal, appears as the more spiritual element. In the Church itself, however, the former bears more the stamp of protestantism, and the latter that of catholicism; and in the state, the one will represent the democratical, the other the monarchical principle. Democracy will always concentrate in itself; it tends as much as possible to be its own legislator, and shuns every power which attempts as a superior to regulate and order by general abstraction; it dissolves and divides until it comes to the single individual, to the last element of the community. It therefore considers authority as nothing, and makes its own conviction the judge of its actions; the community has a delegated power. Unity is formed by an unanimous plurality, and has otherwise no ideal consistency or power. But the essence of the monarchical principle is renunciation and self-denial. It arises in a synthetical form by a succession of abstractions up to the highest power, and then descending again, considers all that is inferior as flowing from that first synthesis, the unity, concentrating the whole in itself. The essential character of monarchy is therefore belief and obedience, applied to that single generality which was produced by the sacrifice of all particulars, as in history all times are united in general living tradition.

But since every state must in its beginning take root in nature, we perceive in the constitutions of antiquity, especially in those of Greece, and, in modern times, in those of the New World, the element of democracy uppermost. In the same manner with respect to the Church we find in the former polytheism, in the latter sectarianism. The Greek constitutions were in all their elements of family, community and state, purely automatous, and the indispensable monarchical part was added by an aristocracy, which was itself only a more limited democracy.

All ancient democracies were founded for the most part by an unconscious instinct, which put nations in motion like the wandering stork; those that were settled built their huts near the water like the beaver, and sent forth colonies like the bees; in the interior of these societies everything was regulated after the periods and cycles of nature; the authorities represented the descending and ascending energies of nature. Rome founded in her interior upon the same principle, introduced externally the system of monarchy into her great empire, but still restricted by the genius of the ancient world; the provinces essentially obeyed, and the will of all nations was concentrated in that of Rome, in the same manner as the Jupiter of the capitol reigned over all the deities of the conquered world.

The Germans issuing from their forests, stormed the bulwarks of this empire, and gradually ingrafted the spiritual unity of monarchy upon their natural state. When Charlemagne had settled the tranquillity of the western world, he formed the first empire in the spirit of the new christian age. He, the first Prince "by the grace of God and the choice of the People," still nobly honored the principle of old German liberty, allowed it every development, and uniting it with the christian monarchical principle, formed the first really organic state, embracing man in all his physical and mental faculties.

In subsequent times, however, the unity which this sovereign, during his long wars, had, perhaps, too strictly maintained, became gradually loosened, and the automatous principle, gaining strength, divided the body of the state into branches forming a gradually rising series of unities, of which each inferior appeared the root of a superior. The feudal system of the middle age was then established; the officers of the crown uniting with the democracy of the landholders, produced the seven degrees of aristocracy, of which the Emperor, as the highest unity, formed the head. Thus all proprietors giving up their property to the community, in order the better to secure its use to themselves, by the protection of the whole, in the same manner as natural liberty is renounced at the formation of society, they formed that impenetrable mass of power which condemned all non-proprietors, or all whom they could conquer by the force of arms, to a mild sort of slavery. With this mixture of the two principles, Germany passed brilliantly through the second period of her middle age, and was elevated to the head of Christendom. But in the course of time this system, which had been organised by the development of democracy, was also to be destroyed by that still spreading power. After the powerful Suabian Emperors became extinct, the imperial dignity being elective, and that of the officers of the crown hereditary, violence and disorder constantly increased. The Ecclesiastical and Lay Princes then acquired more and more strength, because they contained most of the principle of unity. But this accession of power they obtained on the one hand at the expense of the imperial power, which they gradually undermined; and on the other at the expense of the vassals, whom they either impoverished or bribed into their interest.

Territorial sovereignty now gradually developed itself. In the first place the invention of gunpowder enabling the Princes to dispense with the bravery of their vassals, they transformed them into courtiers, or hirelings in their armies. Secondly, the discovery of America, pouring its streams of gold into society, was followed by the system of taxation which soon rendered governments independent of the grants of landholders. Finally, the reformation entirely subdued the Church, and rendered it dependent on the state. Thus the empire was divided into a host of greater and lesser tyrants, who scarcely tolerated the appearance of a chief over themselves, but constantly encroaching downwards, destroyed the democratical principle in all below themselves.

The better to effect this purpose, those systems of centralisation were invented, by which governments took every thing under their control; the least trifle was destined to be regulated from the centre; the police extended its powers into the very private life of society; the Church itself was made a tool of this policy. But insulted nature soon took vengeance on the supporters of this infatuated system. Those central departments required beings of a higher nature than are usually found among the generality of mankind, and yet were mostly occupied by creatures who, with respect to energy and perception, were below mediocrity; whilst from beneath the insulated authority could receive neither assistance nor restoration.

Thus, however, in proportion as it greedily swallowed up every thing its strength was gradually lost, and the machine becoming more intricate, the weak spring that had to set the whole in motion, was inadequate to overcome the resistance. At the same time all instincts and energies being destroyed, the whole political economy became an artificial work of the understanding without life and nature. In like manner as landed property first went for coin, and then for paper, all organic energy became a dead letter, which had but little to do with the real world, and the state resembled those galvanised animals which, without life, awfully perform all its functions.

Whilst this system was in its full growth its antidote was secretly preparing. It proceeded from the efforts of the lower vassals and freeholders of the empire. Under their protection, the freemen incorporated themselves in companies in the cities, and these societies formed in the Hanse Union a corporation of a higher order. Meantime the revolution in Switzerland formed an independent peasantry. The increase of money multiplied the number of free proprietors, and soon transferred the greater part of the soil to the free commons. The service in the armies gave them honorable distinctions, printing gave them knowledge, and the sciences formerly monopolised by the higher orders, and finally by the reformation they obtained freedom of conscience.

Thus the democratical element powerfully grew up in the same ratio as the monarchical externally extended, and internally weakened itself; and while the latter, attempting encroachments upon the former, attacked the liberties of the states, it called forth resistance, which gradually brought on a retrograde motion. Thus originated the revolution in England, and the revolt in the Netherlands; and in our times, the French revolution. But as by the dissolution of the empire the system of sovereignty in Germany was brought to perfection, the democratical element has been carried to the highest pitch of discontent; and it may be easily conceived, that so great a degree of exasperation calls for conciliation, if a violent explosion is wished to be avoided.

Were we to compare the present state of Germany with any situation of organic life, we should say, that it most resembled that of the magnetic Somnambulism; for in that state all free agency is destroyed, and all motion and actions are directed by the inferior organs, without being influenced by any intellectual authority, the mind being in a dreaming state.

But as in that situation inferior life acquires what is lost by the superior, it receives new instinct; a new sense is awakened, whereby it easily obtains a knowledge of itself and the surrounding world; thus we perceive in the third estate, particularly since the impulse given by the wars of liberation, the same change of effects. It has acquired all the faculties which formerly belonged to the higher organism of the state. It has manifested in public opinion that knowledge, which guides the organs, even against their will, which understands all the relations of the world, nay, even its own ailings, and administers the proper remedies to remove them.

To allay this ferment, the two principles must be united, so that the democracy may ascend to the monarch, who, in his infallibility, stands at the head of society; and the latter must descend to the former as the base of the whole. The two elements should form a central co-operation, which would give preponderance both to the monarchical and democratic principle.

The communities should be unrestrained in their internal administration, and uninfluenced in the election of their officers; the mayor or justice of the peace only being confirmed by government; the former guided by ancient custom, and the latter by the general statutes of the land: both as magistrates independent of the community are attached to government only by the positive tie of the law.

The officers of the administration and judicature form the connecting link which brings all these communities into one system of unity. Their operations are threefold; first, the general superintendence of the execution of the law in the communities, merely preventing the *abuse* of liberty, without restraining its use; secondly, the regulation of the general concerns of their respective departments, acting, not with so much freedom as the communities themselves, yet with a certain degree of independence; and, lastly, implicit submission and obedience to the complete control of the executive power in all that is legal and just.

Every department would thereby bear a monarchical relation to that immediately below it, and, as it ascends in the hierarchy of power it ought to be more and more concentrated; certain magistrates being placed in the centre, communicating on the one hand with the local authorities, and on the other with the different branches of the ministry. But in the administration of justice this office should be divided; the decision respecting the fact should be left to a jury, and the application of the law to a judge.

But as the administration of local concerns will be best performed by the inhabitants themselves, all minor officers up to the procurators or presidents of the superior departments should be freely elected by them. To guard against the ascendency of the populace, they should be chosen only by such as are possessed of real property; government simply having the power to confirm one of three that are proposed; but the superior officers should be nominated by government, and hold their appointments during pleasure, whilst those that are elected could only be dispossessed of them by a legal process.

But in order to afford the people a share in the framing of those laws which are to regulate all public functions, provincial assemblies should be called from among the people to regulate their local affairs, and general assemblies to co-operate with the ministry in the regulation of the concerns of the whole nation. Thus the system will be strengthened and supported by the energies of those automatous institutions which are the powerful growth of the native soil.

This appears to be the only means of regaining what we have lost; of calming the public mind; and bringing that extensive, wavering, unsettled activity back again into its proper channel;

thus by restoring the rights of the people, obedience will be secured, and that free submission, which is the only bulwark of the State, will be obtained.

By allowing free communication of thought, bound only to truth in facts, and moral equity in opinion, and its abuse left to the decision of an impartial jury; by placing every branch of the constitution under the jealous control of the nation; by abolishing the uncertain control of the Crown, allotting to every public authority its limited duties, performed on its own responsibility, and as far as possible personally discharged,—the chief sources of those discontents, the malady of all States, will be removed.

By abolishing the empty forms, the parchment bonds, which afford the monarchy, unless it resort to brute force, only a doubtful and wavering authority over the democracy, a real organic bond will again keep the crumbling bodies together in sound active life, and mutually supporting each other, all will contribute to the common good.

7. Metternich on Students, Professors, and the Press, 1819

Metternich's letter of June 17, 1819, to his intimate aide and associate Friedrich von Gentz marks the development of a policy of internal conservatism and enforced quiet into an instrument that served Austria's more traditional and pragmatic foreign-policy interests as well. Here Metternich, writing about agitation among students, intellectuals, and publicists, proposes the elements of the Teplitz Convention (and of the repressive Carlsbad Decrees that followed) which seem to warrant placing the Convention itself in the next section, "Europe and the States." [Metternich, *Memoirs*, III (1881), 286–292.]

THE STUDENT, taken in himself, is a child, and the *Burschenschaft* is an unpractical puppet-show. Then, I have never—and of this you are a witness—spoken of the students, but all my aim has been directed at the professors. Now, the professors, singly or united, are most unsuited to be conspirators. People only conspire profitably against things, not against theories. The last, indeed, may grow to power, but this can never be the case if they leave the sphere of theology. Where they are political, they must be supported by deed, and the deed is the overthrow of existing

institutions, and the *ôtez-vous de là que je m'y mette*.[1] This is
what learned men and professors cannot manage, and the class
of lawyers is better suited to carry it on. I know hardly one
learned man who knows the value of property; while, on the
contrary, the lawyer class is always rummaging about in the
property of others. Besides, the professors are, nearly without
exception, given up to theory; while no people are more practical than the lawyers.

Consequently, I have never feared that the revolution would
be engendered by the universities; but that at them a whole
generation of revolutionaries must be formed, unless the evil is
restrained, seems to me certain. I hope that the most mischievous
symptoms of the evil at the universities may be met, and that
perhaps from its own peculiar sources, for the measures of the
Government will contribute to this less than the weariness of
the students, the weakness of the professors, and the different
direction which the studies may take. But this feeling will never
restrain me from taking steps from above; and, indeed, what
seem to me the only possible measures are taken.

If we are together I can give you many satisfactory explanations of the course of the business, which at a distance I could not
communicate to you without an enormous correspondence, and
even then must remain futile and imperfect.

The greatest and consequently the most urgent evil now is the
press. The measures referring to it which I intend to bring forward at the Carlsbad Congress I will tell you all the more gladly
as I wish you to give me your opinion on my ideas without reserve, and put yourself in a position to help me effectually in
Carlsbad, where the business must begin without delay.

My proposals are, briefly, the following:—All the German
Courts shall unite in measures which seem necessary for the
maintenance of the public peace, and from a full sense of the
right of mutual support which is the foundation of the German
Bund.

They here start from the fundamental idea of the Bund, which
consists of Germany and the Sovereign States, that have agreed
mutually to support and help each other, and which, while they
are separate in administrative respects, form one common power
against foreign countries.

---

[1] "Get out and make room for me."—Ed.

The inward peace of the Bund may be endangered and even destroyed by one of the German States attacking the sovereign power of the others. But this can also be done by the moral action of the Government on others, or through the intrigues even of a party. If this party should be supported by a German State—or only find protection in one of them—if with this protection it finds means to rest its lever against neighbouring States on a neighbouring State, then the inner peace of the Bund is threatened, and the Prince who allows this disorder in his country is guilty of felony against the Bund.

All the German Governments have arrived at the conviction that, at the present time, the press serves a party antagonistic to all existing Governments. The nationalities spread over all Germany make it impossible for single States to guard their frontiers from this evil; if this is the fact for single Governments, it will be no less so for all German Governments if but one German State—let it be even the smallest among them—shut itself out from the acceptance of common measures for the maintenance of the general peace.

The Bund has the right of calling upon every single member to fulfill the common duties. In case that member is not found ready of himself, the Bund has the right of compelling him.

From the constitution of the Bund it also arises that everything that is possible to independent sovereigns and European States is not possible to the sovereign States of the German Bund.

For instance, France and England certainly can permit the freedom of the press, and even assert the principle that this freedom is an indispensable condition of the real representative system.

In France and England laws can be made which confine the abuse of the press in relation to the constitution of those two kingdoms.

I doubt, however, whether either of those States would consider it a fundamental idea of the freedom of the press to tolerate all works which are systematically concocted and disseminated in one of the States, even to the generation of rebellion, by a party that is undermining the existing institutions of the other State. In this case the English Government would certainly complain to the French (and *vice versa*) of the toleration of foreign instigators of rebellion; and if the Government complained to did not render its assistance, the Government complaining has the undoubted right to declare war, and so obtain help and redress, or at the least to stop all intercourse between the two States.

These remedies, grounded on the rights of peoples, are not practicable in Germany. What can be done among European Powers in this respect by repression, must be accomplished in the German Bund by preventive laws.

In these propositions there is no Obscurantism, and therefore they are not to be assailed as such. Even the instigators of rebellion, indeed, feel this, and will not object to them. They may decry such a state of things as a great evil for Germany, and express a wish for the only alternative known to me—the union of all Germany in one whole, undivided body. This wish has already become the fundamental principle of the fraternisation of practical German revolutionists.

Since, however, this can only be fulfilled by a single German monarchy, or one German free State, it is to be supposed that no German Government will be found, from German feeling, to submit to be chased from Court and home—an inevitable condition to be expected by the victim to the love of carrying out that idea.

The means to this end seem to me to be the following:—

1. There must be a settled difference made between books (real works), and journals and pamphlets.

Scientific matter characterises the former, and, where this is not evident, the number of sheets. Thus, for instance, I take for granted that a Dissertation on Trigonometry consisting of three or four sheets might be reckoned as a *work*; while a political work, to be reckoned as such, must contain at least five-and-twenty sheets.

Periodicity and the political or moral subject-matter decides their character.

2. It is reserved to every German State to decide whether they will have a censorship of all literary productions which appear within their limits, or whether they will pass repressive laws.

In the second case the law must be for the whole Bund one and the same law: that is, every State which permits the freedom of the press for works must accept the law which the Bund has passed for all States in the same position.

3. All journals, pamphlets, &c., &c., in Germany must be under a censorship.

4. Where freedom of the press for works is permitted, the local

Government (*Landesregierung*) must through their public prose-
cutor carry on the suit which any other German Government
may bring in a diplomatic way against either the author or publisher. This suit must be instituted and carried on in the name
of the local Government, and the subject of complaint must be
considered and treated by it as affecting that Government itself.

In the same way every German Government must be responsible for its own censorship. Every complaint against the latter
must be considered as a complaint of Government against Government.

5. The usual regulations as to the printing of the author's name,
or at least the place where the work is printed, and the publisher's
name, must everywhere be observed.

No publication can be allowed at any bookseller's in Germany
except under these conditions. Every anonymous writing in the
Bund falls under confiscation.

These are my principal ideas, and I hardly think that any reasonable objection can be made to them. I deplore, indeed, that the
censorship cannot be instituted for all writings without exception.
But I am convinced that in many German States great opposition
would be made if it were applied to true works. The most
pressing evil is, however, certainly met by a firm administration
of my proposals, and I doubt not that they will be accepted by
the majority of eminent men. The most important German States
—as, for instance, Prussia and Bavaria, Saxony and Hanover, even
Baden—have to make no backward step in principle, for they all
have either a general censorship or at the least a censorship of the
journals. In Bavaria the latter is even constitutional: the Government, too, from its incomprehensible toleration, is more culpable
than any other.

Postscript—I beg your indulgence if in my letter you find some
undigested expressions. I have much to do, and I hope that in
reading, and still more in estimating, my ideas on the laws respecting the licence of the press, you will hold more by the spirit
than the words; but I submit both to your better knowledge and
experience.

II

Europe and the States

The state system Metternich tried to establish in Europe was one of collective security among the governments, as distinguished from free competition among sovereign states in pursuit of their individual interests. For its success the system required that governments hold some common interest to be more important than separate state ambition. Rulers and governments had to believe that competition among them would create dangers so great as to overbalance the opportunities competition might offer. The basis found for the system's operation was fear of change—fear of the revolution and war that might be unleashed by open state competition.

The effectiveness of the system consequently depended on emphasizing the dangers of domestic disorder and interstate rivalries, and on maintaining in authority those governments which felt vulnerable to dangers of that kind. Both requirements led to the principle of "intervention" in the domestic affairs of individual states, in the name of Europe, to dramatize and suppress disorder and to sustain anti-revolutionary governments.

When the victorious statesmen convened in 1814, their task appeared to be the more traditional one of dividing the spoils, by a process of bargaining that would result in a kind of equilibrium among states—the principle of the "balance of power." The Bourbon Pretender was made Louis XVIII of a French constitutional monarchy whose power potential roughly matched that of Czarist Russia. Austria's basic strength fell short of that of either France or Russia, and close behind Austria came her traditional rival in the Germanies, the Kingdom of Prussia. Great Britain, whose power was maritime and financial, was mainly concerned to ensure that the Continent should not fall under the domination of any one power.

But within months, two events had interrupted the bargaining. One was a separate agreement between Russia and Prussia, in pursuit of their separate state interests, to extend Russian power westward through a satellite Polish kingdom, and to extend Prussia southward by the annexation of the Kingdom of Saxony. Both aspects of this project seriously threatened Austria: Russia was its great rival to the east, and Prussia its great rival in Germany. Eventually, the issue was compromised, but not without giving Metternich a clear look at the danger to which separate alliances, especially between Prussia and Russia, exposed Austria. The other event was Napoleon's Hundred

Days, when France went over to the outlawed emperor *en masse*, showing that revolutionary imperialism was not dead. The fears revived by the Hundred Days suggested the antidote to the problem of separate alliances—if suggestion was needed—and the basis for collective security, as well as for Austrian state security.

Prussia as a rival was doubly dangerous to Austria. First, it was a potential ally to a restless Russia, and, second, it might, especially under a reformist government, be tempted to make use of German radical nationalism in pursuit of its state interests, at Austria's expense. Metternich nurtured and exploited Frederick William III's fear of revolution to make of Prussia a willing supporter rather than a rival, and to bring about the fall of the Prussian reformist ministry. The main instrument he used was nationalist student radicalism, and the principle he established was joint intervention to suppress disorder and political change in Germany. That was the Metternich system on the German scale; it was established in agreements at Teplitz and Carlsbad in 1819. From that base and on that model the system was extended to Europe, so that Russian ambition might be contained as Prussian had been. The principle of European intervention was established at the conferences at Troppau and at Laibach in 1820 and 1821, on the basis of revolutions in Spain and Italy. Austria and Bourbon France sent armies into Italy and Spain, respectively, to restore conservative régimes there, and the Czar's enthusiasm for Russian intervention everywhere was sidetracked.

The price of the Troppau containment of Russia, though, was the separation of England from the European concert. The British domestic political system did not favor general principles of international counterrevolution, and British interests did not accord with Continental intervention in places open to British naval and commercial influence. England's independence of the conservative concert was confirmed by her cooperation with the North American Republic to prevent Continental intervention in the New World, on the principles expressed in the Monroe Doctrine (1823)—a document which, according to Metternich, "set altar against altar." With Great Britain firmly and securely outside the Continental alliance, the French Revolution of 1830 and the liberal Orleanist monarchy that followed opened the way to a division of Europe into liberal and conservative blocs, replacing the conservative concert Metternich had striven to build. The international division matched and reinforced the division in political principles and domestic institutions, and the division on principle helped define the two international blocs. That was the context for the developments in European thought, economic life, and politics during the latter years of Metternich's Europe.

A CHRONOLOGY

1818   Congress of Aix-la-Chapelle
1819   Teplitz Convention and Carlsbad Decrees. End of the Prussian reform ministry.

1820	Revolutions in Spain and Italy
1820–21	Congresses of Troppau and Laibach
1821	Austrian intervention in Italy
1822	Congress of Verona
1823	French intervention in Spain. The Monroe Doctrine.
1824–30	Ultraconservative régime of Charles X in France
1830	July Revolution in France

BIBLIOGRAPHY

G. de Bertier de Sauvigny, *Metternich and His Times* (London, 1962).
A. J. May, *The Age of Metternich, 1814–1848* (rev. edn., New York, 1963).
D. Perkins, *A History of the Monroe Doctrine* (Boston, 1963).
P. W. Schroeder, *Metternich's Diplomacy at Its Zenith, 1820–1823* (Austin, Tex., 1962).
C. K. Webster, *The Foreign Policy of Castlereagh, 1815–1822* (2nd. edn., London, 1934).

8. Friedrich von Gentz, "Considerations on the Political System Now Existing in Europe," 1818

Friedrich von Gentz (1764–1832), antirevolutionary publicist, took pride in the realism of his political appraisals. As Metternich's most intimate consultant on foreign affairs, he was retained by the rulers of the Danube principality of Wallachia for services that included frequent reports on European politics. The memorandum below is one of these, probably written early in 1818. It provides an introductory sketch of the European political scene as it might be described by an informed and sophisticated observer. To relate the document with others that appear in this section, it may be useful to note the role Gentz assigns to Austro-Prussian cooperation in the European international system, and beyond that, what the ultimate bases of European unity are assumed to be. And you may wish to evaluate Gentz's analysis by checking his predictions against what actually came to pass. [Friedrich von Gentz, *Dépêches inédites du Chevalier de Gentz, aux hospodars de Valachie*, I (Paris, 1876), 354–379. Translation by the editor.]

THE POLITICAL system existing in Europe since 1814 and 1815 is a phenomenon without precedent in the world's history. In place of the principle of equilibrium, or more accurately of counterweights formed by separate alliances, the principle that has governed and too often has also troubled and bloodied Europe for three centuries, there has succeeded a principle of general union, uniting all the states collectively with a federative bond, under the guidance of the five principal Powers, four of which have equal shares in that guidance, while the fifth at this time is still subject to a kind of tutelage, from which it will soon emerge to place itself upon a par with its custodians. The states of the second, third, and fourth rank submit tacitly, though nothing has ever been stipulated in this regard, to the decisions made in common by the preponderant Powers; and so Europe seems really to form a grand political family, united under the auspices of a high tribunal of its own creation, whose members guarantee to themselves and to all parties concerned the peaceful enjoyment of their respective rights.

This scheme of things has its inconveniences. But it is certain that, could it be made durable, it would be after all the best possible combination to assure the prosperity of peoples, and the maintenance of the peace, which is one of its first prerequisites. The strongest objection to the present system is the obvious difficulty of preserving over a long period of time the harmony among the heterogeneous elements that compose it. The most divergent interests, the most conflicting tendencies, and the most contradictory aspirations, views, and secret thoughts are pulled together and for the moment submerged in the common action of a league, which more resembles a coalition created for a particular purpose, than it does a true alliance based on clear and permanent interests. It required unique circumstances to bring such a league into being; it would be contrary to the nature of things and of men for it to replace for long that condition of opposition and conflict which the diversity of positions, interests, and opinions will always impose upon a group of independent Powers, each of which necessarily has its own characteristics and its own system. This perspective is far from unimportant. For one cannot avoid the fact that the collapse of a system now in effect, no matter what new system follows it, will immediately give rise to a state of uncertainty, anxiety, and danger, and will open the way to a new general conflagration with unpredictable results and duration.

Therefore, the most important concern a statesman can have today is the probable duration of this European league, which for the moment has filled the chasm of political dissension but cannot fill it forever, or even for very long. This basically is the only important question of our times; for the peace, the destinies, and the future existence of the peoples of Europe are directly and wholly bound up with it. As long as this kind of general federation exists, questions of the most difficult sort can be worked out smoothly, one way or another, without causing perceptible shocks. But the moment when this system dissolves will be one of the most critical and most terrible that lie before us.

Contemporary opinion is generally doubtful that the present state of affairs can remain stable. It is not believed that an edifice that had its origins in wholly extraordinary events, and which rests upon one single common interest, though that interest be the greatest of all, can survive amid so many surrounding factors for disunity, one or another of which could cause an explosion any day. Even those who possess neither the talents nor the position from which to judge so difficult a question are led by a vague foreboding to regard the Grand Alliance as a meteor always on the verge of extinction; mistrust is part of the spirit of our times. And be it noted besides that the reasons for doubting the stability of the union of sovereigns are much more evident, much easier for the public to grasp, than the less visible reasons for holding the opposite view. But I, having reflected often and deeply on this matter, and possessing all the materials for informed judgment, do not share the conjectures and alarm constantly nourished by many persons. I am persuaded that the European federation—for that is the most accurate term for the present system—is not threatened with immediate ruin. I should not answer for a half-century; but I should not hesitate to answer for ten or even twenty years, a long enough interval I think for everyone to think out the future, and to prepare in time the position that another order of things will require. My opinion is based not on the structure of the system, the extreme fragility of which I myself recognize, but on the situations of the principal Powers that compose it, situations such that no one of these Powers can safely, without risking imminent ruin, leave the circle of its present connections.

The five Powers at the head of the federation are the only ones who could destroy the general system by changing their policies. Squabbles and changes among the others could never have that effect.

Spain and Portugal in one corner, and Sweden and Denmark

in the other, are much too weak and much too far from the center of Europe for their actions to affect the decisions of the great Powers.

The Kingdom of the Netherlands is inevitably bound by the conduct and the relations among its great neighbors; being suspended among France, Britain, and Germany, it can have no desire but peace, and no principle but to be on good terms with everybody.

The states of Germany, now that there no longer are and no longer can be liaisons between themselves and France, are no more than satellites of the two preponderant bodies; and as long as Austria and Prussia work together, the other German courts can only follow their direction.

The states of Italy are squeezed between Austria and France, and deprived of any will of their own.

The Ottoman Porte would undoubtedly have the power to make war against Russia, unimpeded by vague ties with the European federation. But if the Porte should decide some day to attack Russia without provocation from that Power, the result probably would be only a separate war that would not disturb the general system at all. The case would be very different if Russia were the aggressor; in that case, to which I shall return later, the present European system would move inevitably toward catastrophe.

Of the five Powers, which, according to this preliminary description, are the only ones in position to cause decisive change, there are three—Austria, Prussia, and Britain—who would regard such change as total disaster, and would do anything to prevent it. The other two, France and Russia, *could* have, even in *less* than ten or twenty years, more or less attractive reasons for leaving their present positions; but they are held there by more important considerations, or by insurmountable hindrances. This I shall undertake to prove.

Austria, for the past two years, has adopted so pacific a policy that she must most seriously fear any alteration in the European system that might tend directly or indirectly to draw her into new wars. She has reduced her military forces even beyond the limits and proportions that prudence allows. She has neglected her army in all respects; and if, as all the signs indicate, she continues on this false path for several more years, it may be expected that when summoned one day to take action, she will manage only by painful efforts to reconstitute that army, which is in a process of steady decay. Her finances are recovering little by little; and after two or three years she will be able, in this important respect, to get caught up with her affairs. But that would not make it any easier for her to meet the costs of a serious war. She would have no liquid funds, emergency taxes would not pay for half a campaign, sources of credit are dried up for a long time to come, and nobody, from now on, can count on British subsidies. Therefore, everything combines to bind Austria to a peaceful system. She cannot depart from it without incurring inconveniences and very real dangers, it is pure profit for her to maintain the present state of affairs as long as possible, and, because her central position allows her to play so brilliant a role in the European alliance, she will surely be one of the last to abandon that alliance.

Prussia perhaps would find a few more favorable opportunities than Austria in an overturn of the present system. Still she, too, has important reasons to fear it. Her army is less disorganized than Austria's; and, because she has had the good sense to keep fully organized the militia units that did her such good service in the last war, she would have less difficulty reconstituting an effective army, and it would take her less time. But her provinces are too exhausted to produce an army of over a hundred thousand men, and she is without the means to pay them. Although she is much less burdened with debt than Austria, her finances are by no means flourishing; clear proof of this is that she is now negotiating under very onerous conditions, through English bankers and others, a loan of eighteen million crowns [about fifty million francs], just to cover the deficit of the past two years. Prussia's geographical position has become, despite her recent acquisitions, more difficult and precarious than ever before. Her provinces are vulnerable from all directions. If she strips her western defenses, her Rhine possessions and the whole north of Germany are exposed to French invasion; if she withdraws her forces on the Polish side, she will be in Russia's power. The Prussian government fortunately has recognized that her only safety lies in an intimate combination with Austria, a combination which assures to these two Powers the means of joint disposition over the forces of the rest of Germany. This system has prevailed over the alternative of a Russian alliance, which has never had any basis but temporary needs and circumstances. Such an alliance no longer has a single partisan in Prussia; the King himself, however attached personally to the Emperor Alexander, seems to have given it up for good. But the combination with Austria necessarily implies the maintenance of the general system. For Austria, even while working steadily to cement her ties with Prussia and to organize the Germanic Confederation in the interests of the two Powers, still seeks in this only the maintenance of the peace, and considers her association with Prussia and the whole of Germany (an association which today forms the basis of her own policy) to be *framed*, so to speak, in the larger scene of European federation, as the guarantee of general tranquility; and Prussia will cease to walk the same path as Austria on the day she thinks of upsetting that system. Thus Prussia, however one looks at her, is just as interested as Austria in taking care to avoid anything that might compromise the peace; and the government at Berlin fears war, and is right to fear it, as much as and perhaps more than Austria.

England is guided absolutely by the same principles and the same interests. She has reached her highest point; happy if she can stay where she is, menaced by incalculable dangers if she seeks to move out of her position, or if commanding circumstances force her to do so. The debt structure has been pushed to its extreme limits in England. The best-informed men see no possibility of extending those limits within ten or fifteen years. If it is possible within that time to redeem two or three hundred millions of the public debt, then new loans can be considered; otherwise any efforts in this direction must necessarily have the most serious consequences. In the past twenty years England has grown used to making war on a gigantic scale; each of the recent years has cost her a hundred million pounds sterling and more. She cannot accept a secondary role; she must be in the first rank, or else completely inactive. The British government understands its position perfectly; it is steeped in it. In the near future it foresees, not without dread, serious dissensions and perhaps war with the United States of America, a formidable rival whose power is growing before our eyes, and whose interests and plans conflict with those of England in every part of the globe. Thus many important considerations combine to make the British ministry tremble at the very thought of a new war in Europe. She will use every means she has, and even bear heavy sacrifices, to avoid so dangerous a risk. England is the pivot of the European federation; it is she who founded the system, out of her very accurate and very prudent calculation of the great danger to which a new general convulsion would expose her; and also it is she who sustains it, cultivates it, who nurses it always with notable attention, solicitude, and skill. Though she is eternally jealous of France and no less alarmed by the progress of Russia, she carefully avoids giving these two Powers the slightest cause for hostile sentiments. At the same time she treats the German Powers as her true and permanent allies; but even while flooding them with incontestable proofs of her warm confidence, she always reinforces their inclination toward peace, toward avoiding anything that might compromise their good understanding with France and with Russia. This prudent and restrained course is not restricted to the present ministry. It is the necessary outcome of the events that have brought England to the position, brilliant and dangerous at the same time, where she now finds herself; and no matter what ministers govern that country, they will pursue the same policy, perhaps with less skill, aplomb, and dignity than the present ones, but they will always pursue it, at least until a time when the liquidation of a considerable part of the public debt, and of the interest charges and the enormous taxes it carries with it, may permit her to shift to a new course.

I come finally to the two great Powers at the extremities of Europe. These, I admit, do not have the same interest as the others in maintaining the present system. But considering their own situations and their relations with neighboring Powers, there is reason for reassurance regarding the fears they inspire in us.

Let us begin with *France*. Certainly she cannot genuinely enjoy a state of affairs to which she has been forced to submit so as to escape more cruel evils, but which for her has been only a source of humiliation, loss, and bitterness. France will never forget the unprecedented fall that has dropped her from limitless heights of grandeur into nothingness; she will never forget the treaties of 1815, nor the rigor with which fulfillment of those treaties has been demanded, despite the honorable forms devised by the Powers to mask their hard reality. The desire to avenge these insults is in every Frenchman's heart; and though party spirit has smoth-

ered this among some of the noisier ones, of whom there are not
many anyway, sooner or later it will become the dominant sentiment among all elements of the nation. This European federation,
in which so many other Powers have seen and still see their security and their best guarantee, has been nothing but a burden for
France, and can never be an advantage for her. France herself
occupies an important place in it; that is the best thing she can
do for the moment. But she has no need of it for the future.
Her interest is, on the contrary, to dissolve it as soon as possible;
her only chances for recoupment and success lie in divisions
among the great Powers, divisions which would put her in a
position to choose her allies along traditional political lines, and
to recover her strength at the expense of her enemies. These
are all incontestable facts; and the personal character of the King,
the personal characters of his ministers, solemn treaties, special
agreements—all that is of small and transitory weight in such calculations.

It is also true that, Russia excepted, France is the European
Power that has fully recovered its strength most quickly. She has
suffered much, but she has immense resources; and, more important than anything else, her government can command the full
application of her resources better than any other, because her
administrative system far surpasses any other, and because it finds
a perfect instrument for the execution of great projects in a people who are cultivated, intelligent, capable of great things, and
governed now by a free and strong constitution. The existence
of a party that stands, so to speak, outside the constitution and
never ceases to harass and torment the Government is today the
only weak point, the only vulnerable side of France; but in the
eternal nature of things that party must burn itself out in time.
The fiscal wounds will be healed sooner than expected, the army
will be rebuilt within a few years, and the France of 1825 will
no longer resemble the France of 1815 in any way.

But despite all these advantages, France would have great difficulty revising the political system of Europe to suit her tastes,
and until she has accomplished that necessary preliminary, as long
as she is in fact isolated, and a member only of that general association which today takes the place of particular and explicitly
stated alliances, she can undertake nothing substantial. And the
men who direct her affairs are not adventurers who would seize

upon romantic projects. For a very long time to come this Power will be the object of general distrust. The fears and precautions of all Europe will be directed against her for some time yet, and with the slightest hint of an aggressive enterprise, she will revive the league that defeated her in 1814. For a long time yet war against France would be the one popular war in Europe, the only one that would, despite wide hardships, find no lack of supporters, participants, and sacrifice. Governments have learned to compare and balance the dangers that could come upon them from the French side and from the Russian; but the peoples have eyes only for France. The hatreds and fears that France has inspired everywhere will not be quieted so soon.

The French government is too intelligent and too perceptive not to judge and appreciate this state of affairs. First of all, it needs a number of years to recover from its wounds. Five or six years will be absolutely necessary for this. At the end of this time, even if one supposes the French government really determined to recover a major role in the affairs of Europe, it will have to find a way to detach itself from the Grand Alliance, and to substitute for it relations based on common interests with one or the other principal Power—conditions that will not be easy to fulfill. Without achieving this first, France can undertake nothing, or certainly will fail in her undertakings. As long as the league survives among the other Powers, France, even supposing full recovery of her strength, must confine herself to speculations about the future. This reasoning, in which I have left out of account the shocks that the death of the King or other internal events might cause, confirms me in the opinion that it will not be France that overturns the present system; but I am persuaded at the same time that she will profit from the destruction of the system, when other circumstances cause it to fall.

I enter upon the ticklish subject of *Russia* with far less assurance. There, where the absolute will of a single man decides everything and where, to add to the difficulty, the character of that man is problematical, judgments and conjectures find no solid foundations, and permit no better than guesswork. Be that as it may, it is well worth the trouble frankly to declare the pros and cons on a matter so important, without claiming too strong a probability for one side or the other.

The Emperor Alexander, despite all the zeal and enthusiasm he has consistently shown for the Grand Alliance, is the sovereign who could most easily get along without it. He needs nobody's support; if his position be threatened, at least it cannot be threatened from outside his Empire, for all Europe fears his power and has reason to fear it. For him the Grand Alliance is only an implement with which he exercises in general affairs the influence that is one of the main objects of his ambition. It is a comfortable and tractable implement, which he makes use of with great skill, but which he will destroy on the first day he thinks he can replace it with something more direct and more effective. His interest in the preservation of the system is not, as is true of Austria, Prussia, or England, an interest based on necessity or fear; it is a free and calculated interest, which he is in a position to renounce as soon as a different system should offer him greater advantages.

The Emperor of Russia is, moreover, the one sovereign fully in a position to undertake major enterprises at any time. He is at the head of the one standing army really capable of action in Europe today. Nothing could resist the first assault of that army. It is unnecessary to repeat here what we have long known about the geographical situation of Russia and that of her neighbors. None of the obstacles that restrain and thwart the other sovereigns—divided authority, constitutional forms, public opinion, etc.—exists for the Emperor of Russia. What he dreams of at night he can carry out in the morning.

Surely, it takes very considerable counterarguments to give reassurance against dangers as evident as these. But let us see the reverse of the coin.

First, one would have to know whether the Emperor Alexander has the will or desire to bring about changes, and overturn the present system. People say the man is impenetrable, and therefore everybody feels free to judge his intentions. I do not wish to fall into the same error; but I have considered the question long enough to know how difficult it is to resolve it. I know all there is to be said about his consuming energy, his ambition, his dissimulation. But I also know of qualities in him of quite another stamp. His chivalrous loyalty would never permit him an act of betrayal. He sets great store by the good opinion of men, perhaps even more than he does by glory as such. The titles of

Peacemaker, Protector of the Weak, or Regenerator of the Empire have more charm for him than Conqueror. Religious sentiments, which are *not* hypocritical, have for many years so predominated in his mind that all is subordinated to them. A prince in whom good and bad are mixed in so singular a manner must necessarily be the object of many doubts, and it would be rash to say what his conduct would be in this or that possible situation. But when I think of him placed in definite given circumstances, it seems to me less rash to judge what he would do and what he would not do in response to those circumstances. He considers himself the founder, the creator of the European federation; he would like to be considered its chief. For two years he has not dictated a memorandum or a diplomatic document without extolling this system as the century's glory, and as the salvation of the world. Is it probable, is it possible that in the face of all these testimonials, which fill the archives of governments, which are the substance of a hundred proclamations, in the face of a public opinion that respects and fears him, and of a religion he honors, he should embark upon unjust and pointless enterprises, to destroy a work from which he expects his immortality? I cannot easily believe in a revolution that abrupt. Though many people say that all that is a game and a comedy, I have a right to ask for proof. Why should he not be devoted to this system by principle and by preference? Why should he not prefer this kind of glory, which, moreover, fits very well with a secret thought of peaceful supremacy, to the risks of wars and turmoil, whose outcome must always seem doubtful to one who cannot, like Napoleon, hope to make the outcome certain by virtue of military talents of the first order?

Let us suppose all the same that there should occur such an abrupt change in the ideas and sentiments the Emperor has so far expressed that he should decide to defy public opinion, the scruples of conscience, the most solemn testimony, and the most sacred engagements. We then come to another question. Would he have the means to accomplish projects of aggrandizement and domination, on a base so uncertain and so impermanent?

Financial distress, the common malady of all European governments, lies heavy upon the Russian as well; and emergency funds, in the quantity needed for extended campaigns, would be sought in vain, inside or outside the Empire. You could reply to this that the Russian armies, pushed beyond the frontiers by vigorous and swift operations, would no longer cost the country anything, and would find enough to live on. But this argument forgets that the requisition system, easy to apply in a passing invasion, does not suit a war or an occupation of long duration, and that the abuse the French made of this system made them an object of hatred among the peoples, and that a conqueror obliged to base his plan of operations on requisitions would immediately become generally odious, and would find within a year the same fate Napoleon had after fifteen years of unprecedented victories.

As long as Austria and Prussia hold together, Russia will not be able to undertake limited and isolated campaigns. To attain any end comparable to the vast projects attributed to her, she would have to move on an immense front, from the Memel to the Carpathians. Five hundred thousand men would not be too many for such an undertaking. At the beginning she would find little resistance; for, as I observed before, defenses would not be good. But little by little the opposing forces would form; all Germany, more attached to her independence than ever, would be aroused, and would provide Austria and Prussia with the help needed for swift re-establishment of the equilibrium. Without counting the cooperation of England—cooperation more formidable for Russia than a land army of two hundred thousand men—the Russian armies, after a few brilliant and sterile successes, would find themselves everywhere repulsed, and the Emperor Alexander, having lost all the fruits of his former policy, would reap from the one he had embraced only regrets, embarrassments, and dangers from which he could not extricate himself for the rest of his life.

The one single expedition Russia could undertake without directly encountering these enormous difficulties would be the one said to have threatened the Porte for a long time. It is certain that, given the present condition of the other Powers, Russian armies could have crossed the Danube and been in full march against Constantinople without bringing on the slightest hostile movement at their rear or on their flanks. But such successes, even supposing them much easier than they are in reality, would be no less ephemeral and illusory. For if Austria, Prussia, and England stay in agreement—France counting for nothing in this calculation—the Powers can never allow the Porte's territory to be invaded or dismembered by the Russians. Their opposition might be slow, but it need only be sure, to keep the Emperor from exposing himself to a reaction whose consequences might be quite as disastrous for him as those of a vain effort against Germany. It is this consideration that makes me persist in the belief that the present system, even though the Porte is not included in it, is one of the strongest guarantees of its security and its rights, and in the belief that the Holy Alliance, which seems to be regarded with an evil eye in Constantinople, and which is after all only a fanciful ornamentation on the real federation, is one of the Porte's greatest assets.

We see then that in the last analysis the position of Russia, despite the immensity of resources, is infinitely more like that of France than might have been supposed. Just like France, Russia cannot undertake anything without having *previously* changed the European system, by detaching one or another of its essential members and making it her permanent ally. Only then could she break out of line and try her strength, be it against Germany or the Porte. If Prussia had stayed with Russia in the situation of 1814 [cooperation against Austria], it would today be up to the Emperor Alexander to choose among the roles of protector, of dictator, or of tyrant over Europe. This danger is past; and though the government at Vienna has made some mistakes, it has fully expiated them by the active part it took in Prussia's healthy repentance. In whatever hands the direction of that Power's affairs may fall, she will not soon return to her old erroneous ways. Russia can no longer hope to interest England in any project whatever that is contrary to the general interest. All that remains to her, then, as a last resort and a last bugbear, is a separate alliance with France. Such an alliance is possible; it is even one of the least unlikely and the most frightening possibilities of the future. But it needs time and much time for it to ripen. And as the two Powers have no point of contact whatever, the intervening States and England would be guilty of negligence or weakness difficult to imagine, should they let themselves be taken unawares by so fatal a combination.

These reflections lead to a conclusion as remarkable as it is reassuring. What at first glance seems the weakest part of the present system is precisely what gives it force. France and Russia

are today the only two Powers who could threaten Europe with
a new upheaval, and they are rendered incapable of harm as long
as the *middle line*, formed by Powers whose only interest and
whose only desire is peace, is not broken. Austria, Prussia, and
England, each little disposed today and little prepared for a serious
war, comparatively and individually impotent, peaceful by necessity, but still strong enough for joint resistance, are the true ram-
part of the common security of Europe; and the colossi that
occupy the two extremities, breaking against this central dike for
as long as it lasts, must for a long time to come seek their advantage and their glory in preserving an order of things that they
cannot hope to destroy.

Add to these considerations the general situation of the peoples, their horror of war, the attention that must be paid to them,
the penury of all the governments, the evident inclinations of the
cabinets at London, Vienna, and Berlin, and what the soundest
data and the most reasonable calculations tell us of the reigning
principles in France and in Russia—I think that very great proba-
bilities join in pointing to the maintenance of the general peace,
and of the political system, which, with all its imperfections and
all its faults, is today its foundation and its guarantee.

9. Intervention in Germany: Teplitz and Carlsbad, 1819

The Vienna Act of 1815 setting up the German Confederation had included, as a sop to German liberal sentiments, which the authors did
not yet dare fully to antagonize, a provision (Article 13) that the
several German states would establish representative constitutions. The
governments of some of the smaller states in the South, seeking popularity with their subjects and political independence from their
greater neighbors, did provide constitutions and elected assemblies.
Metternich's anxiety at what might develop from this trend led to his
meeting with the Prussian king and government at Teplitz in the
summer of 1819, soon after the Kotzebue murder. The policies agreed
upon there by Austria and Prussia are the political essentials of the
Carlsbad Decrees, adopted by the Diet of the Confederation in September, establishing close controls over universities and the press.
[Metternich to the Emperor Francis: Metternich, *Memoirs*, III (1881),
299–308; the Teplitz Convention: Heinrich von Treitschke, *History of
Germany in the Nineteenth Century*, trans. Eden and Cedar Paul, III
(London, 1917), 628–631.]

Metternich to the Emperor Francis. Teplitz, August 1, 1819

MY REPORT of yesterday will have thrown as much light as was for the moment possible on the state of my negotiations here.

To-day I am able to lay before your Majesty their definite results.

Having ascertained the wishes of the King of Prussia, I entered into conference with Prince von Hardenberg, Prince von Wittgenstein, and Count von Bernstorff, in order to place as clearly as possible the foundation of our future course before them. To this conference I also invited Count Zichy.

My plan consists in the main of the following propositions:—

1. The almost inconceivable perverseness of the course of most of the German Governments (the Prussian above all) has given such an impetus to the revolutionary spirit that perhaps the last period has arrived when help is still possible.

Formerly the German revolutionists were as much separated as the States in which they lived; that under such circumstances no effectual blow could be struck by them was soon clear to the conspirators. The military party in Prussia at first thought of aggrandising themselves by the conquest of Prussia; the civil party in Prussia limited themselves to employing their efforts for the transformation of Prussia. Some men (and it is noticeable that they are nearly all persons engaged in teaching) go much further, and from a revolutionary point of view take the right road. They direct their eyes to the union of all Germans in one Germany.

For this the generation already educated cannot serve them; they therefore turn their attention to those who are to be educated, a plan which commends itself even to the most impatient, for the student generation includes, at the most, a space of four years. Now, the systematic preparation of youth for this infamous object has lasted already more than one of these generations. A whole class of future State officials, professors, and incipient literary men, is here ripened for revolution.

If we now reflect that in the Prussian Government the most numerous and important positions, both in the centre of the Government, and in the provinces (especially is this the case in the Rhine provinces), are occupied by pure revolutionists, it is not to be wondered at if Prussia is considered quite ripe for revolution.

Two circumstances have unexpectedly assisted this deep laid

plan—the disaffection, almost amounting to madness, of the press in general, and the introduction of demagogic Governments in South Germany. What Prussia's weakness had prepared for years, Bavaria accomplished with one blow, Baden imitated, and Wurtemberg sought to extend still further.

2. To complete this work it now only requires to set up a democratic Government in Prussia. That this measure is not yet full depends on the personal timidity of the King and—I say without hesitation—the systematic efforts with which I have made it my duty to frighten the King from every step which must have resulted in the inevitable overthrow of all the existing institutions. To this end it was necessary that the King, and even the high officers of the State, should be imbued with the most undoubting confidence in the true friendship of your Majesty, and to obtain for myself personally the good opinion of the King. How thoroughly this has succeeded is shown by the present result.

3. As the first steps were attained by your Majesty's personal course in German affairs as well as in your Majesty's personal attitude towards the King, I made use of the last meeting of the Courts at Aix-la-Chapelle to make myself at home in the internal affairs of Prussia; and your Majesty will remember the steps which I then took to explain to the King himself his position with regard to his people—or rather with regard to the administration—and to draw his attention to the difference between the principles which must cost him the throne and those which may yet save him. The salvation of the Prussian monarchy may therefore probably date from Aix-la-Chapelle.

That this evil by its extension produces the means of its own extinction is also seen in Prussia. Moral, like physical, evil always reaches such a height, if it is not destroyed in its first germ, or at any rate in its very first period, that at last its weakness becomes plainly evident. The illusion disappears, its imminent and entire dissolution is palpable, and courage often comes in the last hours to the help of the most dejected, and it is fortunate if then the elements of relief are still at their disposal.

This is the present position of the King of Prussia. It is known to your Majesty that, by one of those happy chances which often occur in the life of States as in the lives of men, my journey to Carlsbad happened at the moment of a decision most important for Prussia. That I consider the present crisis momentous for the whole of Germany I have shown your Majesty by my plan, not only of going to Carlsbad myself, but of there conferring with the ministers of the chief German Courts. But a good resolution generally leads to manifold benefits, and so it has here turned out.

That the great conspiracy overspreading the whole of Germany would be unmasked just at this moment was so little foreseen by me that it was part of my plan to discover it at Carlsbad. In the same way your Majesty's idea of going straight to Vienna, instead of to Milan, was of those happy inspirations the object of which can only be known beforehand by Providence.

4. I came here by the pressing invitation of the King, and found him, as I mentioned in my last despatch to your Majesty, in an excellent and, for him, unusually confidential mood. How much this disposition has been increased by my efforts here was yesterday made most evident. The day before yesteday I had begged the King to grant me another audience. Yesterday morning the King came to me himself with Prince Wittgenstein. In a conversation of two hours, and in the presence of that excellent and faithful witness, I unfolded my views, feelings and convictions with the same candour with which I always make it my duty to speak to your Majesty. I thoroughly penetrated the mind of the King, and found the means of exciting in him the most active principle of his character—the repressive—to such a degree that we may hope he will never take the most hazardous of all steps, the introduction of a constitution for his kingdom, without granting me a preliminary examination of what is to be done.

In order to lead the King to right principles, I had prepared a short work which clearly pointed out the true difference between such institutions as the Diets and a so-called representative system. I thought it all the more necessary to place this work in the King's own hands as I saw that he had placed the greatest value on a far more superficial paper which I had presented to Prince Wittgenstein, as well as to the State Chancellor at Aix-la-Chapelle.

I take the liberty of sending your Majesty a copy of the above-named paper. If your Majesty condescends to look it over, you will be convinced that only the utterance of a few sentences—only a few blunders in the choice of the system to be followed—is needed to frustrate for ever any possible rescue of the good cause.

5. During my conversations here with the first Prussian statesmen, I have convinced myself of the following evident facts.

Prince von Hardenberg is morally, as well as physically, in a state of weakness bordering on childhood. He desires what is right, he knows even what is right, but there are in him two elements always most dangerous for a statesman of the highest grade, even if his strength of mind were greater than ever was the Prince's. The one is an extraordinary impulse toward liberalism: the other an unfortunate inclination to get strange people about him. It may be said without exaggeration that at the present time there is not a man near him whose opinions are not either of the purest democracy, or who is not already an active participator in the conspiracy against the very throne of Prussia itself.

The King is thoroughly informed of the state of things. There are in Prussia also two negative powers in conflict—the weakness of the King with that of the State Chancellor. The first is the least dangerous, for the King's weakness is coupled with indolence: that of the Chancellor, with the greatest activity.

Count Bernstorff is thoroughly right-feeling in principle. He is, however, extremely weak, and he has such a deep consciousness of his painful position that he is quite enfeebled by it.

Prince Wittgenstein thinks as I do: he is in the main active, but not nearly so much so as he should be. His influence on the King is far more thorough since the last discoveries so well conducted by him.

The director of the Royal Cabinet, Albrecht, is a quiet and extremely well-meaning man. In Aix-la-Chapelle he already began to draw near to me, and has here laid aside all timidity in this respect. His part is negatively very important, for he makes it his duty to restrain the King from many inconsiderate steps. . . .

I do not wish my presence here to be limited to an empty convention; therefore I have written out the sketch of an agreement, and laid it before our second conference.

This document contains the basis on which alone I seek the safety and prosperity of Germany, and at the same time is a proof that Prussia herself joins with us. The principal features of this basis are as follows. I start from the point of view—

1. That to me purely Austrian must, in the abstract, stand closer than Austro-German affairs.

A good and vigorously managed union of States (*Bundes-Verhältnisse*) is certainly the best and truest weapon of defence for your Majesty's own State: and more, there is no other political combination which can outweigh or replace the advantages arising from this union of States. The more firmly these propositions are established, the more true it is that the same element which if well managed will lead to safety, may through mismanagement or bad and careless execution become highly dangerous.

Therefore from these propositions arises the rule, a real rule of life for Austria—

That we must do everything to regulate and maintain the prosperity of the Bund, or, in case this should prove impossible, we must, relying on our own strength, assume a position very different from that we are taking to-day towards the German Princes outside the Bund.

Faithfully to follow out this principle we must first show most exactly the true position of affairs, and then point out the appropriate ways and means to improve the defects in the Bund.

The course to be followed is clearly laid down in the agreement signed with Prussia.

It is divided into two periods—

(a) The present meeting of the ministers of the most important German Courts at Carlsbad;

(b) A second meeting at Vienna supplementary to the first.

At the first our principles must be made generally known, and the necessary temporary measures founded on them.

Among these I reckon—

(a) The suspension of the licence of the press;

(b) The appointment of commissions for the investigation of the German universities, and the removal of notoriously bad professors;

(c) The formation of a special judicial commission, acting in the name of the whole Bund, to investigate the conspiracy discovered against the Bund.

The second meeting can only be devoted to discussions not of a kind to be accomplished in a few hours or days. Among these I include the correction of the thirteenth article of the Act of Confederation.

All that is most necessary here is provided for by the engagement of Prussia to grant no representation of the people—that is, not to give themselves up with one stroke to the Revolution.

Your majesty will have been long convinced (and the present Report will show this truth afresh) how little I reckon on any firmness in the proceedings of Prussia as to their home affairs. This much, however, is certain, that all danger is for the moment averted, and with this state of things comes the possibility that future evil may be avoided by vigorous measures at the present time. My great desire, therefore, in regard to Prussia, is to make use of this present time, and I cling to this firmly.

The means of leading the revolutionised South German States back to a better footing are so critical in their application that they require the most firm and calm examination, and it is only thus that the desired result can be attained. I hope by this hasty but plain representation to convince your Majesty that this matter, which from the harmony of Austrian and Prussian views begins so prosperously, chiefly depends on this—

To save the German Bund by the help of Austria, or to leave Austria the possibility—difficult as it may be—to save herself.

I feel sure that I shall never be called upon to solve more difficult problems than the present. But they do not come of my choice; the evil exists and must be conquered: the causes of the evil lie deep; they must therefore be grasped from the root: this outbreak already overspreads all Germany; the fight must therefore take place in the open field. In these assertions there is no exaggeration: they are the expression of pure truth.

METTERNICH

The Teplitz Convention

AGREEMENT CONCERNING THE PRINCIPLES BY WHICH THE COURTS
OF AUSTRIA AND PRUSSIA HAVE DETERMINED TO BE GUIDED
IN THE INTERNAL AFFAIRS OF THE GERMANIC FEDERATION

GENERAL PRINCIPLES

(1) The Germanic Federation exists as a political body whose leading characteristics are clearly expressed in articles 1 and 2 of the federal act.

It exists as a genuinely European institution, and as one important to the maintenance of equilibrium and of general repose, and it enjoys the general guarantee which, in virtue of the Vienna congress act, secures the existence of every European state.

(2) Austria and Prussia are independent European powers, and by their German lands are simultaneously states of the Germanic

Federation. In virtue of the first quality, and in especial as principal participators in the work of the Vienna Congress and in all the political negotiations of recent years, they are called upon to supervise the political existence of the Germanic Federation and to adhere to the same. In virtue of the second quality, it is their duty to direct particular attention to the appropriate development and to the firm establishment of internal federal affairs.

(3) In so far as the Germanic Federation exists and must exist as a European political institution, in its interior no principles must find application which would be incompatible with its existence.

(4) The Germanic Federation is represented as a whole by the federal assembly.

The federal assembly is, consequently, in relation to the Federation and to its inner essence, and with especial regard to articles 1 and 2 of the federal act, the supreme political authority in Germany. Its legal decisions must be inviolably executed and maintained as laws of the Federation.

SPECIAL APPLICATION OF THESE PRINCIPLES

(5) Experience has shown that, owing to an unhappy lack of confidence on the part of some of the German governments, and owing also to numerous subsidiary views counteracting the designs of the Federation, the federal bond has lacked the firmness which a Federation, as such, ought to possess. This unfortunate state of affairs can be remedied in no other way than by a close union of the courts, and the courts of Austria and Prussia are resolved to utilise the moment in which the systematic activities of a revolutionary party threaten, not merely to effect the dissolution of the Federation, but to destroy the very existence of all the German governments, to bring about this closer union.

(6) The presence of the ministers of the leading German courts must be taken advantage of in favour of a closer agreement. Should the attempt lead to happy preliminary results, the attempt must be made to perfect this understanding through a meeting of the German cabinets at the earliest possible date particularly with a view to a majority of the votes, and especially in relation to cases where such a majority is not decisive, to secure as restricted a decision as possible—also to secure an arrangement for vigorous executive measures.

(7) The most urgent matters, those about which agreement must first of all be secured, are the following:

A. Emendation of Ideas in respect of Article 13 of the Federal Act[1]

Prussia is resolved not to apply this article in its literal sense to her own domains until her internal financial affairs shall have been fully regulated; that is to say, she is determined that for the representation of the nation she will not introduce any general system of popular representation incompatible with the geographical and internal configuration of her realm, but that she will give her provinces representative constitutions (*landständische Verfassungen*), and will out of these construct a central committee of territorial representatives.

As to the measures which ought to be taken to induce the German states which under the name of estates (*Ständen*) have already introduced systems of popular representation to return to a state of affairs better adapted to the circumstances of the Federation—this is a matter about which, before all, it will be well to await the proposals of the governments concerned. These proposals should then be weighed by the two courts, and not adopted until after due consideration of the many-sidedness of the problems involved.

B. General Arrangements concerning Article 18 of the Federal Act

The two courts agree in their views regarding the principles of the subjoined project, and they will support the same in order to secure its general adoption by their allies and its application in the form of a federal law.

This law, passed by the federal assembly, must if possible be put into effect before the beginning of this year's recess.

In order to secure the necessary measures for effecting their purpose (which is to restrict to the utmost the daily misleading of the people) the German governments must pledge one another mutually that none of the newspaper editors who have to-day become notorious shall be given access to new editorships; and they must pledge themselves in general to reduce the excessive number of newspapers.[1]

C. Measures concerning Universities, Gymnasia, and Schools

In order to pay due regard to what is best for the sciences and for the moral education of youth, it is desirable that a committee

---

[1] Article 13 promised representative constitutions to the German states—Ed.

should be formed composed of tried men belonging to those states which have universities, and that this committee should elaborate a well-thought-out proposal concerning the dispositions by which the above-specified purposes may best be secured. These dispositions should deal with matters of discipline, not only in respect of the students, but also, and in especial, in respect of the teachers.

As an indispensable measure, the two courts will impress upon federal allies the absolute necessity that professors whose sentiments are notoriously bad and who are involved in the intrigues of the later-day disorders among the students shall be immediately deprived of their chairs, and that no person who is thus discharged from any German university shall receive an appointment at a university in any other German state. But the evil must also be attacked at the root, and therefore this measure must be applied to the schools as well.

Paying due regard to the prejudices which inspire many of the German governments against a closer and most wholesome union between the two leading German courts, these latter mutually pledge one another to keep the present agreement permanently secret, and to restrict their activities to the endeavour, not merely to make the principles herein expounded the guide of their own conduct, but further to use their united energies in order to secure the widest possible application of these principles, in unison with their German federal allies.

With these ends in view, and in order to use their utmost energies to secure them, the undersigned have drawn up the present convention with their own hands.

C. F. VON HARDENBERG
F. VON METTERNICH

Teplitz,
August 1, 1819

10. Principles and Personalities in the Metternich System

Metternich's role in the history of European conservatism took shape in the years 1819 and 1820, when he was developing Austrian state policy into a Europe-wide system of opposition on principle to political change. His description of himself as a statesman, his view of the

personalities and ideas with which he was contending, and the political
ideas he endeavored to assert—all these are evidence for assessing and
understanding his role. His reputation as ideologue rests mainly on the
"Confession of Faith" addressed to the Czar Alexander in 1820, during
the Troppau Conference. Interpretation of that document may be
aided by Metternich's estimate of the man to whom it was addressed—
the mystical Czar-autocrat of mighty Russia, who had to be persuaded
and contained or all was lost.

The autobiographical memoir that appears first was probably written
in 1844, and the sketch of Alexander in 1829. [Metternich, *Memoirs*,
I (1880), 34–38, 314–334; III (1881), 453–476.]

Metternich's view of himself

HERE, AT the commencement of the account of my public life, I
propose to admit into the narrative only what relates to myself, or
rather what may serve to fill up the gaps in the official correspondence; for although the latter alone gives a true picture of the work
of a statesman, yet in such documents many details find no place.
I wish that those of my readers who may be in a position to have
access to the Imperial archives may consult the documents of the
time in connection with the present work; and, drawing from this
double source, they will more easily appreciate the great epoch
during which destiny had laid upon me the difficult task of playing
an active part on the world's stage. But before I relate the many
remarkable occurrences which have signalised my career, I will
candidly state the principles on which the actions of my political
life have been based. This statement will serve to clear up many
points in the history of my time and explain my own actions.

That a public career was distasteful to me I have already mentioned. Convinced that everyone ought to be prepared to answer
for the deeds of his own life; penetrated by the consciousness of
the enormous difficulties of propping up a society which was
falling to pieces on every side; disapproving, before the tribunal of
my own conscience, of almost all the measures which I saw
adopted for the salvation of the social body, undermined as it was,
by the errors of the eighteenth century; lastly, too diffident to believe that my mind was of so powerful a stamp that it could improve whatever it undertook: I had determined not to appear on a
stage on which the independence of my character rebelled against
playing a subordinate part, though I did not consider myself
capable of taking the part of a reformer.

The care with which my education had been directed to the

wide field of politics had early accustomed me to contemplate its vast extent. I soon remarked that my mode of thinking of the nature and dignity of this sphere was essentially different from the point of view from which all this was regarded by the enormous majority of those who are called to play great political parts. Here I may be allowed to propound the few principles to which I have always reduced the science commonly known by the name of Politics and Diplomacy.

Politics is the science of the vital interests of states. Since, however, an isolated state no longer exists, and is found only in the annals of the heathen world, or in the abstractions of so-called philosophers, we must always view the society of nations as the essential condition of the present world. Thus, then, each state, besides its separate interests, has also those which are common to it with other states. The great axioms of political science proceed from the knowledge of the true political interests of all states. In these general interests lies the guarantee of their existence, while individual interests to which the transitory political movements of the day assign a great importance, and the care of which constitutes political wisdom in the eyes of a restless and short-sighted policy, possess only a relative and secondary value. History teaches us that whenever the separate come into conflict with the general interests of a state, and the latter are neglected or mistaken in the zealous and extensive prosecution of the former, this is to be regarded as an exceptional or unhealthy condition, whose development or speedy amendment ultimately decides the destiny of the state, that is, its impending decline or its recuperative prosperity. That which characterises the modern world, and essentially distinguishes it from the ancient, is the tendency of nations to draw near to each other, and in some fashion to enter into a social league, which rests on the same basis with the great human society developed in the bosom of Christianity. This foundation consists of the precept of the Book of Books, "Do unto others as ye would they should do unto you." This fundamental rule of every human fraternity, applied to the state, means in the political world reciprocity, and its effect is what in the language of diplomacy is called *bons procédés*, in other words mutual consideration and honourable conduct. In the ancient world, policy isolated itself entirely, and exercised the most absolute selfishness, without any other curb than that of prudence. The law of retaliation set up eternal barriers and founded eternal enmities between the societies of men; and

upon every page of ancient history is found the principle of
mutual evil for evil. Modern history, on the other hand, exhibits
the principle of the solidarity of nations and of the balance of
power, and furnishes the spectacle of the combined endeavours of
several states against the temporary predominance of any one to
impede the extension of this principle, and to constrain it to return
to the common law. The establishment of international relations
upon the basis of reciprocity, under the guarantee of respect for
acquired rights, and the conscientious observance of plighted faith,
constitutes, at the present day, the essence of politics, of which
diplomacy is only the daily application. Between politics and
diplomacy there exists, in my opinion, the same difference as between science and art. Just as men daily transgress the laws of civil
society, nations only too often act in opposition to the eternal precepts which govern their alliance. The faults of men and the faults
of states are subject to the same punishments; their whole difference lies in the gravity of the offence, which is proportionate to
the importance of the individuals.

When we master these truths, what becomes a selfish policy, of
the policy of fantasy, or of the policy of miserable greed, and
especially what becomes of that which seeks profit apart from the
simplest rules of right; which mocks at the plighted word, and,
in short, rests solely on the usurpations of force or craft?

After this confession of faith, it may be conceived what I have
always thought of politicians of the stamp or, if we will, of the
authority of a Richelieu, a Mazarin, a Talleyrand, a Canning, a
Capo d'Istria, or a Haugwitz, and of many more or less famous
names. Resolved not to walk in their steps, and despairing of opening a path in harmony with my own conscience, I naturally preferred not to throw myself into those great political affairs, in
which I had far more prospect of succumbing materially than of
succeeding: I say materially, for I have never been afraid of failing
morally. The man who enters public life has always at command
a sure resource against this danger, that is—retirement.

Metternich's portrait of Alexander I, Czar of Russia

To draw a picture of the Emperor Alexander is a most difficult
undertaking.

Napoleon expressed his opinion of this prince in a manner the
most apt and striking. In one of our conversations, in the year

1810, he asked me whether I knew the Emperor of Russia intimately. I answered that I had had no personal interview with him, except at the time of his residence in Berlin, in 1805. "Well," replied Napoleon, "the course of events may bring you and this Prince together again; the Emperor Alexander is an attractive person, quite the man to exercise a singular spell over those with whom he comes in contact. If I were given to yielding to mere impressions, I could like him with all my heart. With so many intellectual advantages and dazzling qualities, there is something in him for which I have no name, and which I cannot better express than by saying that there is always something wanting in him. The most singular thing is, that one cannot foresee, in any given case or special affair, what will be wanting, because that which is wanting changes perpetually."

In foreseeing that the course of events would bring me into close contact with the Emperor Alexander, Napoleon had spoken prophetically, without believing, assuredly, that the fulfilment of his prediction was so near as it really was. Three years afterwards, I was in the most intimate relations with the Emperor of Russia. These relations lasted for thirteen years in a constant interchange of real confidence, of more or less expressed coldness, and of personal and open disagreements. Each of these phases has enabled me to see the correctness of Napoleon's judgment.

Relations so lasting and yet so variable have given me an opportunity of forming an exact idea of the character of this monarch.

For my part, I cannot better give the impressions I received than by summing them up in this sentence; that Alexander's character showed a peculiar mixture of masculine virtues and feminine weaknesses.

The Emperor Alexander certainly possessed mind, but his mind, refined and keen as it was, had no depth; he was as easily led astray by an excess of distrust as by an inclination to erroneous theories. His judgment was always influenced by fanciful ideas; he seized upon them as if by sudden inspiration, and with the greatest eagerness; and they soon gained weight enough to rule him, and make the subjection of his will an easy matter to their originators.

Such ideas soon came to be regarded by him as systems; quick as his mind was, even to an extraordinary versatility, these systems did not assimilate, they followed one another in rapid succession. Devoted to the system whose turn it was, he arrived at the exact opposite by intermediate steps, of which he was not aware, and nothing remained of the convictions with which he had been penetrated but the remembrance of the obligations under which they had placed him to different individuals. Hence arose the number of insurmountable embarrassments which were always pressing on the mind and heart of the Emperor; and the frequent favours bestowed on men and things quite opposite to one another; hence the difficulty to most spectators of understanding his attitude, who was not in a position to penetrate into the true causes of such strange appearances.

The Emperor Alexander's life was worn out between devotion to certain systems and disappointment in their results; the feelings prompted by both moods were spontaneous and vigorous and, strange as it may sound, their course showed a certain periodicity, of which I shall afterwards give pertinent examples.

He was a man of his word, entering with facility into the obligations of the ideas for the moment paramount; he knew how to avoid with delicacy those who might lead him in an opposite direction; but since his mind, from taking up systems so easily, was constantly undergoing changes, this very regard for his given word placed his conscience, as well as his whole attitude, in a situation as painful to himself as injurious to the public cause.

Many contemporaries have wrongly ascribed to Alexander the possession of a restless ambition. In his character there was neither sufficient strength for true ambition, nor sufficient weakness for mere vanity. He acted generally from conviction, and if he seemed now and then somewhat full of pretension, this was connected more with the little victories of a man of the world than with his success as the ruler of a great empire.

His youth passed in a time which is unequalled in the annals of Russia. The government of Catherine gave him the example of a brilliant despotism; in that of Paul, he was himself several times nearly a victim to a despotism mean even in its very choice of forms. It suffices to know what Russia was under these two governments, to conceive that a mind like Alexander's would find there neither models for imitation nor men to advise him.

La Harpe[1] was entrusted by Catherine II with the first education of Alexander. It is, therefore, not surprising that wrong ideas of

[1] Frédéric César de la Harpe (1754–1838) was a Swiss-born intellectual radical, often thought to be Alexander's main contact with revolutionary circles.—Ed.

liberalism and philanthropy long dominated the pupil of such a master; or that such a wonderful mixture as the lessons of a liberal mentor with the practice of the Russian government must lead his judgment and his action in a wrong direction, far, indeed, beyond the limits in which experience could help him.

The method of education followed by La Harpe was far more suited to fill the mind of his pupil with doctrines wrong in themselves, and ridiculous in their application, than to enrich it with positive knowledge. Convinced, no doubt, that the empire which his pupil would one day be called on to govern was not sufficiently advanced in civilisation to bear immediately the practice of these doctrines, he thought of preparing in the future autocrat a mighty lever, to secure the upheaval of other countries which he considered more ripe for the purpose, and especially his own fatherland, Switzerland. The part of a philanthropic monarch appeared to Alexander the one which would secure to him the palm of certain glory—a glory which was easy to gain by a monarch who was removed from the dangers with which other thrones and the old institutions of Central Europe were surrounded.

Simple in his enjoyments, cool in temperament, with many tastes which were, if I may say so, somewhat plebeian, Alexander was too easily guided not to be taken advantage of by such leaders.

A long observation of the moral peculiarities of this monarch and of his political course led me to discover, what I have called above, the periodicity of his thoughts. This periodicity followed a measure of about five years. I do not know how to express this observation more exactly.

The Emperor seized an idea, and followed it out quickly. It grew in his mind for about two years, till it came to be regarded by him as a system. In the course of the third year he remained faithful to the system he had adopted and learned to love, listened with real fervour to its promoters, and was inaccessible to any calculation as to its worth or dangerous consequences. In the fourth year the sight of those consequences began to calm down his fervour; the fifth year showed an unseemly mixture of the old and nearly extinct system with the new idea. This new idea was often diametrically opposite to the one he had just left. To prove this remark, I will give the following historical facts.

My first connection with the Emperor Alexander took place at the time of my embassy to Berlin in 1805. I found him then liberal in the largest sense of the word, and a bitter enemy of Bonaparte, he loaded him—in his double quality of despot and conqueror—with execrations. In the year 1807 a great change came over his mode of thinking. In 1808 his personal feelings even inclined towards the Emperor of the French. The year 1812 brought a new change in his mood: even if Napoleon had not made war on Russia, Alexander's feelings for him would nevertheless have died away. The old ideas of philanthropy and free-thinking had not only regained the power over his mind, but they even took fire from the spirit of the time. In 1814 they had reached their highest point. In 1815 they had already given way to religious mysticism. In the year 1817, this new turn of mind underwent a great change; and in 1818, I found the Emperor a zealous champion of monarchic and conservative principles, a declared enemy of every revolutionary tendency, and already on his way to return to religious mysticism. He followed this direction till 1823. Then the embarrassments arose which his own counsellors had prepared for him by their policy in the affairs in Greece, and he was able everywhere to see the increase of revolutionary principles, whose germs he, in his blindness, had himself scattered in his own empire in past years. All these painful circumstances caused a visible languor in his mind and feelings. A great weariness of life began to show itself in him. His body, apparently so active, suffered under these moral influences. It was during his residence in Verona towards the end of the year 1822, that Alexander confided to the Emperor Francis, his sure presentiment that his life would not be of long duration. The evil made rapid steps, and in 1825, Alexander died of thorough weariness of life.

There is no doubt that amongst the causes which contributed to shorten his days was that bitter conflict of feelings caused by the prospect of a trial of conspirators, the principal culprits among whom might reproach the Emperor with having been the cause of their error.

By giving this picture of the very peculiar personality of this prince, about whom the world would otherwise with difficulty form a right judgment, I believe I supply the key to many apparently insoluble problems.

All the constancy of the Emperor Alexander's affections seemed concentrated in the feeling which he had for the Emperor Francis.

The particulars which I can supply in this respect will fill up this sketch of the monarch's character, and also throw some light on his relations to me.

The two Emperors were for the first time in personal contact on the battle-fields of Moravia in the autumn of the year 1805. The misfortune which the bad arrangements of the Austrian generals brought about at the beginning of the single campaign of this war was completed by the Russian generals at its close. The Emperor Alexander, young and without any experience of war, lent his ear to high-flown and quite unpractical plans, rather than to the calm and prudent advice which suited the vigorous understanding of the Emperor Francis. Everything which this monarch had foreseen and predicted to his ally was fulfilled in sad succession. This fact was always present to the mind of the Emperor Alexander, and laid the first foundation of that close and complete confidence which he never afterwards ceased to bestow on his friend.

Many subsequent political events made it impossible that this feeling on the part of his Imperial Majesty should always be expressed: but in reality it always existed. The events of the years 1814 and 1815 gave rise to direct and continuous relations between the two monarchs, which at last grew into a sincere hearty personal friendship.

A friendship which has stood every trial, and which nothing could shake, in spite of the most important political interests, and, strangest of all, a thorough difference in the personality of the two friends, is a problem which can only be solved by a true insight into the character of the two monarchs.

The Emperor Francis united in himself the most valuable positive qualities. His calmness, impartiality, soundness of judgment, and unvarying and tranquil temper inspired Alexander with a feeling of devotion which almost resembled the veneration of a child. This feeling was afterwards heightened by a colouring quite peculiar to the mind of this prince. It was religious. The Emperor Alexander considered his friend as a monarch after the will of God, as the representative of God's will, and of godly wisdom, and almost worshipped him. On several occasions, when the Emperor Francis directly opposed the personal inclinations of Alexander, the opinion of the wise monarch sufficed to arrest the decisions of Alexander, and to decide him either to relinquish or change them.

The devotion of the Emperor Alexander to the Emperor Francis continued to the end of his life to be one of his predominant sentiments.

In everything relating to private life Alexander followed the most pure and simple tastes, bearing, however, the stamp of distinguished elegance. With the sciences he did not concern himself, and I never saw in him a leaning to any of them. Amongst the fine arts, he cared only for architecture. His short sight and slight deafness did not allow him to devote himself to the cultivation of those arts the full enjoyment of which depends on the perfection of senses which were partially denied to him. He liked work belonging to the Cabinet, provided it did not go beyond political affairs or military details. He had an evident dislike to merely administrative subjects; and if he ever took part in them, it could only be that he was influenced by the political theories which then attracted his mind. The history of the administration of his empire during the whole of his reign proves how powerful and how hurtful those influences were.

To the outlines of this sketch I will add some illustrations taken from my intercourse with the Emperor. They will not be without value as forming a standpoint from which to consider the history of the time, and they will also serve to confirm the opinion I have expressed as to the mind and character of this prince.

I shall begin by making the general statement that nothing could be so little in harmony as the direction of the Emperor's mind and my own. Our tastes also—with the exception of a certain agreement in the choice of our social relations—were exactly opposite, and probably nothing would have led to a lasting and often intimate connection but our overwhelming interest in the questions which were impending.

I have already said that my first direct relations with the Emperor took place in Berlin in the year 1805. Alexander had come to this city to represent in person the cause and interests of the Austro-Russian alliance. Association in the same cause easily brings two men together, whatever may be the difference of their positions.

The Emperor was accustomed to handle the great political questions himself, thus being—as he was fond of saying—his own minister, and from that time we entered into close and subsequently even into familiar relations.

Peace was concluded at the end of the same year between Austria and France, and since Count Stadion, then Ambassador at St. Petersburg, had accepted the direction of foreign affairs at home, Alexander wished me to represent Austria at his court. A singular concatenation of circumstances led to my nomination as Austrian Ambassador in France. When I again met the Emperor, on the Bohemian frontier, seven years later, I found him apparently reserved towards me. The reasons for this I have explained in another part of these Memoirs. With the charming kindness and cordiality peculiar to him, the Emperor seemed to reproach me with infidelity in my friendship. The conclusion of the alliance dispersed these clouds; but a real intimacy in our personal relations began to revive only after the unhappy result of the first military undertaking of the Allies against Dresden. The efforts which I had vainly made in harmony with the Emperor Francis and Field-Marshal Prince Schwarzenberg to avoid this operation, the frankness of my declaration on this subject to the Emperor Alexander, perhaps also the fulfilment of my predictions, laid the foundation of an increased intimacy.

In spite of the decided opposition of our views on many subjects and notwithstanding many important circumstances, and the discomfort which might so naturally have arisen, nothing disturbed our intimate and daily relations in the course of the campaign—relations, indeed, of a kind rarely occurring between the Sovereign of one great empire and the head of the cabinet of another.

During the whole time of the war operations I spent the evenings with his Imperial Majesty. We remained alone together from eight or nine in the evening till midnight in unrestrained conversation, which included the most different subjects in private life as well as the great moral and political questions and the affairs of the day. Thorough frankness in our interchange of opinions about everything gave to this intercourse the charm of perfect ease.

I never concealed the truth from the Emperor, either about himself or anything else which had, in my eyes, the high value of a principle. Only too often I had to combat some favourite idea of his, which he maintained with great emphasis; our discussions were sometimes very animated—the narrative of our stay in Langrès is a proof of this. Yet our intercourse never suffered from this, but was long continued and maintained with the same frankness and heartiness.

Whilst we were staying in Paris in 1814 I had many discussions with Alexander as to the principles which Louis XVIII ought to follow. As the Emperor Alexander was at that time enthusiastic for liberal ideas, our opinions were often in direct opposition about what would be most likely to contribute to the establishment of internal peace in France under the government of the Bourbons.

After the Peace of Paris I went to England at the same time as the Emperor of Russia and the King of Prussia. Whilst we stayed in that country my personal relations with the Emperor preserved the same character of intimacy. Considerable differences between Alexander and George IV, then Prince Regent, often placed me in a difficult position. Being kindly regarded by both princes and a confidant of their daily and personal troubles, my efforts were necessarily directed to prevent their mutual irritation from growing into a serious dissension. The Emperor, in truth, was always in the wrong: his sensitiveness was constantly kept alive by the Grand-Duchess Katherine, who had been in England some weeks before the arrival of her brother. The conduct at that time of this Princess, who was gifted with very estimable qualities of mind and heart, has always been a problem to me. No doubt, one of the motives of her journey was to break off the marriage agreed upon between the Prince of Orange and the heiress to the English throne, and to place her own sister on the throne of Holland. But this object, which indeed she attained, will not account for all which was strange and unpleasant in her behaviour, nor for the conduct to which she persuaded the Emperor Alexander.

I may here give an anecdote which will throw some light on the often strange and inexplicable character of the Emperor Alexander's mind.

His Imperial Majesty liked to flatter the most distinguished persons belonging to the English Opposition. One day he asked Lord Grey to lay before him a work on the formation of an Opposition in Russia. After the audience, Lord Grey called on me, to ask an explanation of a caprice as unintelligible in its object as unpractical in its execution, "Does the Emperor intend to introduce a Parliament into his country? If he really means to do so—and I should take good care not to advise it—he need not concern himself about an Opposition, it would certainly not be wanting."

It was the Vienna Congress which brought a change in my relations with the Emperor.

The creation of a kingdom of Poland which should include under the Russian sceptre the whole district of the Duchy of Warsaw, and the surrender of the kingdom of Saxony to Prussia, had been agreed upon at the negotiations in Kalisch, between the Emperor Alexander and King William III.[1] This was known to us. The incorporation of Saxony with Prussia was contrary to the Emperor of Austria's fixed principles, and would also cause much lamentable irritation between his empire and Prussia. The Emperor Francis being determined, at the very outset, to oppose this proposition firmly, he, however, thought it prudent to delay all discussion on the subject till after the conclusion of the Peace with France: reserving it till the Congress, which was to regulate the reconstruction of the different Powers of Europe.

This important question had somewhat disturbed the relations of the two courts. Each of them hesitated to speak of it. Thus several weeks passed, even after the meeting of the Congress, without the question being mentioned on either side. The first approaches to the subject were made by the Emperor Alexander to Lord Castlereagh. The latter informed me immediately, and I advised a decided refusal. Some days afterwards the Emperor spoke himself to me about it. I found him a little embarrassed. My decided answer met with only a feeble resistance, and he at last expressed a wish that I should speak to the Prussian Chancellor myself on the matter. The very day of my conversation with his Imperial Majesty, Prince Hardenberg made a communication to me on the point, which he supported by a written one. My verbal and written explanations were the same as I had already given to the Emperor. Prince Hardenberg found all his calculations crossed, and himself placed in a painful position. The Prussian Chancellor considered the affair lost, in consequence of my informing him of the slight importance which the Emperor Alexander had seemed to attach to the question of the incorporation of Saxony in his conversation with me. Perhaps, too, he had misunderstood my words from being slightly deaf and very nervous; and he therefore felt himself obliged to appeal to the Emperor himself, who in his turn may have felt hurt by some misrepresentation of my words.

This affair gave rise to the most extraordinary and hasty conduct on the part of the Emperor Alexander. The day after my explana-

[1] Frederick William III of Prussia.—Ed.

tion with the Prussian Chancellor, the Emperor, my master, sent
for me at a very early hour. His Majesty informed me that the Emperor Alexander had just left him after a very animated conversation in which that prince, thinking himself personally offended by
me, had told his Majesty his decision to challenge me to a duel. The
Emperor added that he had endeavoured to point out to Alexander
how very strange such a proceeding would appear; but, seeing that
his remonstrances were without success, he had told him at last that
if he persisted in his design, he would certainly find me ready to
obey the challenge, which, though my reason would no doubt
condemn, my honour would command me to accept. His Majesty
told me at last that he had most vigorously urged the Emperor to
have a third explanation with me before giving the challenge, to
which Alexander at last agreed.

I declared to his Imperial Majesty that I should await with tranquillity the further steps of the Emperor of Russia, and had hardly
returned to my house when Count Ozarowsky, one of Alexander's
Adjutants-General, was announced. He told me that he was
charged by his Imperial master to call upon me to declare to the
Prussian Chancellor that I had been mistaken in what I had told
him about my conversation with the Emperor Alexander. I begged
the adjutant to tell his Imperial master that I should never recall
one word of the correctness of which I was certain; but that, if
Prince Hardenberg had misunderstood me, and had therefore repeated my words incorrectly, I should be ready to remove the mistake. Count Ozarowsky retired. A few moments afterward his
Imperial Majesty sent word to me that he would not appear at the
ball in my house, to which all the Princes and all the members of
the Congress were invited for that very day.

The same day I saw the Russian ministers, and informed Count
Nesselrode of what had happened. He said he had not received any
instructions from the Emperor with regard to this affair. The conferences went on as if no difficulties at all had been raised, and their
result was that half of Saxony remained to its King.

This strange incident caused no disturbance in the course of the
important discussions of the Congress. Even the open friendship
which existed between the two Imperial courts did not suffer any
injury from it; but this was not the case with regard to the personal relations between the Emperor of Russia and myself. Alexander, who went a great deal into society, liked especially certain

more intimate circles, which, I too, used to visit. Thus hardly a day passed without my meeting him. We did not take any notice of each other. The peculiarity of this conduct before the crowd of spectators who at that time frequented the *salons* of Vienna was gradually effaced by custom. The members of the Imperial Russian family were present as usual at the balls and parties at my house. The Emperor only appeared amongst us no more. The public grew accustomed to the idea that the Emperor was out of humour with me; but since business affairs did not suffer, even the restless curiosity of diplomatists could find nothing to gratify it in a state of things in itself so odd. I often received hints to take some steps to approach his Majesty, but I thought it best to leave the return to the natural order of things to be effected by time.

This disagreement lasted, in fact, till the moment when a great event changed the prospects of the whole of Europe.

The first news of Napoleon's leaving the island of Elba reached me on the sixth of March, at six o'clock in the morning, by an express sent from the Austrian Consul-General from Genoa. The report gave nothing but the simple announcement of the fact. I repaired immediately to the Emperor, my master. His Imperial Majesty commanded me to take the news without delay to the Emperor of Russia and the King of Prussia. It was the first time for nearly three months that I had presented myself to the first of these monarchs. He received me at once. I told him the news of the great event in execution of the wishes of the Emperor, my master. The Emperor Alexander expressed himself with calmness and dignity, in the same manner as his august ally. We did not require much time to deliberate about the measures that had to be taken. The decision was prompt and decided.

Having settled this subject, the Emperor said to me: "We have still to adjust a personal difference. We are both Christians, and our sacred law commands us to forgive offences. Let us embrace, and let everything be forgotten."

I replied to the Emperor that I, on my part, had nothing to forgive, but only to forget painful occurrences, that, according to all justice, his Imperial Majesty must be in the same condition; that I therefore did not accept the forgiveness, but agreed to forget.

The Emperor embraced me, and dismissed me with the request that I would be his friend once more.

In our subsequent frequent relations no mention was ever made of our former disagreement. Our intercourse soon returned to its former intimacy. This was maintained during our meetings in 1815, and again at Aix-la-Chapelle in 1818.

I have still to mention a circumstance which occurred in 1822, which, perhaps, throws more light than any other on the character of Alexander.

About six weeks after the meeting in Verona, I went to see the Emperor one evening, to talk over the affairs of the day. I found him in a state of great excitement, and hastened to enquire the cause. "I am in a strange position," said his Imperial Majesty. "I feel compelled to speak to you on a subject which I think most important, and I am at a loss how to do it." I answered that I could well understand that some important affair occupied his thoughts, but that I could not see how, if he wished to speak to me about it, he could have the least difficulty in doing so.

"It is," replied the Emperor, "because the subject does not concern the ordinary domain of politics: it regards us personally, and I fear lest you should not exactly understand what I mean." It was only after a real effort that the Emperor was able to address me in the following memorable words:—"People wish to separate us, and to tear asunder those bonds which unite us; I consider these bonds sacred, for they unite us for the general good. You desire the Peace of the world, and I have no other ambition but to maintain it. The enemies of Europe's peace are right in this, and in regard to the strength of the resistance which our agreement opposes to their malicious plans. They desire to remove this hindrance in any way possible, and, conscious that they will not succeed by open means, they resort to indirect methods. I am overwhelmed with reproaches for having relinquished my independence, and allowed myself to be guided by you."

I answered the Emperor warmly, that what he had done me the honour to say was not new to me, and that I did not hesitate to return his confidence by a confession which would only confirm the truth of what he had just said. "You are accused, Sire, of giving yourself up entirely to my advice; and, on the other hand, I am accused of sacrificing the interests of my country to my relations to your Majesty. One accusation is of as much value as the other. The conscience of your Majesty is as pure as mine. We serve one and the same cause, and this cause is that of Russia and of Austria, as well as of society in general. I have long been the butt of the various parties, and I consider the cordial relations of our two courts as a bulwark, which alone can withstand the inroads of a general confusion. On the other hand, you will judge from the extreme reserve of my attitude what importance I attach to the preservation of this intimacy. Does your Majesty wish anything altered in this respect?"

"I expected this from you," interrupted the Emperor. "If I have felt some difficulty in confessing the embarrassments in my position, it is not because I am not perfectly resolved to defy them; what I feared was, that you might begin to hesitate."

We then went into many details of the intrigues of one party, of which there were many disciples in Russia, even in the circle immediately surrounding the Emperor.

At the end of our long conversation he made me promise formally "not to be intimidated by any rumour, but to remain faithful to the most intimate alliance with him," and he begged me "to accept from him the not less formal promise of the inviolable constancy of his trust in me."

To loosen the harmony which united the two Emperors and their cabinets had been the design of some persons in this faction, as well as of some ambitious men, and of the many Russian courtiers who thought little and desired much. In direct connection with the Liberalism of the day, these men followed its impulse and became its tools, when they, in their blind self-conceit, imagined themselves its leaders. An alliance having no other object but the protection of true political freedom, which was founded on regard for the real independence of States, and desired only public peace and the removal of all desire for conquest and disturbance, such an alliance was not likely to suit the crowd of sophists and self-seekers.

The insurrection in Greece was afterwards provoked by these men. According to the calculations of the agitators, this was to act as a wedge to separate the Powers, and especially the two Imperial Courts; and as a means of dissolving the alliance. These calculations were correct, but they were fulfilled in a sense which was quite unexpected. The monarch who, in his own kingdom, had worked so much into the hands of the Revolutionists, succumbed mentally and bodily in the fight. The Emperor Alexander died of weariness of life. Seeing himself deceived in all his calculations, under the necessity of himself striking at a class of his own subjects who had been led astray and instigated by men and principles whom he himself had long supported, his heart broke, and the events which clouded the accession of his successor remained a proof of the troubles which embittered the last moments of Alexander.

The true historian will find it difficult to judge aright the character of this Prince. So many sharp contradictions will pass before him that his mind will with difficulty gain the firm standpoint so necessary for those who feel it their noble task to write history.

The mind and heart of this Prince included such opposite moral qualities that the strength of character which he possessed was not sufficient to maintain the balance of his different inclinations.

Every part of his life was marked by errors and mistakes sufficient to bring exposure to himself and the public cause. Always carried away by enthusiasm, and always changeable in the direction of his mind, Alexander never enjoyed one moment of real repose. He had valuable qualities: his disposition was noble, and his word was sacred. These advantages were counterbalanced by great deficiencies.

Had he been born in ordinary society, his qualities would not have attracted notice; but on the throne it is otherwise. If he had been the Ruler of any other country but Russia, neither his faults nor his virtues would have been so apparent. Alexander much needed support; his mind and heart needed to be led and guided. Whilst every Prince has difficulty in finding really unselfish servants, independent enough in character and position to rise to the part of a friend, an Emperor of Russia is in a position less favorable to do so than any other monarch.

The reign of Alexander, we must not forget, occurred in a time overflowing with numberless difficulties for the heads of all governments; and if this could be said of all Princes of that time, it was particularly the case with Alexander.

Before his time, the germ of a false civilisation had been sown on the soil of his vast Empire, which, despotically governed and in want of every real institution, contained a mass of people sunk in complete darkness. This germ Paul I would fain have smothered. To his short reign followed that of Alexander. Well-known Revolutionists, after having guided his education, exercised an evil influence on the mind of the young monarch. Alexander, without experience and full of vain theories, caused evil where he only intended good. He deceived himself, and the discovery of his errors brought him to the grave.

A mind subject to such changes must be considered frail and sensitive; a strong mind it cannot be.

Metternich's "Confession of Faith" to Alexander I

METTERNICH TO THE EMPEROR FRANCIS, TROPPAU, DECEMBER 2, 1820

May it please your Majesty to receive enclosed my "Confession of Faith" to the Emperor Alexander.

I beseech your Highness to read this short diplomatic composition in the sense in which I have drawn it up, and which is known to your Majesty.

METTERNICH

The enclosed herewith returned.

FRANCIS

Troppau, December 2, 1820

METTERNICH TO THE EMPEROR ALEXANDER, TROPPAU, DECEMBER 15, 1820

Sire, I have the honour to send to your Imperial Majesty the enclosed statement. I received your Majesty's commands, and have fulfilled them with an ardour which gives full liberty to my thoughts. Your Imperial Majesty will find it complete on all the questions most worthy of the meditations of every public man, of every man entrusted with grave interests—in short, of every man sufficiently enlightened to feel that to a world of folly he should oppose another full of wisdom, reason, justice, and reformation. I should have despised my self, Sire, long ago, if I did not say what I think. What in a private individual might appear a merit is simply a duty to a man in my position.

What is contained in this statement would excite a disdainful smile from the superficial persons who, full of complacency at their own imperfect knowledge, are impudent criticisers of the first interests of Society—that crowd of bawlers with crude ideas, who are the victims of their own errors, and false prophets, whenever they allow themselves to predict anything but groundless errors. This same smile would appear on the lips of a better class of men—

those men who think that the most useless of all enterprises is to
say what is self-evident. My conviction, Sire, is that it is always the
duty of men who wish to do good to speak, for at all times, and
above all at times disturbed by passion, those men who wish to do
evil, the vain and the foolish, will speak. It is therefore necessary
not to abandon the moral atmosphere to them altogether.

Deign, Sire, while receiving this paper, dictated by my conscience, to accept the homage of my profound respect.

CONFESSION OF FAITH
METTERNICH'S SECRET MEMORANDUM TO THE EMPEROR
ALEXANDER

"*L'Europe,*" a celebrated writer has recently said, "*fait aujourd'hui
pitié à l'homme d'esprit et horreur à l'homme vertueux.*"[1]

It would be difficult to comprise in a few words a more exact
picture of the situation at the time we are writing these lines!

Kings have to calculate the chances of their very existence in the
immediate future; passions are let loose, and league together to
overthrow everything which society respects as the basis of its
existence; religion, public morality, laws, customs, rights, and
duties, all are attacked, confounded, overthrown or called in question. The great mass of the people are tranquil spectators of
these attacks and revolutions, and of the absolute want of all means
of defence. A few are carried off by the torrent, but the wishes of
the immense majority are to maintain a repose which exists no
longer, and of which even the first elements seem to be lost.

What is the cause of all these evils? By what methods has this
evil established itself, and how is it that it penetrates into every vein
of the social body?

Do remedies still exist to arrest the progress of this evil, and
what are they?

These are doubtless questions worthy of the solicitude of every
good man who is a true friend to order and public peace—two
elements inseparable in principle, and which are at once the first
needs and the first blessings of humanity.

Has there never been offered to the world an institution really
worthy of the name? Has truth been always confounded with

[1] "Europe today arouses pity among men of intelligence and revulsion
among men of virtue."—Ed.

error ever since society has believed itself able to distinguish one from the other? Have the experiences bought at the price of so many sacrifices, and repeated at intervals, and in so many different places, been all in error? Will a flood of light be shed upon society at one stroke? Will knowledge come by inspiration? If one could believe in such phenomena it would not be the less necessary, first of all, to assure oneself of their reality. Of all things, nothing is so fatal as error; and it is neither our wish nor our intention ever to give ourselves up to it. Let us examine the matter!

THE SOURCE OF THE EVIL

Man's nature is immutable. The first needs of society are and remain the same, and the differences which they seem to offer find their explanation in the diversity of influences, acting on the different races by natural causes, such as the diversity of climate, barrenness or richness of soil, insular or continental position, &c. &c. These local differences no doubt produce effects which extend far beyond purely physical necessities; they create and determine particular needs in a more elevated sphere; finally, they determine the laws, and exercise an influence even on religions.

It is, on the other hand, with institutions as with everything else. Vague in their origin, they pass through periods of development and perfection, to arrive in time at their decadence; and, comforming to the laws of man's nature, they have, like him, their infancy, their youth, their age of strength and reason, and their age of decay.

Two elements alone remain in all their strength, and never cease to exercise their indestructible influence with equal power. These are the precepts of morality, religious as well as social, and the necessities created by locality. From the time that men attempt to swerve from these bases, to become rebels against these sovereign arbiters of their destinies, society suffers from a *malaise* which sooner or later will lead to a state of convulsion. The history of every country, in relating the consequences of such errors, contains many pages stained with blood; but we dare to say, without fear of contradiction, one seeks in vain for an epoch when an evil of this nature has extended its ravages over such a vast area as it has done at the present time. The causes are natural.

History embraces but a very limited space of time. It did not begin to deserve the name of history until long after the fall of great empires. There, where it seems to conduct us to the cradle of

civilisation, it really conducts us to ruins. We see republics arise
and prosper, struggle, and then submit to the rule of one fortunate
soldier. We see one of these republics pass through all the phases
common to society, and end in an almost universal monarchy—that
is to say, subjugating the scattered portions of the then civilised
world. We see this monarchy suffer the fate of all political bodies:
we see its first springs become enfeebled, and finally decay.

Centuries of darkness followed the irruption of the barbarians.
The world, however, could not return to barbarism. The Christian
religion had appeared; imperishable in its essence, its very existence
was sufficient to disperse the darkness and establish civilisation on
new foundations, applicable to all times and all places, satisfying all
needs, and establishing the most important of all on the basis of a
pure and eternal law! To the formation of new Christian States
succeeded the Crusades, a curious mixture of good and evil.

A decisive influence was shortly exercised on the progress of
civilisation by three discoveries—the invention of printing, that of
gunpowder, and the discovery of the New World. Still later came
the Reformation—another event which had incalculable effects, on
account of its influence on the moral world. From that time the
face of the world was changed.

The facilitation of the communication of thoughts by printing;
the total change in the means of attack and defence brought about
by the invention of gunpowder; the difference suddenly produced
in the value of property by the quantity of metals which the discovery of America put in circulation; the spirit of adventure
provoked by the chances of fortune opened in a new hemisphere;
the modifications in the relations of society caused by so many and
such important changes, all became more developed, and were in
some sort crowned by the revolution which the Reformation
worked in the moral world.

The progress of the human mind has been extremely rapid in
the course of the last three centuries. This progress having been
accelerated more rapidly than the growth of wisdom (the only
counterpoise to passions and to error); a revolution prepared by
the false systems, the fatal errors into which many of the most
illustrious sovereigns of the last half of the eighteenth century fell,
has at last broken out in a country advanced in knowledge, and
enervated by pleasure, in a country inhabited by a people whom
one can only regard as frivolous, from the facility with which they
comprehend and the difficulty they experience in judging calmly.

Having now thrown a rapid glance over the first causes of the present state of society, it is necessary to point out in a more particular manner the evil which threatens to deprive it, at one blow, of the real blessings, the fruits of genuine civilisation, and to disturb it in the midst of its enjoyments. This evil may be described in one word—presumption; the natural effect of the rapid progression of the human mind towards the perfecting of so many things. This it is which at the present day leads so many individuals astray, for it has become an almost universal sentiment.

Religion, morality, legislation, economy, politics, administration, all have become common and accessible to everyone. Knowledge seems to come by inspiration; experience has no value for the presumptuous man; faith is nothing to him; he substitutes for it a pretended individual conviction, and to arrive at this conviction dispenses with all inquiry and with all study; for these means appear too trivial to a mind which believes itself strong enough to embrace at one glance all questions and all facts. Laws have no value for him, because he has not contributed to make them, and it would be beneath a man of his parts to recognise the limits traced by rude and ignorant generations. Power resides in himself; why should he submit himself to that which was only useful for the man deprived of light and knowledge? That which, according to him, was required in an age of weakness cannot be suitable in an age of reason and vigour, amounting to universal perfection, which the German innovators designate by the idea, absurd in itself, of the Emancipation of the People! Morality itself he does not attack openly, for without it he could not be sure for a single instant of his own existence; but he interprets its essence after his own fashion, and allows every other person to do so likewise, provided that other person neither kills nor robs him.

In thus tracing the character of the presumptuous man, we believe we have traced that of the society of the day, composed of like elements, if the denomination of society is applicable to an order of things which only tends in principle towards individualising all the elements of which society is composed. Presumption makes every man the guide of his own belief, the arbiter of laws according to which he is pleased to govern himself, or to allow some one else to govern him and his neighbours; it makes him, in short, the sole judge of his own faith, his own actions, and the principles according to which he guides them.

Is it necessary to give a proof of this last fact? We think we have furnished it in remarking that one of the sentiments most natural to man, that of nationality, is erased from the Liberal catechism, and that where the word is still employed, it is used by the heads of the party as a pretext to enchain Governments, or as a lever to bring about destruction. The real aim of the idealists of the party is religious and political fusion, and this being analysed is nothing else but creating in favour of each individual an existence entirely independent of all authority, or of any other will than his own, an idea absurd and contrary to the nature of man, and incompatible with the needs of human society.

THE COURSE WHICH THE EVIL HAS FOLLOWED AND STILL FOLLOWS

The causes of the deplorable intensity with which this evil weighs on society appear to us to be of two kinds. The first are so connected with the nature of things that no human foresight could have prevented them. The second should be subdivided into two classes, however similar they may appear in their effects.

Of these causes, the first are negative, the others positive. We will place among the first the feebleness and the inertia of Governments.

It is sufficient to cast a glance on the course which the Governments followed during the eighteenth century, to be convinced that not one among them was ignorant of the evil or of the crisis towards which the social body was tending. There were, however, some men, unhappily endowed with great talents, who felt their own strength, and were not slow to appraise the progressive course of their influence, taking into account the weakness or the inertia of their adversaries; and who had the art to prepare and conduct men's minds to the triumph of their detestable enterprise—an enterprise all the more odious as it was pursued without regard to results, simply abandoning themselves to the one feeling of hatred of God and of His immutable moral laws.

France had the misfortune to produce the greatest number of these men. It is in her midst that religion and all that she holds sacred, that morality and authority, and all connected with them, have been attacked with a steady and systematic animosity, and it is there that the weapon of ridicule has been used with the most ease and success.

Drag through the mud the name of God and the powers instituted by His divine decrees, and the revolution will be prepared!

Speak of a social contract, and the revolution is accomplished! The revolution was already completed in the palaces of Kings, in the drawing-rooms and boudoirs of certain cities, while among the great mass of the people it was still only in a state of preparation.

It would be difficult not to pause here to consider the influence which the example of England had for a long time exercised on France. England is herself placed in such a peculiar situation that we believe we may safely say that not one of the forms possible to that State, not one of its customs or institutions, would suit any Continental State, and that where we might wish to take them for models, we should only obtain inconvenience and danger, without securing a single one of the advantages which accompany them.

According to the bent of minds in France, at the time of the convocation of the *notables*, and in consequence of the direction which public opinion had received for more than fifty years—a direction which, latterly, had been strengthened and in some sort adapted to France by the imprudent help which her Government had given to the American revolution—all reform in France touching the very foundations of the monarchy was soon transformed into a revolution. What might have been foreseen, and what had been foretold by everybody, the Government alone excepted, was realised but too soon. The French Revolution broke out, and has gone through a complete revolutionary cycle in a very short period, which could only have appeared long to its victims and to its contemporaries.

The scenes of horror which accompanied the first phases of the French Revolution prevented the rapid propagation of its subversive principles beyond the frontiers of France, and the wars of conquest which succeeded them gave to the public mind a direction little favourable to revolutionary principles. Thus the Jacobin propaganda failed entirely to realise criminal hopes.

Nevertheless the revolutionary seed had penetrated into every country and spread more or less. It was greatly developed under the *régime* of the military despotism of Bonaparte. His conquests displaced a number of laws, institutions, and customs; broke through bonds sacred among all nations, strong enough to resist time itself; which is more than can be said of certain benefits conferred by these innovators. From these perturbations it followed that the revolutionary spirit could in Germany, Italy, and later on in Spain, easily hide itself under the veil of patriotism.

Prussia committed a grave fault in calling to her aid such dangerous weapons as secret associations always will be: a fault which
could not be justified even by the deplorable situation in which
that Power then found itself. This it was that first gave a strong
impulse to the revolutionary spirit in her States, and this spirit
made rapid progress, supported as it was in the rest of Germany
by the system of foreign despotism which since 1806 has been there
developed. Many Princes of the Rhenish Confederation were
secretly auxiliaries and accomplices of this system, to which they
sacrificed the institutions which in their country from time im-
memorial had served as a protection against despotism and democracy.

The war of the Allies, by putting bounds to the predominance
of France, was vigorously supported in Germany by the same
men whose hatred of France was in reality nothing but hatred
of the military despotism of Bonaparte, and also of the legitimate
power of their own masters. With wisdom in the Governments
and firmness in principles, the end of the war in 1814 might nevertheless have insured to the world the most peaceful and happy
future. Great experiences had been gained and great lessons, which
might have been usefully applied. But fate had decided otherwise.

The return of the usurper to France, and the completely false
steps taken by the French Government from 1815 to 1820, accumulated a mass of new dangers and great calamities for the
whole civilised world. It is to the first of these misfortunes that
is partly due the critical state in which France and the whole social
body is placed. Bonaparte destroyed in a hundred days the work
of the fourteen years during which he had exercised his authority.
He set free the revolution which he came to France to subdue; he
brought back men's minds, not to the epoch of the 18th Brumaire,
but to the principles which the National Assembly had adopted in
its deplorable blindness.

What Bonaparte had thus done to the detriment of France and
Europe, the grave errors which the French Government have since
committed, and to which other Governments have yielded—all
these unhappy influences weigh heavily on the world of to-day;
they threaten with total ruin the work of restoration, the fruit of
so many glorious efforts, and of a harmony between the greatest
monarchs unparalleled in the records of history, and they give rise
to fears of indescribable calamities to society.

In this memoir we have not yet touched on one of the most active and at the same time most dangerous instruments used by the revolutionists of all countries, with a success which is no longer doubtful. I refer to the secret societies, a real power, all the more dangerous as it works in the dark, undermining all parts of the social body, and depositing everywhere the seeds of a moral gangrene which is not slow to develop and increase. This plague is one of the worst which those Governments who are lovers of peace and of their people have to watch and fight against.

DO REMEDIES FOR THIS EVIL EXIST, AND WHAT ARE THEY?

We look upon it as a fundamental truth, that for every disease there is a remedy, and that the knowledge of the real nature of the one should lead to the discovery of the other. Few men, however, stop thoroughly to examine a disease which they intend to combat. There are hardly any who are not subject to the influence of passion, or held under the yoke of prejudice; there are a great many who err in a way more perilous still, on account of its flattering and often brilliant appearance: we speak of *l'esprit de système;* that spirit always false, but indefatigable, audacious and irrepressible, is satisfactory to men imbued with it (for they live in and govern a world created by themselves), but it is so much the more dangerous for the inhabitants of the real world, so different from that created by *l'esprit de système.*

There is another class of men who, judging of a disease by its outward appearance, confound the accessory manifestations with the root of the disease, and, instead of directing their efforts to the source of the evil, content themselves with subduing some passing symptoms.

It is our duty to try and avoid both of these dangers.

The evil exists and it is enormous. We do not think we can better define it and its cause at all times and in all places than we have already done by the word "presumption," that inseparable companion of the half-educated, that spring of an unmeasured ambition, and yet easy to satisfy in times of trouble and confusion.

It is principally the middle classes of society which this moral gangrene has affected, and it is only among them that the real heads of the party are found.

For the great mass of the people it has no attraction and can have none. The labours to which this class—the real people—are obliged to devote themselves, are too continuous and too positive to allow them to throw themselves into vague abstractions and ambitions. The people know what is the happiest thing for them: namely, to be able to count on the morrow, for it is the morrow which will repay them for the cares and sorrows of to-day. The laws which afford a just protection to individuals, to families, and to property, are quite simple in their essence. The people dread any movement which injures industry and brings new burdens in its train.

Men in the higher classes of society who join the revolution are either falsely ambitious men or, in the widest acceptation of the word, lost spirits. Their career, moreover, is generally short! They are the first victims of political reforms, and the part played by the small number among them who survive is mostly that of courtiers despised by upstarts, their inferiors, promoted to the first dignities of the State; and of this France, Germany, Italy, and Spain furnish a number of living examples.

We do not believe that fresh disorders with a directly revolutionary end—not even revolutions in the palace and the highest places in the Government—are to be feared at present in France, because of the decided aversion of the people to anything which might disturb the peace they are now enjoying after so many troubles and disasters.

In Germany, as in Spain and Italy, the people ask only for peace and quiet.

In all four countries the agitated classes are principally composed of wealthy men—real cosmopolitans, securing their personal advantage at the expense of any order of things whatever—paid State officials, men of letters, lawyers, and the individuals charged with the public education.

To these classes may be added that of the falsely ambitious, whose number is never considerable among the lower orders, but is larger in the higher ranks of society.

There is besides scarcely any epoch which does not offer a rallying cry to some particular faction. This cry, since 1815, has been *Constitution*. But do not let us deceive ourselves: this word, susceptible of great latitude of interpretation, would be but imperfectly understood if we supposed that the factions attached quite the same meaning to it under the different *régimes*. Such is certainly not the case. In pure monarchies it is qualified by the name of "national representation." In countries which have lately been brought under the representative *régime* it is called "development," and promises charters and fundamental laws. In the only State which possesses an ancient national representation it takes "reform" as its object. Everywhere it means change and trouble.

In pure monarchies it may be paraphrased thus:—"The level of equality shall pass over your heads; your fortunes shall pass into other hands; your ambitions, which have been satisfied for centuries, shall now give place to our ambitions, which have been hitherto repressed."

In the States under a new *régime* they say:—"The ambitions satisfied yesterday must give place to those of the morrow, and this is the morrow for us."

Lastly, in England, the only place in the third class, the rallying cry—that of Reform—combines the two meanings.

Europe thus presents itself to the impartial observer under an aspect at the same time deplorable and peculiar. We find everywhere the people praying for the maintenance of peace and tranquillity, faithful to God and their Princes, remaining proof against the efforts and seductions of the factious who call themselves friends of the people and wish to lead them to an agitation which the people themselves do not desire!

The Governments, having lost their balance, are frightened, intimidated, and thrown into confusion by the cries of the intermediary class of society, which, placed between the Kings and their subjects, breaks the sceptre of the monarch, and usurps the cry of the people—that class so often disowned by the people, and nevertheless too much listened to, caressed and feared by those who could with one word reduce it again to nothingness.

We see this intermediary class abandon itself with a blind fury and animosity which proves much more its own fears than any confidence in the success of its enterprises, to all the means which seem proper to assuage its thirst for power, applying itself to the task of persuading Kings that their rights are confined to sitting upon a throne, while those of the people are to govern, and to attack all that centuries have bequeathed as holy and worthy of man's respect—denying, in fact, the value of the past, and declaring themselves the masters of the future. We see this class take all sorts of disguises, uniting and subdividing as occasion offers, helping each other in the hour of danger, and the next day depriving each other of all their conquests. It takes possession of the press, and employs it to promote impiety, disobedience to the laws of religion and the States, and goes so far as to preach murder as a duty for those who desire what is good.

One of its leaders in Germany defined public opinion as "the will of the strong man in the spirit of the party"—a maxim too often put in practice, and too seldom understood by those whose right and duty it is to save society from its own errors, its own weaknesses, and the crimes which the factious commit while pretending to act in its interests.

The evil is plain; the means used by the faction which causes these disorders are so blameable in principle, so criminal in their application, and expose the faction itself to so many dangers, that what men of narrow views (whose head and heart are broken by circumstances stronger than their calculations or their courage) regard as the end of society may become the first step towards a better order of things. These weak men would be right unless men stronger than they are come forward to close their ranks and determine the victory.

We are convinced that society can no longer be saved without strong and vigorous resolutions on the part of the Governments still free in their opinions and actions.

We are also convinced that this may yet be, if the Governments face the truth, if they free themselves from all illusion, if they join their ranks and take their stand on a line of correct, unambiguous, and frankly announced principles.

By this course the monarchs will fulfil the duties imposed upon them by Him who, by entrusting them with power, has charged them to watch over the maintenance of justice, and the rights of all, to avoid the paths of error, and tread firmly in the way of truth. Placed beyond the passions which agitate society, it is in days of trial chiefly that they are called upon to despoil realities of their false appearances, and to show themselves as they are, fathers invested with the authority belonging by right to the heads of families, to prove that, in days of mourning, they know how to be just, wise, and therefore strong, and that they will not abandon the people whom they ought to govern to be the sport of factions, to error and its consequences, which must involve the loss of society. The moment in which we are putting our thoughts on paper is one of these critical moments. The crisis is great; it will be decisive according to the part we take or do not take.

There is a rule of conduct common to individuals and to States, established by the experience of centuries as by that of everyday life. This rule declares "that one must not dream of reformation while agitated by passion; wisdom directs that at such moments we should limit ourselves to maintaining."

Let the monarchs vigorously adopt this principle; let all their resolutions bear the impression of it. Let their actions, their measures, and even their words announce and prove to the world this determination—they will find allies everywhere. The Governments, in establishing the principle of *stability*, will in no wise exclude the development of what is good, for stability is not immobility. But it is for those who are burdened with the heavy task of government to augment the well-being of their people! It is for Governments to regulate it according to necessity and to suit the times. It is not by concessions, which the factious strive to force from legitimate power, and which they have neither the right to claim nor the faculty of keeping within just bounds, that wise reforms can be carried out. That all the good possible should be done is our most ardent wish; but that which is not good must never be confounded with that which is, and even real good should be done only by those who unite to the right of authority the means of enforcing it. Such should be also the sincere wish of the people, who know by sad experience the value of certain phrases and the nature of certain caresses.

Respect for all that is; liberty for every Government to watch over the well-being of its own people; a league between all Governments against factions in all States; contempt for the meaningless words which have become the rallying cry of the factious; respect for the progressive development of institutions in lawful ways; refusal on the part of every monarch to aid or succour partisans under any mask whatever—such are happily the ideas of the great monarchs: the world will be saved if they bring them into action— it is lost if they do not.

Union between the monarchs is the basis of the policy which must now be followed to save society from total ruin.

What is the particular object towards which this policy should be directed? The more important this question is, the more necessary it is to solve it. A principle is something, but it acquires real value only in its application.

The first sources of the evil which is crushing the world have been indicated by us in a paper which has no pretension to be anything more than a mere sketch. Its further causes have also there been pointed out: if, with respect to individuals, it may be defined by the word *presumption*, in applying it to society, taken as a whole, we believe we can best describe the existing evil as the *confusion of ideas*, to which too much generalisation constantly leads. This is what now troubles society. Everything which up to this time has been considered as fixed in principle is attacked and overthrown.

In religious matters criticism and inquiry are to take the place of faith, Christian morality is to replace the Law of Christ as it is interpreted by Christian authorities.

In the Catholic Church, the Jansenists and a number of isolated sectarians, who wish for a religion without a Church, have devoted themselves to this enterprise with ardent zeal: among the Protestant sects, the Methodists, sub-divided into almost as many sects as there are individuals; then the enlightened promoters of the Bible Societies and the Unitarians—the promoters of the fusion of Lutherans and Calvinists in one Evangelical community—all pursue the same end.

The object which these men have in common, to whatever religion they may ostensibly belong, is simply to overthrow all authority. Put on moral grounds, they wish *to enfranchise souls* in the same way as some of the political revolutionists who were not actuated by motives of personal ambition wished to *enfranchise the people*.

If the same elements of destruction which are now throwing society into convulsion have existed in all ages—for every age has seen immoral and ambitious men, hypocrites, men of heated imaginations, wrong motives, and wild projects—yet ours, by the single fact of the liberty of the press, possesses more than any preceding age the means of contact, seduction, and attraction whereby to act on these different classes of men.

We are certainly not alone in questioning if society can exist with the liberty of the press, a scourge unknown to the world before the latter half of the seventeenth century, and restrained until the end of the eighteenth, with scarcely any exceptions but England—a part of Europe separated from the continent by the sea, as well as by her language and by her peculiar manners.

The first principle to be followed by the monarchs, united as they are by the coincidence of their desires and opinions, should be that of maintaining the stability of political institutions against the disorganised excitement which has taken possession of men's minds; the immutability of principles against the madness of their interpretation; and respect for laws actually in force against a desire for their destruction.

The hostile faction is divided into two very distinct parties. One is that of the Levellers; the other, that of the Doctrinaires. United in times of confusion, these men are divided in times of inaction. It is for the Governments to understand and estimate them at their just value.

In the class of Levellers there are found men of strong will and determination. The Doctrinaires can count none such among their ranks. If the first are more to be feared in action, the second are more dangerous in that time of deceitful calm which precedes it; as with physical storms, so with those of social order. Given up to abstract ideas inapplicable to real wants, and generally in contradiction to those very wants, men of this class unceasingly agitate the people by their imaginary or simulated fears, and disturb Governments in order to make them deviate from the right path. The world desires to be governed by facts and according to justice, not by phrases and theories; the first need of society is to be maintained by strong authority (no authority without real strength deserves the name) and not to govern itself. In comparing the number of contests between parties in mixed Governments, and that of just complaints caused by aberrations of power in a Christian State, the comparison would not be in favour of the new doctrines. The first and greatest concern for the immense majority of every nation is the stability of the laws, and their uninterrupted action—never their change. Therefore let the Governments govern, let them maintain the groundwork of their institutions, both ancient and modern; for if it is at all times dangerous to touch them, it certainly would not now, in the general confusion, be wise to do so.

Let them announce this determination to their people, and demonstrate it by facts. Let them reduce the Doctrinaires to silence within their States, and show their contempt for them abroad. Let them not encourage by their attitude or actions the suspicion of being favourable or indifferent to error: let them not allow it to be believed that experience has lost all its rights to make way for ex-

periments which at the least are dangerous. Let them be precise and
clear in all their words, and not seek by concessions to gain over
those parties who aim at the destruction of all power but their own,
whom concessions will never gain over, but only further embolden
in their pretensions to power.

Let them in these troublous times be more than usually cautious
in attempting real ameliorations, not imperatively claimed by the
needs of the moment, to the end that good itself may not turn
against them—which is the case whenever a Government measure
seems to be inspired by fear.

Let them not confound concessions made to parties with the
good they ought to do for their people, in modifying, according to
their recognised needs, such branches of the administration as require it.

Let them give minute attention to the financial state of their
kingdoms, so that their people may enjoy, by the reduction of public burdens, the real, not imaginary, benefits of a state of peace.

Let them be just, but strong; beneficent, but strict.

Let them maintain religious principles in all their purity, and not
allow the faith to be attacked and morality interpreted according
to the *social contract* or the vision of foolish sectarians.

Let them suppress Secret Societies, that gangrene of society.

In short, let the great monarchs strengthen their union, and prove
to the world that if it exists, it is beneficent, and ensures the political
peace of Europe: that it is powerful only for the maintenance of
tranquillity at a time when so many attacks are directed against it;
that the principles which they profess are paternal and protective,
menacing only the disturbers of public tranquillity.

The Governments of the second order will see in such a union
the anchor of their salvation, and they will be anxious to connect
themselves with it. The people will take confidence and courage,
and the most profound and salutary peace which the history of any
time can show will have been effected. This peace will first act on
countries still in a good state, but will not be without a very decided influence on the fate of those threatened with destruction,
and even assist the restoration of those which have already passed
under the scourge of revolution.

To every great State determined to survive the storm there still
remain many chances of salvation, and a strong union between the

States on the principles we have announced will overcome the storm itself.

11. Intervention in Europe: Troppau, 1820

Within months after the system of joint intervention to suppress radicalism had been established for Germany at Teplitz and Carlsbad, revolutions drove the rulers of Spain and of Naples from their thrones. Metternich, especially concerned for Austria's interests in Italy, called for a Congress of the Powers at Troppau. England and France, with Mediterranean interests of their own, were reluctant and sent only observers. But that left Metternich free to concentrate his attention on the Czar Alexander, whose purposes and attitude were uncertain. At a private interview Metternich persuaded the Czar of the rightness of his political views, and established a kind of personal supremacy over the Russian ruler (see Metternich's estimate of the Czar and the "Confession of Faith" addressed to him at Troppau, pp. 96–127). The result was the Troppau Protocol, endorsed by the three eastern powers and freeing Austria to suppress the Italian revolts. The French constitutional monarchy did not formally accept the document, but soon intervened in Spain in accordance with its principles. The British position, marking the first serious break in the European concert, is described in Castlereagh's interview with Lieven. [Text of the Troppau Protocol: Walter A. Phillips, *The Confederation of Europe* (2nd edn., London, 1920), pp. 208–209, by permission of Longmans, Green & Co.; the Circular Dispatch and Metternich's letter to Rechberg: Metternich, *Memoirs*, III (London, 1881), 444–450; Castlereagh's interview with Lieven: C. K. Webster, *The Foreign Policy of Castlereagh, 1815–1822* (London, 1925), pp. 568–573. Translation by the editor.]

Preliminary Protocol of Troppau, presented by Metternich to the Congress of the Powers at Troppau, November 15, 1820

States which have undergone a change of Government due to revolution, the results of which threaten other states, *ipso facto* cease to be members of the European Alliance, and remain excluded from it until their situation gives guarantees for legal order and stability. If, owing to such alterations, immediate danger threatens other states, the Powers bind themselves, by peaceful means, or if need be by arms, to bring back the guilty state into the bosom of the Great Alliance.

Circular Despatch of the Courts of Austria, Russia, and Prussia,
to their Ambassadors and Agents at the German
and Northern Courts, Troppau, December 8, 1820

The events of March 8 in Spain, and July 2 in Naples, and the
catastrophe in Portugal, must cause in all those who have to care
for the peace of States a deep feeling of grief and anxiety, and, at
the same time, a necessity for meeting, in order to consider in common how best to meet the evils which threaten to break out all
over Europe.

It was natural that these feelings should be very active in those
particular Powers which had lately conquered revolution, and now
saw it raising it head again; and also natural that these Powers, in
resisting the revolution for the third time, should resort to the same
means which they had used so happily in the memorable combat
which delivered Europe from a twenty years' yoke.

Everything justified the hope that this union, formed under the
most dangerous circumstances, crowned with the most brilliant
success, fostered by the negotiations of 1814, 1815, and 1818, as it
had released the European continent from the military despotism
of the representative of revolution, and brought peace to the world,
would be able to curb a new force not less tyrannical and not less
to be despised—the power of rebellion and outrage.

These were the motives, and the purpose, of the meeting in
Troppau. The former are so evident that they do not require an
explanation: the latter is so honourable and beneficial that doubtless
the wishes of all honourable men will follow the allied Courts in
their noble career.

The business which is imposed on them by the most sacred obligations is great and difficult; but a happy presentiment bids them
hope for the attainment of their aim by a firm maintenance of the
spirit of those treaties to which Europe owes peace and unity
among her States.

The Powers exercise an indisputable right in contemplating
common measures of safety against States in which the Government has been overthrown by rebellion, and which, if only as an
example, must consequently be treated as hostile to all lawful constitutions and Governments. The exercise of this right becomes
still more urgent when revolutionists endeavour to spread to neigh-

bouring countries the misfortunes which they had brought upon themselves, scattering rebellion and confusion around.

Such a position, such proceedings are an evident violation of contract, which guarantees to all the European Governments, besides the inviolability of their territories, the enjoyment of those peaceful relations which exclude the possibility of encroachment on either side.

The allied Courts took incontestable fact as their starting-point, and those ministers who could be at Troppau itself supplied with definite instructions from their monarchs, therefore made an agreement as to the principles to be followed as to States whose form of government has been violently disturbed, and as to the peaceful or forcible measures to be adopted to lead such States back into the Bund.

The results of their deliberations they communicated to the Courts of Paris and London, that those Courts might take them into consideration.

Since the Neapolitan revolution takes daily fresh root; since no other endangers so directly the peace of the neighbouring States; since no other can be acted upon so immediately, the necessity of proceeding on the above-mentioned principles with regard to the kingdom of Both the Sicilies soon became evident.

To bring about conciliatory measures to that end, the monarchs assembled at Troppau resolved to invite the King of Both Sicilies to meet them at Laybach, a step which would free the will of his Majesty from every outward constraint, and put the King in the position of a mediator between his deluded and erring subjects and the States whose peace was threatened by them. Since the monarchs were determined not to acknowledge Governments created by open rebellion, they could enter into a negotiation with the person of the King only. Their ministers and agents in Naples have received the necessary instructions for that purpose.

France and England have been asked to take part in this step, and it is to be expected that they will not refuse their consent, since the principle on which the invitation rests is in perfect harmony with the agreements formerly concluded by them, and is also a pledge of the most upright and peaceable feelings.

The system established between Austria, Prussia, and Russia is no new one; it rests on the same maxims which formed the foundation of the agreements by which the union of the European States

in the Bund has been effected. The hearty concord existing between the Courts which form the centre of this confederation can
only be strengthened by it. The Bund will be maintained on the
same footing as that on which it was placed by the Powers to
whom it owes its existence, and as it has been gradually accepted
by all, from the conviction entertained of its evident and undoubted advantages.

No further proof, however, is required that the Powers have not
been guided in their resolutions by the thought of conquest or the
desire of interfering with the internal affairs of other Governments.
They want nothing but to maintain peace, to free Europe from the
scourge of revolution, and to avert, or shorten as much as possible,
the mischief arising from the violation of all the principles of order
and morality. Under such conditions they think themselves justified in claiming the unanimous approbation of the world as a reward for their cares and their efforts.

Metternich to Count Rechberg, Foreign Minister of Bavaria, Vienna, December 31, 1820

I take advantage, my dear Count, of the first moment at my disposal, which is the last of my stay here, to give you some account
of what has been done and what is going to be done. . . .

Here are the facts in all their simplicity.

Any catastrophe such as that of Naples presents different periods, whether regarded from a domestic or foreign point of view.
The revolt breaks out; it is indubitable and evident; it is the beginning of a conflagration; if they are in good order, take your
fire-engines there; ask no questions; do not hesitate; extinguish the
fire; success will be certain. Do not take empty fire-engines, but
let them be well filled.

Then comes the second period. The revolt takes the appearance
of Reform. A feeble sovereign swears to put a knife to his throat.
A chorus of Liberals and Radicals join in his hymns; the sovereign
is praised to the skies; and the people seem to adore him. Milk and
honey are to flow in all the veins of the State abandoned to
anarchy; tyrants alone could hinder the development of so fine a
work!

This is the history of the months of July to November.

Our fire-engines were not full in July, otherwise we should have set to work immediately.

In the second period, it did not seem to us that our neutral attitude was sufficient; the Naples affair threatened Italy, Austria, Europe equally. It is therefore for the latter to declare itself in principle with us. We take upon ourselves the material part. To go to Naples is nothing at any time, but to remain at Naples and re-establish order in the kingdom of the Two Sicilies is certainly more difficult.

Europe has frankly and well seconded us. We, who were free to hold whatever language we liked, have spoken: those of our allies who could do the same have done so. Those who are more bound by forms have acted according to our principles. The Neapolitan revolt and all its charms have been put in quarantine. You have done more than even the great English and French. You have sent back the agent of the Carbonari who came to boast to you of the happiness of his country; you have done this, my dear Count, and it was worthy of you.

Agreed in their principles at Troppau, the three Cabinets have carried them into effect. The idea of inviting the King to meet us at Laybach was acceptable. This invitation was made on very simple, but the only correct grounds. You know the autograph letters of the Sovereigns: they are all friendly, for no one is an enemy of the King. The *ostensible* instructions for our plenipotentiaries were more precise. They were ordered to declare—

1st. That the Powers would never recognise anything which is the work of the rebellion.

2nd. That before resorting to extreme measures, they desire to exhaust every means of conciliation, *not between the rebellion and lawful power, but between the real interests of the kingdom and those of Italy and Europe.* That, knowing but one proper instrument for a work so great and salutary, his Majesty the King was invited to meet the three monarchs.

3rd. That at Naples it is asserted that the King is free. That the King, being free, should feel it his duty to take upon himself this great work; that if the King did not come he would be surrendered.

4th. That as the King's person is not on this occasion to be replaced by any other, the invitation is personal. That our ambassadors would in consequence refuse passports to any other individual, were it even a Prince of the Royal House; that on the other hand, it would depend upon the King to be accompanied by whomsoever his Majesty should think fit.

5th. That the King, if he were prevented from leaving the Kingdom, should be placed under the safeguard and responsibility of every Neapolitan.

The order has gone, and there is not a folly that our agents have not committed. Unhappily, there is not a single head among them. These stormy times, my dear Count, are weak in heads. . . .

Report by Prince Lieven, Russian Ambassador in London,
of an interview with Foreign Minister Castlereagh
concerning the Troppau Protocol

December 8, 1820

He could not, he said, disguise from me his regret at seeing the three Courts sign a document as important as this protocol without the knowledge of the representatives of the other two cabinets; but, above all, he could not hide his lively apprehensions regarding the actual purposes of the protocol. He did not know, he added, how to interpret it. Should it be considered the basis of an action treaty, and thus the basis of a new alliance, or is it only a statement of a confidential understanding among the cabinets concerning present circumstances and future possibilities? In the latter case, the only cause for apprehension would be that the secret of the cabinets must not be exposed. But the former case would give very legitimate causes for alarm, for nothing could have a graver or more deplorable effect on Europe in its present state.

The three Courts would be creating a new political system that would invalidate all existing engagements. They would be erecting an authority that other Powers would find it impossible to recognize; but more than that, they would be giving birth to a contrary system that would make them find opposition in places where today they find only a sincere wish to assist and to agree. . . .

If the principles indicated in that document were proclaimed, he continued, the fundamental laws of our monarchy would oblige us not only to declare ourselves as being against them, but also to make protest against these doctrines. We should find ourselves forced to do this, however convinced we might otherwise be of the rectitude and the sincerity of the views expressed. You would be proclaiming before the universe that you have taken unto your-selves the exclusive privilege of meddling in the internal affairs of independent States, States to whom existing agreements guarantee the very rights you intend to violate. You even agree among your-selves to use coercive means.

[Lieven argued that the intention was only to exclude offending states from the alliance, and to intervene with force only as a last resort when a neighboring state is threatened.]

I do not question, answered the Secretary of State, the inten-tions of the monarchs—no one does more justice than I to the gen-erous motives that guide them—but I must judge and condemn now what we shall soon be forced to judge and condemn before our Parliament. Thus, in reply to your observations, I must observe in my turn that principles like these, agreed upon and recognized by three autocratic sovereigns, in fact open all countries to invasion by their armies. They would themselves assume the right to deter-mine the need for their intervention, and to decide upon the ex-pediency and the occasion for employing their instruments of compulsion. Upon what principle can one justify the right of Powers to erect, at their own initiative and desire, a tribunal so threatening to the independence of nations?

The distinctions to be made on such essential points are so deli-cate, that just as it would be impossible for them to define and pre-dict all the cases to which they would apply their principles, so too would it become easy for the enemies of order to interpret them in an exaggerated sense, a sense that would suit their projects the better, and to lead the nations, the governments, and even the very authors of a system generous in principle into dangerous error. Could England, even, find safety in this system of coercion? Suppose some change should come about in this country, suppose the present public agitation should seem to you the kind of situa-tion that requires your intervention, suppose an English monarch should ask your help. Would not any of these hypothetical cir-cumstances authorize the Alliance to intervene in the internal affairs of Great Britain? What minister, I ask you, could sanction principles that might lead to such results? and could he stay in office a single day if he did not declare himself hostile to them?

Just what great advantages does this system offer to balance off the disastrous threats it raises?

[Lieven answered that it would head off future disturbances and
unite the forces of order against them.]

As I have repeated more than once, Viscount Castlereagh said
to me, it is not the goals and the intentions of the monarchs that I
am speaking against, but the forms and means they wish to apply.
The same object might be achieved in more natural ways, ways
more in conformity with the spirit of our times. Your action
against Naples will do more than anything else to make your views
and your resolution known, without consolidating opinion by
harsh statements of principle, hostile to the independence of nations. Deeds will have more effect than words, and will not hand
over such dangerous weapons to the seditious.

Let Austria, at the moment when she acts (should that indeed
be the course of wisdom), openly make her reasons known to her
allies. She has legitimate ones; the evidence she has of the plots of
the Carbonari are by themselves sufficient grounds to justify
energetic measures for the preservation of her influence. The other
Powers, answering the declaration from the Court at Vienna, can
state their opinions on the case that has provoked the declaration,
and in that way they will be able to express their views with far
more energy and effect, because each will be speaking in the language appropriate to its own situation; this they would not be
able to do in any joint proclamation, in which the particular problems of each must necessarily weaken and impede the force of
thought and expression.

In our century the spirit of faction knows how to turn everything to the advantage of its dangerous doctrines. Here the monarchs would be gratuitously giving it weapons that it could easily
turn against them. In our times actions count for more than systems, and rules of practice more than laws in writing. Your principles thus proclaimed would establish a new law among nations.
A collective declaration in which three absolute sovereigns assume
the right to condemn a free people and to follow up their con-
demnation with the dispatch of an army called European to wage
war on Neapolitan territory would immediately give to the factious, and even to those who are not, easy means of representing
you as odious and arbitrary, and of awakening in the Neapolitan
nation a spirit of resistance and an enthusiasm whose consequences
are difficult to foresee. One should remember the effect of the
proclamation of the Duke of Brunswick[1] at the beginning of the

Revolution; it is well known that it was this imprudent document that gave the first impetus to the warlike and conquering spirit of the French. By all means, act where action is necessary, but no proclamations that generalize your principles; they can only obstruct the purposes you set yourselves.

We assuredly are not a government of revolutionary principles, and so our desires cannot differ from yours; but the procedure you are adopting can force us against our will to become the center and the rallying point of the revolutionaries. You raise two standards where for the health of Europe there should be only one. I repeat: act, but do not dictate laws. You will always find us ready and willing to second you whenever our help becomes necessary; and we shall be able to find in each particular situation sound reasons for our support. But do not put us in an arena where we must fight you; do not compel us to block you, and thus lose everything.

All that I have been saying to you from the British point of view will apply equally to France, with the difference that she more than we must take into consideration the situation of the King vis-à-vis his nation—a situation that would be exposed to very great dangers by a schism in European politics. It would be easy to state that this league of sovereigns is based on hatred and distrust of the French, and to attribute every measure of the French government that does not suit the interests of the factious, and which obstructs their plans, to the King's dependence on the support and the help of this league. New seeds of discord thus will be disseminated in that country, the home and the source of the revolutionary madness that torments all the others; and it will be given over to new upheavals, while the specific engagements that guarantee its tranquility are nullified and destroyed.

One cannot ignore the fact that Spain already gives concrete proof of the fear and distrust that this union of the Sovereigns inspires in the peoples. Our last reports from Madrid, which I promptly transmitted to Lord Stewart [British representative at Troppau], inform us of the uneasiness the King's ministers are beginning to feel, lest that monarch be already influenced by hope

[1] As commander of the German and émigré armies invading revolutionary France in 1792, Brunswick had announced the goal of the war to be the restoration of authority to the French royal family. The "Brunswick Manifesto" gave the war against France the character of a war against Revolution, rallying French patriotism behind the revolutionary movement and leading to the deposition and execution of the King.—Ed.

for foreign assistance. And, however resolved they may seem to support the rights of the monarchy, it now seems that because of their apprehensions regarding the results of the meeting at Troppau, they are more inclined than they ever before have appeared to be to surround themselves with new guarantees against the encroachments of the royal authority upon the liberties of the nation.

The standing and the impressive might of the three Powers and, even more important, the virtuous characters of their rules are precious assets for Europe. They are in better position than the other major Courts to act quickly when a situation requires it, and thereby to assure the maintenance of peace and order in Europe; but the greater their powers, the more they must not abuse them. This is a decisive moment for the governments; they cannot afford to make mistakes. Look at the state of public sentiment in all countries—the more one thinks about it the more appalled one is by the immense harm that would come from a single false step.

I have never regretted more than now not being in the Emperor's presence, so as to place my thoughts before him. My belief in all that I have been saying to you is so strong that I have no doubt, the Emperor being so accessible to the frank language of truth, that the opinions I impart to His Imperial Majesty cannot but bear conviction to a judgment as enlightened as his. On every occasion the Emperor has reaffirmed his immutable principle of contracting no more new engagements, of forming no new connections alongside those which exist, and seeking no guarantees outside the general Alliance. This determination of his is in fact the anchor of European security. Why do it injury? . . .

12. Canning on Intervention, 1826

The British opposition to intervention shown in Castlereagh's reaction to the Troppau Protocol evolved under his successor in the Foreign Office, George Canning (1770–1827), into British leadership of a liberal "camp" in international affairs. Canning was a dramatic popular figure, a House of Commons man, who was quite ready to use the weapons of patriotic and liberal enthusiasm both at home and in his foreign policy—to Metternich's disgust and horror. In 1823, confronted by French intervention in Spain to restore the conservative Bourbon régime, which Canning was unable to prevent, he asserted the principle of nonintervention. In the terms of the Monroe Doctrine, the non-intervention principle was directed against any wish the Continental powers might have to suppress revolutionary régimes in Latin America —that was something Canning and the British fleet *could* prevent. By 1826, the principle of nonintervention had been extended to mean that England would intervene actively to defend a liberal Portuguese government against its domestic enemies, or against the Spanish Bourbons, or against the Troppau powers. What this implied for Metternich's Europe is made clear in Canning's famous speech in the British Parliament. [H. Temperley, *The Foreign Policy of Canning, 1822–1827* (2nd edn., London, 1966), pp. 539–540, 579–585. By permission of Frank Cass & Co. Ltd.]

Canning to Sir William À Court, British envoy extraordinary in Spain

September 18, 1823

THE BRITISH GOVERNMENT will not, in any case, undertake any guaranty [sic] whatever, either of territory or internal Institutions.

The scrupulousness with which England is in the habit of fulfilling her obligations makes it the more necessary for her not to contract them lightly. A guaranty is one of the most onerous obligations which one state can contract towards another. A defensive Alliance binds the Government contracting it to come to the aid of its Ally, in case of an unprovoked attack against his Dominions: and to make in his behalf, every reasonable and practicable exertion,—practicable in extent, and reasonable in duration. But it does not bind the assisting Government to the alternative of either a successful result, or an indefinite prolongation of the War. A guaranty, strictly construed, knows no limits either of time, or of degree. It would be, unless distinctly restricted in that respect, claimable in a War commenced by the Power to whom the guaranty is given, as well as in a War of unjust aggression against that Power; and the integrity of the territory of that Power must be maintained, at whatever cost the effort to maintain it is prolonged: nay, though the guaranteed Power itself should contribute almost nothing to maintaining it. If . . . the engagement is to be restricted in these particulars, it would constitute a unilateral defensive Alliance, but it would cease to be a guarantee. Objectionable as a territorial guarantee is shown to be, the objections to a guaranty of internal institutions are infinitely stronger. It is diffi-

cult to say whether these objections apply with greater force to
the party giving, or to that which receives, such a guaranty.

The very principle on which the British Government so earn-
estly deprecated the War against Spain, was, that of the right of
any Nation to change or to modify its internal Institutions.

Is that War to end in His Majesty's consenting to assume to
Himself the province of defending, against all Challengers, from
within, as well as from without, the Institutions, whatever they
might be, which the War may leave standing in Spain?

Is His Majesty to guaranty the [liberal] Constitution of 1812,
indifference to which, to say the least . . . is the single point upon
which anything like an Agreement of opinion has been found to
exist in Spain? or is He to guaranty the antient despotism, the
restoration of which, with all its accompaniments, appears to be the
object of by far the largest party in the Country? or is it to be in
behalf of some new system, struck out at a heat, at the winding up
of affairs at Cadiz, that the faith of Great Britain is to be pledged,
and that Her blood and treasure are to be forthcoming? or is it only
to the undoubted right of the Spanish Nation to reform its own
Government, that the sanction of His Majesty's is to be added?
If such a guarantee were anything more than the mere affirmance
of an abstract proposition, against whom would it have practically
to operate? clearly against the Spanish themselves: and in the endless struggles which might be expected from the then distracted
state of parties in that Country, against every party by turns?

Could anything be more unbecoming than the assumption of
such a right by a foreign Power? Could anything be more intolerable to the Country with respect to which it was assumed?

It is hardly necessary to add that while His Majesty must decline
accepting such a right for Himself, he could not acknowledge it in
any other Power.

The exercise of such a right must necessarily lead to an inter-
meddling with the affairs of the guaranteed State, such as to place
it, in fact, at the mercy of the Power who gives the guarantee.

Russia, in former times, guaranteed the Constitution of Poland.

The result is known—and it was inevitable.[1] The natural and

---

[1] Russian guarantee of the old Polish aristocratic constitution in 1792, against
a reform party, had led to rival invasions of Poland by Russia and Prussia,
to partition of Poland among the eastern Powers, and to a Polish national
uprising led by Kosciuszko.—Ed.

necessary course of things must, in such a case, overbear even the most sincere and studied abstinence from interposition on the part of the guaranteeing Power.

There can be no doubt that His Majesty's Allies will feel how little such an arrangement would be compatible with the Engagements by which they stand bound to each other: to maintain the State of territorial possession established at the Peace, and the rights of independent Nations.

Canning's speech in Commons on Portugal, December 12, 1826

It will be for Spain, upon a communication of the step now taken by His Majesty, to consider in what way she will meet the call. The earnest hope and wish of His Majesty's Government is, that she may meet it in such a manner as to avert the consequences of the Message before us.

Sir, I set out with saying that there were reasons which induced me to think that nothing short of a point of national faith or national honor, I will not say would justify, but would make desirable at the present moment, any voluntary approximation to the possibility of a dangerous war. Let me be understood, however, distinctly, as not meaning to say I dread war in a good cause (and in no other may it ever be the lot of this country ever to engage!) from a distrust of the strength of the country to commence it, or of her resources to maintain it. I dread it, indeed—but on far other grounds: I dread it from a consciousness of the tremendous power Great Britain possesses of pushing hostilities in which we may be engaged, to consequences which I shudder to contemplate. (*Hear, hear, hear*) Some years ago, in the discussion of the negociations respecting the French war against Spain, I took the liberty of adverting to this topic. I then stated that the position of this country in the present state of the world was one of neutrality, not only between contending nations, but between contending principles; and that it was by neutrality alone that we could maintain that balance, the preservation of which I believed to be essential to the peace and safety of the world. I then said that I feared that the next war which should be kindled in Europe, would be a war not so much of armies, as of opinions. Four years' experience has confirmed rather than altered my opinion. It is, to be sure, within narrow limits that this war of opinion is at present confined: but it *is* a war of opinion that Spain (whether as Government or as nation) is now waging against Portugal; it is a war which has commenced in hatred of the new institutions of Portugal. How long is it reasonable to expect that Portugal will abstain from retaliation? I fear that the next war to be kindled in Europe, if it spread beyond the narrow limits of Spain and Portugal, will be a war of most tremendous character—a war not merely of conflicting armies, but of conflicting opinions. (*Cheering*)

I know that if into that war this country enters (and if she do engage, I trust it will be with a most sincere desire to mitigate rather than exasperate, and to contend with arms, rather than with the more fatal artillery of popular excitation), she will see under her banners, arrayed for the contest all the discontented and restless spirits of the age, all those who—whether justly or unjustly—are dissatisfied with the present state of their own countries. The consciousness of such a situation excites all my fears, for it shows there exists a power to be wielded by Great Britain, more tremendous than was perhaps ever brought into action in the history of mankind. (*Hear*) But, though it may be "excellent to have a giant's power it may be tyrannous to use it like a giant." The knowledge that we possess this strength is our security; and our business is not to seek opportunities of displaying it, but to content ourselves with letting the professors of violent and exaggerated doctrines on both sides feel that it is not their interest to convert their umpire into their competitors. (*Hear*) The situation of this country may be compared to that of the Ruler of the Winds.

The consequence of letting loose the passions at present chained and confined, would be to produce a scene of desolation which no man can contemplate without horror; and I should not sleep easy on my couch, if I were conscious that I had contributed to precipitate it by a single moment.

This, then, is the reason—a reason very different from fear—the reverse of a consciousness of disability—why I dread the recurrence of hostilities in any part of Europe; why I would bear much, and would forbear long; why I would (as I have said) put up with almost any thing that did not touch national faith and national honor, rather than let slip the furies of war, the leash of which we hold in our hands—not knowing whom they may reach, or how far their ravages may be carried. Such is the love of peace which the British

Government acknowledges; and such the necessity for peace which the circumstances of the world inculcate. I will push these topics no farther.

I return, in conclusion, to the object of this Address. Let us fly to the aid of Portugal, by whomsoever attacked; because it is our duty to do so; and let us cease our interference where that duty ends. We go to Portugal, not to rule, not to dictate, not to prescribe constitutions—but to defend and preserve the independence of an ally. We go to plant the standard of England on the well-known heights of Lisbon. Where that standard is planted, foreign dominion shall not come.

[Responding to the question of whether his Government should not have intervened in 1823, in the name of the balance of power, to defend the Spanish liberal government and prevent French restoration of the Spanish Bourbon monarchy, Canning resumes:]

I confess to think that the effects of the French occupation of Spain have been infinitely exaggerated.

I do not blame these exaggerations; because I am aware that they are to be attributed to the recollections of some of the best times of our history; that they are the echoes of sentiments which, in the days of William and Anne, animated the debates and dictated the votes of the British Parliament.[1] No peace was in those days thought safe for this country while the crown of Spain continued on the head of a Bourbon. But were not the apprehensions of those days greatly overstated? Has the power of Spain swallowed up the power of maritime England? or does England still remain, after the lapse of more than a century, during which the Crown of Spain had been worn by a Bourbon, niched in a nook of that same Spain —Gibraltar; an occupation which was contemporaneous with the apprehensions that I have described, and which has happily survived them?

Again, Sir, is the Spain of the present day the Spain of which the statesmen of the times of William and Anne were so much afraid? Is it indeed the nation whose puissance was expected to shake England from her sphere? No, Sir, it was quite another Spain

---

[1] England had fought the War of the Spanish Succession (1702–1713) to prevent the crowns of Spain and of France from being united in the Bourbon family.—Ed.

—it was the Spain within the limits of whose Empire the sun never set—it was Spain *"with the Indies"* that excited the jealousies and alarmed the imaginations of our ancestors.

But then, Sir, the balance of power! The entry of the French army into Spain disturbed that balance, and we ought to have gone to war to restore it! I have already said that, when the French army entered Spain we might, if we chose, have resisted or resented that measure by war.

But were there no other means than war for restoring the balance of power? Is the balance of power a fixed and unalterable standard? Or is it not a standard perpetually varying, as civilization advances, and as new nations spring up and take their place among established political communities? The balance of power a century and a half ago was to be adjusted between France and Spain, the Netherlands, Austria, and England. Some years afterwards, Russia assumed her high station in European politics. Some years after that again, Prussia became not only a substantive, but a preponderating monarchy. Thus, while the balance of power continued in principle the same, the means of adjusting it became more varied and enlarged. They became enlarged, in proportion to the increased number of considerable states—in proportion, I may say, to the number of weights which might be shifted into the one or the other scale. To look to the policy of Europe, in the times of William and Anne, for the purpose of regulating the balance of power in Europe at the present day, is to disregard the progress of events, and to confuse dates and facts which throw a reciprocal light upon each other.

It was not Spain they (our ancestors *temp.* Queen Anne) feared; India [the West Indies] was the cause of their apprehension; and I admit that if, when France made that attack, Spain had still been placed in possession of the same resources, there might have been ground for a more decisive interference. I will admit, for argument's sake, that the occupation of Spain by France was a disparagement to the character of this country; I will admit even that it was a blow to the policy which ought to be maintained in the regulation of the balance of power. What, then, was to be done? There were two means to be adopted in our resistance to it, one of them was to attack the French troops which entered Spain; the other was to render the Conquest harmless as far as regarded us, and valueless, or something worse, actually injurious, to the possessor. I say, then, that if we have been for the present dispossessed of anything in our situation as forming part of the balance of power, we are fully compensated. Was it necessary to blockade Cadiz, I say, to restore the situation of England? No. I look at the possessions of Spain on the other side of the Atlantic; I LOOK AT THE INDIES AND I CALL IN THE NEW WORLD TO REDRESS THE BALANCE OF THE OLD. (*Great cheering*)

It is thus, Sir, that I answer the accusation brought against His Majesty's government, of having allowed the French army to usurp and to retain the occupation of Spain. That occupation, I am quite confident, is an unpaid and unredeemed burden to France. It is a burden of which, I verily believe, France would be glad to rid herself. But they know little of the feelings of the French Government, and of the spirit of the French nation, who do not know that, worthless or burdensome as that occupation may be, the way to rivet her in it would be, by angry or intemperate representations, to make the continuance of that occupation a point of honor.

I believe, Sir, there is no other subject upon which I need enter into defence or explanation. The support which the Address has received, from all parties in the House, has been such as would make it both unseemly and ungrateful in me to trespass unnecessarily upon their patience. In conclusion, Sir, I shall only once more declare that the object of the Address which I propose to you is not war—its object is to take the last chance of peace. If you do not go forth on this occasion to the aid of Portugal, Portugal will be trampled down, to your irretrievable disgrace—and then will come war in the train of national degradation. If, under circumstances like these, you wait till Spain has matured her secret machinations into open hostility, you will in a little while have the sort of war required by the pacificators—and who shall say where that war will end?

III

A New Generation: The Nations

The passages included in this section are self-explanatory in many ways, because the authors were intent on explaining themselves. They identified themselves as members of a new generation, and therefore as spokesmen of the future in contrast with the past. They were vitally conscious of history, but not so as to recapture the past; rather, they projected history into the future—their future—and future history was to correct the wrongs of the past.

For most of them the persisting wrongs of the past could be lumped together as the Vienna Settlement and its perpetuation in Metternich's Europe. Curiously, the revolutionary and Napoleonic era, which they remembered only dimly or not at all, was part of what they meant by the future, while the situation in which they lived was something out of the past. The system established was conservative, and it was "artificial"; for the true course of future history had been signalized by the currents of change and the popular movements of revolutionary days. Metternich's Europe was at odds with history and with the coming generation—with Young Europe. Young Europe meant the nations, for just as the new generation yearned to express itself against the conventions of the past (or present), so it believed that the historical, "natural," national communities yearned to express themselves against Metternich's Europe.

Revolutionary and Napoleonic times, during which the new generation imagined history to have been running free, had introduced popular patriotism as a historical force. The power that lay in the nation had been seen in the successes of the French *patrie*, and in the Spanish popular resistance that arose against French domination though the Spanish régime crumbled. German reformers had sought to draw on popular patriotism to help them against Napoleonic France. Even shopkeepers' England and Holy Russia found national pride in their defiance to and defeat of revolutionary French imperialism.

But nationality had been ignored and rejected in the Vienna territorial settlement and in the interventionist Metternich system. In Italy and in Germany, the Congress statesmen had established nests of separate states under jealous petty sovereigns. If the Italian nation or people and the German nation or people were real and historical, then these arrangements and their beneficiaries were artificial and archaic.

Poland had been placed under Russian domination. And Poland's
separate national existence was dramatized rather than extinguished by
the history of its partitions and the hollowness of its pretended separate
identity under Russian rule. The Austrian Empire was by its nature a
denial of nationality, with its conglomeration of German, Czech,
Hungarian, Italian, Polish, and South Slav peoples. As for France, the
Vienna Settlement and the Bourbon Restoration were the work of
victorious enemies, a defeat and a suppression of the *patrie* that had
overthrown the Bourbons and brought the nation's most glorious days.
Metternich's Europe feared revolution, war, history, and heroes, but to
the new generation these meant freedom, greatness, and the future.

The new generation, then, the Young Europe of the nations, is not a
statistician's name for people of a certain age. It is a name for a very
talented and vigorous body of people who thought of themselves and
of Europe in these ways. Usually they were young (to begin with),
because young people as a rule are less adapted to the existing order
of things, and less committed to it professionally and socially. For
similar reasons they were likely to be intellectuals, by profession or
inclination—poets, artists, essayists and novelists, academics and the
academically trained—for intellectual life puts a premium on saying
something new, and on cutting away what is old and contrived, irra-
tional and unnatural. Young intellectuals knew something about the
world but did not feel themselves part of it. The *status quo* principle
of Metternich's Europe, in a sense, extended their youth into middle
age, because it did not encourage men of this temperament to grow into
the world. They communicated with one another, and were kept
adolescent until the sudden demands of opportunity and responsibility
in 1848.

The national revolutions of the twenties and thirties, nearly all of
them suppressed or diverted by Metternich's Europe, were landmarks
in the history of the new generation, and so many added reasons for
their alienation from the European system. The names Greece (where
Byron died), Poland, Germany, and Italy were slogans, ideals, even
battle cries against the existing system, for none of them existed but
in the future. Recurring revolution showed where freedom and the
future and greatness lay, and they pointed to freedom's and the future's
and greatness's enemy.

A CHRONOLOGY

Felicité de La Mennais (Lamennais)	1782–1854
George Gordon, Lord Byron	1788–1824
Friedrich List	1789–1846
Heinrich Heine	1797–1856
Adam Mickiewicz	1798–1855
Alexander Pushkin	1799–1837
Victor Hugo	1802–1885
Edgar Quinet	1803–1875
Giuseppe Mazzini	1805–1872

BIBLIOGRAPHY

G. Brandes, *Main Currents in Nineteenth-Century Literature* (6 vols., New York, 1901–1905).
N. H. Clement, *Romanticism in France* (New York, 1939).
G. O. Griffith, *Mazzini: Prophet of Modern Europe* (London, 1932).
C. J. H. Hayes, *Nationalism: A Religion* (New York, 1960).
J. G. Legge, *Rhyme and Revolution in Germany* (New York, 1919).
E. Newton, *Romantic Rebellion* (New York, 1962).
R. H. Thomas, *Liberalism, Nationalism, and the German Intellectuals* (Cambridge, England, 1952).

13. The Decembrist Insurrection in Russia, 1825

Victory over Napoleon brought Russian armies deep into western Europe. Soon after their return to Russia, certain young army officers, mostly of noble birth, began to form secret revolutionary political societies. They favored such reforms as the abolition of serfdom and land redistribution, a constitutional monarchy, or even a Russian republic. When Alexander I died in December 1825, and confusion surrounded the succession, leaders of the secret societies started a military revolt. It was ill-planned and uncertain, and the new Czar Nicholas I (1825–55) suppressed it the same day. In the long investigations and interrogations that followed, the Decembrists showed themselves most eager to confess and describe their actions. In this letter Peter Kakhovsky (1797–1826), a leading Decembrist, explains the spirit that lay behind the rising. He was executed with four other leaders the following July; the rest were sent into exile. [Kakhovsky to General Levashev, reprinted from *The First Russian Revolution, 1825* by Anatole G. Mazour, with the permission of the publishers, Stanford University Press. Copyright 1937, renewed 1964, by Anatole G. Mazour, pp. 274–277.]

YOUR EXCELLENCY,
Dear Sir!
The uprising of December 14 is a result of causes related above. I see, Your Excellency, that the Committee established by His Majesty is making a great effort to discover all the members of the secret Society. But the government will not derive any notable benefit from that. We were not trained within the Society but were already ready to work when we joined it. The origin and the root of the Society one must seek in the spirit of the time and in our state of mind. I know a few belonging to the secret Society but am inclined to think the membership is not very large. Among my

many acquaintances who do not adhere to secret societies very few are opposed to my opinions. Frankly I state that among thousands of young men there are hardly a hundred who do not passionately long for freedom. These youths, striving with pure and strong love for the welfare of their Fatherland, toward true enlightenment, are growing mature.

The people have conceived a sacred truth—that they do not exist for governments, but that governments must be organized for them. This is the cause of struggle in all countries; peoples, after tasting the sweetness of enlightenment and freedom, strive toward them; and government, surrounded by millions of bayonets, make efforts to repel these peoples back into the darkness of ignorance. But all these efforts will prove in vain; impressions once received can never be erased. Liberty, that torch of intellect and warmth of life, was always and everywhere the attribute of peoples emerged from primitive ignorance. We are unable to live like our ancestors, like barbarians or slaves.

But even our ancestors, though less educated, enjoyed civil liberty. During the time of Tsar Aleksei Mikhailovich the National Assembly, including representatives of various classes of the people, still functioned and participated in important affairs of the State. In his reign five such Assemblies were summoned. Peter I, who killed everything national in the State, also stamped out our feeble liberty. This liberty disappeared outwardly but lived within the hearts of true citizens; its advancement was slow in our country. Wise Catherine II expanded it a little; Her Majesty inquired from the Petersburg Free Economic Society concerning the value and consequences of the emancipation of peasants in Russia. This great beneficial thought lived in the heart of the Empress, whom the people loved. Who among Russians of her day and time could have read her INSTRUCTION without emotion? The INSTRUCTION alone redeems all the shortcoming of that time, characteristic of that century.

Emperor Alexander promised us much; he, it could be said, enormously stirred the minds of the people toward the sacred rights of humanity. Later he changed his principles and intentions. The people became frightened, but the seed had sprouted and the roots grew deep. So rich with various revolutions are the latter half of the past century and the events of our own time that we have no need to refer to distant ones. We are witnesses of great events. The discovery of the New World and the United States, by virtue of its form of government, have forced Europe into rivalry with her. The United States will shine as an example even to distant generations. The name of Washington, the friend and benefactor of the people, will pass from generation to generation; the memory of his devotion to the welfare of the Fatherland will stir the hearts of citizens. In France the revolution which began so auspiciously turned, alas, at the end from a lawful into a criminal one. However, not the people but court intrigues and politics were responsible for that. The revolution in France shook all the thrones of Europe and had a greater influence upon the governments and peoples than the establishment of the United States.

The dominance of Napoleon and the war of 1813 and 1814 united all the European nations, summoned by their monarchs and fired by the call to freedom and citizenship. By what means were countless sums collected among citizens? What guided the armies? They preached freedom to us in Manifestoes, Appeals, and in Orders! We were lured and, kindly by nature, we believed, sparing neither blood nor property. Napoleon was overthrown! The Bourbons were called back to the throne of France and, submitting to circumstances, gave that brave, magnanimous nation a constitution, pledging themselves to forget the past. The Monarchs united into a Holy Alliance; congresses sprang into existence, informing the nations that they were assembled to reconcile all classes and introduce political freedom. But the aim of these congresses was soon revealed; the nations learned how greatly they had been deceived. The Monarchs thought only of how to retain their unlimited power, to support their shattered thrones, and to extinguish the last spark of freedom and enlightenment.

Offended nations began to demand what belonged to them and had been promised to them—chains and prisons became their lot! Crowns transgressed their pledges, the constitution of France was violated at its very base. Manuel, the representative of the people, was dragged from the Chamber of Deputies by gendarmes! Freedom of the press was restricted, the army of France, against its own will, was sent to destroy the lawful liberty of Spain. Forgetting the oath given by Louis XVIII, Charles X compensates *émigrés* and for that purpose burdens the people with new taxes. The government interferes with the election of deputies, and in the last elections, among the deputies only thirty-three persons were not in the service and payment of the King, the rest being sold to the Ministers. The firm, courageous Spanish people at the cost of blood rose for the liberty

of their country, saved the King, the Monarchy, and the honor of
the Fatherland; of their own volition the people themselves received Ferdinand as King. The King took the oath to safeguard the
rights of the people. As early as the year 1812, Alexander I recognized the constitution of Spain.

Then the Alliance itself assisted France by sending her troops,
and thus aided in dishonoring her army in the invasion of Spain.
Ferdinand, arrested in Cadiz, was sentenced to death. He summoned Riego, swore to be once more loyal to the constitution and
to expel the French troops from his territory, and begged Riego to
spare his life. Honest men are apt to be trustful. Riego gave guaranty to the Cortes for the King, and he was freed. And what was
the first step of Ferdinand? By his order Riego was seized, arrested,
poisoned and, half-alive, that saint-martyr hero who renounced the
throne offered to him, friend of the people, savior of the King's
life, by the King's order is now taken through the streets of Madrid
in the shameful wagon pulled by a donkey, and is hanged like a
criminal. What an act! Whose heart would not shudder at it?
Instead of the promised liberty the nations of Europe found themselves oppressed and their educational facilities curtailed. The
prisons of Piedmont, Sardinia, Naples, and, in general, of the whole
of Italy and Germany were filled with chained citizens. The lot of
the people became so oppressive that they began to regret the past
and to bless the memory of Napoleon the conqueror! These are the
incidents which enlightened their minds and made them realize
that it was impossible to make agreements with Sovereigns. . . .

The story told to Your Excellency that, in the uprising of December 14 the rebels were shouting "Long live the Constitution!"
and that the people were asking, "What is Constitution, the wife
of His Highness the Grand Duke?" is not true. It is an amusing
invention. We knew too well the meaning of a constitution and we
had a word that would equally stir the hearts of all classes—
LIBERTY!

The events of December are calamitous for us and, of course,
must be distressing to the Emperor. Yet the events of this date
should be fortunate for His Imperial Highness. After all, it was
necessary sometime for the Society to begin its activities, but
hardly could it have been so precipitate as in this instance. I swear
to God, I wish the kind Sovereign prosperity! May God aid him
in healing the wounds of our Fatherland and to become a friend
and benefactor of the people. . . .

Most obedient and devoted servant of Your Excellency,
1826   PETER KAKHOVSKY
February, 24th day

14. Adam Mickiewicz, "The Books of the Polish Nation," 1832

Adam Mickiewicz (1798–1855) was born into the lesser Polish gentry of the Lithuanian and Russian border region, which had recently been annexed into the Russian Empire by the Third Partition of Poland (1795). At the University of Vilna (also in Russian Lithuania) he studied history and literature, and together with other students formed a secret society for self-improvement and the cause of Polish patriotism. In 1823 he was arrested and sent to St. Petersburg and from there to Moscow, where he entered the personal service of the governor general of the city. There he wrote romantic poetry in Polish and was lionized by cultivated Moscow society. His poetry of the twenties was not markedly political, but after the Polish Revolution of 1830 to 1831 Mickiewicz, now in Paris, turned to patriotic themes. His poem, "The Books of the Polish Nation," was written and published in Paris; Mickiewicz never saw Warsaw. [Adam Mickiewicz, *Konrad Wallenrod and Other Writings*, tran. Jewel Parish and others (Berkeley, Calif., 1925), pp. 133–143. By permission of the University of California Press.]

The Books of the Polish Nation
From the Beginning of the World to the
Martyrdom of the Polish Nation

IN THE beginning there was belief in one God, and there was freedom in the world. And there were no laws, only the will of God, and there were no lords and slaves, only patriarchs and their children.

But later the people denied the one God, and made for themselves idols, and bowed themselves down to them, and slew in their honor bloody offerings, and waged war for the honor of their idols.

Therefore God sent upon the idolaters the greatest punishment, which is slavery.

And one half of the people became the slaves of the other half, although all had sprung from one Father. For they had denied that origin and had devised for themselves various Fathers; one said that he sprang from the earth, and another from the sea, and others from other things.

And when, thus warring, some were taking others into slavery, they all fell together into the slavery of the Roman Emperor.

The Roman Emperor called himself God, and proclaimed that there was no other law in the world except his will; what he approved, that was to be called virtue, and what he condemned, that was to be called sin.

And philosophers were found who strove to prove that the Emperor in so doing did well.

And the Roman Emperor had nothing under him nor over him that he must respect.

And all the earth became slaves, and there was never such slavery in the world, either before, or after; save in Russia in our days.

For even among the Turks the Sultan must respect the law of Mohamet, nor can he interpret it himself, but for that there are Turkish priests.

But in Russia, the Emperor is the head of the faith, and in what he commandeth men to believe, in that they must believe.

And it came to pass that when slavery had grown strong in the world, there came on a turning point for it; even as the solstice, the turning point of night, in the longest and darkest night, such was the turning point of slavery in the time of the Roman bondage.

At that time there came to earth Jesus Christ, the Son of God, teaching men that all are born brothers, children of one God.

And that he is the greatest among men, who serveth them and who sacrificeth himself for their good. And whosoever is better in any way, so much the more ought he to sacrifice. But Christ, being best of all, was to sacrifice his blood for them through the bitterest suffering.

So Christ taught that naught is to be held in respect on earth, neither human wisdom, nor office, nor riches, nor a crown; but that sacrificing oneself for the good of men is alone to be held in respect.

And whosoever sacrificeth himself for others shall find wisdom and riches and a crown on earth, in heaven, and everywhere.

But whosoever sacrificeth others for himself, that he may have wisdom, and office, and riches, shall find folly and wretchedness and damnation on earth, in hell, and everywhere.

And finally Christ said: "Whosoever will follow after me shall be saved, for I am Truth and Justice." And when Christ taught in this manner, the judges, who judged in the name of the Roman Emperor, were terrified; and they said: "We drove out justice from the earth, and behold it returneth: let us slay it and bury it in the earth."

Then they martyred the holiest and most innocent of men, and laid him in the tomb, and they cried out: "Justice and truth are in the world no longer; who now will rise against the Roman Emperor?"

But they cried out foolishly, for they knew not that having committed the greatest sin, they had already filled up the measure of their iniquities; and their power came to an end in the time when they exulted most.

For Christ arose from the dead, and, having driven out the Emperors, set up his cross in their capital city; and at that time the lords freed their slaves and acknowledged them as brothers, and the kings, anointed in the name of God, acknowledged that the law of God was over them, and justice returned to the earth.

And all the nations that believed, whether they were Germans, or Italians, or French, or Poles, looked upon themselves as one nation, and this nation was called Christendom.

And the kings of the different nations looked upon themselves as brothers, and marched under the one sign of the cross.

And he who was a man of knightly rank rode out to war against the heathen in Asia, that he might protect the Christians in Asia and win back the sepulcher of the Savior.

And they called this war in Asia the war of the cross.

And although the Christians did not make war either for glory or for the conquest of lands or for riches, but for the deliverance of the Holy Land, yet God rewarded them for this war with glory and lands and riches and wisdom. And Europe became enlightened and set in order and enriched. And God rewarded her for that she had made a sacrifice of herself for the good of others.

And freedom spread abroad in Europe slowly but steadily and in order; from the kings freedom passed to the great lords, and, these being free, they bestowed freedom upon the nobility, and from the nobility freedom passed to the cities, and soon it would have come down to the people, and all Christendom would have been free, and all Christians, like brothers, equal with one another.

But the kings corrupted all.

For the kings became evil and Satan entered into them and they said in their hearts: "Let us take heed: lo, the people are attaining understanding and plenty, and they live uprightly, so that we cannot punish them, and the sword rusteth in our hands; but the people are attaining freedom and our power weakeneth, and as soon as they mature and become wholly free, our power will be at an end."

But the kings in so thinking thought foolishly, for if kings are the fathers of the nations, then the nations, like children, on coming of age go out from under the rod and guardianship.

And yet if the fathers are good, children grown up and wholly free deny not their fathers; nay, when their fathers' hair hath become gray they honor and love them the more.

But the kings desired to be like savage fathers dwelling in the forests, who yoke their children to carts like beasts and sell them to merchants for slaves. So the kings said: "Let us strive that the people may always be foolish, and thus not know their powers; and that they may quarrel among themselves and thus not unite with one another against us."

Then they called to the men of knightly rank: "Why do ye go to the Holy Land? It is far; fight rather one with another." And the philosophers at once strove to show that it was folly to fight for the faith.

Then the kings, renouncing Christ, made ready new gods that were idols, and set them up in the sight of the people, and bade them bow down to them and fight for them.

And so the kings made an idol for the French and called it *honor;* and this was the same idol that in pagan times was called the golden calf.

Then their king made an idol for the Spaniards, which he called *political preponderance,* or *political influence,* or power and authority, and this was the same idol that the Assyrians had worshiped under the name of Baal, and the Philistines under the name of Dagon, and the Romans under the name of Jupiter.

And then their king made an idol for the English that he called *sea power and commerce,* and this was the same idol that of old was called Mammon.

And then an idol was made for the Germans that was called *Brotsinn* or *welfare,* and this was the same idol that of old had been called Moloch and Comus.

And the peoples bowed down to their idols.

And the king said to the French: "Arise and fight for *honor*." So they arose and fought five hundred years.

And the English king said: "Arise and fight for Mammon."

So they arose and fought full five hundred years. And the other nations fought also, each for its own idol.

And the nations forgot that they had sprung from one Father. And the Englishman said: "My father is *ship* and my mother is *steam*." And the Frenchman said: "My father is *continent* and my mother is *bourse*." And the German said: "My father is *workshop* and my mother is *pothouse*."

And those same people who said that it was folly to fight for the faith against the pagans, those same people fought for a scrap of paper called a treaty, fought over a seaport, over a city; like serfs who fight with clubs over the boundary of an estate which they do not possess but which their lords possess.

And those same people who said that it was folly to go to distant lands in the defense of their fellow men, those same people sailed over the sea at the bidding of their kings, and fought over a factory, over a bale of cotton, and over a sack of pepper. And the kings sold them for money into lands across the sea.

And the people became corrupt, so that from among the Germans, and the Italians, and the French, and the Spaniards, only one Christian man was to be found, a wise man and a knight. He was by birth a Genoese.

He exhorted them that they should cease fighting at home, but should rather win back the sepulcher of the Lord and Asia, which had become a desert plain, but which might be a populous and fair country in Christian hands. But all laughed at that man of Genoa and said: "He dreams, and is foolish."

Therefore that godly man departed himself for the war; but in that he was alone, and poor, he therefore wished first to discover lands where gold is produced; and after having gathered riches from there, to hire an army, and reconquer the Holy Land. But all when they heard him cried out: "He is mad."

Yet God saw his good intent, and blessed him; and that man discovered America, which became the land of freedom, a holy land. That man was called Christopher Columbus, and he was the last knight of the cross in Europe, and the last who undertook an enterprise in the name of God, and not for himself.

But in Europe meanwhile idolatry had increased. And just as

the pagans worshiped at first different virtues in the form of idols, and then different vices, and then men and beasts, and then trees, stones, and different figures that they drew, so also it happened in Europe.

For the Italians devised for themselves an idol goddess, whom they called *Political Balance of Power.* And this idol the pagans of old had not known, but the Italians were the first to establish its worship among themselves, and fighting over it they became weak and foolish and fell into the hands of tyrants.

Then the kings of Europe, seeing that the worship of this goddess *Balance of Power* had exhausted the Italian nation, introduced her quickly into their kingdoms, and spread abroad her worship and bade men fight for her.

And the Prussian king drew a *circle* and said: "Lo, here is a new God." And they bowed down to this *circle* and called this worship *political rounding.*

And nations created in the image of God they bade men regard as stones and clods, and to clip them off, so that one might weigh the same as another. And the state, the fatherland, the people, they commanded men to regard as a piece of money that men clip for the sake of roundness.

And philosophers were found who praised everything that the kings had devised.

And of these false wise men, the priests of *Baal,* and of *Moloch,* and of *Balance of Power,* two were the most famous.

The first was called *Machiavelli,* which signifieth in Greek a man *desirous of war,* in that his doctrine led to continual wars, such as were among the pagan Greeks.

And the other liveth to this day, and he is called *Ancillon,* which signifieth in Latin *son of the slave woman,* in that his doctrine leadeth to slavery, such as was among the Latins.

Finally in idolatrous Europe there rose three rulers; the name of the first was *Frederick the Second* of Prussia, the name of the second was *Catherine the Second* of Russia, the name of the third was *Maria Theresa* of Austria.

And this was a Satanic trinity, contrary to the Divine Trinity, and was in the manner of a mock and a derision of all that is holy.

Frederick, whose name signifieth *friend of peace,* contrived wars and pillage throughout his whole life, and was like Satan eternally panting for war, who in derision should be called Christ, the God of peace.

And this Frederick in mockery of the ancient knightly orders, established a godless order, to which in derision he gave the watchword *suum cuique*, or render to each man what is his; and the badge of this order his servants wore, who seized upon and pillaged that which belonged to others.

And this Frederick in mockery of wisdom wrote a book which he called *Anti-Machiavelli*, or the adversary of Machiavelli, but he himself acted according to the teaching of Machiavelli.

Now *Catherine* signifieth in Greek pure, but she was the lewdest of women, and it was as though the shameless Venus had called herself a pure virgin.

And this Catherine assembled a council for the establishing of laws, that she might turn lawmaking into a mockery, for the rights of her neighbors she overthrew and destroyed.

And this Catherine proclaimed that she protected freedom of conscience or tolerance, that she might make a mock of freedom of conscience, for she forced millions of her neighbors to change their faith. And *Maria Theresa* bore the name of the most meek and immaculate Mother of the Savior, that she might make a mock of humility and holiness.

For she was a proud she-devil, and carried on war to make subject the lands of others.

And she was godless, for while praying and confessing her sins she took into slavery millions of her neighbors.

Now she had a son Joseph, who bore the name of a patriarch, the patriarch who did not permit himself to be seduced by the wife of Potiphar, and who freed from slavery his brothers who had sold him into slavery.

And this Joseph of Austria incited his own mother to evil, and his brothers, the Poles, who had defended his empire from Turkish slavery, he took into slavery.

The names of these three rulers, *Frederick, Catherine*, and *Maria Theresa*, were thus three blasphemies, and their lives three crimes, and their memory three maledictions.

Then this trinity, seeing that not yet were the people sufficiently foolish and corrupt, fashioned a new idol, the most abominable of all, and they called this idol *Interest*, and this idol was not known among the pagans of old.

And the nations became corrupt, so that among them was found only one man who was a patriot and a soldier.

He persuaded them that they should cease warring for *Interest*, but rather that they should protect the freedom of their neighbors; and he himself went away to war, to the land of freedom, to America. The name of this man is Lafayette. And he is the last man of the men of old in Europe in whom there still dwelleth the spirit of self-sacrifice, the remnant of the Christian spirit.

Meanwhile all nations were bowing down to *Interest*. And the kings said: "If we spread abroad the worship of this idol, then as nation fighteth with nation, so afterwards city will fight with city, and then man with man.

"And people will again become savage, and we shall again have such power as the savage kings had of old, idolaters, and such as the Moorish kings and the cannibal kings now have, that they may eat their subjects."

But the Polish nation alone did not bow down to the new idol, and did not have in its language the expression for christening it in Polish, neither for christening its worshipers, whom it calls by the French word *egoists*.

The Polish nation worshiped God, knowing that he who honoreth God giveth honor to everything that is good.

The Polish nation then from the beginning to the end was true to the God of its ancestors.

Its kings and men of knightly rank never assaulted any believing nation, but defended Christendom from the pagans and barbarians who brought slavery.

And the Polish kings went to the defense of Christians in distant lands, King Wladislaw to Varna, and King Jan to Vienna, to the defense of the east and the west.

And never did their kings and men of knightly rank seize neighboring lands by force, but they received the nations into brotherhood, uniting them with themselves by the gracious gift of faith and freedom.

And God rewarded them, for a great nation, Lithuania, united itself with Poland, as husband with wife, two souls in one body. And there was never before this such a union of nations. But hereafter there shall be.

For that union and marriage of Lithuania and Poland is the symbol of the future union of all Christian peoples in the name of faith and freedom.

And God gave unto the Polish kings and knights freedom, that all might be called brothers, both the richest and the poorest. And such freedom never was before. But hereafter there shall be.

The king and the men of knightly rank received into their brotherhood still more people; they received whole armies and whole tribes. And the number of brothers became as great as a nation, and in no nation were there so many people free and calling each other brothers as in Poland.

And finally, on the Third of May, the king and the knightly body determined to make all Poles brothers, at first the burghers and later the peasants.

And they called the brothers the nobility, because they had become noble, that is had become brothers with the Lachs, who were men free and equal.

And they wished to bring it about that every Christian in Poland should be ennobled and called a Nobleman, for a token that he should have a noble soul and always be ready to die for freedom.

Just as of old they called each man accepting the gospel a Christian, for a token that he was ready to shed his blood for Christ.

Nobility then was to be the baptism of freedom, and every one who was ready to die for freedom was to be baptized of the law and of the sword.

And finally Poland said: "Whosoever will come to me shall be free and equal, for I am FREEDOM."

But the kings when they heard of this were terrified in their hearts and said: "We banished freedom from the earth; but lo, it returneth in the person of a just nation, that doth not bow down to our idols! Come, let us slay this nation." And they plotted treachery among themselves.

And the King of Prussia came and kissed the Polish Nation and greeted it, saying: "My ally," but already he had sold it for thirty cities of Great Poland, even as Judas for thirty pieces of silver.

And the two other rulers fell upon and bound the Polish Nation. And Gaul was judge and said: "Verily I find no fault in this nation, and France my wife, a timid woman, is tormented with evil dreams; nevertheless, take for yourselves and martyr this nation." And he washed his hands.

And the ruler of France said: "We cannot ransom this innocent nation by our blood or by our money, for my blood and my money belong to me, but the blood and money of my nation belong to my nation."

And this ruler uttered the last blasphemy against Christ, for

Christ taught that the blood of the Son of Man belongeth to all our brother men.

And when the ruler had uttered these words, then the crosses fell from the towers of the godless capital, for the sign of Christ could no longer shine upon a people worshiping the idol *Interest*.

And this ruler was called Casimir-Périer, a Slavic first name and a Roman last name. His first name signifieth corrupter or annihilator of peace, and his last name signifieth, from the word *perire* or *périr*, destroyer or son of destruction. And these two names are anti-Christian. And they shall be alike accursed among the Slavic race and among the Roman race.

And this man rent the league of peoples as that Jewish priest rent his clothes upon hearing the voice of Christ.

And they martyred the Polish Nation and laid it in the grave, and the kings cried out: "We have slain and we have buried Freedom."

But they cried out foolishly, for in committing the last sin they filled up the measure of their iniquities, and their power was coming to an end at the time when they exulted most.

For the Polish Nation did not die: its body lieth in the grave, but its spirit hath descended from the earth, that is from public life, to the abyss, that is to the private life of people who suffer slavery in their country and outside of their country, that it may see their sufferings.

But on the third day the soul shall return to the body, and the Nation shall arise and free all the peoples of Europe from slavery.

And already two days have gone by. One day passed with the first capture of Warsaw, and the second day passed with the second capture of Warsaw, and the third day shall begin, but shall not pass.

And as after the resurrection of Christ bloody offerings ceased in all the world, so after the resurrection of the Polish Nation wars shall cease in all Christendom.

15. Giuseppe Mazzini on "Young Italy," 1832

Giuseppe Mazzini (1805–72) was born at Genoa, where his father was a physician and a professor at the university. He first studied medicine, until his horror at the dissection room turned him to law, in which he took his degree in 1826. "For a short time," he writes, "my mind was somewhat tainted by the doctrines of the foreign materialist school; but the study of history, and the intuitions of conscience—the only tests of truth—soon led me back to the spiritualism of our Italian fathers." He joined the underground revolutionary Carbonari movement, and was imprisoned for six months during the abortive Italian revolts of 1830 and 1831, to which he alludes bitterly in the passage below. While in prison, he planned the new revolutionary society "Young Italy," which was to have connections with similar groups in other countries, as a part of "Young Europe." In 1849 he became a member of the republican triumvirate that governed Rome until it was deposed by the French and the papal government was restored. [Giuseppe Mazzini, "Della Giovine Italia," in *Scritti editi ed unediti di Giuseppe Mazzini*, II (Imola, 1907), 100–113. Translation by the editor.]

We stand at the edge of an era, and it is not an era of *transition*, as the men of revolution have preached until now. The era of *transition* is a stage that necessity imposes on the nations so that they may rise from dumb servitude to liberty. Liberty is too holy a thing for the soul of a slave to understand, or for his heart to become its sanctuary, until he has first been reconsecrated to *moral existence* by long trials and long suffering. But we have consummated this era. Forty years of striving, baptism in tears and blood, and the European development that has taken place before our eyes, have borne the fruit of wisdom and courage; and ours is a country which gives unusual swiftness to the talents of her sons, and a quicker beat to their hearts.

We have beheld Europe. Everywhere the cry for new things has arisen, an appeal to new emotions, a summons to new principles, which the century has put in ferment. Everywhere it is one battle, and the contenders are divided under two banners; and now only victory can be the arbiter, for one group strives to call full halt at the very first signs of the regenerative *idea*, and the other strives to advance, and to press principles onward to their legitimate consequences. The first, encouraged by the silence of the masses, blind by nature, inert by nature, exalts repose as the supreme good, without mentioning that death too is repose; the second, relying on reason and on faith in human destiny, declares that movement is a law, a necessity in the life of nations. It is an implacable war, because between the system we call old and the new generation there stands, as token of eternal cleavage, a prodigious revolution on a

European scale, swallowed up in a day by a few cowards and mercenaries, reduced to a change in the names of things and no more—there stands *universal Association* having been forced to fall back a step, victim of such deceptions that a century of slaughter would not suffice to atone for them, if it were not that one hour of liberty has the power to erase the past. The war is implacable because the fate of half of Europe hangs on the outcome, and there can be no peace, for Europe knows well how stubborn a system of inertia is when faced by unalterable will. Europe has read the consequences by the light of the flames of Bristol, and written them in the blood of the people of Lyons[1]— and why should we try, hoping for some compromise, to hide the truth from our brothers, to disown the banner that the century has put in our hands, to deny a universal and obvious fact that is apparent in the smallest events, in the journals, in the books, in the strivings of every people in every place? Unity! We desire it, but unity only among good people, and unity founded on truth. The other kind, which some still call for in their timidity or their folly, without saying how it is to be achieved, is a union of corpses with a living thing; it smothers the light of life in the living, but gives no spark to what is dead.

We have beheld Italy—Italy, the purpose, the soul, the consolation of our thoughts, the country chosen of God and oppressed by men, twice queen of the world and twice fallen through the infamy of foreigners and the guilt of her citizens, yet lovely still though she be dust, unmatched by any other nation whatever fortune has decreed; and Genius returns to seek in this dust the word of eternal life, and the spark that creates the future. We have tried to see her with an objectivity as cool as intense longing and the need to grasp her internal nature will allow—and our hearts beat strong within our breasts, for we have young passions, and pride in the name Italian lifts our souls within—but we enjoined our hearts to silence, and saw her as she was—vast, strong, intelligent, fertile with the elements of rebirth, beautiful in memories such as could create a second universe, peopled with spirits great in sacrifice, and great in victory—but laid to waste, divided, mistrustful, ignorant, wavering irresolute between the threats of tyranny and the treacherous flattery of the many who with their adulation of her antique

---

[1] There had recently been bloodily suppressed riots in Bristol and Lyons. —Ed.

MAZZINI ON "YOUNG ITALY"

grandeur put her to sleep lest she seek new grandeur—and all the forces of her several parts counterbalanced against one another, neutralized by lack of unity and lack of faith—qualities which neither the ten centuries of wretchedness that resulted from pro-vincial jealousies, nor the power of intellect, nor the fervor of imagination, have so far made to prevail among us—and to create them, what is wanted more than anything else is the authority of a principle that is lofty, regenerative, universal, applicable to all the parts of Italian civilization, and that reforms and purifies them all into one design—of a single and potent principle in which are focused all the rays, all the elements of life, a faith in which souls may be made virginal again, and conscience may whisper destiny to the masses—because what we lack today is not the means for action, but accord and ties among the means: not substance, but motion to impel it, not power, but the conviction that we are powerful. We have beheld Italy, dallying in the confines of the *social* world of *individualism*, while yet remaining subject to the influence of the Middle Ages. The idea of *personality*, the sense of individual independence rooted in every man, and repugnance at dissolving the unity within oneself into the vast unity of the na-tional conception, have been predominant, very good principles in themselves, but adverse, when pressed too far, to the common pro-gress. Better not to speak of sad things, yet this individualistic tendency was present even in the passion for liberty, which, though in its better aspect it appeared as hatred against fetters, appeared also as violent reaction and vengeance for minor offenses. Very few loved liberty as love, liberty as the ordained purpose of man, liberty as the single means of social progress. Very few seemed conscious of the high mission every human being has by nature toward humanity. It was awareness of this mission that created giants like Mirabeau, Bonaparte, Robespierre, the men of the Convention— and as long as they followed it, they were great—and because it is hard to distinguish the point at which this mission was effaced by other motives, posterity will acclaim them as great.—But for Italy, as we have seen her, materialism, destroying all dignity of the origin and of the destiny of man, dried up life at the heart; or else in-difference, wasting all thirst for truth, captured many of those souls, more numerous in Italy than anywhere else, who live and die martyrs to an idea. Hence the lack of faith, of faith in self, of faith in the right, and in the future; because man, confined by the

ruling *individualism* within the restricted sphere of his own affairs,
overwhelmed by the vastness of the concept, either resigns himself
to live as a slave, or finds freedom in death on the scaffold.—And
these vices, which long servitude, and Rome, imposed on Italy,
have blocked all endeavors more terribly than the German bayonets.

And we looked at the past, to see whether we could find the
remedy there. Now the past has taught us not to despair, the past
has taught us how many things and which things are only artifices
of tyranny and relics of servitude of the spirit—no more than that.
The learning of our forefathers was exercised more in the realm
of principles than of application. Perhaps the flame of fatherland
and liberty with which they burned showed them how vast the
arena was. But circumstances stifled the conception, and their
efforts took on neither the energy, nor the magnitude, nor the
harmony that such work requires. Harmony of principles and
actions was necessary—and the movements that broke out were
partial instead, and provincial. But without a universal movement,
triumph will always prove impossible; without the universality of
prior accord, the movement will not break out simultaneously,
nor ever be truly Italian—and for the envies and the animosities
that still exist among the provinces to be erased once and for all,
all must be fraternalized in the brotherhood of movement, of
danger, of victory. They should have propagated the reforming
spirit, the need for renewal, over all the branches of Italian civilization—and they limited reform to one single branch of the human
intellect, and rejected progress in the others—and the men who
preached political liberty and freedom from the old habits of submission proclaimed a crusade for the hopeful notions of emancipation found in the old philosophical and literary theories; they stole
from the English the balance of power and the principles of constitutional monarchy, while they vilified as slaves of the north and
traitors to the fatherland anybody who tried to point in his studies
and in his writings to that liberty which was not lost in the north—
nor did they pay any mind to the need to prepare for intellectual
independence the men they wanted to bring to the concept of
political independence; for man is *one*, and the intellect cannot be
trained in two contradictory systems at the same time. The great
regeneration they had in mind needed to feed upon sublime sacrifice, strong examples, and total repudiation of the individual for

the sake of a principle. They should have elevated man to the level of a generality, raised him to a concept so lofty that it could encompass the whole of human nature. They should have written down lists of his rights and duties, given him an awareness of his noble origins, set up for him a *social* mission, and revealed it to him in the blue of the starry heavens, in the grand harmony of creation, in the physical universe reduced to the image of a powerful thought, in the ruins of the past, in the generative ideas of the religions, in the prophecies of the poets, in the ray of light where Genius touches the earth, in the restless emotions of the heart, which above all things knows it was born free, mighty in faculties, in energy, king of the world and of matter, never subject to any laws but the eternal ones of progressive and universal reason. They should have purified his passions and inspired them with love, infused him with enthusiasm, which wings the spirit toward the beautiful, and raised before his path virginal hope, with its smile sustained in the face of martyrdom—but they held him back in materialism, a frigid credo, disheartening and individualist, refuge of every man against the bullying of superstition and sacerdotal tyranny, but within which he cannot remain except the flower of his spirit be withered. They held him in the fetters of an endless struggle, teaching him to look upon himself as dominated, blindly and inexorably, by the facts, whereas the need was to convince him that there was within him a force independent of the facts, master of the facts, ruler of that very destiny. They put him in a realm of alternate *action* and *reaction,* while what was needed was to implant in his breast an awareness of invincible *progress,* and of triumph. They mocked the old beliefs, but made no effort to substitute new ones. They extinguished enthusiasm, and tried to arouse it with words. They spoke to the multitudes of the homeland, and yet destroyed faith, homeland of the spirit, faith in a law higher than mere betterment, faith in a concept of everlasting movement that embraces and advances the whole spectrum of human phenomena, the faith that created the power of Rome, the vast dominion of Islam, the eighteen centuries of Christianity, the Convention, Sand, and Greece renewed, the faith that gave back lost dignity to the slave, and cried to him: *Act! act! God wills it! God, who created thee in His image, and breathed into thee a spark of His omnipotence!* This is what the first reformers of a nation sunk into the depths ought to have tried, if those first had been able to do more than dimly glimpse renewal and die for it. Then, coming down to practice, it was necessary to have the people, to arouse the masses; and for that, the people had to be convinced that these efforts were undertaken for them, for their betterment, for their material prosperity, because the uneducated population does not act for the sake of bare words, but for something real; and to convince them of these purposes, it was necessary to bring them into the movement, talk to them, cast into the arena that ancient and feared word Republic, the only one perhaps that speaks to the people as a promise of good will, an idea with practical *utility*. And these men trembled before the people, they despaired of their ability to guide it, stirred up as it was. And they worked to smother its roar, or to attract it they produced abstruse theories of the balance of forces, and metaphysical notions of ordained destiny, so that the outcome would be eternal calm for the state, and constitutions borrowed from other countries, now proven to be incapable of enduring, out of harmony with traditions, habits, emotions. Revolutions are prepared with education, they are matured with care, they are carried out with energy, and they are hallowed by their dedication to the common good. But these most recent revolutions broke out unexpected, unprepared, artificially connected; they aimed at the triumph of one class over another, of a new aristocracy over an old—and no thought was given to the people. Then, they proceeded on the basis of artificial principles, putting the interpretation of them in the hands of astute authorities, frightened of everything, despairing of any help from diplomacy, or from foreigners—the first essentially a dishonest art, the other essentially suspect, useful sometimes for the strong, but never for the weak. We saw men revile kings, setting up laws and agreements that openly showed distrust of them and that limited their power—and at the same time these men put unlimited trust in their promises, as though tyrants had a God in whose name they could swear. We saw the aristocracy attacked in constitutions, and nevertheless called to the summit of affairs, as though this caste could ever commit suicide. We read on the banners the name of Italy, while we saw disowned brothers who had risen nearby in the same cause, in the same hour, in a common effort. We heard the cry of territorial independence, while the barbarian guarded the doors; and meanwhile the policy of the new governors was dominated by the hope of avoiding that war which nature has made eternal between master and slave, which breaks his chains—and youth was curbed when it sought to move into a larger arena—they decreed togas instead of arms. These were errors born of the fault of cowardice on the part of the very ones vilely deceived and betrayed, errors sprung more perhaps from the positions and the infamy of the European cabinets than from those of the men at the head of our affairs, but such that for shrewd politicians of wide experience to persist in them now must be the part of incompetence or of treason.

And then—we looked around ourselves, and then—we launched ourselves into the future. The spirit wearied by long delusions took new heart in the awareness of an eternal mission; it rekindled in the sentiment of patriotic fervor, of the passion for liberty, which is life for us. The errors of the fathers had come from the will of their age; but why should we persist in the errors of the fathers? The years mature new destinies; and we, contemplating the movement of the age, glimpse a new generation, fervent in hope—and hope is fruit in the bud—inspired to new things by the *spiritual* breath of the era, stirred by a pervasive need for strong shocks and sensations. And as a means to create this generation, amid the confusion of the systems, amid the anarchy of principle, from the individualism of the Middle Ages, from the mire in which Italian life is held fast, we saw emerging here and there men who lived and died for an idea. We saw arising souls who, like Prometheus, protest against the fate that oppresses them and confront it alone; we saw, appearing, visions that bore prophecies of the future on their brows, beings of a higher nature, which nature always casts upon the earth at the end of one epoch to connect it with a new. And all the whole generation needs to achieve greatness, together with these privileged few, is a concentration of beliefs and tendencies, a unity of direction, a *parole* that is fertile, energetic, uncontaminated by hate or fear, that will reveal the will of the century, clear and powerful.—

This *parole* we shall speak.

• This will we shall try to interpret. All the tendencies that seem visible in the age, and which we have identified in the course of this article, we shall develop in our journals with all the ardor of people who expect nothing and fear nothing from political parties, and who seek nothing on earth but a goal and a way to attain it. And from these tendencies which now exist in embryo, from all the inevitability clearly apparent in past events, and from all the inspirations of the age will come, let us hope, a system that will gather within itself the coming generation. It is simply a system, let us say it again, that we have tried to identify with the name *Young Italy;* but we chose this term because the one term seems to marshal before the youth of Italy the magnitude of its duties and the solemnity of the mission that circumstances have entrusted to it, so that it will be ready when the hour has struck to arise from its slumber to a new life of action and regeneration. And we chose it because we wanted to show ourselves, writing it, as what we are, to do battle with raised visors, to bear our faith before us, as the knights of medieval times bore their faith on their shields. For while we pity men who do not know the truth, we despise men who, though they know the truth, do not dare to speak it.

Undefiled by connections or by private grudges, hearts burning with generous wrath but open to love, with no other desire than to die for the progress of humanity and for the liberty of the fatherland, we need not be suspected of personal ambition or of envy. Envy is not one of youth's passions. Who among us cares for individuals? Who makes war on names? The age of names is finished. We are in the age of principles; only them do we defend or attack, only on this battlefield are we inexorable. There is the pivot of the future; there stand our dearest hopes. The generations pass; names and the battles that surround them are drowned in the popular torrent, in its flood. We draw a veil over the things that have happened—who can make them not exist? But the future is ours; the theories of the past we refute by the age that presses upon us. We raise our banner between the old world and the new. Let him who will, rally to this banner; let him who will not, live on memories, but let him not seek to resurrect from them another banner, fallen, ragged.

If, among the men whose birth in an era earlier than ours makes them think that we or our principles might exclude them from the movement, there be any who have gray hairs on their heads but enthusiasm in their hearts, men who moving with the times are awake to the progressive unfolding of the revolutionary elements, and who in accordance with this development modify the scope of their activities, oh let them come to us! Let them view dispassionately our theories, our actions, our achievements— and come to us! Come, and bare before us the honorable wounds won in the fields of the fatherland's battles. We shall kiss those holy wounds, we shall venerate those white hairs, we shall accept their counsel, and, rallying around them, we shall display them to our enemies with pride, proclaiming: "We have the voice of the past and that of the future for our cause!"

Peace then! To peace our souls are devoted. In the name of the fatherland—in the name of all that is most sacred—we cry peace! Let the charge of sowing discord fall upon the heads of those men who proclaim themselves free, but allow no progress in human affairs, who talk of concord and then smother ideas frankly offered under malign interpretations and suspicions, who preach unity and spatter venom on efforts to achieve it. With these, there can be no accord.

Youth, my brothers—take comfort and be great! Faith in God, in the right, and in ourselves!—that was the cry of Luther, and it moved half Europe. Raise this cry—and forward! Events will show whether we are mistaken when we say the future is ours.

16. Edgar Quinet, Introduction to the epic poem "Napoléon," 1836

Edgar Quinet (1803–75) was the son of a Protestant mother and a soldier of the Army of the Rhine. He spent much of his literary career fighting down the suspicion that the defeat at Waterloo had marked a historic decline in the greatness an dthe world mission of France. When the Revolution of 1830 produced only the dull and cautious July Monarchy of Louis Philippe, he turned to seek reasons for the decline, and means for regenerating French greatness in the new century. He wrote poetry, essays, and history, adn taught literature at Lyons and at the Collège de France in Paris. Like many other French poets of his time (see Pommier, "Progress" below, pp. 299–305), he tried to create a kind of poetry that would reflect and express the modern age in subject matter, in theme, and in its aesthetic principles. And like many other young Frenchmen, he found in Napoleon Bonaparte a symbol not only of France's past greatness but also of her hope for future greatness, and of enmit ytoward Metternich's Europe. [Edgar Quinet, *Napoléon* (Paris, 1836), pp. i–xx. Translation by the editor.]

READERS WHO remember a work published under the title *Ahasvérus*[1] will recognize, despite the difference in subject matter, that the poem these lines serve to introduce is, in a way, complementary

---

[1] Quinet's prose poem *Ahasvérus*, on the Wandering Jew theme, appeared in 1833; it attracted considerable attention, but was generally not well received.—Ed.

to the first, and that they converge in the same whole. *Ahasvérus*, in the thinking of him who wrote it, represented by its subject the poetry of the past, of general history, of that eternal man in whom all men are embodied, and who is called humanity. The poem that now follows it belongs to the poetry of the present; it has as its subject the individual *man*, the hero, Napoleon. To these two fragments there will later be added a third part, which will complete the meaning of the preceding. Until that is accomplished, the humble monument that the author would like to have raised will be exposed to many attacks, of which perhaps some, especially the accusation of irreligious tendencies, might have been repulsed if the connections holding the several fragments together had been made clear from the beginning.

For if it be asked, first, by what right an author with no special warrant has dared touch the subject I here enter upon, I shall answer that the grandest subjects are not always the most difficult to treat, that the duty of the poet is not to invent poetry but to express it, that the most vast subjects, God, Nature, the hero, are the customary themes of the songs of the humblest and commonest poets. If it is one of the subjects sacred to the memory of peoples, they will never rebuff those spirits which cultivate them with honest devotion. Finally, I shall add that, having spent the earliest and best years of my life in the arms of soldiers and in the camps of the Empire, I have not been completely free to choose my memories. It has often occurred to me, as it has occurred to other men of my times, too, to think that it would have been good to die in those holy battles of 1814 and 1815, when what was at stake moved all together, not just each alone, but like them I was too young for that; and as many subsequent events have confirmed rather than effaced this regret, I have tried at least to preserve in myself and in a few others the remembrance of so many glorious dead. And if I have failed here in my undertaking, I hope I can be accused by neither victors nor vanquished of having thoughtlessly profaned their memory.

A more specious ground for rejecting this work without examining it would be the idea almost universally held that the French mind is incompatible with the epic, and that our language lacks the heroic genius. To assign that opinion its proper weight, it may be helpful to notice at what time it was formed. Everyone knows today that the France of the North and of the South produced in the Middle Ages more epical monuments than any other country in Europe; the day is not distant when publication of the manuscripts of the twelfth and thirteenth centuries will leave no doubt of it whatever. The writers of the century of Louis XIV, pressed in other directions, neglected the question of the epic almost completely. The question did not seem settled in France until after the experience of Voltaire. It was not then recognized that the criticisms aimed at the *Henriade*[2] were an indictment of the age in which it was written, far more than of the genius of the French language itself. The eighteenth century, ready to dissolve all tradition, was the reverse of the epical epochs; it was in no way possible for the wars of the regency to arouse the quenched heroism anywhere. By an effort of entirely individual genius, Voltaire rose to brilliant imitations of Alexandrine and Roman poetry. But one man tries in vain; in this kind of poetry, if the thought and will of all do not do half the work, then the work is impossible.

Since the *Henriade*, a revolution has taken place. The whole past overturned, colossal wars, the world in flames, a new power establishing a new epoch—not only a world transformed, but history become heroic. Shall all these things have left the highest problem of art in the same situation where it was? Surely not. If history has assumed an epic character, poetry will do the same. In any case it is not overbold to try to follow the path so obviously laid open by events. Would it not be strange if the people said to be the most heroic in action were the only ones lacking the genius for heroic things in their literature?

This genius, if fact, is in a nation nothing other than the feeling it has about itself and about the action it exercises upon the world. And we know of none that has been completely deprived of this. Not every people has had a Homer, but all have had more or less rough fragments like the *Iliad*. If this element is not to be found in French literature, then that seems the most convincing proof that the full development of French literature has not been attained, that on the contrary it still has a whole phase to go through.

However this may be, the preceding ideas are the ones that have sustained the author in his task. I am not unaware that this task is one of the kind that cannot be entirely accomplished by one man alone. Here it is right that many perish so that one may survive, and

[2] Voltaire's *Henriade* (1723) was an effort at an epic in Alexandrine couplets on the career of Henry IV of France.—Ed.

the first who tries to accomplish this work almost inevitably falls victim. How many unknown poets before Dante, Ariosto, Camoens! Yet their work, if it was sincere, was by no means in vain. Even here, if any part of this rough monument merits being preserved, the future will rule over the remains and make its mark upon them. Instead of seeking out subjects so remote from us, why have so many poets in France and outside France not applied themselves to this theme, which is the theme of all the peoples and all the contemporary nationalities? Why do we not find, around this mighty object of the love and the hatred of everybody, a new battle of rhapsodists or minstrels? One would think that the peoples, having fought so well with the sword, would today have no less noble a field of rivalry in this battle of poetry and of national memories.

For my part, finding myself by chance one of the first to be fully engaged in this pursuit, and being without the guidance of any established model, I have had to start over and do afresh my work of the day before many times. In a very wandering life, I have tried to visit most of the battlefields it has been possible for me to see; I have informed myself as best I could about the kinds of passions each people brought to the struggle. My strongest endeavor, in a situation where it would have been so easy to become absorbed in the glory of one individual, has been to be unjust to nobody. This theme is a grand field of the dead, where each must rest in peace within his noble tomb. . . .

[After a technical discussion of the meter and verse forms chosen, Quinet continues:]

Because epic poetry is, properly speaking, the poetry of providence or of divine judgment in history, it is not enough for it to show or portray the things with which it is concerned; it must also unveil their causes and their mysteries. Thence comes its need for the presence of deity, which in the language of the critics is called the need for the *marvelous*. This necessity has been understood in such a way as to cause the belief that modern times are inappropriate to the epic, on the grounds that the marvelous is lacking. Here, clearly, the appearance of things has been confounded with the reality. The epic, no doubt, must be full of God; one cannot take a step into it without feeling the celestial presence there. But where the schoolmen err is in their belief that this real presence must necessarily be manifest, as among the ancients, in the form of a tangible personage, like Mercury or a dragon, or by an idealization, called Fame, Discord, etc. This is falling back into a dead idolatry. It is not the idol but the god that the epic requires. It is not divine presence in the form of a dead personality that I miss in your empty poem. What I ask is that the actions take place amid divine thought, and that this thought be, so to speak, the scene of the events. This is the first and only law of the marvelous; and this, too, is why Bossuet is epic, and why Voltaire put the drama in place of the epic.

A second consequence, which follows from the first, is this. If the events that make up the subject of the epic take place in the midst of divine intelligence, it follows that these events themselves are illuminated by its light; that is, the epic personage must appear very different from the dramatic personage. The same character, conceived under these two points of view, is expressed quite differently, though the circumstances are otherwise quite similar. In the drama, man appears from an exclusively human point of view. He is prey to all the uncertainties of earthly reality, he acts within the narrow limits of time and history, and the more the poet is immersed with him in these obscurities, the more nearly he achieves his aim. With the epic personage it is quite otherwise. He has overleaped history; he belongs to a higher realm. That is what the ancients meant when they called him a demigod. The idea remains, we lack the word. The hero has entered the domain of immutable things. He has one foot on Olympus; he is on the threshold of eternity. Therefore, the duty of the poet is not simply to make him talk as he really talked as a human; nor should he only make him say the things his mouth did not say but his heart thought. He should go on to make him reveal the secret of his life, though he himself did not know it. In a word, the poet should make providence and universal intelligence speak through his character, far more than the voice of a solitary and capricious individual. The epic personage is not just a person; a type, a century, an epoch, are comprehended in him, and must be expressed by him. Some represent a people, others a race, and still others, all humanity at a given time; but whatever they do, they are never alone with themselves, long separated from the Deity, as the hero of the drama is.

Any doubt of this will disappear if one compares the Agamemnon of Homer with the Agamemnon of Aeschylus, or the Cid of the Spanish romances with the Cid of Corneille.

The relation between the epic and history is implicit in the preceding. The epic does not copy history, it does not contradict it; it transforms it. It takes hold of the memories of men, things eternally alive, and prepares a new formation for them. The task of the historian is to be transported into the past, to be identified with it; the task of the poet is to impose, on that which is no more, the face of that which is, to immortalize past, present, and future in a single moment, which is the moment of art. The historian works with a fact that has been, that never again will be, that cannot be other than what it was; the poet works with a tradition that is, that still lives, that develops and grows through his work. More than any other art form, the epic is conjoined organically with civilization, because it is itself the continual transformation of the past into the future, or rather the vision of life itself, at its source and in its development. And so the greatest poets have been the mightiest instruments of change in the ideas, customs, memories, and creeds of their epochs. Homer transformed the old Olympus, Dante transformed Catholicism, and Raphael, most epic of the moderns, transformed everything he touched.

Moreover, as the epic grew out of the ode, it follows that it is more or less mixed with lyric poetry, depending on how far it is from its beginnings. The Oriental epic does not bear the same relation to lyric poetry that the Greek epic does, nor the latter the same as the Latin epic. In the Orient, the hymn absorbs the recital. In Greece, hymn and recital attained almost perfect balance in Homer. Among the Romans, Virgil preserves hardly a trace of the sacred element. Description has taken the place of religion. He is the first epic poet who deprived the words "I sing" of their proper and literal meaning. From that moment, the antique lyre was mute. The poet talked. He ceased to sing.

All that is ephemeral or artificial in the transmutations of mankind disappears in the epic. From among events it can use only those bearing the mark of necessity and celestial will. Those that drift with the caprice of the crowd, and only halfway happen, do not exist for the epic. In the same way not all heroes fulfill the conditions it demands of its own. The dramatic poet welcomes characters that are changing, contradictory. The uncertainty of human passions often serves to form and elaborate his development; but that is where epic poetry is diametrically different from dramatic poetry. Not only must its heroes represent a system of facts and general sentiments, but to enter on the brazen road of the epic, their characters must also be immutable. All irresolution is forbidden them. For these personages the term pillar of stone was invented. Thus one sees why history provides so few figures who can endure, without bending, the hard test of the epic.

It also follows from the foregoing that the poetry called *fictional* often demands reality even more than history does. The poet, you say, gives immortality; what that means is that the poet, among a multitude of objects, some perishable, some made to last, distinguishes automatically between what is passing and what is eternal, though the universe be still plunged deep in uncertainty. . . .

[After a brief history of the epic form, from antiquity to the nineteenth century, Quinet resumes:]

If the epic is one of the essential conditions of the world spectacle, and if it is no other than the events themselves, developing within universal intelligence, it follows that the epic is itself as imperishable as nature and as history; but it has often happened that critics have confused the epic itself with the form of it accepted by the ancients, and they have more than once denied the presence of epic elements moving under their very eyes, when what they have seen has not conformed with the model in their minds. Others have thought that in our times the epic has taken refuge entirely in the novel. It cannot be denied here that, as the principle of individuality has been developed to excess in modern times, that hurried epic of internal and hidden life which is called the novel has had to acquire among the arts an importance unknown to the ancients, but the heroic poem and the novel are two forms of the modern epic that coexist in the same manner as the city and the family. Moreover, it is one of the first laws of the poetics of the novel not to let its heroes be effaced by the heroes of history or of the world. Beyond its characters one doubtless glimpses the empires and peoples that pass in the distance, but neither the peoples who pass, nor the states that crumble or arise, nor the mighty adventures of the human race, can become its immediate theme, and it would perish on the day when, ceasing to be individual, it made itself in a true sense social and heroic. The difference between the novel and the epic is the difference between man and humanity. The two forms are identifiable in antiquity as the *Odyssey* and the *Iliad*. Among the moderns, Boccaccio has not dethroned Dante. Richardson does not exclude Milton. Cervantes does not destroy Camoens.

If further confirmation of what has been said were needed, I should add that even in our own times there are epic forms that the novel will never be able to absorb, no matter what it does. These elements are the songs of the people. It is known that throughout Europe there recur these songs in which each nation, spontaneously, in its common tongue, gathers together the phases of its history and the effects of its history upon it. These verse songs taken together form the true people's epic of modern times; they would be for modern society what the songs of the Cid were for Spanish society of the Middle Ages. Now it is clear that the novel cannot, without ceasing to exist, become a literal echo of these voices, these rhythms; it has other preoccupations. Even if it should turn in this direction, I still ask how the popular form— cadenced, metrical—could be fully reproduced in its prose? And I ask, by what reversal of ideas could it happen here that unwritten literature should be more expert than the literature of books, and that the people should have today a more cultivated form than the poet and the artist?

In our times the epic is no longer the property of one people to the exclusion of another. It does not dwell entirely with one, but is in us all. It is found in that life of hate or love that bears all together toward the unity of the future world. Thus it follows that if the peoples act and appear today in the social poem, the poetical rules for that art cannot be strictly contained in the rules appropriate for any one of them. The formal *art of poetics* that rules the epic cannot exist hereafter for anyone, neither French- man, nor German, nor Englishman, nor Spaniard, nor Italian. Here the artist should rely, no longer on a particular body of rules, but on that very law which derives from the modern world. Milton no more than Boileau can lay out this new *art of poetics*, nor Klopstock more than Ariosto. This law is to be found nowhere but in the total observation of contemporary humanity.

Now, if we envisage the social world in its relations with art and poetry, we find it presents to the artist and to the poet two instruments of quite different natures, among modern peoples.

Some are still situated, where art is concerned, in that primitive simplicity which precedes formed literatures. These are the Slavs in all their branches, the Russians, the Serbs, the Hungarians, the Albanians, the modern Greeks, and then the eastern peoples, Turks, Circassians, Arabs. Among them art is still a song; the epic is found there in its simplest and most elementary form. Other peoples on the contrary, and these are the ones where the social initiative is found, have left the spontaneous form in poetry, and have arrived in the philosophical and scientific epoch. These are France, Germany, England, Italy, Spain. Even there both elements, conscious art and primitive poetry, sometimes meet, as happens in certain mountainous areas of Italy, Spain, Ireland, Scotland, and French Brittany.

The first conclusion to be drawn from this is that the poet who seeks to reproduce contemporary humanity will be obliged to satisfy these two orders of things. Just as the Greek epic brought within itself the differences and the varied geniuses of the Ionians, Dorians, Easterners, Westerners, just so the poet of our times must represent at the same time the spontaneous genius and the conscious genius, the popular element and the philosophic element, in modern humanity. For him the problem of his art is to combine, without destroying, the two forms appropriate to these opposed elements, so as to make from them a third, which will be the basis for the rules of the future.

Art, in France, has so far assumed three main characters, and passed through three eras. It was sacerdotal up to the tenth century, and feudal until the Renaissance. After the Renaissance it was exclusively monarchical. The era it still has to pass through is the era of democracy. Under this form, it shall be more especially, as is the France of our times, social and cosmopolitan.

Each of these periods has had its hero, whom it reconstituted after its manner. In the sacerdotal period, Arthur; feudalism, Charlemagne; monarchy, Louis XIV; democracy, Napoleon.

Napoleon, however one looks upon him, with love or with hatred, satisfies the first requirement for the epic personage, which is to encompass within himself a total generation. His historical character is to represent the development of individuality in modern times. That must be his poetical character as well. As soon as you put him in your poem he rules it; he absorbs all, as if it were his empire. And Alexandrine or feudal poetics cannot in any way be applied to him. He does not have the relations with companions that Achilles has with Ajax, or Charlemagne with the twelve peers. In his epic only three characters are really to be found—himself, the people, the world. Only among these three does dialogue occur; any other hero who intrudes sinks beneath their weight. No doubt other names and other personalities can move and act incidentally in the poem, but none can remain and fix himself at the side of the hero; isolation is his law, even in the kingdom of the imagination. The poetical force of the men who surround him resides in the peoples; make them separate, and they are destroyed.

In a word, the action in the modern poem is not shared, as with the ancients, among several personalities acting on the same plane, but rather between one personality on the one side and all the world on the other. Here is one of the first laws one encounters, I believe, whenever one considers the matter.

Moreover, it is not poetry's goal merely to depict Napoleon as he appeared to his contemporaries. That would be a retreat into history and an abdication. Between Napoleon and us arises an element that must be taken into account. This element is the time that separates us from him. Napoleon necessarily appears to us in a quite different perspective from that in which he appeared to his contemporaries. We who never saw him cannot place ourselves in the exact position of the generation that preceded us, unless we put archeology in the place of poetry. The forms in which the past appears to men of our own times are the true reality of the poet. Besides, each people has already made its own Napoleon, in its own tradition. The Napoleon of the East is not the Napoleon of the North, nor the one of the North the one of the South; but from these different types must emerge and take form, little by little, the epic Napoleon, who will be no other than the Napoleon of history, seen across the mutations of space and of time.

In the France of the future, the wars of the Revolution and Empire will constitute the heroic age of democracy; and just as Charlemagne, at the dawn of feudalism, became the hero of feudal poetry, so Napoleon in the same way will become the hero of the poetry of the people.

But as democracy moves beyond its heroic age and enters into the exercise of its rights, it has, like all the dominant forces that have preceded it, its art and its artists; but it can no longer *be* those. Peoples have their poets when they themselves are no longer poets.

Thus folk songs, which were discussed above, are lost every day, and are not recovered; and with the passage of time the very memory of them fades. In these circumstances, as in all such situations, the poet naturally becomes the echo of extinguished voices. He instinctively raises to the forms of conscious art and written poetry this traditional and oral poetry; and his mission is to transcribe in his fashion the songs of the last rhapsodists whom civilization is going to destroy.

17. Felicité de Lamennais, from
The People's Own Book, 1837

Felicité de Lamennais (or de La Mennais, 1782–1854) was a French priest, born in St. Malo in Brittany of a shipowning family ennobled by Louis XVI. He began his literary career as an advocate of royalism and the absolute authority of the Catholic Church. During the reign of Charles X (1824–30) he renounced royalism and turned to a belief in democracy held together and sustained by religious faith and love of fellow man; in 1830 he founded the journal *L'Avenir* (*The Future*) with the motto "God and Liberty." In about 1834 he broke with the organized Church and became the popular and eloquent apostle of a libertarian social democracy in which a spontaneous sense of human community and morality would take the place of coercion and materialism, and in which national harmony would replace privilege and power. [Felicité de La Mennais, *The People's Own Book*, trans. Nathaniel Greene (Boston, 1839), Chap. XIII, pp. 129–139.]

THE SOCIAL state, natural to man, establishes relations between families whence arises a new order of duties, duties toward one's country.

Our country is the common mother, the unity in which isolated individuals are merged and blended; it is the sacred name that expresses the voluntary fusion of all interests into one sole interest, of all lives into one perpetually-enduring life.

And this fusion, the prolific source of inexhaustible blessings, the origin of a continual and otherwise impossible progress,—this fusion, the effect of which is indefinitely to increase the conservative force, the power of development, productive energy, security, prosperity,—how is it effected? By the devotion of each to all, the sacrifice of self, in fine by love, which, stifling abject selfishness, accomplishes the perfect union of the members of the social body.

Now, you already know that the true society, founded upon the natural equality, is by its nature and can in fact be but the fraternal organization. Every other political institution, whatever may be its form, contains something that is illegitimate and fatal: illegitimate, because necessarily violating imprescriptible rights; fatal, because in violating them it attacks the very foundations of order, and thus provokes intestine feuds, civil wars, which no power can hinder from breaking out sooner or later.

Your first duty toward your country, then, is to labor with untiring zeal to establish, in its entire integrity, the great and salutary principle of the absolute equality of rights, whence all public and private liberty emanates; to combat privilege incessantly until you shall have completely vanquished it.

To permit attacks upon the sole legitimate sovereignty, that of the people, a suspension of its exercise, a substitution of domination for free association, to bend the knee to a master, is to betray the holy cause of right and of humanity, to deny the name itself of country. The stall where beasts of service eat and sleep, is not a country.

If, under whatever pretext, you permit the establishment of categories among the essentially equal members of the community, the creation of classes invested with certain prerogatives to the exclusion of the rest of the people, you sanction a criminal usurpation of power by virtue of which they will arrogate to themselves the right of establishing similar categories, you basely sacrifice your own right and that of your brethren, you renounce for yourselves and for them the quality of man, you prostrate yourselves, on the ruins of the true society, at the feet of tyranny.

What is the object of the association of originally independent families? A stronger guaranty of equality and of liberty, the better assured reign of justice, the promotion of the common good by an organization of the common labor, by a development of the indefinite power of knowledge and action of which humanity contains the germ.

Now, what is necessary for this? Good laws. Would you then know what the laws are, observe by whom they are made. If they are framed by some few, they will be almost exclusively for the advantage of the few; if by all, they will be made for the good of all, in accordance with eternal principles, with elevated and fruitful sympathies, the sacred interests from which the social institution emanates. Give yourselves therefore no rest until all cooperate in the perfecting of the laws by the choice of those who make the laws.

You will then no longer be excluded from the administration of public affairs, nor delivered, without protection, into the hands of those who now domineer over you; you will no longer be chased from assemblies where your interests are discussed, upon whose decisions your very existence may depend, as a vile animal is driven from the presence of men; you will no longer form a caste politically proscribed; you will then indeed have a country.

And your country, in whose bosom all the different families are united, should have a place in your love above that of either one of those families. Otherwise, you would rend the tie by which they are all united; you would treat the entire body as subordinate to one of its members; you would, so far as your influence extends, destroy society by bringing it again under the influence of selfishness, which would annihilate its foundations.

To your country, then, belongs all that you are, and all that you have, your heart, your arm, your goods, and even your life. He who hesitates to die for her is forever infamous.

At the same time you should remember that you ought to prefer mankind even to your country; for there are the same relations between countries as between families, and they involve the same duties. The human race is essentially one, and perfect order will never exist, the evils that desolate the earth will never entirely disappear, until nations, overthrowing the fatal barriers that separate them, form but one great and sole society.

Exclusive patriotism, that which is but the selfishness of nations, has not less fatal consequences than individual selfishness: it isolates, it divides the inhabitants of different countries, and prompts them to mutual injury instead of mutual aid; it is the father of that bloody and horrible monster called WAR.

What more opposed to nature and her laws than the name of stranger? Do we not all call ourselves brothers? And how can brothers be strangers?

Justice and charity are due from the people of one country to those of another. The rights of each people should be respected, and assistance afforded when necessary either for defence against attacks or for re-conquering that of which they have been despoiled. The people that suffers its neighbors to be oppressed by another people, digs the grave of its own liberty.

Employ then all your efforts for the reconciliation of differences between nations, for strengthening the bonds of union, and for the destruction of those prejudices which tend to prolong their separation. Each one of them, according to its genius, situation, climate, has its particular function assigned to it by Providence for the progressive improvement of humanity. Far from creating obstacles, all ought to second it, laboring as it does for all in laboring for itself. No one of them suffices for itself; they subsist and develop themselves by the assistance they mutually lend each other. It is not true, as repeated by those who deceive to enslave them, that they have opposing interests: they have not, unless it be accidentally, and by consequence of some disturbance of their natural relations. Re-establish those relations; the welfare of the one is the welfare of the other, as, in a well-ordered family, the welfare of one of its members is the welfare of all, his prosperity their prosperity.

When rain falls in the region where the Nile has its source, the river swells and overflows, gradually covering the valley it enriches. That its fertilizing waters may reach the more distant lands, must they not first bathe those immediately on its banks?

Selfishness will always exist under one form or another; were not the sacred interests of entire humanity placed above the minor interests of persons and of nations, progress, arrested in every direction, could not be even imagined, for want of some ultimate object. Were not the whole human race its term, our love, like our devotion, blind, feeble, imperfect, would every moment stray and fail. Individuals, families, nations, what are they but parts of a great whole? Otherwise there would be no reason for their being. Unity, ultimate and complete, in which all the relations are co-ordered, all rights concentred, all duties harmonized, is man himself in the plenitude of his imperishable being.

18. Heinrich Heine, from *Germany: A Winter's Tale,* 1844

Heinrich Heine (1797–1856) was born of Jewish parents in Düsseldorf. He was intended by his parents for a commercial career, and was sent to a wealthy banker uncle in Hamburg, where he promptly showed himself unfit for business. Heine was set upon being a lyric poet instead, and succeeded in becoming one of the half-dozen most brilliant lyricists in any modern European language. When a scurrilous attack he had made upon a rival poet was banned in Prussia in 1831, Heine—who

had never been able to strike roots in Germany—went to Paris. There
he spent the rest of his life, in conscious exile. He joined the most
advanced and scintillating intellectual circles of Paris; he wrote for
the best French and German journals, and his poetry was on and off
the German censors' lists throughout his life. Sentimental journeys in
1843 and 1844 to the Germany he had renounced produced *Germany:
A Winter's Tale*, in which the ironic revelation of the Jewish exile's
love for his fatherland accents the liberal criticism of the German
régime of Metternich's Europe. The book was immediately successful
in Germany, and officially banned throughout the country. [Heinrich
Heine, *Works*, XI (London, 1905), trans. Margaret Armour, 1–10,
29–34.]

Departure from Paris

Paris, adieu, beloved town,
　　To-day I turn a rover,
And leave you happy here behind,
　　With pleasure brimming over.

My German heart has fallen sick—
　　Within my breast I feel it—
And in the North the doctor dwells
　　Whose skill alone can heal it.

He's famous for his wondrous cures,
　　To health he'll soon restore me,
But drastic are his bitter drugs;
　　I shrink from what's before me.

Farewell, ye merry folk of France,
　　My brothers happy-hearted;
Though foolish yearning drives me forth,
　　We shall not long be parted.

Imagine! For the smell of peat
　　I long with real anguish;
For turnips, Lünenburger cakes
　　And sauer-kraut I languish.

I yearn for watchmen, councillors,
　　Black bread in all its crudeness,

For tobacco, parsons' daughters blonde—
 I even yearn for rudeness.

I long to see my mother, too;—
 I frankly own I'm human—
'Tis fully thirteen years since last
 I saw the dear old woman.

Farewell, my wife, my lovely wife;
 I must perplex and grieve you—
So close I fold you to my heart,
 Yet, none the less, I leave you.

With this terrible thirst that drives me far
 From bliss, I dare not trifle;
I feel I must fill my lungs once more
 With German air, or stifle.

In convulsive throes this pain would end—
 This wild impetuous burning—
My foot, to tread on German ground,
 Quivers and shakes with yearning.

By the end of the year, completely cured
 Of this malady most unpleasant,
I'll be back, I promise, in time to buy
 The loveliest New Year's present.

CAPUT I

When I crossed from France to Germany
 'Twas the mournful month and dreary
When November winds are stripping bare
 The forests worn and weary.

As we drew toward the boundary
 I felt my pulses leaping
Within my bosom for delight;
 I think I started weeping.

And when I heard the German tongue,
  'Twas with such curious gladness
I seemed to feel my heart's blood ebb
  Without regret or sadness.

A little maiden with a harp
  Entuned a common ditty;
The voice was false, but the pathos true;
  It touched my heart to pity.

She sang of love and lovers' woes,
  Of loss, and fates that sever,
Of meetings in a better land
  Where grief is purged for ever.

She sang our mortal vale of tears,
  The joys that end in sadness,
The world where souls, redeemed at last,
  Attain eternal gladness.

She sang the epopee of heaven,
  The song of loss and sighing,
With which they lull the populace,
  Big booby! when it's crying.

I know the song, the text, and the men
  Who wrote the song, and taught her;
I know that in private they drank their wine,
  And preached in public water.

I will write you a new, a sweeter song;
  You shall sing it without a quaver;
We will build the kingdom of heaven on earth—
  'Tis a better plan and a braver.

We shall then be happy and starve no more:
  We whom the earth was spoiled for;
No longer shall lazy bellies waste
  What busy hands have toiled for.

Oh, here below there's not only food
   In abundance for every comer,
But beauty and pleasure and lollipops,
   And the myrtle and rose of summer.

The sugar plums, as soon as they're ripe,
   Shall to each and all be given,
And angels and sparrows may have our share
   Of the vague delights of heaven.

And if after death our wings should sprout,
   We'll pay you a visit with pleasure,
And help you to eat your tarts and cakes,
   And similar laid up treasure.

As sweet as the viol and flute shall ring
   My song, when that other's supplanted.
The passing bell shall be tolled no more,
   Nor the *Miserere* chanted.

To the Genius of Freedom, Europe, the Maid,
   Her virgin heart has yielded;
They have plighted their troth, and, heart on heart,
   With a first fond kiss have sealed it.

And a wedding true it will be, though the priest
   May pronounce no blessing hollow.
Long live the bridegroom and the bride,
   And the children that shall follow!

Oh, a wedding song is this new song;
   There's gladness in every line there;
And stars, at the Holy Sacrament,
   Arise in my soul, and shine there.

They are rapturous stars that blaze and pass
   In streams of flame and wonder—
I feel such vigour in my blood
   I could split the oaks asunder.

For, now I have stepped on German sod,
  A magic sap steals through me;
The giant has touched his mother again,
  And her love and her strength renew me.

CAPUT II

While thus the maiden trilled and strummed,
  The joys of heaven forestalling,
My box the Prussian douaniers
  Were carefully overhauling.

They poked among handkerchiefs, shirts, and hose;
  They rummaged in likely places;
They were nosing about for prohibited books,
  And jewelry and laces.

Ye fools, who turn my boxes out,
  There's nothing there forbidden;
The contraband I travel with,
  In my head is safely hidden!

You will find neither Mechlin nor Brussels lace,
  'Tis with what's in my head I trick you;
I warrant, were I to unpack my point,
  It would prettily tease and prick you!

I carry the royal diamonds there
  Of the Future, and need not falter:
The gems of the new, the unknown God,
  That shall blaze upon his altar.

Oh, many a book I have stowed away;
  I am speaking in moderation
When I tell you my brain is a warbling nest
  Of books for confiscation.

Believe me, in Satan's library
  Not one is worse or stranger;

Hoffmann von Fallersleben's[1] own
   Are not so fraught with danger.

A traveller standing by remarked
   We had reached the chain of duties
Known as the Prussian Zollverein,[2]
   And enlarged upon its beauties.

"By the Zollverein," he went on to say,
   "Our national life is founded,
And our poor divided Fatherland
   To one whole at last is rounded.

"The Zollverein gives a unity
   Which is obvious and real;
The unity born of the censorship
   Is the deeper, the ideal.

"The censorship unifies thought and soul.
   What we want—and the goal is sighted—
Is a Germany welded to one great whole,
   Without, within, united."

* * *

CAPUT VIII

From Cologne to Hagen some fifteen and six
   Is the fare, rather under than over.
The diligence chanced to be full, so I rode
   In a special chaise, without cover.

'Twas a late autumn morning both chilly and dull
   Through the mud the carriage went wheezing.
But, in spite of the wretched weather and road,
   I found it all rather pleasing.

Ah, this is my native air indeed,
   By which my hot cheek fanned is,

---

[1] A patriotic poet, author of "Deutschland, Deutschland über Alles."—Ed.
[2] The tariff union among German states.—Ed.

And this mud of the highway in which I sink
  The mud of my Fatherland is!

The horses kept wagging their tails like friends,
  As if theirs had always been my road.
Atalanta's apples were not more fair
  Than their pellets of dung on the high-road.

We posted through Mühlheim, a pretty town;
  The people are busy and staid there.
In the May of eighteen thirty-one,
  I remember, a visit I paid there.

There was bud, then, and blossom on bush and on
    bough,
  The sunbeams were laughing and winking,
The birds were all singing and yearning in song,
  And the people were hoping and thinking,

"These lanky, lean warrior-guests of ours
  We shall soon be allowed to fire on.
When they take to their horses their stirrup-cup
  We'll pour them from bottles of iron.

And Freedom her banner of red, white and blue
  Will wave over dancing and revel;
She may even fetch Bonaparte up from the grave
  In defiance of Death and the Devil."

But alas! the knights are still to the fore,
  And plenty of geese, whose haunches
Were lean as a lathe when they entered the land,
  Now go with their jolly round paunches.

Pale as pictures of Faith, Hope, Charity,
  Were the dogs when they settled down here;
But since then they have tippled their noses red
  On the goodly wine of our town here.

And freedom has sprained her ankle bone,
  And alas! the revel tarries,

And sadly the tricolor of France
   Looks down from the towers of Paris.

The Emperor rose from the dead, 'tis true,
   But the English worms had made him
A peaceful and a quiet man,
   And again in the tombs they laid him.[3]

I saw the procession, the gilded car;—
   Amid the crowd stood staring;—
Saw the golden goddess of Victory
   The golden coffin bearing.

Up the Champs Elysées, over the snow,
   Where the heavy mists hung blinding,
On through the Arc de Triomphe proud
   The solemn train came winding.

The musicians' fingers were stiff with cold,
   And the music suffered badly;
The eagles on their standards seemed
   To nod me a greeting sadly.

The people looked like so many ghosts,
   Lost in their memories hoary;
Again they dreamed the magic dream
   Of world-imperial glory.

I wept that day. I wept when I heard,
   From the heart of a loving nation,
The "Vive l'Empereur!" ring out, as of old,
   In deathless adoration.

CAPUT IX

We left Cologne at a quarter to eight—
   The start was somewhat early.

---

[3] In response to Bonapartist enthusiasm, in 1840 the government of Louis
Philippe brought back the remains of Napoleon I to France and interred
them at the Invalides.—Ed.

When Hagen was reached, where we halted to dine,
  It was three o'clock, or nearly.

The table was spread, I was glad to see,
  With the good old German dishes.
My sauer-kraut, hail! Your homely smell
  As sweet as a man could wish is.

My mother stewed her chestnuts so—
  I loved them with childish devotion.
And my native cod-fish, be greeted! How well
  You swim in your buttery ocean!

O the Fatherland must be dear to all,
  Unless to the heart of dullard!
Of bloaters and eggs I am also fond,
  Fried brown and rightly coloured.

How the sausages spluttered for glee in the fat!
  Roast fieldfares, like angels rejoicing,
A melodious song from their apple-sauce sang,
  The sweetest of welcomes voicing.

"All hail, compatriot! Long you have roamed,"
  They twittered and warbled together,
"And wandered afar in a foreign land,
  With birds of a foreign feather."

A goose was put down with the other good things,
  A creature quiet and kindly;
Perhaps in the days when we both were young,
  She had yielded her heart to me blindly.

Her gaze was so wistful and faithful and sad—
  I was sorry I could not commend her—
I am willing to vouch for her beautiful soul,
  But her body was far from tender.

A boar's head was served on a pewter plate;
  'Twas a dish with which none could quarrel.
The snouts of our bores at home, I see,
  Are garlanded still with laurel!

19. Friedrich List on a *National System* of *Political Economy*, 1840

Friedrich List (1789–1846) was born of an artisan family in a small town in southwestern Germany. Through his own talents and energies he rose to early prominence in the Württemberg government in the years surrounding the victory over Napoleon, taught political economy and administration at the University of Tübingen, and became a liberal member of the Württemberg Diet. He worked actively for German economic unity and development. With the consolidation of Metternich's Europe he fell out of favor, resigned his professorship in 1820, was banned from the Diet, and finally escaped imprisonment only by emigration to America in 1825. There he studied the Hamilton system of national economic development. After his return to Germany in 1832, protected by a commission as United States Consul, he became the leading advocate of an economic system in which national unity and protection against the outside would be combined with liberal principles of free trade and free development within Germany. As means to both ends, unity and development, he especially favored the construction of railroads. In the *National System*, List undertook a systematic exposition of his views. His Introduction should serve as a link between the liberal nationalism of his generation and the economic issues that drew increasing attention in the later thirties and the forties— and with which the following two sections of this book are concerned. List committed suicide as a result of overwork and frustration in 1846. [Friedrich List, *National System of Political Economy*, trans. G. A. Matile (Philadelphia, 1856), pp. 61–63, 70–82.]

Introduction

Et la patrie et l'humanité!

No BRANCH of political economy presents a greater diversity of views between men of theory and men of practice, than that which treats of international commerce and commercial policy. There is, however, in the domain of this science no topic, which, in regard to the well-being and civilization of nations, as well as to their independence, power and duration, presents the same degree of importance. Poor, weak, and uncivilized countries have not unfrequently attained power and wealth by a judicious commercial system, whilst others have sunk from a high rank for want of such a system; nations have even lost their independence, and their

political existence, because their commercial policy had not aided
the development and the consolidation of their nationality.

In our day, more than at any former period, among all the questions which belong to political economy, that of international commerce has acquired a preponderant interest; for the more rapidly
the genius of discovery and of industrial improvement, as well as
that of social and political progress advances, the more rapidly is
the distance between stationary nations and those which are progressive increased, and the greater is the peril of remaining behind.
If in time past it required centuries to monopolize that important
branch of industry, the manufacture of wool, some ten years have
sufficed in our time to obtain ascendency in the much more considerable manufacture of cotton; and now the start of a few years
may enable England to absorb all the flax industry of the continent
of Europe.

At no other epoch has the world seen a manufacturing and commercial power possessing resources so immense as those in the control of the power which now holds sway, pursuing designedly a
system so consistently selfish, absorbing with such untiring energy
the manufacturing and commercial industry of the world, the important colonies, the domination of the seas, and subjecting so
many people, as in the case of the Hindoos, to a manufacturing and
commercial yoke.

Alarmed by the consequences of that policy, nay, constrained
by the convulsions it has occasioned, we have seen in our century,
Prussia, a continental nation, as yet imperfectly prepared for manufacturing industry, seeking her welfare in the prohibitory system
so condemned by theorists. And what has been her reward? National prosperity.

On the other hand, encouraged by promises of theory, the
United States of America, which had made a rapid growth under
the protective system, have been induced to open their ports to the
manufacturers of England; and what fruits has this competition
borne? A periodical visitation of commercial disaster.

Such experience is well calculated to provoke doubts of the
infallibility which theory arrogated to itself, and of the absurdity
it imputes to practice; to create fears lest our nationality be in
danger of perishing by an error of theory, like the sick man, who
by conforming to a printed prescription died of an error of the
press: to arouse suspicion that this boasted theory has attained its

large growth only for the Trojan-Horse purpose of concealing arms and soldiers, and inducing us to take down, with our own hands, the walls which protect us.

At least this truth is evinced: during the half century in which this great question of commercial policy has been discussed in all civilized nations, in books and in legislative halls, by the shrewdest minds, the abyss, which, since Quesnay and Smith has separated theory from practice, not only has not disappeared, but has actually grown wider every year. What kind of science is that which sheds no light upon the path which practice must follow? Is it reasonable to suppose that the professors of this science, by the mighty power of their intelligence, have everywhere become exactly acquainted with all that pertains to social life and industry, whilst the men of the world, mingling freely in all the outward concerns of life, unable to comprehend the truth discovered and brought to light by the former, have continued from generation to generation to mistake evident errors for truth? Is it not better to acknowledge that practical men, too much inclined in general to adhere to the actual, would not so long and so obstinately have resisted theory, if theory itself had not been in opposition to truth and nature.

Indeed we do not hesitate to aver that the contradiction between theory and practice in regard to commercial policy, is as much the fault of theory as of practice.

Political economy, in matters of international commerce, must draw its lessons from experience; the measures it advises must be appropriate to the wants of our times, to the special condition of each people; it must not, however, disavow the exigencies of the future nor the higher interests of the whole human race. Political economy must rest consequently upon Philosophy, Policy, and History.

For the interests of the future and the welfare of men, philosophy requires a more intimate union and communion of nations, a renunciation of war so far as possible, the establishment and development of international law, transition of the *jus gentium* to a federal law, freedom of communication among nations, as well in moral as in material concerns; lastly, the union of all nations under some rule of law, or in some aspects of the subject, a universal association.

In the case of any particular people, a wise administration, with extended views, pursues special objects, seeking guarantees for independence and for duration, measures calculated to hasten progress in civilization, well-being, and power, and to improve social condition so that the body politic shall be completely and harmoniously developed in all its parts, perfect in itself, and politically independent. . . .

[After describing some concrete technical problems of international trade and their incompatibility with prevalent economic theory, List proceeds:]

The author will begin, as theory does not begin, by interrogating History, and deducing from it his fundamental principles; this being done, an examination of former systems will follow, and his tendency being especially practical, he will, in conclusion, furnish a sketch of the later phases of commercial policy.

For greater clearness, we give here a cursory view of the principal results of his researches and meditations:

The association of individuals for the prosecution of a common end is the most efficacious mode towards ensuring the happiness of individuals. Alone, and separated from his fellow-creatures, man is feeble and destitute. The greater the number of those who are united, the more perfect is the association, and the greater and the more perfect is the result, which is the moral and material welfare of individuals.

The highest association of individuals now realized, is that of the state, the nation; and the highest imaginable, is that of the whole human race. Just as the individual is happier in the bosom of the state than in solitude, all nations would be more prosperous if they were united together by law, by perpetual peace, and by free interchange.

Nature leads nations gradually to the highest degree of association; inviting them to commerce by variety of climate, soil, and productions; and by overflowing population, by superabundance of capital and talents, it leads them to emigration and the founding of distant colonies. International trade, by rousing activity and energy, by the new wants it creates, by the propagation among nations of new ideas and discoveries, and by the diffusion of power, is one of the mightiest instruments of civilization and one of the most powerful agencies in promoting national prosperity.

The association of nations by means of trade is even yet very imperfect, for it is interrupted, or at least weakened, by war or selfish measures on the part sometimes of one and sometimes of another nation.

A nation may by war be deprived of its independence, its wealth, its liberty, its constitution, its laws, of its own special features, of that degree of culture and national well-being to which it may have attained; it may be wholly enslaved. Nations are thus the victims of each other, and selfish policy is continually disturbing and delaying the economical development of nations.

To preserve, to develop, and to improve itself as a nation is consequently, at present, and ever must be, the principal object of a nation's efforts. There is in that nothing false or selfish; it is a reasonable tendency, agreeing perfectly with the real interests of humanity; for it leads naturally to universal association, which is an advantage to men, so far as nations have reached the same degree of culture and power, and, consequently, so far as it may be realized, by way of association or confederation.

A universal association proceeding from the overbearing influence and wealth of a single nation, based, consequently, upon the subjection and dependence of all others, would result in the annihilation of separate nationalities and national emulation; it would hurt the interests and wound the feelings of nations which deem themselves on the way to independence and the attainment of great wealth as well as of high political importance; such an association would be only a repetition of what has already occurred in the attempt to subjugate the world, made by the Romans; an attempt that would be more successful in our days by means of manufactures and commerce, instead of, as formerly, by the sword; though either mode would restore the world to barbarism.

The civilization, political education, and power of nations, depend chiefly on their economical condition; and, reciprocally, the more advanced the economy, the more civilized and powerful will be the nation, the more rapidly will its civilization and power increase, and the more will its economical culture be developed.

In the economical development of nations, it is necessary to distinguish the following principal stages: the savage state, the pastoral state, the agricultural state, the agricultural and manufacturing state, and finally, the agricultural, manufacturing, and commercial state.

It is obvious that a nation possessing an extensive territory, enriched with varied resources and a numerous population, uniting agriculture and manufactures with an external and internal trade, is beyond comparison more civilized, politically more developed, and more powerful than any merely agricultural country. But manufactures constitute the basis of external and internal trade, of navigation, of an improved agriculture, consequently of civilization and political power; and should any nation succeed in monopolizing all the manufacturing activity of the world, and in checking all other nations in their economical development by reducing them to the mere production of agricultural commodities and raw materials, and other indispensable local productions, it would undoubtedly attain to very wide, if not to universal, dominion.

A nation that greatly values its independence and its safety, must make a vigorous effort to elevate itself as fast as possible, from an inferior to a higher state of civilization, uniting and perfecting as quickly as possible its own agriculture, manufactures, navigation, and commerce.

The transition from the savage to the pastoral, and from the pastoral to the agricultural state, as well as the first progress in agriculture, is very efficiently promoted by free intercourse among manufacturing and commercial nations.

The elevation of an agricultural people to the condition of countries at once agricultural, manufacturing, and commercial, can only be accomplished under the law of free trade when the various nations engaged at the time in manufacturing industry shall be in the same degree of progress and civilization; when they shall place no obstacle in the way of the economical development of each other, and not impede their respective progress by war or adverse commercial legislation.

But some of them, favored by circumstances, having distanced others in manufactures, commerce, and navigation, and having early perceived that this advanced state was the surest mode of acquiring and keeping political supremacy, have adopted and still persevere in a policy so well adapted to give them the monopoly of manufactures, of industry and of commerce, and to impede the progress of less advanced nations or those in a lower degree of culture. The measures enforced by such nations, taken as a whole, the prohibitions, the duties on imports, the maritime restrictions, premiums upon exports, &c., are called the protective system.

The anterior progress of certain nations, foreign commercial legislation and war have compelled inferior countries to look for special means of effecting their transition from the agricultural to the manufacturing stage of industry, and as far as practicable, by a system of duties, to restrain their trade with more advanced nations aiming at manufacturing monopoly.

The system of import duties is consequently not, as has been said, an invention of speculative minds; it is a natural consequence of the tendency of nations to seek for guarantees of their existence and prosperity, and to establish and increase their weight in the scale of national influence.

Such a tendency is legitimate and reasonable only so far as it renders easy, instead of retarding, the economical development of a nation; and it is not in opposition to the higher objects of society, the universal confederation of the future.

As human association ought to be considered under two points of view, that is to say, the cosmopolitan, embracing all the human race, and the political or merely national, every economy, private or public, ought to be considered under two different aspects, the individual, social and material power, by means of which riches are produced, and the interchangeable value of the products of industry.

There is, consequently, a cosmopolitan economy and a political economy, a theory of interchangeable value, and a theory of productive power. These doctrines are distinct in their essence, and require to be developed separately.

The productive power of nations is not solely dependent on the labor, the saving, the morality, and the intelligence of individuals, or on the possession of natural advantage and material capital; it is dependent also upon institutions and laws, social, political, and civil, but, above all, on the securities of their duration, their independence, and their power as nations. Individuals would be in vain laborious, economical, ingenious, enterprising, intelligent, and moral, without a national unity, without a division of labor and a co-operation of productive power. A nation cannot otherwise attain to a high degree of prosperity and power, nor maintain itself in the permanent possession of its intellectual, social, and material riches.

The principle of the division of labor has been hitherto but imperfectly understood. Industrial production depends much less on the apportioning of the various operations of a manufacture among several individuals, than on the moral and material association of those individuals for a common end.

This principle applies not only to a manufacture or to a rural industry; it extends also to every kind of national industry, agricultural, manufacturing, and commercial.

The division of labor and the combination of productive power take place in a nation when the intellectual power is applied so as to co-operate freely and efficiently with national production, when manufacturing industry and trade are equally and harmoniously developed.

A merely agricultural people in free intercourse with manufacturing and trading nations will lose a considerable part of their productive power and natural resources, which must remain idle and unemployed. Its intellectual and political culture, and its means of defence, will thus be limited. It can possess neither an important navigation, nor an extensive trade; its prosperity, as far as it results from external commerce, may be interrupted, disturbed, or annihilated by foreign legislation or by war.

On the other hand, manufacturing industry is favorable to science, art, and political progress; it promotes the general welfare, increases population, public revenue, and the power of the country; it enables the latter to extend its influence to all parts of the world, and to found colonies; it sustains fisheries and navies, mercantile and national. By it only, can agriculture rise to any high degree of efficiency and perfection.

Agriculture and manufacturing industry united in the same nation, under the same political power, live in perpetual peace; they are disturbed in their reciprocal action neither by war nor by foreign legislation; they ensure to a nation the continued development of its prosperity, civilization, and power.

Agriculture and manufacturing industry are subjected by nature to special conditions.

The countries of the temperate zone are especially fit for the development of manufacturing industry; for the temperate zone is the region of intellectual and physical effort.

If the countries of the torrid zone are little favored in reference to manufactures, they possess, on the other hand, the natural monopoly of many precious commodities which the inhabitants of the temperate climates greatly prize. The exchange of the manufactured products of the one for the commodities of the other constitutes a division of labor and a co-operation of productive power throughout the chief commercial nations, and mainly constitutes the great international trade of the world.

A country of the torrid zone would make a very fatal mistake should it try to become a manufacturing country. Having received no invitation to that vocation from nature, it will progress more rapidly in riches and civilization if it continues to exchange its agricultural productions for the manufactured products of the temperate zone.

It is true that tropical countries sink thus into dependence upon those of the temperate zone, but that dependence will not be without compensation if competition arises among the nations of temperate climes in their manufacturing industry in their trade with the former, and in their exercise of political power. This competition will not only ensure a full supply of manufactures at low prices, but will prevent any one nation from taking advantage by its superiority over the weaker nations of the torrid zone. There would be danger and damage in this dependence only so far as manufactures, important branches of trade, foreign commerce, and maritime power should become the monopoly of a single nation.

Nations of the temperate zone possessing extensive territory enriched with varied resources have lost one of the richer sources of prosperity, civilization and power, if they do not succeed in realizing a national division of labor and a co-operation of national productive power, as soon as they possess the necessary conditions, economical, intellectual, and social, for accomplishing it.

By economical conditions, we understand an advanced stage of agriculture, which cannot be sensibly stimulated by the export of its products; by moral conditions, a high moral culture among individuals; by social conditions, we mean legal security to citizens for their persons and properties and the free exercise of their moral and physical faculties; institutions regulating and facilitating trade, and suppressing all restraints upon industry, liberty, intelligence, and morality, as for instance, feudal institutions.

It is of the utmost concern for a nation uniting such advantages first fully to supply its own wants, its own consumption, with the products of its own manufactures; then to form direct connections progressively with the countries of the torrid zone, transmitting to them, upon its own vessels, its manufactured products, receiving in exchange their commodities.

In comparison with this exchange of the manufactured products of the temperate for the agricultural productions of the torrid zone, other international trade is of a secondary importance, if we but except the trade in a few special articles; wine, for instance.

The production of raw materials and commodities among the great nations of temperate climes has no real importance but in regard to internal trade. An uncultivated nation may at the beginning advance its agriculture by the exportation of wheat, wine, flax, hemp, and wool; but no great nation ever arrived at wealth, civilization, and power, by such policy.

It may be stated as a principle, that a nation is richer and more powerful in proportion as it exports more manufactured products, imports more raw materials, and consumes more tropical commodities.

Productions of the tropics serve to manufacturing countries of temperate climes not only as raw materials and alimentary commodities, but also, and especially, as stimulants for agricultural and industrial labor. The nation which consumes the greatest quantity of tropical commodities will always be that of which the agricultural and manufacturing production is relatively the most considerable, and that which consumes the greatest quantity of its own products.

In the economical development of nations by means of external trade, four periods must be distinguished. In the first, agriculture is encouraged by the importation of manufactured articles, and by the exportation of its own products; in the second, manufactures begin to increase at home, whilst the importation of foreign manufactures to some extent continues; in the third, home manufactures mainly supply domestic consumption and the internal markets; finally, in the fourth, we see the exportation upon a large scale of manufactured products, and the importation of raw materials and agricultural products.

The system of import duties being considered as a mode of assisting the economical development of a nation by regulating its external trade, must constantly take as a rule the principle of the industrial education of the country.

To encourage agriculture by the aid of protective duties is vicious policy; for agriculture can be encouraged only by promoting manufacturing industry; and the exclusion of raw materials and agricultural products from abroad has no other result than to impede the rise of national manufactures.

The economical education of a country of inferior intelligence and culture, or one thinly populated relatively to the extent and the fertility of its territory, is effected most certainly by free trade with more advanced, richer, and more industrious nations. Every commercial restriction in such a country aiming at the increase of manufactures is premature, and will prove detrimental not only to civilization in general but the progress of the nation in particular. If its intellectual, political, and economical education, under the operation of free trade, has advanced so far that the importation of foreign manufactures and the want of markets for its own products has become an obstacle to its ulterior development, then only can protective measures be justified.

A nation without extensive territory and of otherwise limited resources, which does not control the mouths of its rivers or which has not suitable boundaries, cannot resort to the protective system, or at least cannot employ it with full success. It must be first enlarged by way of conquest or negotiation.

Manufacturing industry is concerned with so many branches of science and art, it implies so much experience, practice, and adaptation, that the industrial training and education of a country can proceed but slowly. All excessive or premature protection is expiated by a diminution of national prosperity.

No commercial policy is more dangerous and reprehensible than a sudden resort to absolute prohibition of foreign products. It may, however, be justified when a country, separated from others by a long war, finds itself almost in a compulsory state of prohibitions in regard to foreign products, and under the absolute necessity of offering a high premium to the industry which will enable it to supply its own wants.

The return from such a condition must be by gradual transition from the prohibitive to the protective system, and should be effected by means of duties fixed by anticipation and decreasing gradually. On the other hand, a nation which is to pass from free trade to the protective system should commence with low duties to be afterwards raised by degrees according to a suitable scale.

Duties thus fixed by anticipation must be strictly maintained by the government; it must be careful not to diminish them before the appointed time, and equally careful to raise them if they should prove insufficient.

Duties upon imports so high as absolutely to exclude foreign competition are prejudicial to the country which adopts them; for they suppress all rivalry between domestic and foreign manufactures, and encourage indolence among the former.

When, under the rule of suitable and progressive duties, the manufactures of a country do not thrive, it is an evidence that the country does not yet possess the conditions requisite to a manufacturing people.

Duties designed to favor an industry should never be put so low as to endanger the existence of the latter from foreign competition. It should be a rule to preserve what exists—to protect national industry in its trunk and in its roots.

Foreign competition should not have more than its share in the annual increase of consumption. Duties should be raised when foreign commodities supply the greatest part or the whole of the increased annual consumption.

A country like England, which is far in advance of all its competitors, cannot better maintain and extend its manufacturing and commercial industry than by a trade as free as possible from all restraints. For such a country, the cosmopolitan and the national principle are one and the same thing.

This explains the favor with which the most enlightened economists of England regard free trade, and the reluctance of the wise and prudent of other countries to adopt this principle in the actual state of the world.

A quarter of a century since, the prohibitive and protective system of England operated to her detriment and to the advantage of her rivals.

Nothing could be more prejudicial to England than her restrictions upon the importation of raw material and food.

Union of customs and commercial treaties are the most efficient means of facilitating national exchanges.

But treaties of commerce are legitimate and durable only when the advantages are reciprocal. They are fatal and illegitimate when they sacrifice one country to another; when one country, to purchase advantage for its agriculture, sacrifices a manufacturing industry already well advanced; such a treaty was that of Methuen,[1] a compact in which one party took the lion's share.

The treaty concluded between England and France in 1786 was one of those leonine treaties. And all the propositions made since by England and France to other countries are of the same nature.

If protective duties enhance for a time the price of domestic manufactures, they secure afterwards lower prices by means of internal competition; for an industry that has reached its full development can safely reduce its prices far below those which were

[1] 1702 treaty between England and Portugal, exchanging manufactured woolens for Portuguese wine.—Ed.

necessary to ensure its growth, and thus save to its consumers the whole expense of transportation and the whole profits of trade which are consequent upon imports of the same articles from other countries.

The loss occasioned by protective duties consists, after all, only in values; whilst the country thus acquires a power by which it is enabled to produce a great mass of values. This loss in values must be considered as the price of the industrial training of the country.

Protective duties upon manufactured products do not press heavily upon the agriculture of a country. By the development of manufacturing industry the wealth, population, consumption of agricultural products, rent, and exchangeable value of real estate are vastly increased, whilst the manufactured products consumed by farmers gradually fall in price. The gain thus realized exceeds, in the proportion of ten to one, the loss which agriculturalists incur by the transient rise of manufactured products.

Internal and external trade flourish alike under the protective system; these have no importance but among nations supplying their own wants by their own manufacturing industry, consuming their own agricultural products, and purchasing foreign raw materials and commodities with the surplus of their manufactured articles. Home and foreign trade are both insignificant in the merely agricultural countries of temperate climes, and their external commerce is usually in the hands of the manufacturing and trading nations in communication with them.

A good system of protection does not imply any monopoly in the manufacturers of a country; it only furnishes a guarantee against losses to those who devote their capital, their talents, and their exertions to new branches of industry.

There is no monopoly, because internal competition comes in the place of foreign competition, and every individual has the privilege of taking his share in the advantages offered by the country to its citizens; it is only an advantage to citizens as against foreigners, who enjoy in their own country a similar advantage.

But this protection is useful not only because it awakens the sleeping energies of a country and puts in motion its productive power, but because it attracts the productive power of foreign countries, including capital, both material and moral, and skilful masters as well as skilful men.

On the other hand, the absence of manufacturing industry in a nation long civilized, the productive powers of which cannot be sensibly excited by the export of raw materials and agricultural products and by the importation of foreign manufactures, exposes it to numerous and serious inconveniences.

The agriculture of such a country must necessarily suffer; for the surplus population, which, in a great manufacturing development, finds means of living in factories and creates a large demand for agricultural products, thus affording substantial profits to agriculture, will be reduced to the labor of the fields, and thence will follow a subdivision of farms and a small culture, both as prejudicial to the power and the civilization of a country as to its wealth.

An agricultural people consisting chiefly of proprietors of small estates can neither fill the channels of internal trade with large quantities of commodities nor furnish a large consumption for manufactured goods; in such a country every one is limited almost to his own production and his own consumption. In circumstances like these, no complete system of communications can be established, and the immense advantages which they afford are lost to the country.

Hence ensues necessarily, moral and material, individual and political weakness. The danger is aggravated when neighboring nations pursue a different policy; some making progress in every respect, others retrograding; some hoping for a brighter future, the courage and enterprise of their people being aroused; the absence of hope extinguishing by degrees in others all courage, intelligence, and enterprise.

History is not without examples of entire nations having perished, because they knew not and seized not the critical moment for the solution of the great problem of securing their moral, economical, and political independence by the establishment of manufacturing industry and the formation of a powerful class of manufacturers and tradesmen.

IV

Population and Poverty

Growth of population, increase in poverty, growth of urban industry—
Metternich's Europe could not be sure just how they fit together, nor
can historians now. Did factories come because population growth
created a floating labor surplus that could be marshaled into cities to
exploit the productive potential of steam engine and machine? Perhaps;
for men did not readily become factory laborers when there was
room for them and their sons on the land or in the old established trades.
Or did poverty come from the herding of men into factory towns,
where they were at the mercy of the demands of the machine and of
the computations of profit by the owners of machines, computations
that determined what wages should be paid or whether the wheels
should turn at all? For it was the spectacle of the urban poor that
made the problems of population and poverty most dramatically apparent. Or did population grow because improved forms of production
and accumulating capital provided work and sustenance for increasing
numbers of people? For there had to be some material explanation for
the growth of population far beyond the limits once imposed by famine
and disease.

But hardly anybody doubted that these developments were related
and were characteristic phenomena of the nineteenth century. And it
seemed clear that they were happening spontaneously, in the sense that
they were quite independent of the régime called Metternich's Europe.
A régime of the *status quo* was not equipped to cope with dynamic
problems that arose outside its sphere of political action. Once again,
the tendencies and demands of history stood in contradiction to Metternich's Europe.

Population and poverty were critical dangers Europe was obliged
to confront. Institutions had to be adapted or created to meet them.
Industrialization might be a promise and a proof that the Metternich
system was doomed; this theme will be treated in the section following,
on Machines, Motion, and Progress. But first, the problems of visibly
rising population and poverty: where did they come from, and why
did they seem both irresistible and historic?

Probably the main reasons why historians cannot agree on the
causes of the European population explosion of modern times is that
a great many factors combined in irregular ways, so that no one or

two specific factors can be shown to be the determining ones. Whether one considers medical improvements, sanitation, nutrition, marriage customs, employment opportunity, or any of a dozen other possibilities, it can always be shown that population grew in places where the factor being considered was absent. Uncertainty as to cause is probably one reason why contemporaries thought of population growth as a historical trend projecting indefinitely into the future, for it took on the character of an independent, self-generating force.

General population statistics were neither reliable nor widely available before the middle of the nineteenth century, and the way most people knew the population was growing was that they saw what seemed an increasing "excess" of population. That is, they saw poverty; and the most likely place to see mass poverty was among the economically insecure of the cities. Probably the living standards of the urban poor were no lower than those of the rural poor were and always had been, but the city poor were there to be seen in a mass, and they created more serious social and political problems than the less concentrated and less volatile rural poor. The old, stable European communities had been equipped with laws, customs, and social pressures to keep their numbers commensurate with the economic resources locally available, and to keep the poor in check. It was probably in large part the weakening of these structures and the overflow from them that provided the apparent population excess and the migration to the great towns. Even though the birth rate on the land might be higher than that in the town, migration from country to town usually resulted in a much faster growth of urban population than of rural.

Contemporary observers were probably right in the long run to identify the food supply—basic subsistence—as the main control of population, governing its growth and setting its limits. For most of the elemental creators and sustainers of life—including sexual vigor, successful pregnancy and childbirth, the ability to found and raise a healthy family, and resistance to disease—were critically affected by the nutritional resources available. To think of population and its changes, therefore, was to think of hunger. The basic population theory of the time was one set forth by the Rev. Thomas Robert Malthus (1766–1834), who argued that population would tend naturally to grow faster than food supply, except insofar as it was checked by famine, disease, war, or vice (or, dubiously, by "moral restraint"). The theory confirmed the population-poverty equation that lay before a casual observer's eyes. Economic doctrines like that of David Ricardo (1772–1823) held that wages must naturally hang at a minimum subsistence level—that is, that the working population (economists and their friends excepted) must always live on the verge of starvation; for if wages were to rise above that level, the working class would reproduce faster and drive wages back down to the margin again. It followed that to try to improve the economic condition of the poor, of the "masses" that nobody knew very well, was like trying to sweep back the sea with a broom. The sea only stopped where its waves broke exhausted on the shore.

Population grew, and poverty was inevitable. That guaranteed perpetual and growing reservoirs of social discontent. Population grew, and went to the cities; and even though it may have been attracted there by employment opportunities, still the worker and his family were bound to remain on the edge of starvation, and unstable—everyone remembered the Paris of revolutionary days. Or could rapid sustained growth of industry and commerce and agricultural productivity support or even draw ahead of the increase in population, and create a new economic world? But whichever it should be, industrial revolution or revolution in the streets, both portended an inevitable end to Metternich's Europe.

A CHRONOLOGY

1798	Malthus, *Essay on the Principles of Population*
1816–17	Locally severe famine
1817	Ricardo, *On the Principles of Political Economy*
1830–33	Cholera
1834	English New Poor Law
1846–47	Potato-rot: widespread famine

POPULATION OF EUROPE

1750	140 million
1800	187 million (the ten largest cities: 3,286,000)
1810	199 million
1820	213 million
1830	234 million
1840	251 million
1850	267 million (the ten largest cities: 7,847,000)

BIBLIOGRAPHY

M. C. Buer, *Health, Wealth, and Population in the Early Days of the Industrial Revolution* (London, 1926).

W. L. Langer, "Europe's Initial Population Explosion," *American Historical Review*, LXIX (1963), 1–17.

T. R. Malthus, *Essay on the Principles of Population* (many editions).

A. Redford, *Labor Migration in England* (Manchester, 1964).

A. F. Weber, *The Growth of Cities in the Nineteenth Century* (Ithaca, N.Y., 1963).

C. B. Woodham-Smith, *The Great Hunger: Ireland, 1845–1849* (New York, 1962).

20. Article on "Population," from the *Staats-Lexikon*, 1846

The following article should generally introduce the question of population as it appeared in the 1840's. The *Staats-Lexikon* was a multivolume encyclopedia designed mainly for the use of German civil servants, and for the library shelves of the politically conscious. It appeared first in the 1830's, and went through several revised and expanded editions. Most of the articles were prepared by academics, political writers, and public officials, and were firmly liberal in tone. When an article on "Population" submitted by the prominent German political writer Robert von Mohl turned out to be a gloomy one, lamenting the headlong growth of population and (rather hopelessly) suggesting measures to hold it down, the editors commissioned a second article on the same topic, "because this subject is one of the foundations of political science." Wilhelm Schulz, author of this second article, had as a youth participated in the last battles against Napoleon, had studied at the University of Giessen (as had Karl Follen and Heinrich von Gagern), and had gone on to write extensively on politics and economics. Notice how his article on "Population," characteristically for *Staats-Lexikon* articles, raises political questions such as civil liberties and national progress and power, questions that he and his editors assumed a modern discussion of population should treat. [*Das Staats-Lexikon. Encyklopädie der sämmtlichen Staatswissenschaften, für alle Stände*, ed. Carl von Rotteck and Carl Welcker. 2nd edn., II (Altona, 1846), 481–494. Translation by the editor.]

THE PEOPLE [*Volk*] constitutes the creative living substance and, therefore, the end purpose of the state. A single and yet many-channeled stream, out of whose current individuals seem briefly to emerge, only soon to vanish again, and yet a stream in which every individual plays a definite part and adds an impulse with lasting effect—so the population flows from its dim unknown sources, eternal beginnings and endings, over the lands of the earth. And as this stream floods and recedes, political conditions change with it, and so do the relative positions and powers of states.

Countless races of men have ranged themselves in unbroken sequence through the history of the world. From the ever-renewing life of the peoples, death here plucks away teeming youth, there withered age, now the blossom, and then again the ripened fruit. And when we look objectively at the separate instances within the incessant interchange, the eye is bewildered by the motley variety;

it seems as if blind accident strews the seed of man over the earth with one hand, while with the other it plies the sickle endlessly, in aimless harvest. But as soon as we enlarge our view to encompass the course of the human race in its great entirety, then we recognize that here too, as in all beginnings and endings, a regular order exists; we see how within the limits drawn by a higher hand, room is left for the free wills of men, even though human wills can never, to the end of time, destroy the law itself. The scholar [Süssmilch, 1761] who was the first or one of the first to turn his attention to this movement had good reasons to entitle it "the *divine* order in the variations in the human race." Since his time, added experience, observations, and comparisons have made it possible to know many more of the principles of this order. Yet we must admit that the veil is far from being raised, and that a wide field for investigation remains open in the statistics of population development. For as is true of all researches into physiology and psychology, Nature's secrets of procreation and birth are not fully revealed, so that many secrets of the laws of the propagation of the human race remain hidden from our understanding, riddles for whose answers future generations will seek again and again in their hunger for knowledge.

Men are the children of the earth and live from what it produces. But the earth itself is only one part of a system of heavenly bodies; and all analogies from our experience, and certain clues to the history of our own earth, must persuade us that this system, too, in all its members, has its periods of unfolding, of growth, and of decline. Is the totality of those forces that control the propagation of the human race now in a period of growth? Despite all irregularity in detail, the statistical observations possible so far agree that the answer is yes, at least for modern times, and at least for those peoples that have attained a higher stage of culture.

In view of the organic relation of constant giving and receiving that exists between the earth and its creatures, it may be said that maladjustment between the *whole* human race and its means of subsistence is, if not in the nature of things impossible, still most unlikely. Merely the simple common experience that the adult person always maintains on the whole the same bodily weight, apart from minor fluctuations, until at last death returns his body to the nourishing earth, indicates that in animal life a simple transition of substances takes place. For no matter what happens to these substances in the process of consumption, the most exact findings of organic chemistry show that though their forms be changed they still, directly or indirectly, serve as media for the creation of new nourishment, so that in Nature's household no nourishment is ever lost. Now, ever since Malthus made his famous statement that in every twenty-five years the population increased in the geometrical progression, 1, 2, 4, 8, 16, etc., while total foodstuffs could only increase in the arithmetical progression 1, 2, 3, 4, 5, people have played with the notion that in the end an overpopulation of the whole earth was possible, in which all the ties of social order must dissolve, and where amid murderous anarchy all culture must be brought to the grave by a new uncontrolled rule of violence. But in fact observation of natural laws provides no grounds for such a surmise; nor are there grounds for the hazy opinion that Eternal Wisdom overlooked this defect in its law of propagation, a mistake, however, that human wisdom has succeeded in recognizing if not correcting. If on a field where a thousand stalks of grain could grow, there were only one stalk, there would be nothing to prevent a new stalk from sprouting from each sound grain, so that the increase would proceed in geometric progression until at last the whole field would be covered. Now the earth is the field, which the seed of man is far from covering, and so we need not see even a distant threat in the growing increase of population. If finally a denser crowd spreads over the earth's surface, then the size of the population will inevitably strike a balance with the sources of nourishment. Either the free wills of men on higher stages of culture will impose the required rational restraints on the sexual drive, so that it will no longer act like a blind power, or else it may be that as the human race grows older its power of procreation will undergo a general decline. This latter view seems justified enough when we grasp the full idea of an inseparable and mutual interrelation between Nature and human life.

The possibility of a partial and temporary overpopulation of individual states or areas can by no means, however, be ignored. Although in Nature's great household, however dense the crowd, no nourishing substance is lost, still actual subsistence depends on the prior *relative* distribution of the materials creating nourishment. Agricultural production, which comes especially into question here, cannot be indefinitely raised within a limited space by increased application of fertilizers alone. Therefore, any given space can sustain only a population of appropriate size, so that at times a space can be overfilled with people. And, of course, similar simple relative overpopulation can sometimes occur where recent changes in economic relations subject significant parts of the population, perhaps whole classes, to shortages and poverty. Just as an individual, then, lives through in his youth a period of more or less rapid, often far too rapid growth, resulting often in peculiar ills, so too can it happen in the growth of whole peoples. Partial overpopulation then is only a passing affliction of development, a kind of children's illness in the life of nations, which can be overcome and dispelled with good will and the application of the right remedies. At the same time, the increase in the total population of the earth is a sign that the human race as a whole is still in the period of its youth, old though we may feel in worldly wisdom and world history, and boast though we may of experience, which really is still relatively brief.

ABSOLUTE AND RELATIVE POPULATION

A distinction is made between *absolute* population, that is, the number of people existing on some given space, and *relative* population, or the proportion between the number of inhabitants and the area upon which they live [population density]. Calculations of the total surface of the earth range between nine and ten million square [German] miles.[1] Of this almost three-quarters is covered with water and about 2½ million square miles are land. A significant part of the latter is still entirely unknown, so that estimates of the total population of the earth must be uncertain. The usual figures range from 700 million or 800 million to 1 billion or 1.1 billion. The earth is suitable for agriculture only as far as sixty degrees latitude north and south; in other zones people can scrape together a laborious and precarious existence only with hunting, fishing, or a barren kind of herding. In the still thinly populated tropical areas, on the other hand, according to Humboldt, over fifty persons could support themselves on about an acre planted with bananas of the larger kind, while the same space in Europe does not yet suffice for two persons. The density of the population varies greatly in the different regions and countries, and will continue to do so in future centuries, although the sharpest contrasts may be gradually vanishing in a large part of the world. Thus for

[1] The German mile equaled about five British or American miles.—Ed.

example the relative population of America is still less than 1/21 that of Europe, and that of Australia only about 1/90. Asia has on the average only 500 inhabitants per square mile, Africa hardly more than 200. The density in certain European countries on the other hand, such as Ireland and Belgium, reaches from 5,000 to almost 8,000; and over even much larger expanses, an average population of 3,000 per square mile is not unusual. It is true that for large regions, as for example the still largely unknown continent of Australia and the interior of Africa, it is still impossible to measure the capacity to support population with any degree of probability; and the polar regions, as well as the greater part of the desert and steppe areas, especially of Africa and Asia, must be regarded as fully uninhabitable. But even taking all this into account, it would surely not be too bold a hypothesis to assume that the development of population could reach a point in the course of a few centuries where there might be an average density of 1,500 per square mile. In such a case the earth's population would amount to 3.75 billion, three times the present figure. Who could predict the political and social consequences of just this one change in the conditions of human life? For in all countries of the cultivated world, the increase in population, this bodily growth of peoples, is almost inevitably bound together with a spiritual growth. Asia, indeed, shows us some heavily populated realms, such as China, where oppressive despotism prevails and whose inhabitants from generation to generation seem trapped within narrow bounds of traditions and attitudes. But the means of intellectual intercourse there are quite different from those in Europe and America, quite apart from the hereditary difference of temperament. Merely the form of the Chinese written language, and the far greater difficulties involved in using it, oblige the intellectually active to expend the greater part of their energy only to get command of the intellectual achievements of their forebears. And so it is all the more likely that the few who wish to and can go beyond this shall, as offenders against the traditional order, fall victim to the retaliation of the despot, who is the defender of tradition. A quite different situation prevails in Europe and America, partly because of the natural mental equipment and character of the inhabitants, but also because they are made up of many different but related states or groups of states, among which there are intellectual frictions and activity through their printing presses and other means of communication. Here the denser the population becomes, the more the intellectual centers multiply, and the exchange of opinion proceeds so much the faster. Denser masses come to agree more readily on common views than tribes spread over great expanses. That is why among a large people living close together, there are formed stronger and more distinct parties, which attain a greater sense of strength from the fact of their growth, and which consequently are the more ready and able to convert predominant views into action. And at the same time, a denser mass is much more sensitive to the more general measures a government applies to a people. When a country doubles its population, the effects of wise decrees, and of the opposite kind, are doubly felt. The nerves of the body politic are then more stimulated; and as an ever more decisive public opinion forms accordingly, it becomes all the more dangerous to oppose it, and all the more necessary to give unimpeded course to the free movement of spirits, so that in truth the public interest comes unmistakably to the fore. Considering only the single fact of growing population, therefore, we may be firm in the conviction of growing freedom, and may be sure that despite the arbitrary wills of individuals, the nations will raise themselves more and more to be masters of their destinies. . . .

[After a description of the physical world, which undertakes to show that population is densest in northern moderate climates and where the open seas are readily accessible, the author continues:]

The differing populations among the states has raised the further question: What size population best serves the purposes of the state? It is clear enough that no one general answer can be valid, because not only the general but even the particular interests of states change, and so too do the means to attain them. Moreover, the same mass of population may in different situations have very different political value. The clear unchanging purpose of the state is freedom in union, or the development of each member of the state in regular harmonious relation with its totality and unity. To achieve this end a constant, organic, living interchange is necessary, of such a kind that the central authorities, in whom the unity of the state is expressed, are an *articulation* of the people, so that they for their part may *articulate* in accordance with the impulse received. Thus it is clear that the size of the population *can* reach the point where the living circulation between the members and the political center pulses too sluggishly. But it is also clear that no uniform standard for this can be ascertained. State purposes, for example, might be attained even with a very numerous population, if this population, through improved means of communication, is able to carry on a lively exchange within itself and with the monarchic or democratic or whatever other kind of political head it may have. This will be the case especially when the population's nationality, religion, and so on do not comprise too many disparate elements, constituting in themselves a tendency toward separation. On the other hand, the disadvantages for states whose populations are too small are clearly visible. Not only do they find themselves constantly dependent on greater powers, but also they cannot find within themselves, not always at least, sufficient intelligence and those specific talents necessary for satisfactory maintenance of the various functions of government. This lack is often evident enough in the smaller German states and in the smaller cantons of Switzerland. And so there state costs become relatively higher, because not *all* expenses can be adjusted to the small size of the population, because in political budgets as well as private ones, the smaller economic unit is relatively the more expensive one. Many useful institutions are quite impossible in states that are too small, or not so valuable as they might be in larger political organizations. For example, the introduction of the jury system has survived even in the little canton of Geneva, even though in such a cramped space the parties must stand in harsh confrontation with each other; and in this lies a really important hint that the objections some people make to introducing this sound institution are based, if not on ill will, then surely on prejudice and lack of understanding. But it remains true, all the same, that only in large states can the problem of biased judgments be taken care of by removing the case from the normally competent jury for trial in another district; that is, only larger states can avoid the drawbacks a small state may experience in all its institutions, including even the jury system. Finally, a state with a very small population lacks freedom of action in that it is not in a position to initiate important social reforms. Suppose it is a question, say, of effective measures against the ever more glaring disproportion between rich and poor, perhaps through progressive taxes on incomes or estates, or through regulation of the wages or hours of labor. There is more reason to fear in smaller states than in larger that these measures would result in the emigration of capital and sharp disturbances in production and in all economic areas. Considering the present organization of justice and of the various branches of administration in most European countries, it may be said that the *usual* political requirements and interests can be adequately served with a population of half a million or more, as in the middle states of the German Confederation. But this is not nearly enough for unusual undertakings, nor for the protection of political independence against the outside. In fact, the era of petty states is close to its end. For through the same law by which great industry swallows up small, by a law that rules *all* branches of human activity, small states themselves must become less and less important politically, with the progress of culture and the related development of power. One need only think of changes in military methods and the growing application of industry to warfare. In feudal times, any knight could defy even numerous enemies from behind the walls of his castle, and thus maintain a kind of political independence. But then the introduction of gunpowder opened the way for the creation of larger states; and with the support of newer inventions and discoveries it is still working in the same direction. For even armies work now more than ever with machinelike power; and just as when a steamship of forty horsepower must go to the bottom when it is struck by one of four hundred, whatever the gallantry of its crew, so it is when a great army collides with one that is too small. The conscious purpose or the instinct of self-preservation, consequently, urges peoples splintered into many states toward closer union. But there is at the same time a strong effort to maintain or validate natural characteristics, and thus a hatred for the deadly monotony of centralization. Both can be reached together only in the form of a federal state, an organism of organisms, a political association of associations. All fragmented nations, like the Germans and the Italians, strive visibly toward this form as the model of their political futures. Switzerland, too, seeks first a stronger and deeper unity within herself, so that perhaps at a later time she may join a larger national and state community, not to relinquish her independence but to maintain it.

Very significant differences in population densities are to be found not only between different continents, but also within the European state system, and even between countries on nearly the same cultural level. In the year 1840 the Austrian monarchy had on the average 3,025 inhabitants per square mile, Prussia 2,863; the states of the German Confederation without Austria and Prussia, 3,660; France 3,604; Switzerland 3,103; Holland and Belgium 6,158. All data respecting changes in population come under the new statistical term *movement* or development of population. Components of the movement are births and deaths, and also immigration and emigration, though the latter in their volume so far have been of less importance for the European states. The number of births depends mainly on the number and the fertility of marriages, because in existing experience illegitimate births have contributed a distinctly smaller number. In moderate climates, full puberty begins with men at 22 years, with women at 17, and it ceases at 60 and at 48 respectively. The question arises: If marriages were made at the age when full puberty is reached, how many children would result from the working of pure natural law? It is obvious that this question *cannot* be answered on the basis of individual cases, nor by simple calculation of the regular period of pregnancy and *possible* conception after childbirth; for the physiological possibilities of procreation and birth cannot be determined in that way. Here there are no certain points of reference, and for Mohl to assume that on the average ten children can come from every marriage is only a rough hypothesis. The proportion is actually quite different, partly indeed because most marriages are formed at a later age, partly because the prevailing diet also influences procreative powers, and partly because economic considerations especially can lead to voluntary restraints on the satisfaction of the sexual urge in marriage. It is well-known that the so-called two-child family is traditional in some areas, and sporadically at least this kind of restraint seems quite common, especially in the countryside. Also, not only are there fewer marriages in years of shortages and famine, but fewer legitimate children are born. Thus both the annual number of marriages and their average fertility vary a great deal in the various states according to circumstances. For example it is calculated that in Russia there is annually one marriage for every 92 inhabitants (according to other calculations one for every 110); in densely populated Württemberg there is only one marriage for every 143 to 145 inhabitants. As for the average fertility of marriages, Bickes [1833] tries to divide the European states into three categories. In the first category there are more than 5,000 children for every 1,000 marriages; in the second 4,200 to 4,999; in the third fewer than 4,200. The greater part of Italy, Württemberg, Bohemia, and Portugal belong to the first category; Hessen, Austria, the Netherlands, Mecklenburg, Prussia, and Russia belong to the second; and most of the other states belong to the third category.

The average ratio of annual births to total population in the chief European states ranges between 1:22 and 1:32. Death rate ranges from 1:47 to 1:33. All observations agree that the over-all death rate has declined markedly in Europe during the course of the last century. This is a result of the introduction of smallpox vaccination, progress in medicine and obstetrics, the improvement and increase of healing institutions, and doubtless, too, of generally healthier living habits, resulting from the spread of enlightenment among great masses and the removal of many prejudices and customs injurious to health. In the nature of the case, reforms in sanitation policy especially must have their greatest effect when they are applied to great masses, specifically, in the great cities, where the death rate is still highest, but was far higher before. In London, for example, the average life span was calculated at no more than 6 years for 1728-1739, but it was no less than 26 years in 1820-1829, so that there was a difference of 20 years. The present average life span in Russia is 21 years; in Prussia 30 years (Rau says only 27); in Switzerland 35; in France 32; in Belgium 37 (Quitelet says only 32); in England 39 (Rickman says only 33). From these figures it is apparent that human life becomes more secure as cultural level rises together with the density of population, whereby the means of subsistence and mutal aid and support are multiplied. Political bodies thus appear to be life assurance companies in the most exact and positive sense, and the effectiveness of these organizations grows with the relative number of their members, as indeed all associations are in every way superior when their size permits a specialized functional structure. Existing data permit the assumption that under favorable circumstances the *average* life span can be raised to 40 years, so that a third of mankind would reach their sixtieth year, and a half their thirtieth year; whereas at present the *probable* life span in otherwise thriving states, as for example Belgium, amounts to only 25 years, which is to say that after this interval half the people born in a given year have died. Women have an advantage over men in

average life span, and married persons over unmarried. The kind
of occupation also causes many variations. In England for the
years 1810 to 1820 the death ratio in nineteen purely agricultural
districts was 1:57; in thirteen mixed districts 1:56; and in the ten
purely manufacturing districts 1:54. In Germany it has been found
that clergymen have the best expectation of reaching advanced age,
then peasants, soldiers, physicians. Even more striking are the
differences in death rate according to economic means. Villermé
divided the departments of France into rich and poor on the basis
of taxes paid, and found the death rates to be 1:46 and 1:34 respectively.

The growth of the European population since the beginning of
the eighteenth century has much more to do with the reduction of
mortality resulting from cultural progress than with increased
fertility and frequency of marriages. The fact is that in a number
of European states the number of marriages at least in recent times
has decreased rather than increased. Yet for 1815 to 1830, a period
of peace only partially interrupted by war, Charles Dupin calculated the average annual increase in the European population to
be 12,000 for every million then living; Bickes reckoned 12,390.
From 1815 to 1840 the population of the Austrian Monarchy rose
from 28,179,000 to 36,800,000; in Prussia (1816 to 1840) from
10,588,000 to 14,400,000; in the other states of the German Confederation (1822 to 1840) from 13,575,000 to 15,460,000. The
population of France between the years 1816 and 1840 rose from
29,850,000 to 34,700,000; that of the Low Countries (Belgium and
the Netherlands) since 1815, from 5,278,000 to 6,940,000; Switzerland since 1822, from 1,855,000 to 2,250,000. The famine years
1816 and 1817 held down the population increase immediately
after the peace of 1815; and then the cholera of the years 1831 to
1836 significantly raised mortality in some places. On the whole,
recent statistical data seem to indicate periodic waves in both the
factors that enter into the movement of population. Hoffmann, for
example, found in Prussia during the three four-year periods between 1820 and 1831 a constant increase in mortality—2.63 per
cent, then 2.68, then 2.91, then 3.21. This highest death rate was
only partly a direct result of the cholera, because the districts most
severely hit, considered separately, show an increase only 4/7 as
great as the increase in mortality over-all. A contrary observation
is claimed for Munich in the year 1836, in that the numbers who

died of *other* diseases in the parallel months of 1835 are said to be significantly smaller. But the observations from the Prussian Monarchy extend over a larger area and a longer time. Also it is known that higher mortality was almost general in Europe before the cholera years. It appears therefore that the human organism taken as a whole, just like individuals, is affected by temporary maladies; and that sweeping pestilence for individual groups in the ranks of peoples are to be considered only as extreme symptoms of a more general evil. In the same four three-year periods there was a simultaneous decline of births in Prussia from 4.37 per cent, to 4.25, then 4.04, then 3.83. But in the fruitful years 1832 to 1834 there was a reversal in both respects, wherein the death rate dropped to 3.16 per cent and the birth rate rose to 3.95 per cent. During that whole unfavorable time, however, there was still a progressive growth of population, though at a slower rate. And because, moreover, the wounds left by bloody wars and sweeping pestilence are quickly healed, when with the reduced competition for jobs and sustenance the number of marriages promptly rises, and because at the present stage of culture the science and institutions of healing must be expected to advance rather than retreat, and the over-all causes for the significant general decline in mortality will continue to operate in the future—for these reasons one must expect, with the greatest confidence, that the population of Europe will continue to grow for a long time to come.

The figures used so far to describe the increase have taken into account the annual emigration to foreign continents. Especially in recent years this has indeed risen significantly, in what is still a small part of Europe, specifically the British Isles and several German states; but it would have to become much greater still to exert a very marked influence on the development of population. For many decades Ireland has had the most emigrants, and yet hardly any other European country has increased its population at such a rate, so that only in the past decade has a small decline set in. Also, a greater volume of emigration, just like greater mortality from war or pestilence, and for the same reasons, would bring about a proportional rise in marriages and births; and so for this reason alone, one should not rate its importance too high. In France, nearly twenty-five years of war carried away a relatively larger number of men at the height of their powers than almost any other country has lost by emigration, however great, in recent times. And yet that same France at the conclusion of peace in 1815 had a larger number of people in the *same* space than it had before the Revolution. This continual growth of population, despite all periodic fluctuations and restraints, is rather a sign that Europe has not yet reached its years of physical maturity. Of course, it is obvious that no single period, and especially not the time of peace from 1815 to 1830, can be taken as a guide to the distant future; for in *this* period, for the reasons given, the increase was especially great. But still one may assume without exaggeration that unless Europe falls victim to far more wars, epidemics, and famines than it has during the past half-century, it will experience an average annual increase of 1 per cent and that therefore—allowing for some slight slackening of growth in later years—its population will double in the course of a century. The increase is much faster yet in the New World, so far as we have accurate figures. The United States almost quintupled its population within fifty years; this, indeed, resulted partly from the continuing settlement of immigrants, most of them at a vigorous age, but also from favorable economic circumstances, which have encouraged numerous and early marriages.

In view of these statistical facts, there has been much discussion in recent times concerning the question of when a population is too thin or too dense, and concerning what policies states should adopt in order to overcome the one defect or the other.

[After a history of population policy from the time of Abraham to the beginning of the nineteenth century, the author proceeds:]

It takes only slight acquaintance with the facts and with the comparative compilations of statistics to recognize that there is no more a universally valid standard for the ideal population density of a state than there is for the ideal total population. According to the same law whereby the well-organized and numerous association achieves and produces more, proportionally, than the less numerous, so it must be maintained, in conformity with experience a thousandfold, that states can only attain the higher stages of morality, and of material and spiritual power, when they have dense populations. Therefore it may be the task of policy to take measures that will lead to the growth of population. Under some circumstances it can become appropriate to encourage immigration from foreign countries by offering special advantages. But here the organic interconnection of all political and social life must always be kept in view; and one must consider what the obstacles to faster growth have been. Where sources of subsistence and nourishment are available, the procreative power of man is so prompt that population growth can always be given a push by improving the general prosperity, through better distribution of the instruments of work and their simultaneous liberation from artificial restraints. Thus, in recent times the removal of restrictions on landed property, and its greater freedom of exchange, as well as the abolition of guild compulsion, which has allowed more families to be established, have had decisive influence on the fast increase in the number of inhabitants of many European states. That France increased its population even during the bloodiest of wars should be attributed mainly to these legislative changes. The whole era that lay in the grip of political and religious despotism was unfavorable to population growth. Despotism depopulated the Iberian Peninsula from the time of Charles V and Philip II onward; in the days of the Carthaginians and Romans there had been a much stronger population there than there was under the last weak kings of the House of Austria. But after the end of their rule a gradual rise began in Spain; it was not even interrupted by the revolution set off by antiquated constraint, and it has continued even through the latest decades of invasion and civil war.

On the other hand, it cannot quite be denied that the population density of a state *could* reach a point leading to disproportion with available means of production within a limited area and thus with the limited nourishment available. And though to believe that overpopulation of the whole earth is possible would be to believe in hobgoblins, still a full-bloodedness could develop in certain limbs of the great body of mankind that would be a specific evil, and require particular remedies. The encouragement and organization of a *continual voluntary* emigration in sufficient volume appears especially appropriate to such a situation, and is quite legitimate. But suppose voluntary emigration should prove inadequate. Can then forced emigration be ordered, or can marriage be restricted, either by specific property requirements or by a minimum age, for example 30 to 32 years for men, so that the generations are farther apart? Every state has the right to adopt the measures necessary for the maintenance of the whole; and if no other way out were open, then the state would have the right to restrict personal liberty in the ways described. But it must be understood that the forced emigration must be applied equally to *all* classes of the population without distinction of wealth or social estate, so far as individuals are eligible, as in the case of universal obligation for military duty. Otherwise the result would be a highly oppressive exemption in favor of a privileged class, just another kind of inequality, which no people that has attained consciousness of its freedom and its rights will endure for long. This kind of privilege to the disadvantage of the poorer part of the population exists in any situation where permission to marry is conditional on proof of a certain amount of property or a certain income. Thus to the burden of a usually undeserved poverty is added coercion, for the purpose of the state, within the holiest sanctuary of the human personality; and scarcely anything could be more intolerable. Someone may reply that nobody has a right to marry and conceive children if he is unlikely to be able to feed them. Man *always* has the right to satisfy, with moderation, the drives planted in him by nature, and for that reason should not be obliged to leave them unsatisfied. Besides, marriage too is an association for joint gain; and the state, with its abstract general restrictions, cannot know in advance whether its prohibition in given cases may not tend to increase poverty rather than prevent it. To make marriage conditional on a certain amount of property, if it were not to appear the most hateful possible oppression of the poor by the rich, would have to presuppose at a minimum that the state, at the same time and in positive ways, would assume the duty of providing for every poor man the work and the tools that would make it possible for him to earn the property required by law for the founding of a family within a reasonable time. A *universal* delay until a certain age for all classes of the citizenry would indeed be no violation of the general principle of equality before the law; but it would lead to a thousand kinds of harassment and difficulty, because one cannot put off uniformly, for a specified period, the very different reasons for needing or wishing to enter family estate. Besides, any restraint on the legitimate satisfaction of one of the most powerful of natural drives will lead certainly to illegitimate or unnatural satisfaction, spreading crime, excesses, and disease; and with this growing corruption more misery and poverty would perhaps be created among the smaller population than might exist in a larger.

Such measures must be considered especially oppressive tyranny when they come from a government still separated from the people, when they are not a decision of the people themselves, not the *moral, self*-restraint of a *free* citizenry. Only under the rule of freedom can bitter necessity lose its sting. But does there exist in any European state—this is an important question of practical policy —such overpopulation that the resulting misery could be met only with these measures of constant coercion? This must be flatly denied. The quite universal statistical evidence is that so far the volume of necessary foodstuffs is increasing not merely as fast as, but even faster than the population. Consequently, food prices have on the whole, apart from certain shortage years, declined rather than risen. Great uncultivated stretches of tillable land lie open not only in the thinly populated states of eastern Europe, but even in the thickly settled western states, like England, France, and Germany. European Russia, Scandinavia, and the Iberian Peninsula have about 72 million people on 97,000 square miles, only 741 per square mile; and it is clear that here there is enough unused space to support a population many times greater. Russia alone, by conservative estimates, encompasses 50,000 square miles, on each of which with proper cultivation 3,000 people could live, so that the population could easily rise to 100 million. In Spain almost half the tillable land is uncultivated. The same is true of Hungary and the whole of southeastern Europe. But even in states on the highest stage of material culture there are substantial areas still available for cultivation. In industrious Saxony only 1.1 million acres are under the plow. Out of 54 million hectares France has between 7 and 8 million untilled; Belgium has 330,000 uncultivated hectares out of 3,422,000. The area of Great Britain, Ireland, and the lesser islands was estimated in 1827 at not quite 77.4 million acres, and the land capable of cultivation but untilled at about 14.6 million. Recent calculations indicate that out of every 100 hectares, 13 are untilled in Belgium, 27 in France, and 26 in the British Isles. It is quite noteworthy, and instructive in the highest degree, that in the British Isles, despite the extraordinarily strong population increase since the middle of the last century, untilled land has not been brought under cultivation at the same rate; the agricultural population has remained constant, and the surplus has turned almost entirely to industry. Yet the average imports of grains from foreign countries has not increased in anything like the same proportion. This remarkable fact is mainly the result of the great qualitative improvement that has brought a gradual revolution to English agriculture. But even more! During the same period, popular consumption in the British Isles—poor hungry Ireland included—has *on the average* improved both in variety and in quantity. Thus the inhabitants *taken as a whole* are better-nourished than before. And even compared with other states, their consumption of the most essential and useful foodstuffs is significantly larger. The annual per capita consumption of meat in the British Isles is 80 pounds, but in France only 40, and in the German states about the same as France. Consumption of bread and flour is only a little lower in the British Isles than in France; and the far larger consumption of beer, that nourishing liquid bread, more than makes up the difference. And nevertheless it is true that there is a greater measure of misery, want, and deprivation in Great Britain and Ireland than anywhere else, despite the annual rise in average production and consumption. Therefore, there is absolutely no question here of overpopulation *with respect to the total means of subsistence*, but there is indeed a question of economic insecurity for large groups of the working population, and a question of bad distribution of work and of income. The same is true of the other European states with relatively smaller populations. Consequently, the European nations everywhere would have sound reasons to reject *forced* emigration or legal efforts to restrict marriage among the poorer classes. Beyond this, they are perfectly entitled to demand that social reforms be instituted, so that the most natural right of every man is not only recognized in theory but validated in practice, the right to have work of a moderate kind that does not exhaust his powers before his time, to secure free and happy existence and achievement.

Absolute population is always a very important factor in estimating the resources of the state. Because of the great variations in the movement of population and thus in its relative density, it has become a standard task of political arithmetic to calculate the probable period for the doubling of population in the several states. These calculations are very uncertain, for the observation of individual states shows us clearly enough that there are fluctuations that depend on thousands of circumstances, which no human wisdom can see in advance. At the beginning of the eighteenth century the English population was stationary or even declining, so that if the decline had continued at the 1700 rate, the population would have disappeared entirely in 500 years. But then it grew slowly until the middle of the eighteenth century, when as a result of reforms in production a faster growth began, though still only in arithmetical progression. Not until the beginning of the nineteenth century did the movement of population receive new impulse from the blossoming of great industry, so that from then on it rose in geometrical progression. Accordingly, England, if its growth had continued at the 1740 to 1750 rate, would have doubled the number of its inhabitants only after 100 years, whereas in fact this doubling was attained between 1820 and 1830, after 70 to 80 years. Now, if one takes the increase of 1810 to 1820 as a point of departure, another doubling would occur after only 48 years. No matter how wide of the mark calculations from data like these may prove to be, they indicate at least the *possibility* of very significant changes in the political power relationships of states, even without territorial changes. According to Moreau de Jonnès, by these terms the Prussian population would double in 39 years; Austria in 44 (by more recent figures 52); Russia with Poland in 48; and France not for 125 years. Accordingly, France, whose present population is about 4/7 that of the Russian Empire, would face Russia after the passage of a century with less than one-third the population of Russia. Such a decline seems even less exaggerated when one considers that the expected population increase in states already densely settled will not for a long time equal that of the larger, more thinly settled countries, which still have significant cultivable spaces. How foolish it is, then, to dream of political balance of power and systems of stability reckoned by present power bases, for these bases themselves will be overturned by swift and irresistible change. From this standpoint too, it is apparent that the smaller and more densely peopled states in the middle part of our continent must continue to lose power relative to the great eastern realms. So much more urgent is the injunction for closer political unity among reasonably similar elements of the countries of Europe still politically fragmented, in Germany, Switzerland, and Italy. . . .

21. Excerpts from the Report of the Parliamentary Commission of Inquiry into the Poor Laws, 1834

The English New Poor Law of 1834 may be looked upon as an effort to use Malthusian doctrines of population and poverty as bases for legislation. The old Poor Law, based on a statute of the forty-third year of Elizabeth I's reign (1601), had been designed mainly to meet the problems of the infirm and of the vagrant sturdy beggar; it had made each parish responsible for its native paupers and for finding work for them if they were able-bodied. But by the nineteenth century this system had proved inadequate. There were many abuses, and many poor, and the poor tax had become more burdensome than most communities seemed able to bear. The "Utilitarian" followers of Jeremy Bentham (1748–1832), notably Edwin Chadwick (1800–1890), accepted the view that the only natural check on surplus population was extreme economic deprivation, and that this simple principle must be the basis for any direct and effective treatment of the modern problem of population and poverty. In 1832, Parliament appointed a commission, of which Chadwick became the dominant member, to investigate the whole matter. Chadwick's report of the existing situation and proposed remedial measures formed the basis of the 1834 law. [*Report from His Majesty's Commissioners for Inquiring into the Administration and Practical Operation of the Poor Laws* (London, 1834), pp. 21, 24–26, 31–33, 44–47, 49–52, 227–229, 240–241, 261–265. The nature of the material has made extensive editing necessary.]

I. Out-door Relief to the Able-Bodied

A. ALLOWANCE

BY THE parish allowing to labourers, who are employed by individuals, relief in aid of their wages.

The word *allowance* is sometimes used as comprehending all parochial relief afforded to those who are employed by individuals at the average wages of the district. But sometimes this term is confined to the relief which a person so employed obtains on account of his children, any relief which he may obtain on his own account being termed "Payment of Wages out of Rates." In the following Report we shall use the word "allowance" in its former or more comprehensive sense.

In some places allowance is given only occasionally, or to meet occasional wants; to buy, for instance, a coat or a pair of shoes, or to pay the rent of a cottage or an apartment. In others it is considered that a certain weekly sum, or more frequently the value of a certain quantity of flour or bread, is to be received by each member of a family.

The latter practice has sometimes been matured into a system, forming the law of a whole district, sanctioned and enforced by the magistrates, and promulgated in the form of local statutes, under the name of *Scales*.

The following are copies of some of the scales:—

COUNTY OF CAMBRIDGE

The Churchwardens and Overseers of the Poor are requested to regulate the incomes of such persons as may apply to them for relief or employment, according to the price of bread; namely,

A single woman, the price of .	.	3	quartern loaves per week
A single man	. 4	.	ditto
A man and his wife . . .	. 7	.	ditto
Ditto . ditto and one child .	8	.	ditto
Ditto . ditto and two children	9	.	ditto
Ditto . ditto and three ditto .	11	.	ditto

Man, wife, four children and upwards, at the price of two quartern loaves per head per week.

It will be necessary to add to the above income in all cases of sickness or other kind of distress, and particularly of such persons or families who deserve encouragement by their good behaviour, whom parish officers should mark both by commendation and reward.

> By order of the Magistrates assembled at the Shire Hall, Cambridge, December 15th, 1821,
> ROBERT GEE,
> CLERK TO THE MAGISTRATES. . . .

In perhaps a majority of the parishes in which the allowance system prevails, the earnings of the applicant, and, in a few, the earnings of his wife and children, are ascertained, or at least professed or attempted to be ascertained, and only the difference between them and the sum allotted to him by the scale is paid to him by the parish. The following extracts from Mr. Tweedy's Report from Yorkshire, and Mr. Wilson's from Durham, show the mode in which this branch of the allowance system is extending itself over the North of England:—

In Gisburn, the rule and practice of the town is to inquire into the circumstances of each case, and to make up the wages of a man and his family to 1s. 6d. per head. This rule is adopted, because it is the rule by which the magistrates govern themselves on application to them. The course of the magistrates is to inquire of a weaver (for instance) how many pieces he can weave per week, and how much he gets for it. A man will say, perhaps, he can weave three pieces in a week, and would get 1s. 3d. a piece for weaving them; then if he had a family of a wife and four children, they would allow him 5s. 3d. a week.—A man had a sickly wife, and was allowed 5s. a week for her and for a woman to attend her. She died, and in about a year he married again; and on the very day of his marriage, said, "Now I have married again, I'll work Gisburn another round"; and he has been as good as his word, having had three children by the second wife, on account of which he received 2*l.* 11*s.* from January to September in last year.

At Dent, in the same neighbourhood, "relief to the able-bodied is afforded by payments of a weekly or monthly sum in the name of a pension, the amount of which is regulated according to the number of a man's family, after the rate of two shillings a head per week: poor people, especially those who have become pensioners, marry early, more frequently under twenty years of age than above; they are induced to this, no doubt, from a reliance upon relief from the poor-rate. Instances have been numerous in which this has been known to be the case, and in a majority of cases relief is applied for on the birth of the *first* child: the most profligate and dissolute are amongst this class, and if they get a little extra pay at any time, they spend it in drinking, leaving their families to be maintained by the township."

At Kettlewell (in Craven) and the neighbourhood, the same system prevails. "The rule of the magistrates is to allow so much as will yield one shilling and sixpence a head per week, and the overseers take this rule therefore as their guide. The overseer has sometimes called upon little farmers for their rates, and found that they had *no* provisions of any kind in the house, *nor* money to buy any; while on the other hand, he has not unfrequently been obliged to give relief to men who, there is no doubt, could have procured work if they had exerted themselves: they speak of it as a matter of right; and, if what they ask be not granted, they threaten to appeal to the magistrate; and, as he lives *fifteen* miles off, the overseers are often induced to yield to their demands, on account of the *expense* of meeting the claim before him."

The places above-named are within the jurisdiction of one bench of magistrates.

At Pateley Bridge many are relieved in degree when the wages they earn are not sufficient. It is reckoned that 1*s.* 9*d.* per head for each member of the family is necessary, except for infants, and that rule the overseers act upon. One magistrate, however, allows 2*s.* 6*d.* each for husband and wife, and 1*s.* 6*d.* for each child. Relief is demanded as a matter of right, and sometimes with insolence. An instance is mentioned as occurring some years ago, in which a man came and said, "We have been getting married; can you find us a house?" and another instance occurred two years ago, in which a man came out of Craven, and claimed relief a few weeks after marriage, and was insolent in his demand.

At Knaresborough the paupers are chiefly weavers of linen and flax dressers; if they are wholly out of work, the rule is to allow a man and his wife 6*s.* a week, and 9*d.* for each child: a single man 3*s.* a week. This rate is allowed, because the magistrates allow it;

but in fact, in many cases, it amounts to *more* than a man, when trade is flourishing, could earn. If a man has partial work, they give him 1s. 6d. or 2s. a week, or as little as they can satisfy him with, knowing that, if he goes before the magistrate, he will allow him such a sum as, with his earnings, will make up the rate above mentioned. Immediately that a man is out of work *now*, he comes for relief; and, if he be not relieved at once, he goes to a magistrate, who grants a summons, and makes a memorandum upon it, directing the overseer to relieve him in the mean time.

In Darlington, in the county of Durham (says Mr. Wilson), allowances to able-bodied labourers are graduated according to the numbers in their families; and whenever the wages of any class of labourers (for example, of the linen weavers, who have latterly been the most distressed) fall below the amount appointed by the scale, the difference is made up as a matter of course by the parish. The scale awards 2s. a head a-week to heads of families, and 1s. 6d. for each of the children under 12 years of age. This is the minimum of allowance paid by the parish in all cases. Suppose a single man to earn 2s. a week, he could put forward no claim to relief. Suppose another, earning the same wages, but possessing besides a wife and six children, then 2s. a head for himself and his wife, and 1s. 6d. a head for each of his children, give a total amount of 13s. weekly. In this second case the *family man* has a recognized claim on the parish for an allowance of 11s. weekly, making up his earnings of 2s. by the above-mentioned graduated scale.

Some remarkable instances of this occurred on Wednesday, January 9th, at the meeting of the parish committee. One applicant owned he had earned 21s. during the last fortnight; but because he had not applied within the last month to the parish, and his average during that period had not been made up (he had four children), he now applied to have the deficit made up, which was done accordingly. Another man was earning 9s. a week; he had six children; 4s. were handed over the table to him immediately.

A third had seven children, with himself and his wife, making nine in family. He stated that his average earnings were 9s. a week. Last week he had been out of work for a day or two, and consequently had earned only 5s. The parish had found two days' work for him, which made up his earnings to 7s.: 7s. 6d. additional were handed to him over the table. . . .

B. THE ROUNDSMAN SYSTEM

By the parish paying the occupiers of property to employ the applicants for relief at a rate of wages fixed by the parish, and depending not on the services, but on the wants of the applicants, the employer being repaid out of the poor-rate all that he advances in wages beyond a certain sum. This is the house row, or roundsmen, or billet, or ticket, or stem, system.

According to this plan, the parish in general makes some agreement with a farmer to sell to him the labour of one or more paupers at a certain price, and pays to the pauper, out of the parish funds, the difference between that price and the allowance which the scale, according to the price of bread and the number of his family, awards to him. It has received the name of the billet or ticket system, from the ticket signed by the overseer, which the pauper, in general, carries to the farmer as a warrant for his being employed, and takes back to the overseer, signed by the farmer, as a proof that he has fulfilled the conditions of relief. In other cases the parish contracts with some individual to have some work performed for him by the paupers at a given price, the parish paying the paupers. In many places the roundsman system is effected by means of an auction. Mr. Richardson states that, in Sulgrave, Northamptonshire, the old and infirm are sold at the monthly meeting to the best bidder, at prices varying, according to the time of the year, from 1s. 6d. a week to 3s.; that at Yardley, Hastings, all the unemployed men are put up to sale weekly, and that the clergyman of the parish told him that he had seen ten men the last week knocked down to one of the farmers for 5s., and that there were at that time about 70 men let out in this manner out of a body of 170.

The following extracts, from the Answers to our printed Queries for rural districts, are further examples of all these forms of relief:—

GREAT HENNY, ESSEX—*William Newport*, Churchwarden; *Edward Cook*, Overseer

Having so many labouring men, the income from the land will not allow us to give more than is sufficient for the best characters to subsist upon, and we are obliged to give the same to the worst. A man of bad character, on account of which he is not employed, having two children or more, applies to the parish at the end of the week for relief, through loss of time, and has the same money given him as the honest labourer receives of his master for his labour for the same week.

HARLOW, ESSEX—*Isaac Rogers*, Overseer

We are obliged to maintain the family if the man is idle.

CASTLE HEDINGHAM—*Ashurst Majendie*, Deputy Lieutenant, Member of Vestry

Rent was, at one period, paid by the parish, by which an artificial price was kept up; since the practice has been discontinued, the rent of cottages has fallen.

GOUDHURST, KENT—*Giles Miller*

Every man having more than three children upon his hands, comes to the parish for support for all above the third: it is granted as a matter of course.

The word "scale" is unknown, but the thing exists as effectually as if it were published by authority at every petty sessions. Every parish officer and pauper knows that a man with his wife and three children is entitled to have his wages "*made up*" (such is the phrase) to 12s. a week; and he is entitled to 1s. 6d. per week for every child beyond three; and without entering into any very rigid account as to the average of his earnings. Extra receipts are supposed to go for clothes and extra payments: in reality, they too often go to the beer shop. . . .

General Remarks on Out-door Relief

We have dwelt at some length on out-door relief, because it appears to be the relief which is now most extensively given, and because it appears to contain in itself the elements of an almost indefinite extension; of an extension, in short, which may ultimately absorb the whole fund out of which it arises. Among the elements of extension are the constantly diminishing reluctance to claim an apparent benefit, the receipt of which imposes no sacrifice, except a sensation of shame quickly obliterated by habit, even if not prevented by example; the difficulty often amounting to impossibility on the part of those who administer and award relief, of ascertaining whether any and what necessity for it exists; and the existence in many cases of positive motives on their parts to grant it when unnecessary, or themselves to create the necessity. The first and third of these sources of mal-administration are common to the towns and to the country; the second, the difficulty of ascertaining the wants of the applicant, operates most strongly in the large towns, and is well displayed in the following extract from the Report of Mr. Chadwick, on the Eastern Division of the Metropolis:—

George Huish, Assistant Overseer of the Parish of Saint George's, Southwark

I have lived in the parish upwards of 40 years, and have served office upwards of 12 years, and before that time I had cognizance of much parochial business with a relation.

The most injurious portion of the Poor Law system is the out-door relief. I do not serve a day without seeing some new mischiefs arise from it. In the smaller parishes, persons are liable to all sorts of influences. In such a parish as ours, where we administer relief to upwards of 2000 out-door poor, it is utterly impossible to prevent considerable fraud, whatever vigilance is exercised.

Has the utmost vigilance been tried?—One man to every 20 would be required to watch the paupers living out of the parish, and one man to watch every 100 living within the parish; which is an expense of inspection which could not be borne. Suppose you go to a man's house as a visitor: you ask, where is Smith (the pauper)? You see his wife or his children, who say they do not know where he is, but that they believe he is gone in search of work. How are you to tell, in such a case, whether he is at work or not? It could only be by following him in the morning; and you must do that every day, because he may be in work one day, and not another. Suppose you have a shoemaker who demands relief of you, and you give it him on his declaring that he is out of work. You visit his place, and you find him in work; you say to him, as I have said to one of our own paupers, "Why, Edwards, I thought you said you had no work?" and he will answer, "Neither had I any; and I have only got a little job *for the day*." He will also say directly, "I owe for my rent; I have not paid my chandler's shop score; I have been summoned, and I expect an execution out against me, and if you stop my relief, I must come home," (that is, he must go into the workhouse). The overseer is immediately frightened by this, and says, "What a family that man has got! it will not do to stop his relief." So that, unless you have a considerable number of men to watch every pauper every day, you are sure to be cheated. Some of the out-door paupers are children, others are women; but, taking one with another, I think it would require one man's whole time to watch every twenty paupers.

Does the practice of obtaining out-door relief extend amongst respectable classes of mechanics, whose work and means of living are tolerably good?—I am every week astonished by seeing persons come whom I never thought would have come. The greater number of our out-door paupers are worthless people; but still the number of decent people who ought to have made provision for themselves, and who come, is very great, and increasing. One brings another; one member of a family brings the rest of a family. Thus I find, in two days' relief, the following names:—"John Arundell, a sawyer, aged 55; his son

William, aged 22, a wire-drawer; Ann Harris, 58, her husband is in Greenwich Hospital; her son John, and his wife, also came separately; so does their son, a lad aged 18, a smith." Thus we have pauper father, pauper wife, pauper son, and pauper grandchildren, frequently applying on the same relief-day. One neighbor brings another. Not long since a very young woman, a widow, named Cope, who is not more than 20 years of age, applied for relief; she had only one child. After she had obtained relief, I had some suspicion that there was something about this young woman not like many others. I spoke to her, and pressed her to tell me the real truth as to how so decent a young woman as herself came to us for relief: she replied that she was "gored" into it. That was her expression. I asked her what she meant by being gored into it. She stated, that where she was living there were only five cottages, and that the inhabitants of four out of five of these cottages were receiving relief, two from St. Saviour's, and two from Newington parish. They had told her that she was not worthy of living in the same place unless she obtained relief too.

Indeed, the malady of pauperism has not only got amongst respectable mechanics, but we find even persons who may be considered of the middle classes, such as petty masters, small master bricklayers, and other such persons, who have never before been seen making application to parish officers, now applying. My opinion is, that they apply in consequence of having witnessed the ease with which others who might have provided for themselves obtain relief. They naturally say, "Why should we be content with half a loaf when we might have a whole one?" A few days ago a man applied for relief, stating that he was in great distress. On inquiry, it was found that he held a situation as packer, and actually received wages of the amount of 20s. per week, at the time he made the application, and had been in the receipt of them for some time previous. We found that one woman had received relief from us for two years, whilst she was receiving from the East India Company a pension of 70l. per annum. In one instance, we discovered that a man, named James Peaton, was receiving relief of six different parishes; he belonged to our parish, and he had picked out five other parishes, which gave relief on the five other days. He made it his entire business to live on parish pensions, and he received one week's pension every day.

Since the inquiry has been made, I have stationed persons at well-known gin-shops to observe the number of paupers who came, and the money they spend; and, from all their statements, I have drawn the conclusion that 30l. out of every 100l. of the money given as out-door relief, is spent in the gin-shops during the same day.

From the preceding evidence it will be seen how zealous must be the agency, and how intense the vigilance, to prevent fraudulent claims crowding in under such a system of relief. But it would require still greater vigilance to prevent the *bona fide* claimants degenerating into impostors; and it is an aphorism amongst the active parish officers that "cases which are good to-day are bad to-morrow, unless they are incessantly watched." A person obtains relief on the ground of sickness; when he has become capable of returning to moderate work, he is tempted, by the enjoyment of subsistence without labour, to conceal his convalescence, and fraudulently extend the period of relief. When it really depends upon the receivers whether the relief shall cease with its occasion, it is too much to expect of their virtue that they shall, in any considerable number of instances, voluntarily forego the pension.

The permanent officers appointed to make inquiries at the residence of the out-door paupers frankly acknowledge, that it is beyond the powers of any individuals to prevent an immense amount of fraud. We add the following instances from Mr. Chadwick's Report:—

Mr. Thorn, assistant overseer of the parish of Saint Giles, Cripplegate, London, states—

> The out-door relief in the city of London would require almost one man to look after every half dozen of able-bodied men, and then he would only succeed imperfectly in preventing fraud. They cheat us on all hands. I have had instances where the masters who have employed out-door paupers have given such answers to my inquiries, as to leave no doubt in my mind that the master concealed the real amount of wages, for fear that if he caused the parish to reduce the man's allowance he should have to pay him higher wages. There is no protection whatever from the growing evil of the increase of the able-bodied out-door poor, which is one of the greatest evils of the system, but in finding them labour out of town.

Mr. Samuel Miller, assistant overseer in the parish of Saint Sepulchre, London, declares that—

> With respect to the out-door relief, there must, from the very nature of it, be an immense deal of fraud. There is no industry, no inspection, no human skill, which will prevent gross impositions belonging to this mode of relief.
>
> By far the greater proportion of our new paupers are persons brought upon the parish by habits of intemperance, and the others are chiefly pauper children or hereditary paupers.
>
> After relief has been received at our board, a great portion of them

proceed with the money to the palaces of gin-shops, which abound in the neighbourhood.

Mr. William Weale, assistant overseer of the parish of Lambeth, whose chief business is the investigation of the cases of out-door paupers, after specifying the modes of examination, concludes by stating, that after all—

However diligent an assistant overseer, or an officer for inquiry, may be, there are numerous cases which will baffle his utmost diligence and sagacity; the only test of these cases is making their condition more severe than that of the lowest class of labourers who obtain their livelihood by honest industry.

Mr. Luke Teather, another officer of great experience in the same business, adds, that as—

It is the study of bad paupers to deceive you all they can, and as they study more their own cases than any inquirer can study each of the whole mass of different cases which he has to inquire into, they are sure to be successful in a great many instances. The only protection for the parish is to make the parish the hardest taskmaster and the worst paymaster that can be applied to. . . .

It appears from all our returns, especially from the replies to question 53, of the Rural Queries, that in every district, the discontent of the labouring classes is proportioned to the money dispensed in poor's-rates, or in voluntary charities. The able-bodied unmarried labourers are discontented, from being put to a disadvantage as compared with the married. The paupers are discontented, from their expectations being raised by the ordinary administration of the system, beyond any means of satisfying them. "They, as well as the independent labourers, to whom the term poor is equally applied, are instructed," says Mr. Chadwick, "that they have a right to a 'reasonable subsistence,' or 'a fair subsistence,' or 'an adequate subsistence.' When I have asked of the rate distributors what 'fair,' or 'reasonable,' or 'adequate' meant, I have in every instance been answered differently; some stating they thought it meant such as would give a good allowance of 'meat every day,' which no poor man (meaning a pauper) should be without; although a large proportion of the rate-payers do go without it." It is abundantly shown in the course of this inquiry, that where the terms used by the public authorities are vague, they are always filled up by the desires of the claimants, and the desires always wait on the imagination, which is the worst regulated and the most vivid in the most ignorant of the people. In Newbury and Reading, the money dispensed in poor's-rates and charity is as great as could be desired by the warmest advocate either of compulsory or of voluntary relief; and yet, during the agricultural riots, many of the inhabitants in both towns were under strong apprehensions of the rising of the very people amongst whom the poor-rates and charities are so profusely distributed. The violence of most of the mobs seems to have arisen from an idea that all their privations arose from the cupidity or fraud of those entrusted with the management of the fund provided for the poor. Those who work, though receiving good wages, being called *poor*, and classed with the really indigent, think themselves entitled to a share of the "poor funds." Whatever addition is made to allowances under these circumstances, excites the expectation of still further allowances; increases the conception of the extent of the right, and ensures proportionate disappointment and hatred if that expectation is not satisfied. On the other hand, wherever the objects of expectation have been made definite, where wages, upon the performance of work, have been substituted for eleemosynary aid, and those wages have been allowed to remain matter of contract, employment has again produced content, and kindness become again a source of gratitude.

II. In-doors Relief

In-doors Relief, that which is given within the walls of the Poor-house, or as it is usually, but very seldom, properly denominated the Workhouse, is also subject to great mal-administration. When Mr. Chadwick's account of Reading was published, many readers thought that the management of the workhouses, described by him, must be an exception to the general rule. It is probable that the smallness of those workhouses prevents their inmates from suffering so much from the misconduct of one another, as is the case in the larger workhouses. But in all other respects, in the absence of classification, discipline, and employment, and the extravagance of allowances, the Reading workhouses seem to be merely fair specimens of the ordinary workhouses in thriving towns. The description of many of the London workhouses, in the Evidence collected by Mr. Codd, is still less favourable than the Report from Reading.

Mr. W. Lee, who has, for seventeen years, held the office of master of the workhouse of St. Pancras, containing more than 1000 inmates, says,—

It is a common remark among our paupers that they live better in the house than they ever lived before; and looking to the cleanliness, the airiness and roominess of the apartments, the goodness of the beds and bedding, and the wholesomeness and quantity of the food, this is probably the case. There are 300 children; if we get them places they throw them up, or misconduct themselves so as to lose them, and return to the workhouse as a matter of course, because they prefer the security and certainty of that mode of life to the slightest exercise of forbearance or diligence. As little or no classification can take place, the younger soon acquire all the bad habits of the older, and become for the most part as vitiated. This is peculiarly the case with respect to young girls. We are obliged to have many prostitutes among our inmates: they decoy the young girls, with whom they have met in the house, to leave it, and addict themselves to the same abandoned course.

Mr. Bryand, clerk to the overseers of St. James's, Westminster, states, that the workhouse contains 811 persons, and that the parish has, besides, about 40 refractory poor in places called farm-houses, who, in consequence of their bad character, are excluded from the regular establishment. The workhouse inmates, therefore, are people of comparatively good character; and Mr. Bryand considers the workhouse to be better managed than most workhouses, or certainly as well.

He goes on to say,—

Our paupers are allowed to leave the workhouse for one day in each week. It is a very common occurrence for both men and women, on the days that they are let out, to return in a state of intoxication. They are let out on the weekly days, about one o'clock, after dinner, and on festival days early in the morning: on these latter days, it not unfrequently happens that paupers, especially women, are brought into the house by constables or policemen, before twelve o'clock, in a beastly state of intoxication; they are received as a matter of course, and the care of the governor and matron is applied, not to their punishment, but to keeping them quiet and peaceable: if they can be rendered so, they are put to bed, and no further notice is taken of the case; if they cannot, and they are very violent and riotous, the heads of the house are obliged to have recourse to assistance to hold them or tie them down in their beds.

We have in the house many women who are known to be prostitutes; we have also notorious thieves. I recollect, in particular, W. Thomas and J. Selburn, now young men; both of them were brought up from infancy in the workhouse; these men are always supported either by the county or in the parish, except what they get by thieving. I am persuaded that parish poor-houses, as at present administered, have the effect of attracting paupers. . . .

III. Remedial Measures

The most pressing of the evils which we have described are those connected with the relief of the Able-bodied. They are the evils, therefore, for which we shall first propose remedies.

If we believed the evils stated in the previous part of the Report, or evils resembling or even approaching them, to be necessarily incidental to the compulsory relief of the able-bodied, we should not hesitate in recommending its entire abolition. But we do not believe these evils to be its necessary consequences. We believe that, under strict regulations, adequately enforced, such relief may be afforded safely and even beneficially.

In all extensive communities, circumstances will occur in which an individual, by the failure of his means of subsistence, will be exposed to the danger of perishing. To refuse relief, and at the same time to punish mendicity when it cannot be proved that the offender could have obtained subsistence by labour, is repugnant to the common sentiments of mankind; it is repugnant to them to punish even depredation, apparently committed as the only resource against want.

In all extensive civilized communities, therefore, the occurrence of extreme necessity is prevented by alms-giving, by public institutions supported by endowments or voluntary contributions, or by a provision partly voluntary and partly compulsory, or by a provision entirely compulsory, which may exclude the pretext of mendicancy.

But in no part of Europe except England has it been thought fit that the provision, whether compulsory or voluntary, should be applied to more than the relief of *indigence*, the state of a person unable to labour, or unable to obtain, in return for his labour, the means of subsistence. It has never been deemed expedient that the provision should extend to the relief of *poverty;* that is, the state of one, who, in order to obtain a mere subsistence, is forced to have recourse to labour.

From the evidence collected under this Commission, we are induced to believe that a compulsory provision for the relief of the indigent can be generally administered on a sound and well-defined principle; and that under the operation of this principle, the assurance that no one need perish from want may be rendered more complete than at present, and the mendicant and vagrant repressed by disarming them of their weapon,—the plea of impending starvation.

It may be assumed, that in the administration of relief, the public is warranted in imposing such conditions on the individual relieved, as are conducive to the benefit either of the individual himself, or of the country at large, at whose expense he is to be relieved.

The first and most essential of all conditions, a principle which we find universally admitted, even by those whose practice is at variance with it, is, that his situation on the whole shall not be made really or apparently so eligible as the situation of the independent labourer of the lowest class. Throughout the evidence it is shown, that in proportion as the condition of any pauper class is elevated above the condition of independent labourers, the condition of the independent class is depressed; their industry is impaired, their employment becomes unsteady, and its remuneration in wages is diminished. Such persons, therefore, are under the strongest inducements to quit the less eligible class of labourers and enter the more eligible class of paupers. The converse is the effect when the pauper class is placed in its proper position, below the condition of the independent labourer. Every penny bestowed, that tends to render the condition of the pauper more eligible than that of the independent labourer, is a bounty on indolence and vice. We have found, that as the poor's-rates are at present administered, they operate as bounties of this description, to the amount of several millions annually.

The standard, therefore, to which reference must be made in fixing the condition of those who are to be maintained by the public, is the condition of those who are maintained by their own exertions. But the evidence shows how loosely and imperfectly the situation of the independent labourer has been inquired into, and how little is really known of it by those who award or distribute relief. It shows also that so little has their situation been made a standard for the supply of commodities, that the diet of the workhouse almost always exceeds that of the cottage, and the diet of the gaol is generally more profuse than even that of the workhouse. It shows also, that this standard has been so little referred to in the exaction of labour, that commonly the work required from the pauper is inferior to that performed by the labourers and servants of those who have prescribed it: So much and so generally inferior as to create a prevalent notion among the agricultural paupers that they have a right to be exempted from the amount of work which is performed and indeed sought for by the independent labourer.

We can state, as the result of the extensive inquiries made under this Commission into the circumstances of the labouring classes, that the agricultural labourers when in employment, in common with the other classes of labourers throughout the country, have greatly advanced in condition; that their wages will now produce to them more of the necessaries and comforts of life than at any former period. These results appear to be confirmed by the evidence collected by the Committees of the House of Commons appointed to inquire into the condition of the agricultural and manufacturing classes, and also by that collected by the Factory Commissioners. No body of men save money whilst they are in want of what they deem absolute necessaries. No common man will put by a shilling whilst he is in need of a loaf, or will save whilst he has a pressing want unsatisfied. The circumstance of there being nearly fourteen millions in the savings banks, and the fact that, according to the last returns, upwards of 29,000 of the depositors were agricultural labourers, who, there is reason to believe, are usually the heads of families, and also the fact of the reduction of the general average of mortality, justify the conclusion, that a condition worse than that of the independent agricultural labourer, may nevertheless be a condition above that in which the great body of English labourers have lived in times that have always been considered prosperous. Even if the condition of the independent labourer were to remain as it now is, and the pauper were to be reduced avowedly below that condition, he might still be adequately supplied with the necessaries of life.

But it will be seen that the process of dispauperizing the ablebodied is in its ultimate effects a process which elevates the condition of the great mass of society.

In all the instances which we have met with, where parishes have

been dispauperized, the effect appears to have been produced by
the practical application of the principle which we have set forth
as the main principle of a good Poor-Law administration, namely,
the restoration of the pauper to a position below that of the independent labourer.

The principle adopted in the parish of Cookham, Berks, is thus
stated:—

> As regards the able-bodied labourers who apply for relief, giving
> them hard work at low wages by the piece, and exacting more work
> at a lower price than is paid for any other labour in the parish. In
> short, to adopt the maxim of Mr. Whately, to let the labourer find
> that the parish is the hardest taskmaster and the worst paymaster he
> can find, and thus induce him to make his application to the parish
> his last and not his first resource. . . .

The next class of specific effects which have followed the application of the principle of keeping the condition of the pauper inferior to that of the independent labourer, is, that it has arrested
the increase of population, which the evidence shows to be produced by the present state of the law and of its administration.

In the parish of Burghfield, Mr. Samuel Cliff, the assistant overseer, states that he was—

> Convinced that the discontinuance of the allowance system had
> saved the parish from destruction; it did this by the immediate check
> which it gave to population. Whilst the allowance system went on, it
> was a common thing for young people to come to me for parish
> relief two or three days after they were married: nay, I have had
> them come to me just as they came out of church and apply to me
> for a loaf of bread to eat, and for a bed to lie on that night, and,
> moreover, for a house for them to live in. But this sort of marriages
> is now checked, and in a few years the parish will probably be
> brought about. If the former system had gone on, we should have
> been swallowed up in a short time.
> Is your knowledge of the individuals resident in your parish such
> that you can state without doubt that there are persons in it, now
> single, who would, under the influence of the system of allowing
> rates in aid of wages, have married had that system been continued?—
> I have no doubt whatever that several of them would have married;
> I know them so well that I am sure of it.

In the Report from Cookham, it is stated, that "some very striking consequences have resulted from the operation of the present
system. In the eight years preceding the operation of the new sys-

tem, the increase of population was very rapid; for the eight years subsequent there was, as compared with the eight years preceding, a positive diminution. Improvident marriages are less frequent." In the Report from Swallowfield, it is stated, that, "the number of improvident marriages is diminished about one-half." In Bingham, the diminution of improvident marriages was about one-half; and yet, in all these three parishes, illegitimate births, instead of having been promoted by the diminution of marriages, have been repressed still more effectually, and in the last, almost extinguished. . . .

From the above evidence it appears, that wherever the principle which we have thus stated has been carried into effect, either wholly or partially, its introduction has been beneficial to the class for whose benefit Poor-Laws exist. We have seen that in every instance in which the able-bodied labourers have been rendered independent of partial relief, or of relief otherwise than in a well-regulated workhouse—

1. Their industry has been restored and improved.
2. Frugal habits have been created or strengthened.
3. The permanent demand for their labour has increased.
4. And the increase has been such, that their wages, so far from being depressed by the increased amount of labour in the market, have in general advanced.
5. The number of improvident and wretched marriages has diminished.
6. Their discontent has been abated, and their moral and social condition in every way improved.

Results so important would, even with a view to the interest of that class exclusively, afford sufficient ground for the general introduction of the principle of administration under which those results have been produced. Considering the extensive benefits to be anticipated from the adoption of measures, founded on principles already tried and found beneficial, and warned at every part of the inquiry by the failure of previous legislation, we shall, in the suggestion of specific remedies, endeavour not to depart from the firm ground of actual experience.

We therefore submit, as the general principle of legislation on this subject, in the present condition of the country:—

That those modes of administering relief which have been tried wholly or partially, and have produced beneficial effects in some districts, be introduced, with modifications according to local circumstances, and carried into complete execution in all.

⸀The chief specific measures which we recommend for effecting these purposes, are—

First, That except as to medical attendance, and subject to the exception respecting apprenticeship hereinafter stated, all relief whatever to able-bodied persons or to their families, otherwise than in well-regulated workhouses (*i. e.*, places where they may be set to work according to the spirit and intention of the 43d of Elizabeth) shall be declared unlawful, and shall cease, in manner and at periods hereafter specified; and that all relief afforded in respect of children under the age of 16, shall be considered as afforded to their parents.

It is true, that nothing is necessary to arrest the progress of pauperism, except that all who receive relief from the parish should work for the parish exclusively, as hard and for less wages than independent labourers work for individual employers, and we believe that in most districts useful work, which will not interfere with the ordinary demand for labour, may be obtained in greater quantity than is usually conceived. Cases, however, will occur where such work cannot be obtained in sufficient quantity to meet an immediate demand; and when obtained, the labour, by negligence, connivance, or otherwise, may be made merely formal, and thus the provisions of the legislature may be evaded more easily than in a workhouse. A well-regulated workhouse meets all cases, and appears to be the only means by which the intention of the statute of Elizabeth, that all the able-bodied shall be set to work, can be carried into execution.

The out-door relief of which we have recommended the abolition, is in general partial relief, which, as we have intimated, is at variance with the spirit of the 43d of Elizabeth, for the framers of that act could scarcely have intended that the overseers should "take order for setting to work" those who have work, and are engaged in work: nor could they by the words "all persons using *no* ordinary and daily trade of life to get their living by," have intended to describe persons "who *do* use an ordinary and daily trade of life."

Wherever the language of the legislature is uncertain, the prin-

ciple of administration, as well as of legal construction, is to select
the course which will aid the remedy; and with regard to the able-
bodied, the remedy set forth in the statute is to make the indolent
industrious. In proposing further remedial measures we shall keep
that object steadily in view.

And although we admit that able-bodied persons in the receipt
of out-door allowances and partial relief, may be, and in some cases
are, placed in a condition less eligible than that of the independent
labourer of the lowest class; yet to persons so situated, relief in a
well-regulated workhouse would not be a hardship: and even if it
be, in some rare cases, a hardship, it appears from the evidence that
it is a hardship to which the good of society requires the applicant to
submit. The express or implied ground of his application is, that
he is in danger of perishing from want. Requesting to be rescued
from that danger out of the property of others, he must accept
assistance on the terms, whatever they may be, which the common
welfare requires. The bane of all pauper legislation has been the
legislating for extreme cases. Every exception, every violation of
the general rule to meet a real case of unusual hardship, lets in a
whole class of fraudulent cases, by which that rule must in time
be destroyed. Where cases of real hardship occur, the remedy must
be applied by individual charity, a virtue for which no system of
compulsory relief can be or ought to be a substitute.

The preceding evidence, as to the actual operation of remedial
measures, relates principally to rural parishes. We shall now show,
from portions of the evidence as to the administration of relief
upon a correct principle in towns, that by an uniform application
of the principle which we recommend, or, in other words, by a
recurrence to the original intention of the poor-laws, other evils
produced by the present system of partial relief to the able-bodied
will be remedied. The principal of the further evils which it would
extirpate is, the tendency of that system to constant and indefinite
increase, independently of any legitimate causes, a tendency which
we have shown to arise from the irresistible temptations to fraud
on the part of the claimants. These temptations we have seen are
afforded—

First. By the want of adequate means, or of diligence and ability,
even where the means exist, to ascertain the truth of the statements
on which claims to relief are founded:

Secondly. By the absence of the check of shame, owing to the want of a broad line of distinction between the class of independent labourers and the class of paupers, and the degradation of the former by confounding them with the latter:

Thirdly. By the personal situation, connexions, interests, and want of appropriate knowledge on the part of the rate distributors, which render the exercise of discretion in the administration of all relief, and especially of out-door relief, obnoxious to the influence of intimidation, of local partialities, and of local fears, and to corrupt profusion, for the sake of popularity or of pecuniary gain.

The offer of relief on the principle suggested by us would be a self-acting test of the claim of the applicant.

It is shown throughout the evidence, that it is demoralizing and ruinous to offer to the able-bodied of the best characters more than a simple subsistence. The person of bad character, if he be allowed anything, could not be allowed less. By the means which we propose, the line between those who do, and those who do not, need relief is drawn, and drawn perfectly. If the claimant does not comply with the terms on which relief is given to the destitute, he gets nothing; and if he does comply, the compliance proves the truth of the claim—namely, his destitution. If, then, regulations were established and enforced with the degree of strictness that has been attained in the dispauperized parishes, the workhouse doors might be thrown open to all who would enter them, and conform to the regulations. Not only would no agency for contending against fraudulent rapacity and perjury, no stages of appeals (vexatious to the appellants and painful to the magistrates) be requisite to keep the able-bodied from the parish; but the intentions of the statute of Elizabeth, in setting the idle to work, might be accomplished, and vagrants and mendicants actually forced on the parish; that is, forced into a condition of salutary restriction and labour. It would be found that they might be supported much cheaper under proper regulations, than when living at large by mendicity or depredation.

Wherever inquiries have been made as to the previous condition of the able-bodied individuals who live in such numbers on the town parishes, it has been found that the pauperism of the greater number has originated in indolence, improvidence, or vice, and might have been averted by ordinary care and industry. The smaller number consisted of cases where the cause of pauperism could not be ascertained rather than of cases where it was apparent that destitution had arisen from blameless want. This evidence as to the causes of the pauperism of the great mass of the able-bodied paupers, is corroborated by the best evidence with relation to their subsequent conduct, which has corresponded in a remarkable manner with the effects produced in the dispauperized parishes of the rural districts. Ill-informed persons, whose prepossessions as to the characters of paupers are at variance with the statements of witnesses practically engaged in the distribution of relief, commonly assume that those witnesses form their general conclusions from exceptions, and that their statements are made from some small proportion of cases of imposture; but wherever those statements have been put to a satisfactory test, it has appeared that they were greatly below the truth. The usual statements of the permanent overseers in towns are, that more than one-half or two-thirds of the cases of able-bodied paupers are cases of indolence or imposture; but it rarely appears that more than five or six in a hundred claimants sustain the test of relief given upon a correct principle. . . .

22. "Developments in the Population of Paris," from the *Revue des deux Mondes*, 1845.

Paris was a great city, in size the largest on the Continent and second only to London in Europe; and Paris, as Metternich's Europe well knew, was the home and the harbinger of European revolution. For both these reasons, the analysis of André Cuchot (1812–90) for the *Revue des deux Mondes* of the Paris population and its development is especially interesting. The *Revue des deux Mondes* was the most brilliant journal in Europe. It might be found in any cultivated home or respectable bookshop in Europe. It had an extraordinarily distinguished list of contributors. Cuchot, though not yet among the most eminent of these, was one of the most active and one of those closest to the editors. He had written extensively, in the *Revue* and elsewhere, on economic and social topics. And he had studied the Paris records carefully, as his article shows. The features to which he draws his readers' attention suggest what he thought it important to know about urban population developments. And it may be instructive to compare his treatment and style with what one might expect of a present-day demographer. [André Cuchot, "Mouvement de la population de Paris," *Revue des deux Mondes* n.s. IX (1845), 718–736. Translation by the editor.]

ON A plain that once was nothing but an evil marsh, under rather a sullen sky, which though fickle is still salubrious, providing 174 days of fine weather in an average year—there is a city that as an intellectual center has no equal, though it is only the world's third city in terms of population. The area Paris occupies today is 34,379,016 square meters, of which 1,469,016 are water. If this area were divided up equally among the Parisians, each of them would have 43 square meters to live on; but air and space are distributed very unequally between the inhabitants of the center and those of the outskirts. Three districts [arrondissements], which include the suburbs, the 1st, the 12th, and the 8th, occupy between 4 million and 6 million square meters; on the other hand, the 4th, 7th, and 9th measure only 500,000 to 700,000, about one-ninth as much. The result of this disproportion is that an inhabitant of the 1st or 8th district has 83 square meters to move about on, while an inhabitant of the 4th or 7th has only a 12-meter area. The differences are even greater if one makes the comparison not among the 12 districts but among the quarters [quartiers], which are, as we all know, 48 in number. If you live in the Champs-Élysées quarter, you get a 190-meter area; if you are one of the working tenants of the Arcis quarter, 7 square meters will have to do.

Statesmen might turn to the size of the Paris population at different times to gauge the level of national vitality. Paris is France's heart; it swells and beats strongly when the country prospers, and it contracts when times are bad. The earliest official census, that of 1694, gives 720,000 souls to the city as a whole, perhaps a less exaggerated estimate than the judicious Vauban believed. At that time the star of the Grand Monarch had not yet paled in the eyes of the nations. The cannon of Fleurus, of Steinkirk, of Neerwinden still echoed in glory; that was the eve of the Peace of Ryswick. Twenty years later, after the losses and humiliations of a disastrous war, after the ravages of famine and epidemics, the population of Paris had suffered a decline, which official documents do not specify, but which must have been considerable. The effects were still felt half a century after the death of Louis XIV, if we can rely on the rough enumeration of 1762, which indicates only 600,000 souls. A slight increase during the reign of Louis XVI bears witness to the sincere efforts of that monarch for the public welfare; and in 1784, an estimate by Necker based on the number of births gives the figure 620,000, a conclusion later confirmed by more precise calculations. Then suddenly the sky darkened and the thunder growled; egoism and fear fell upon the city of luxury and pleasures.

Some chose exile; others hid themselves in provincial obscurity to wait out the tempest. A census of 1789 found only 524,186 individuals in the capital. The decline undoubtedly continued through the bloody days of 1793; for history it is regrettable that no one has determined the figure to which the Parisian population was reduced during the Terror. The return of security, manifest in a gradual rebirth of society, began with the first days of the Consulate; the Paris population was reckoned at 548,000 in 1801, and 580,000 in 1806. This upswing was hardly interrupted by the last reverses of the Empire. With the constitutional monarchy, and with administrative centralization pressed almost to the point of abuse, the capital became a luminous center whose expansion is astonishing. Three years after the restoration, Paris already had a population of 710,000 souls, and in twelve years that number rose steadily to 880,000. The Revolution of July, like that of 1789, temporarily drove out the fearful and the dissatisfied. The census of 1831 gives only 785,862 persons, including the mobile population of the military establishments. When confidence returned the great city became again, as in the past, the rendezvous of men of affairs, the jousting field of the knights of industry, the paradise of idlers; and a new census of 1836 showed 899,313 inhabitants. That meant an increase of 114,000 souls in the course of five years, or about 14 per 100. In the outskirts the increase was even more rapid, with a growth during the same period of almost 25 per 100, not counting the 10,000 to 12,000 persons who spend the six pleasant months of the year in the rural communities of the Seine department. Finally one last census, made in 1841, brings the total population of Paris to 935,361, and the total population of the department to 1,194,603. This increase of 36,000 souls for the metropolis, and almost 100,000 for the rural communities, would almost be a disturbing phenomenon if it did not have a temporary cause, the attraction of the great work on the fortifications. And because the census of 1841 is known to us only in its general results, we have had to base our commentary on the analytical census of 1836.

The most populous district then as now was the 6th, with 93,000 souls, whereas the 9th had half that many. Domiciled in charity asylums were 12,055 individuals; 1,380 convicts were serving their penalties in the prisons; there were 17,051 soldiers in the barracks; and 2,323 persons were in religious establishments. The

10 secondary schools, 4 seminaries, and more than 300 boarding-schools held 9,251 children; five years before there had been more than 13,000. Can that decline be one of the results of the campaign against the university? The mobile population in furnished lodgings was estimated at 35,000 individuals, 500 [sic] of them foreigners. The basic social element, the families, included about 700,000 souls; more than 110,000 persons were attached to the families, some in domestic service, others in various employments. One fact worth noticing is that in 1831 women outnumbered men by about 26,000, while in 1836 there was a surplus of 8,000 men. This shift in five years can only be explained by the immigration of workers from the provinces, and thus is a symptom of industrial activity.

Paris, in fact, is not exclusively the city of the Parisians; it is a national property, the rendezvous of all the French. Its prosperity benefits all the departments, and its splendor shines over the whole land. It was demonstrated in 1833 that half the persons resident in Paris had not been born there. Among the 23,176 who died that year, 10,858 were originally from the provinces, and 17 from our overseas colonies. When one considers that the provincials who come to Paris to carry on a trade are generally grown men, while the population of Parisian origin includes a swarm of children and adolescents, then one comes to the conclusion that within the adult category there are only half as many native Parisians as there are provincials. Multiply the number of deaths in each group by forty, and you obtain a figure that provides a precise idea of the number of the living. By this means, considering that among the 5,274 provincials (whose circumstances could be verified) who died in Paris, 866 belonged to that class called the free occupations, one concludes that more than half, perhaps two-thirds of the persons who live in Paris by their wealth or by their talents came here from all parts of the kingdom. Paris governs France, people say in a tone of reproach. But not so; it is the nation that consents to come to Paris to govern itself. The brilliant salons of Paris society are really a thousand-chambered parliament where 70,000 deputies come to represent French civilization, just as political France is represented by its special deputies at the Palais-Bourbon.

In the ranks of wage occupations, certain geographical regions seem to claim monopoly of certain industries. For example, approximate calculations based on mortuary data show that the number of shoemakers from old Lorraine may be set at more than 5,000. Almost all the rugged progeny of Cantal,[1] about 7,000 in number, compete for places as tinkers, coalmen, water carriers, knife grinders, junkmen. Four thousand masons and sawyers are birds of passage who have their nests in the mountains of Creuse. Most of the wine merchants and barrelmakers come from Yonne and the Côte d'Or [Burgundy]. Women drawn to the sorry means of existence that a great city provides for their sex, as servants, washerwomen, and cleaning women, come in general from the departments immediately surrounding the capital.

The thousand foreigners who die annually in Paris, from all the countries of the world, yield the figure of 40,000 for those residing there, either in transit or permanently. German workers make a group of 6,000 to 7,000; there are even more Belgians. There are about 6,000 Savoyards, 4,000 Swiss, as many English, and somewhat fewer than 600 North Americans.

The exchange between the metropolis and the departments can only be beneficial for France as a whole. Just as Paris receives countrymen, so she sends her children to the provinces. The records of the civil government show that the immigration of outsiders is by no means necessary to maintain her population, or even to increase it. Between 1820 and 1829, the average annual births were 27,992; during the next seven years, a period that includes the two disastrous cholera years, this average rose to 28,475; today it would exceed 30,000. The statisticians calculate that in France one infant is born annually for every 33 persons. For that proportion to be applicable in Paris the city would have to hold 1 million souls. It has been noted that male births, in general, are more frequent; but the balance between the sexes is quickly re-established by a higher death rate among boys during the first two years of life.

Of all the lessons statistics can provide, none is of sadder significance than the comparison of legitimate birth figures with those that result from debauchery or misery. During the period 1827 to 1836, the average number of infants born of legitimate marriages was 18,778, including 500 born in the charity hospitals. Average births out of wedlock were 9,936, of which 4,865 were in the hospitals. Accordingly, more than a third of the population of Paris is born

[1] Province in central France known for its mining and metallurgical industries.—Ed.

outside the law upon which society rests, and among every three Parsians one meets one is likely to see one bastard! Political economy invents marvelous theories about material interests and the augmentation of the public wealth. Would not the best means to enrich a nation be to make it moral? What a crushing burden imposed on the decent portion of society by those who live in disorder! Among 10 infants born in the hospitals, there are 9 whose birth is a punishment for error. Among 37 married women, there is only one who is reduced to delivery in a hospital bed; the proportion is 1 in 2 for the unfortunates who become mothers without being married.

For several years, the number of acknowledged natural children has tended to rise. Toward the last years of the restoration, the figure for this was about 2,300 acknowledged at the time of birth, and 180 subsequent to birth. In 1836, there were 2,667 acknowledgments of the first kind, and 250 of the second. But we cannot see moral progress in this increase; it seems to indicate that respect for marriage as a religious institution is growing weaker among the very men who honorably preserve their sense of paternal responsibility. On the other hand one must see a favorable symptom in the increasing number of children acknowledged by actual marriage subsequent to birth. Where 852 marriages of reparation were identified in 1827, 1,087 were counted ten years later. This favorable development is owed mainly to a charitable society, the Saint-François Régis, whose purpose is to bring about legal and religious sanction for irregular unions, by good advice and gifts of money. Between its foundation in 1826 and January 1, 1844, this society has brought consecration to 11,007 illicit establishments, and legitimacy to almost 9,000 natural children.

The number of marriages is proportional to the absolute population figure. In recent years the average has been about 8,200, which means one marriage for every 110 individuals. A comparison between rich and poor districts shows that prosperity and education do not significantly influence the marriage rate. There are fewer widowers than widows. Is that a reason to believe that the risk of death is greater for the male sex in family life? We do not think so. Many men avoid marriage out of selfishness or on principle, but once they have experienced conjugal intimacy, it becomes difficult for them to resume the bachelor's life, and they promptly seek out new connections. Women, on the other hand, though eager to

marry when they are young, later adjust very well to the independence that widowhood brings. That is why the public records
show many more celibates of the male sex than of the female, and
why conversely there are 54,000 widows compared with 17,000
widowers who have not remarried.

Every time the clock marks twenty minutes, an existence ends and
a time of mourning begins. During the ten-year period 1820 to
1829, the total number of deaths was 238,980, which means an
average of a little under 24,000 per year; the number of female
deaths surpassed that of males by about 4 per cent. The average can
be estimated at 25,000 deaths per year since 1830, or about 69 a
day. Variations must be noted for irregular disasters, such as civil
war or epidemics. Thus we set apart 680 persons killed in the July
Days, 275 killed in the bloody riots of the Saint-Merry cloister,
and 18,602 cholera victims. The history of the 1832 scourge is
written on the mortuary tables now before our eyes. A few cases
broke out in the month of March, and immediately a panic that was
just as contagious and just as dreadful as the sickness subjected the
Parisian population to the most appalling experiences. In April
12,733 victims died. There was relief and a sense of recovery in the
two months following; then a sudden recurrence carried off 2,573
persons. After this second crisis, the contagion gradually faded, but
much more slowly than generally supposed; the death records still
show 505 definite cholera deaths in 1833, and 25 in 1834. It is noteworthy that mortality was much lower than usual during the years
following the cholera, as though the funerals of 1832 were a down
payment to death.

Among the 24,057 persons who died in 1836, records show that
14,645 ended their existence at home, more or less in comfort;
8,326 ended their days in the hospitals, 64 died in the prisons, 289
found their last beds on the chill slabs of the morgue. These figures, which recur with minor variations every year, are profoundly
sad. They show how in a city so proud of its civilization and its
wealth, more than a third of the citizens would perish without care
and perhaps without refuge, if public charity did not take them in
for their last moments. Even among those who breathe their last
on beds that belong to them, only a third have lived in comfort.
This is a conjecture drawn from the burial records of the past year
in the three Paris cemeteries. Among 22,661 burials, not counting
those done at the expense of the hospitals and asylums, there were

1,566 purchases of plots in perpetuity and 4,763 temporary locations. The common trench, sad rendezvous of the poor, swallowed 16,332 corpses.

Even with phenomena that deviate from the natural order, the persistence of totals and the regular recurrence of the same figures astonish the statistician. At the beginning of a year one can predict that a few more than 900 Parisians will die violent deaths, accidental or deliberate. Between 200 and 220 will die by drowning, and 50 by strangulation. Mere fashion holds some sway even in the matter of suicide. Thus, in 1832 the majority of those who brought death upon themselves threw themselves into the Seine; in 1834 and 1835, after certain disasters had struck the popular imagination, gas asphyxiation was preferred. Men account for three-quarters of the table of sudden deaths, but there is one category, death by burning, which belongs almost entirely to the female sex.

Let us now reproduce the movement within that immense hive, where there are buzzing, along with the busy workers, so many evil and sterile wasps. Let us try to classify the inhabitants of Paris by their occupations. The *Recherches statistiques*, newly published by order of the Prefect of the Seine department, divides the population of Paris into five categories, including within each group all the persons who live from the occupation practiced by the head of the family. For example, if a banker's household includes his wife and three children, five persons are counted in the commercial class. By applying that rule to the census of 1831, one reaches the following conclusions:

Free	professions	125,788	or	16%
Commercial	"	70,727		9%
Mechanical	"	337,921		43%
Wage-paid	"	172,890		22%
Military	"	78,586		10%
		785,862 [sic]		100%

That a sixth of the Parisian population belongs to the free professions would be grounds for astonishment if we did not add that this category includes all those who live by return on capital, or as [white-collar] employees, or by their talents. Thus half of this first group consists of landlords and investors, 61,000 in number; but how many scanty properties there are, and how many persons of private means survive only by prodigies of thrift! The 27,000 employees or clerks, with a few exceptions, vegetate in lowly conditions. As for persons engaged in careers that demand cultivation of the mind, few though they are, still there are undoubtedly far too many of them for the opportunities our society offers. The functions based on the science of law—the magistracy, the bar, the notaries—provide careers, often more honorable than they are lucrative, for about 7,000 persons; how many advocates without cases there are among the 977 licensed at the royal court, not counting 760 probationers! It is sad for the physicians but lucky for society that the level of disease does not increase with the number of doctors; where there were 1,090 in 1833, we now have 1,430. Ten thousand souls for the category of architects, sculptors, painters, designers, and engravers would be too low an estimate. As for musicians and men of letters, official documents do not provide the means to count them with sufficient precision. Even though everybody today claims to be a writer, and musicomania is one of the peculiarities of our times, we believe that in general the number of those who try to make a full-time profession out of cultivating the arts or literature has tended to decrease for several years; bitter disenchantment has caused a good many dubious vocations to vanish.

Grouped in the category of *commercial professions* are traders who resell, wholesale or retail, goods that they have not produced, from the banker who sells money, to the second-hand man who cries his wares to people in the streets. This class, calculated at 70,727 persons in 1831, would amount to at least 81,000 today, if one assigns to it a growth proportional to that of the population as a whole. This figure, with females in the majority, implies about 12,000 places of business. It would doubtless be an exaggeration to set that countinghouse aristocracy called high commerce at 2,000 families, or 10,000 heads. Nine-tenths of the individuals in the general category are, rather, small retailers compelled to exploit the pressing needs of the masses that live from day to day. It is painful to note that proprietors of cheap wineshops are the most numerous among them—7,000, counting women and children; then come the grocers with 4,000; the fruiterers, about the same; cafés, 2,400; beef butchers, 2,000; pork butchers, half that many. There are more than 10,000 street peddlers. Petty trade now has enemies whose existence it does not suspect; many economists have denounced it as a plague upon the people. The profit a shopkeeper takes, as intermediary between producer and consumer, is considered all the more invidious a toll because it weighs entirely on the lower classes; and some look to the time, in the name of progress, when the worker will be able to provision himself directly from the factory, on better terms.

But no one who has observed common practices can believe this kind of change possible. What keeps the small retailer in business is the fact that he gives credit. He knows his neighborhood best, he can tell with whom he can be liberal, and so he is surest of getting his accounts paid. For the wife of the honest laborer, high politics consists of managing her credit among the tradesmen she deals with; and is it not an important assurance for families with such uncertain resources to know that there will be, whatever happens, bread for the children and a glass of wine when the father comes home in the evening broken with fatigue and soaked in sweat? Were it not that the poor need credit, costly though it is to them, the petty trades would vanish even before benevolence intervened; they would give way to the absorbent action of the powerful capital interests. Great incorporated houses would close these dirty smoky stalls called *boutiques* by the thousands; we should see the sale of beverages concentrated in certain storehouses, and that of foodstuffs in vast grocery warehouses, just as we already see the sale of almost all textiles monopolized by the great clothing stores.

The third category, the *mechanical professions*, set fourteen years ago at 337,921 persons and now surely to be estimated at 380,000, is the most numerous of all. It includes manufacturers proper, meaning those who undertake by their own efforts, or with paid help, the manufacture of exchangeable products. Studies made by the city government for the establishment of an industrial advisory council provide a classification of Parisian manufactures. It makes a list of 125 well-defined occupations, which can be divided into five groups. The first includes twenty-four industries concerned with the manufacture of yarns and textiles. In that class there are 2,480 "notables," or persons eligible to participate in the election of the council, meaning that they have been active for at least six years, and have never undergone bankruptcy. The second group, including at least twenty metal-working trades, has 5,672 notables, counting only independent producers. It would be astonishing to find 650 master clockmakers and watchmakers, 742 jewelers, 420 makers of musical instruments, 225 bronzeworkers, etc., if we did not know that Paris inspires and satisfies the luxury trade of a large part of Europe. The third group, chemical products, includes forty-six trades, but still amounts to only 2,321 elector-notables. In a fourth group entitled miscellaneous occupations there are thirty-five trades with 4,491 notables. Among the most numerous are master shoemakers, 780; cabinetmakers, 702; heads of establishments concerned with typography or lithography, 778. A final group, not included in the ordinance that established the advisory council, consists mainly of the building trades; it includes 412 masonry contractors, 660 master carpenters, 500 master locksmiths, 462 painter-glaziers, etc.—4,080 notables in all.

Add to these heads of establishments with six years practice and undamaged reputation the 6,000 foremen and licensed artisans, and you come to a total of 26,000 proprietors or directors of shops. This industrial aristocracy, assuming four or five persons per household, amounts to only 120,000 souls. Now, since the industrial population taken as a whole must today exceed 380,000 souls, the difference between the two figures, about 260,000, represents the needy crowd of petty workmen and day laborers. It is regrettable that government publications do not permit us to establish precisely the statistics of the working class. The summary of working certificates, prepared at the prefecture of police for a period of six years (1836 to 1841), includes 118 occupations and yields the following results, in rounded numbers:

New certificates requested	152,000	average per year	25,300
Entry visas for Paris	62,000		10,300
Exit visas from Paris	83,000		13,800
Signed in with masters	258,000		43,000
Signed out with masters	215,000		35,800

This table would give a very false idea of the development of the industrial population. For the Decree of the Year XII [1803], which regulates the trades, has long since fallen into desuetude for lack of penal sanctions against the masters and workers who refuse to abide by it. The majority of the workers, and ordinarily the older and better ones, according to official reports, do not take out certificates; and those who have them very often neglect to have them endorsed by the masters when they change jobs. Nothing could deceive the statistician more than a regulation as badly observed as this one. Therefore it is necessary to return to calculations based on the mortuary tables, for an approximate enumeration of the persons engaged in the more important branches of Parisian industry. A single figure including all family members comes closer to the truth for this class than for the preceding one, because here women and children are often employed. The shoemakers' group seems the most numerous, about 24,000 heads. Then come the tailors, 20,000; the carpenters, 14,000; goldsmiths, jewelers, and related occupations, 12,000; the locksmiths, 10,000; the masons, 8,000; cabinetmakers, 5,000; typographers of various kinds, 8,000; hatters, 5,000; hairdressers, 5,000. When we search for a description of the circumstances of most women, we find at least 40,000 dressmakers and lingerie workers, counting the mistresses of shops; 17,000 laundresses and linen women, working mainly on their own; 6,000 who knit, 5,000 who embroider, 1,500 florists, etc. Commerce, we said, relies in general on the needs of the mass; but running over the list of the various industries one notes that most of them are aimed at the classes for whom luxuries are permissible.

Although most of the individuals in the three preceding categories live by wages, there are grouped under the special title *wage-paid occupations* domestic servants and hired people, the nature of whose services draw them close to domestic life. This lower class, reckoned in 1831 at 173,000 souls, must today include at least 200,000. People without skills who sell their strength from day to day make up 60,000 of these, as many men as women. That coarse and greedy race which descends on Paris every year from the most impoverished cantons of France to monopolize the rude trades of porters, coalmen, water-carriers, and scrubmen forms a special clan of at least 16,000 members. The class of domestics proper exceeds 50,000 persons in number, three-quarters female. One notes that among ten servants only one is married; does not this detail explain a good many irregularities? Special domestic services provide livelihoods also for 20,000 janitors, 11,000 cooks, 10,000 coachmen and stableboys, 3,000 attendants for the sick or for children, etc. This is a sad list; we shall not pursue it further.

The military population, estimated at 80,000 souls, includes in addition to the soldiers of the Paris garrison the military class of all ranks, active or retired. Women and children amount to one-sixteenth of this number, about 5,000 souls.

It is a surprise to find, with the inhabitants of Paris all grouped by occupation, how few easy and comfortable situations there are,

compared with the multitude condemned to marginal and unhappy existence. Comfort and—to take from the vulgar tongue one
of those picturesque expressions that give the body of an idea—
bread baked ahead of time apparently are assured to only one person in ten, like a privilege. This fact acquires the force of a mathematical demonstration from the contrast between the two classes
at the extremes of the scale, the enfranchised class and the class that
must live by begging public charity. On the list of enfranchised
citizens prepared in 1836 for the Seine department, 14,608 names
come from the twelve Paris districts; 70,000 persons at most share
therefore in the comfort implied by a direct tax of 200 francs per
family. Many investors, employees, and artists are rich without
being voters, you will say; but yet how many of the property
owners are in fact driven to the wall by mortgages and bills, people
who have the right to vote without actually having that assured
independence that society presumes them to have! And let us
now contrast these figures with the statistics of the indigent population.

In 1841, 29,282 indigent households were counted, comprising
66,487 individuals. That meant, as in the last days of the restoration, one pauper among 13 persons. Within that average, the proportion varies widely among the several Paris districts. In the 2nd
district there is only one indigent among 33 inhabitants; in the 12th
and in the 8th, one person in 6 claims public charity as a right. A
third of those who die in Paris do not leave enough behind to bury
them with, and so for every three burials the administration must
pay the costs of one. Who would believe, looking upon a holiday
crowd, carefree and proud in their Sunday best, that one in four
is condemned to breathe his last on an asylum bed? Yet that is the
normal proportion of deaths recorded in the institutions open to
paupers. What lodgings can one obtain for a rent of less than 100
francs? The garret in a hovel! But 18,000 households, composed of
2 to 3 persons each, have no other place. A very large number of
laborers live from day to day in miserable furnished lodgings, the
renting of which costs more in the long run than healthier and more
comfortable establishments. This nomad race, estimated ten years
ago at 28,000 heads, now includes 12,000 more because of the great
fortification undertaking. Though the savings bank of Paris receives annually 40 million francs, half of it provided by the classes
that live by wages, the municipal pawnshop for its part has regis-

tered 1.4 million articles whose total value, set at 24 million by the pawnbrokers, must represent an intrinsic value of 50 to 60 million.

Almost all occupations contribute names to the list of unfortunates who have the sad courage to let their wretchedness be officially verified. One notes 164 lettered men among them, designated as clerks, teachers, or writers; ten years ago almost twice as many were listed. Does that mean that the learned professions now offer more opportunities than in the past? We dare not believe so; if we count fewer victims from the literate pursuits that is because, as we said before, overcrowding has tended to diminish. Artists have more resources than writers against the ultimate calamity. The instrumentalist who is not afraid to lower himself joins the orchestras at public dances. Painters whose canvases find no buyers can accept certain decorating tasks. Only 39 musicians asked for a dole; not one indigent was a painter. In the manual trades, the number of indigents produced in each seems roughly proportional to the number of workers employed in each; from this one might conclude that there are not, despite common beliefs, good and bad trades in the absolute; rather, the competition that brings poverty is practically the same in all occupations. Among the heads of indigent households, 2,196 belong to the building trades, which include a score of occupations, from masons to repairers of stoves. Shoemakers registered a total of 1,011; tailors, 447; petty second-hand men, 778; men of toil, whose only resource is to sell their muscular strength by the day, 2,934. Servile occupations give the following totals: janitors, 1,283; coachmen and drivers, 311; rag-pickers and scavengers, 271. It has been noted that domestics proper, those who give service within families, find something to deposit in savings accounts, almost as much by themselves as the whole laboring class. Let us add in turn that perhaps domestics, of all the occupations, contribute the fewest paupers, in proportion to the large number thus engaged. More than 50,000 domestics of both sexes send only 315 indigents to the charitable agencies. There is another figure we cannot add to the list without a feeling of shame for our times, nor without fear for the future of that French culture which likes to think itself the schoolmistress of nations. This figure concerns the printers. In a group that we have estimated at 8,000 souls, including women and children, we assume 3,000 working heads of households. Now, 149 are paupers, 1 in 20, while the proportion among lackeys and servants is 1 in 160! Put on livery and you will have eight times less chance of spending your last days begging than if you enter that profession which in the old industrial hierarchy constituted a sort of aristocracy!

The women obliged to seek charity belong mostly to those vague occupations in which the majority take refuge when they begin to realize that the treasure of their youth has been foolishly squandered. One finds among the inscribed paupers 876 washerwomen, 938 cleaning women, 1,060 old-clothes peddlers, 2,127 needleworkers, and 3,532 unfortunates obliged to admit they have no skills. The number of women left destitute by the desertion of their husbands has developed disturbingly during the past dozen years, if we take this as an indication of general morality. The 1,325 inscribed in 1832 became 1,898 in 1841. So much suffering, so much shame to be borne—and they are not reserved exclusively for the progeny of the great city. Paris, we repeat, is really a gathering place where strangers make half the number. Among 29,000 heads of indigent households, 21,000 originated in the departments. The provinces know Paris only from its reflected splendor, from the echoes of its foolish pleasures. They quit the villages under the spell of a beautiful dream. Their last looks at the old steeple and the thatched roofs, at the fussy suspicious old men, at their wondering and envious young neighbors, are proud looks of pity; as they dream along the road of the fortunes they will make in Paris and the pleasures they will find there, their steps are light and their hearts full of joy. Finally, they reach the enchanted place, and there they find shame and the anguish of beggary.

If society were not impelled to aid the poor out of duty and because its heart is touched, it would have to do so still out of self-interest. Poverty is rarely an immediate provocation to crime; but it leads to crime by disordering conduct, by a degradation that in the end comes to a kind of savagery. The vicious part of the Parisian population has been estimated at 55,000 souls. Out of that number, in which men predominate, 25,000 persons can be brought before the courts for the irregularity of their lives, without being exactly malefactors; the other 30,000 constitute the class whose shameless demoralization and whose criminal impudence are a permanent danger for peaceable citizens. Of those who begin by picking pockets and end with murder, doubtless the great majority are unfortunates who lack the moral strength to resist the evil counsels of poverty. The 20,000 suspect women who are known to be in

Paris—are they not almost always women of the laboring class who have found they cannot make their legitimate resources meet their legitimate needs? From this class come the degraded creatures who learn to make a trade of debauchery. A few years ago the latter were counted at about 8,000, of whom half found ways of avoiding police surveillance.

Let us hurry to get through the nine prisons of Paris, enumerating the various categories of prisoners they enclose. Our figures, based on official reports, give averages for the seven years 1836 to 1842 inclusive: boys detained without prior charge as a measure of paternal correction, 24; confined as a precautionary administrative measure, feeble, dangerous illnesses, or children in early infancy, 432 male and 751 female; imprisoned for debt to the government, 24; debtors incarcerated through prosecution by private creditors, 150 men and 8 women. This last figure shows that our commercial practices are fortunately far from English rigidity. Before the adoption of a bill recently passed on Lord Brougham's motion, the three prisons of London contained 620 debtors, most of whom had been incarcerated for very small sums. The new bill, which stipulated that one did not incur loss of liberty for any sum smaller than 20 pounds sterling, immediately reduced the number of prisoners to 250. There are ordinarily in the prisons of Paris about 1,200 men and 250 women retained on preventive grounds or without definite conviction. Convicted persons paying their penalties in the jails of the department have averaged 1,440. This number breaks down as follows: correctional sentences to one year's imprisonment or less, 841 male and 155 female—included in these figures, shockingly, are 450 children under sixteen years, the Paris gamins. Correctional detention of more than one year must be served in the central prisons. There are commonly 250 convicts in that category in the prisons of Paris who are awaiting transfer, unless they have been authorized to stay there as a favor and by paying their own expenses. The criminal prisoners also detained pending transfer average about 72. In all, 42,000 to 44,000 individuals enter the prisons of Paris annually; an almost equal number leave them, by acquittal, by discharge, by remission of punishment, by transfer, by escape, or by death. This turnover maintains ordinarily 3,000 to 4,000 persons under lock and key. In 1842 the total number of prisoner-days was 1,344,442, and the expense totaled 1,279,909 francs. Additional convicts of Parisian origin, at least 1,200 in number, are in the

workhouses of Saint-Denis and of Villers-Cotterets; 1,258 are in
the various central houses of detention, and about 500 in the peni-
tentiaries.

We must, despite our repugnance, conclude with one last feature
of this sad catalogue of the miseries and infirmities of the great city.
The number of lunatics in the Seine department, at last count, was
3,685. More than two-thirds of these unfortunates, belonging to
the needy classes, must be shut up in the asylums, where their maintenance becomes a public charge. The annual cost of each indigent
lunatic is 545 francs, so that 885,404 confinement-days required a
total expenditure of 1,328,106 francs.

This rapid survey of the population of Paris leaves an impression
that is, it seems to us, touched with uneasiness. Clearly, the capital
of France is tending to become, like London, a great center of activity and a monstrous agglomeration of people. The misuse of
administrative centralization, the convergence of all the railroads
in the metropolis, the intellectual predominance of the Parisian
press and Parisian oratory, the attractions of luxury and fashion—all
these will accelerate this development faster and faster. It used to
be that whatever looked like an increase of population was, for our
fathers, a sign of public prosperity. The time for that benign naïveté
is past. Everyone knows nowadays that the strength of a nation lies
less in the number than in the physical vigor and the moral energy
of the people who compose it; and also we know that the great
centers contain relatively the most suffering and wretchedness.
The danger we dimly perceive is not yet apparent to every eye;
fair illusions sustain a sense of security. Paris has considerable
revenues; her municipal administration is intelligent and energetic.
Great works of improvement and ornamentation have been
achieved; other and still greater projects are under study and will
come with time, for money will not be lacking. This transformation of the old city, which we hardly notice because it is happening
gradually before our eyes, arouses the admiration of strangers who
visit us from a distance. The growth of luxury in private life is still
more astounding. But what, at bottom, are the results of this
splendor? Poverty is somehow eclipsed by it, and seeks darkness to
hide its shame. In the middle class, whoever has any resources uses
them to put up a good front; for appearances have become necessities of life, necessities of vanity for some, necessities for respect
and for credit for the majority. From this rivalry in consumption

results a superficial and deceptive glitter, a universal dazzlement that blinds us to real and profound misery. It is good for public attention to be drawn to this point, and that is why we have tried to give moral significance to the cold and silent figures ranked in the columns of the official documents.

V

Machines, Motion, and Progress

It may be that the perspective of history will show that the development of modern industry and the increased motion of population were the main agents that dissolved the old western world into the new. If it does, then these were the vital enemies of Metternich's Europe. A great many contemporaries believed that they were, for better or for worse. Machines, motion, and progress seemed alien themes to the political régime of Metternich's Europe, and yet they were growing up in its very midst. It looked like a sharpening historical contradiction, and portended historic conflict and resolution.

Europeans were likely to look at England for clues to what the new world would be like, for British commerce and industry were extensively developed and therefore "advanced." Or they might look at the United States, a moving and growing country built by the most "advanced" British elements—America, a new country where no régime like Metternich's Europe had ever existed and which therefore signified what Europe might become when the age of Metternich had succumbed to the future. England and America were schools for the future, and men interested in the future studied them and read about them. The most successful prophets of what the future would bring, men like Alexis de Tocqueville (1805–59), Friedrich Engels (1820–95), and Camillo di Cavour (1810–61), based their prophecies mainly on what they knew of England or America. And countless businessmen and engineers journeyed to see for themselves.

The term Industrial Revolution was apparently first used in the 1820's by certain Frenchmen, deliberately to draw an analogy with their own great Revolution, of 1789 and yet to come. They meant mass machine production, based on mechanical power, served by men who must come to where the machinery and power were and who must work according to their pace. It was a style of production that had begun with cotton textiles in England, in the latter part of the eighteenth century, and then had spread to other manufactures. Each successive technological improvement brought demands for new ones— new processes to prepare materials to feed the machines, iron to build them, coal to make the iron, and, most brilliant invention of all, the steam engine (made of iron and run by coal) to drive the machines and carry their produce on iron rails to the mass markets the machines required. Industrialism acquired the spiraling, self-feeding character apparent in all great historical developments, a character still apparent now, but quite unlike the manufacturing economy of preindustrial times.

That is what made it an industrial revolution. It was under way in France and Belgium by the 1830's, and visible in parts of Germany, Austria, and Italy by the 1840's. Industry's share in the total economy was still small by today's standards, but it was dramatically new; and most important of all, it was only a hint of what surely would come.

For persons not themselves directly engaged in industrial development, its effects were probably most evident in two ways. First, it penetrated the countryside and brought formerly isolated and separated communities into closer contact and regular exchange with the great world and with one another. Second, it concentrated productive efforts in urban centers, drawing its workers from the population at large and making of them a new kind of labor force, whose faces seemed to observers as indistinguishable as the mass goods produced by the machines they served.

The railroad was the main agent of penetration. It reached out toward and through distant and formerly inaccessible places, bringing fuel and materials to the machines and then distributing their products. The investment brokerages and banks it spawned cut through the older, quieter patterns of finance; it made—and lost—fortunes that dwarfed older ones built up privately by painstaking penury and decades or centuries of agricultural exploitation. Railroads were the extended tentacles of industry. The art, poetry, and journalism of the early nineteenth century were filled with the imagery of the huffing locomotive on its stark rails, cutting across diffuse pastoral scenery.

The drawing together of production into urban centers was just as dramatic, and even more portentous. Like the railroad, this process brought the isolated countryside into closer contact with the greater world. More and more sons of the village went to the city for work, and more and more of the goods the village used were obtained from the city. And as the balance of economic activity and population shifted from country toward town, a greater and greater share of the life of European society took place in the dynamic environment of the city, where change and novelty were accepted and even sought after. The "people" were entering the modern world. The machine and the city showed that things did not have to be as they always had been, and that it might be better if they were not.

The concrete evidence of machines, motion, and progress was a mightier challenge to Metternich's Europe than sentimental dreams of liberty had ever been. Not all the dreamers of liberty were sure they wanted so noisy and overwhelming an ally. But for those who, hoping for freedom from the past, accepted the jarring changes of present and future, the coming industrial age promised wider freedom, truer community, and better lives.

A CHRONOLOGY

1769	James Watt's steam engine
1783	Steam engines first used in cotton manufacture
1793	Eli Whitney's cotton gin
1814	George Stephenson's steam locomotive
1825	The world's first steam railroad line, in England
1835	Steam railroads in France, Belgium, and Germany
1835–45	Boom in railroad investment and construction
1830–40	European iron production approximately doubles
1840–50	European iron production grows by about 50 per cent

EUROPEAN RAILROAD MILEAGE IN EXISTENCE

1830	60 miles
1840	2120 miles
1850	14,000 miles

BIBLIOGRAPHY

T. S. Ashton, *The Industrial Revolution, 1760–1830* (rev. edn., New York, 1964).

J. H. Clapham, *The Economic Development of France and Germany* (4th edn., Cambridge, England, 1936).

D. S. Landes, "Technological Change and Development in Western Europe, 1750–1914," *Cambridge Economic History of Europe*, Vol. VI (Cambridge, England, 1965), 274–601.

L. Mumford, *Technics and Civilization* (New York, 1934).

W. W. Rostow, *The Stages of Economic Growth* (Cambridge, England, 1960).

A. P. Usher, *A History of Mechanical Inventions* (rev. edn., Cambridge, Mass., 1964).

23. Dr. Ure on the Philosophy of Manufactures, 1835

Dr. Andrew Ure (1778–1857) took his degree in medicine at Glasgow in 1801, but achieved early success as a lecturer in popular science, notably before Glasgow workingmen's audiences, rather than as a practicing physician. He went on to write many voluminous and enthusiastic works on industry and science for the general public, and although they are almost forgotten now, they were immensely successful in Europe and America during his lifetime. This selection is from the opening chapter of one of them. Ure's scientific judgments, sometimes bizarre, were usually shrewd, practical, and up to date; from 1830 until his death he practiced as a consulting industrial chemist to governments and private companies, in addition to his writing and lecturing. The similarities between Ure's views here and those of Friedrich Engels, which appear in the next selection, are as worthy of notice and reflection as the divergences. [Andrew Ure, *The Philosophy of Manufactures, or, An Exposition of the Scientific, Moral, and Commercial Economy of the Factory System* (London, 1835), pp. 1–9, 13–25.]

Book the First
General Principles of Manufactures

CHAPTER I

GENERAL VIEW OF MANUFACTURING INDUSTRY

MANUFACTURE IS a word, which, in the vicissitude of language, has come to signify the reverse of its intrinsic meaning, for it now denotes every extensive product of art, which is made by machinery, with little or no aid of the human hand; so that the most perfect manufacture is that which dispenses entirely with manual labour. The philosophy of manufactures is therefore an exposition of the general principles, on which productive industry should be conducted by self-acting machines. The end of a manufacture is to modify the texture, form, or composition of natural objects by mechanical or chemical forces, acting either separately, combined, or in succession. Hence the automatic arts subservient to general commerce may be distinguished into Mechanical and Chemical, according as they modify the external form or the internal constitution of their subject matter. An indefinite variety of objects may be subjected to each system of action, but they may be all conveniently classified into animal, vegetable, and mineral.

A mechanical manufacture being commonly occupied with one substance, which it conducts through metamorphoses in regular succession, may be made nearly automatic; whereas a chemical manufacture depends on the play of delicate affinities between two or more substances, which it has to subject to heat and mixture under circumstances somewhat uncertain, and must therefore remain, to a corresponding extent, a manual operation. The best example of *pure* chemistry on self-acting principles which I have seen, was in a manufacture of sulphuric acid, where the sulphur being kindled and properly set in train with the nitre, atmospheric air, and water, carried on the process through a labyrinth of compartments, and supplied the requisite heat of concentration, till it brought forth a finished commercial product. The finest model of an automatic manufacture of *mixed* chemistry is the five-coloured calico machine, which continuously, and spontaneously, so to speak, prints beautiful webs of cloth with admirable precision and speed. It is in a cotton-mill, however, that the perfection of automatic industry is to be seen; it is there that the elemental powers have been made to animate millions of complex organs, infusing into forms of wood, iron, and brass an intelligent agency. And as the philosophy of the fine arts, poetry, painting, and music may be best studied in their individual master-pieces, so may the philosophy of manufactures in this its noblest creation.

There are four distinct classes of textile fibres, cotton, wool, flax, and silk, which constitute the subjects of four, or, more correctly speaking, five distinct classes of factories; first, the cotton factories; second, the woollen; third, the worsted; fourth, the flax, hempen, or linen; and fifth, the silk. These five factories have each peculiarities proceeding from the peculiarities of its raw material and of its fabrics; but they all possess certain family features, for they all employ torsion to convert the loose slender fibres of vegetable or animal origin into firm coherent threads, and, with the exception of silk, they all employ extension also to attenuate and equalize these threads, technically styled yarn. Even one kind of silk which occurs in entangled tufts, called floss, is spun like cotton, by the simultaneous action of stretching and twisting.

The above-named five orders of factories are, throughout this kingdom, set in motion by steam-engines or water-wheels; they all give employment to multitudes of children or adolescents; and they have therefore been subjected to certain legislative provisions, defined in the *Factories Regulation Act*, passed by Parliament on the 29th August, 1833.

It is probable that 614,200 work-people are constantly engaged within the factories of the United Kingdom: of which number 561,900 belong to England and Wales; 46,825 to Scotland; and 5,475 to Ireland. Fully five-tenths of them are under twenty-one years of age, and three-tenths of these young persons are females. It must be remembered, however, that besides these 614,200 inmates of factories, a vast population derives a livelihood from the manufactures of cotton, wool, flax, and silk, such as the hand-weavers, the calico-printers and dyers, the frame-work knitters, the lace-makers, lace-runners, muslin-sewers, &c. &c.

It appears from the Parliamentary Returns of 1831, that in Great Britain, out of a total population of 16,539,318 persons, there are of

Agricultural Labourers and Labouring Occupiers	1,055,982
and of Manufacturing Labourers	404,317
Whence there are 1000 agricultural to 383 strictly manufacturing labourers.	
Persons employed in retail trade, or in handicraft, as masters or workmen	1,159,867
Total adult persons employed in arts and trades	1,564,184
being about fifty per cent more than those engaged in agriculture.	
The capitalist, bankers, professional and other educated men amount to	214,390
Labourers non-agricultural to	618,712
If we include in the agricultural department, the occupiers employing labourers (few of whom, however, work), we shall have to add	187,075
to the above number	1,055,057 [sic]

The total sum of Agriculturists is 1,243,057, being only 80 per cent of the adult males employed in manufactures, arts, and trades.

When we take into account the vastly greater proportion of young persons constantly occupied with factory labour, than of those occupied with agricultural labour, we shall then be led to conclude that at least double the amount of personal industry is engaged in the arts, manufactures, and trade, to what is engaged in agriculture. Considerably upwards of one-tenth of the population of this island is actually employed in manufactures; and probably little more than one-fifteenth in agriculture. This conclusion ought to lead our legislative landlords to treat the manufacturing interests with greater respect than they have usually been accustomed to do. If we consider, moreover, how much greater a mass of productive industry a male adult is equivalent to, in power-driven manufactures, than in agriculture, the balance in favour of the former will be greatly enhanced.

France, which has for upwards of a century and a half tried every scheme of public premium to become a great manufacturing country, has a much less proportion than one employed in trade for two employed in agriculture. M. Charles Dupin, indeed, has been led by his researches into the comparative industry of France and of the United Kingdom, to conclude that the agricultural produce of our country amounted in value to 240 millions sterling, and that of his own to 180 millions sterling, being the ratio of three to two; and that our manufacturing power is inferior to that of France in the proportion of sixty-three to seventy-two; or as seven to eight. There can be no doubt that his agricultural estimate underrates France, as much as his manufacturing estimate underrates Great Britain.

This island is pre-eminent among civilized nations for the prodigious development of its factory wealth, and has been therefore long viewed with a jealous admiration by foreign powers. This very pre-eminence, however, has been contemplated in a very different light by many influential members of our own community, and has been even denounced by them as the certain origin of innumerable evils to the people, and of revolutionary convulsions to the state. If the affairs of the kingdom be wisely administered, I believe such allegations and fears will prove to be groundless, and to proceed more from the envy of one ancient and powerful order of the commonwealth, towards another suddenly grown into political importance than from the nature of things.

In the recent discussions concerning our factories, no circumstance is so deserving of remark, as the gross ignorance evinced by our leading legislators and economists, gentlemen well informed in other respects, relative to the nature of those stupendous manufactures which have so long provided the rulers of the kingdom with the resources of war, and a great body of the people with comfortable subsistence; which have, in fact, made this island the arbiter of many nations, and the benefactor of the globe itself. Till this ignorance be dispelled, no sound legislation need be expected on manufacturing subjects. To effect this purpose is a principal, but not the sole aim of the present volume, for it is intended also to convey specific information to the classes directly concerned in the manufactures, as well as general knowledge to the community at large, and particularly to young persons about to make the choice of a profession.

The blessings which physico-mechanical science has bestowed on society, and the means it has still in store for ameliorating the lot of mankind, have been too little dwelt upon; while, on the other hand, it has been accused of lending itself to the rich capitalists as an instrument for harassing the poor, and of exacting from the operative an accelerated rate of work. It has been said, for example, that the steam-engine now drives the power-looms with such velocity as to urge on their attendant weavers at the same rapid pace; but that the hand-weaver, not being subjected to this restless agent, can throw his shuttle and move his treddles at his convenience. There is, however, this difference in the two cases, that in the factory, every member of the loom is so adjusted, that the driving force leaves the attendant nearly nothing at all to do, certainly no muscular fatigue to sustain, while it procures for him good, unfailing wages, besides a healthy workshop *gratis:* whereas the non-factory weaver, having everything to execute by muscular exertion, finds the labour irksome, makes in consequence innumerable short pauses, separately of little account, but great when added together; earns therefore proportionally low wages, while he loses his health by poor diet and the dampness of his hovel. Dr. Carbutt of Manchester says, "With regard to Sir Robert Peel's assertion a few evenings ago, that the hand-loom weavers are mostly small farmers, nothing can be a greater mistake; they live, or rather they just keep life together, in the most miserable manner, in the cellars and garrets of the town, working sixteen or eighteen hours for the merest pittance."

The constant aim and effect of scientific improvement in manufactures are philanthropic, as they tend to relieve the workman either from niceties of adjustment which exhaust his mind and fatigue his eyes, or from painful repetition of effort which distort or wear out his frame. At every step of each manufacturing process described in this volume, the humanity of science will be manifest. New illustrations of this truth appear almost every day, of which a remarkable one has just come to my knowledge. In the woollen-cloth trade there is a process between carding and spinning the wool, called *slubbing*, which converts the spongy rolls, turned off from the cards, into a continuous length of fine porous cord. Now, though carding and spinning lie within the domain of automatic science, yet slubbing is a handicraft operation, depending on the skill of the slubber, and participating therefore in all his irregularities. If he be a steady, temperate man, he will conduct his business regularly, without needing to harass his juvenile assistants, who join together the series of card rolls, and thus feed his machine; but if he be addicted to liquor, and passionate, he has it in his power to exercise a fearful despotism over the young piecers, in violation of the proprietor's benevolent regulations. This class of operatives, who, though inmates of factories, are not, properly speaking, factory workers, being independent of the moving power, have been the principal source of the obloquy so unsparingly cast on the cotton and other factories, in which no such capricious practices or cruelties exist. The wool slubber, when behind hand with his work, after a visit to the beer-shop, resumes his task with violence, and drives his machine at a speed beyond the power of the piecers to accompany; and if he finds them deficient in the least point, he does not hesitate to lift up the long wooden rod from his slubbing-frame, called a billy-roller, and beat them unmercifully. I rejoice to find that science now promises to rescue this branch of the business from handicraft caprice, and to place it, like the rest, under the safeguard of automatic mechanism. The details of this recent invention will be given in describing the woollen manufacture. . . .

The term *Factory*, in technology, designates the combined operation of many orders of work-people, adult and young, in tending with assiduous skill a system of productive machines continuously impelled by a central power. This definition includes such organizations as cotton-mills, flax-mills, silk-mills, woollen-mills, and certain engineering works; but it excludes those in which the mechanisms do not form a connected series, nor are dependent on one prime mover. Of the latter class, examples occur in iron-works, dye-works, soap-works, brass-foundries, &c. Some authors, indeed, have comprehended under the title *factory*, all extensive establishments wherein a number of people co-operate towards a common purpose of art; and would therefore rank breweries, distilleries, as well as the workshops of carpenters, turners, coopers, &c., under the factory system. But I conceive that this title, in its strictest sense, involves the idea of a vast automaton, composed of various mechanical and intellectual organs, acting in uninterrupted concert for the production of a common object, all of them being subordinated to a self-regulated moving force. If the marshalling of human beings in systematic order for the execution of any technical enterprise were allowed to constitute a factory, this term might embrace every department of civil and military engineering; a latitude of application quite inadmissible.

In its precise acceptation, the Factory system is of recent origin, and may claim England for its birthplace. The mills for throwing silk, or making organzine, which were mounted centuries ago in several of the Italian states, and furtively transferred to this country by Sir Thomas Lombe in 1718, contained indeed certain elements of a factory, and probably suggested some hints of those grander and more complex combinations of self-acting machines, which were first embodied half a century later in our cotton manufacture by Richard Arkwright, assisted by gentlemen of Derby, well acquainted with its celebrated silk establishment. But the spinning of an entangled flock of fibres into a smooth thread, which constitutes the main operation with cotton, is in silk superfluous; being already performed by the unerring instinct of a worm, which leaves to human art the simple task of doubling and twisting its regular filaments. The apparatus requisite for this purpose is more elementary, and calls for few of those gradations of machinery which are needed in the carding, drawing, roving, and spinning processes of a cotton-mill.

When the first water-frames for spinning cotton were erected at Cromford, in the romantic valley of the Derwent, about sixty years ago, mankind were little aware of the mighty revolution which the new system of labour was destined by Providence to achieve, not only in the structure of British society, but in the fortunes of the world at large. Arkwright alone had the sagacity to discern, and the boldness to predict in glowing language, how vastly productive human industry would become, when no longer proportioned in its results to muscular effort, which is by its nature fitful and capricious, but when made to consist in the task of guiding the work of mechanical fingers and arms, regularly impelled with great velocity by some indefatigable physical power. What his judgment so clearly led him to perceive, his energy of will enabled him to realize with such rapidity and success, as would have done honour to the most influential individuals, but were truly wonderful in that obscure and indigent artisan. The main difficulty did not, to my apprehension, lie so much in the invention of a proper self-acting mechanism for drawing out and twisting cotton into a continuous thread, as in the distribution of the different members of the apparatus into one co-operative body, in impelling each organ with its appropriate delicacy and speed, and above all, in training human beings to renounce their desultory habits of work, and to identify themselves with the unvarying regularity of the complex automaton. To devise and administer a successful code of factory discipline, suited to the necessities of factory diligence, was the Herculean enterprise, the noble achievement of Arkwright. Even at the present day, when the system is perfectly organized, and its labour lightened to the utmost, it is found nearly impossible to convert persons past the age of puberty, whether drawn from rural or from handicraft occupations, into useful factory hands. After struggling for a while to conquer their listless or restive habits, they either renounce the employment spontaneously, or are dismissed by the overlookers on account of inattention.

If the factory Briareus[1] could have been created by mechanical genius alone, it should have come into being thirty years sooner; for upwards of ninety years have now elapsed since John Wyatt, of Birmingham, not only invented the series of fluted rollers (the spinning fingers usually ascribed to Arkwright) but obtained a patent for the invention, and erected "a spinning engine without hands" in his native town. The details of this remakable circumstance, recently snatched from oblivion, will be given in our Treatise on the Cotton Manufactures. Wyatt was a man of good education, in a respectable walk of life, much esteemed by his superiors, and therefore favourably placed, in a mechanical point of view, for maturing his admirable scheme. But he was of a gentle and passive spirit, little qualified to cope with the hardships of a new manufacturing enterprise. It required, in fact, a man of a Napoleon nerve and ambition, to subdue the refractory tempers of workpeople accustomed to irregular paroxysms of diligence, and to urge on his multifarious and intricate constructions in the face of prejudice, passion, and envy. Such was Arkwright, who, suffering nothing to stay or turn aside his progress, arrived gloriously at the goal, and has for ever affixed his name to a great era in the annals of mankind, an era which has laid open unbounded prospects of wealth and comfort to the industrious, however much they may have been occasionally clouded by ignorance and folly.

Prior to this period, manufactures were everywhere feeble and fluctuating in their development; shooting forth luxuriantly for a season, and again withering almost to the roots, like annual plants. Their perennial growth now began in England, and attracted capital in copious streams to irrigate the rich domains of industry.

---

[1] The hundred-handed monster of Greek mythology.—Ed.

When this new career commenced, about the year 1770, the annual consumption of cotton in British manufactures was under four millions of pounds weight, and that of the whole of Christendom was probably not more than ten millions. Last year the consumption in Great Britain and Ireland was about two hundred and seventy millions of pounds, and that of Europe and the United States together four hundred and eighty millions. This prodigious increase is, without doubt, almost entirely due to the factory system founded and upreared by the intrepid native of Preston. If then this system be not merely an inevitable step in the social progression of the world, but the one which gives a commanding station and influence to the people who most resolutely take it, it does not become any man, far less a denizen of this favoured land, to vilify the author of a benefaction, which, wisely administered, may become the best temporal gift of Providence to the poor, a blessing destined to mitigate, and in some measure to repeal, the primeval curse pronounced on the labour of man, "in the sweat of thy face shalt thou eat bread." Arkwright well deserves to live in honoured remembrance among those ancient master-spirits, who persuaded their roaming companions to exchange the precarious toils of the chase, for the settled comforts of agriculture.

In my recent tour, continued during several months, through the manufacturing districts, I have seen tens of thousands of old, young, and middle-aged of both sexes, many of them too feeble to get their daily bread by any of the former modes of industry, earning abundant food, raiment, and domestic accommodation, without perspiring at a single pore, screened meanwhile from the summer's sun and the winter's frost, in apartments more airy and salubrious than those of the metropolis, in which our legislative and fashionable aristocracies assemble. In those spacious halls the benignant power of steam summons around him his myriads of willing menials, and assigns to each the regulated task, substituting for painful muscular effort on their part, the energies of his own gigantic arm, and demanding in return only attention and dexterity to correct such little aberrations as casually occur in his workmanship. The gentle docility of this moving force qualifies it for impelling the tiny bobbins of the lace-machine with a precision and speed inimitable by the most dexterous hands, directed by the sharpest eyes. Hence, under its auspices, and in obedience to Arkwright's polity, magnificent edifices, surpassing far in number, value, usefulness, and ingenuity of construction, the boasted monuments of Asiatic, Egyptian, and Roman despotism, have, within the short period of fifty years, risen up in this kingdom, to show to what extent capital, industry, and science may augment the resources of a state, while they meliorate the condition of its citizens. Such is the factory system, replete with prodigies in mechanics and political economy, which promises, in its future growth, to become the great minister of civilization to the terraqueous globe, enabling this country, as its heart, to diffuse along with its commerce, the life-blood of science and religion to myriads of people still lying "in the region and shadow of death."

When Adam Smith wrote his immortal elements of economics, automatic machinery being hardly known, he was properly led to regard the division of labour as the grand principle of manufacturing improvement; and he showed, in the example of pin-making, how each handicraftsman, being thereby enabled to perfect himself by practice in one point, became a quicker and cheaper workman. In each branch of manufacture he saw that some parts were, on that principle, of easy execution, like the cutting of pin wires into uniform lengths, and some were comparatively difficult, like the formation and fixation of their heads; and therefore he concluded that to each a workman of appropriate value and cost was naturally assigned. This appropriation forms the very essence of the division of labour, and has been constantly made since the origin of society. The ploughman, with powerful hand and skilful eye, has been always hired at high wages to form the furrow, and the ploughboy at low wages, to lead the team. But what was in Dr. Smith's time a topic of useful illustration, cannot now be used without risk of misleading the public mind as to the right principle of manufacturing industry. In fact, the division, or rather adaptation of labour to the different talents of men, is little thought of in factory employment. On the contrary, wherever a process requires peculiar dexterity and steadiness of hand, it is withdrawn as soon as possible from the *cunning* workman, who is prone to irregularities of many kinds, and it is placed in charge of a peculiar mechanism, so self-regulating, that a child may superintend it. Thus,—to take an example from the spinning of cotton—the first operation in delicacy and importance, is that of laying the fibres truly parallel in the spongy slivers, and the next is that of drawing these out into slender spongy cords, called rovings, with the least possible twist; both being perfectly uniform throughout their total length. To execute either of these processes tolerably by a hand-wheel would require a degree of skill not to be met with in one artisan out of a hundred. But fine yarn could not be made in factory-spinning except by taking these steps, nor was it ever made by machinery till Arkwright's sagacity contrived them. Moderately good yarn may be spun indeed on the *hand-wheel* without any drawings at all, and with even indifferent rovings, because the thread, under the twofold action of twisting and extension, has a tendency to equalize itself.

The principle of the factory system then is, to substitute mechanical science for hand skill, and the partition of a process into its essential constituents, for the division or graduation of labour among artisans. On the handicraft plan, labour more or less skilled, was usually the most expensive element of production—*Materiam superabat opus;* but on the automatic plan, skilled labour gets progressively superseded, and will, eventually, be replaced by mere overlookers of machines.

By the infirmity of human nature it happens, that the more skilful the workman, the more self-willed and intractable he is apt to become, and, of course, the less fit a component of a mechanical system, in which, by occasional irregularities, he may do great damage to the whole. The grand object therefore of the modern manufacturer is, through the union of capital and science, to reduce the task of his work-people to the exercise of vigilance and dexterity,—faculties, when concentred to one process, speedily brought to perfection in the young. In the infancy of mechanical engineering, a machine-factory displayed the division of labour in manifold gradations—the file, the drill, the lathe, having each its different workmen in the order of skill: but the dexterous hands of the filer and driller are now superseded by the planing, the key-groove cutting, and the drilling-machines; and those of the iron and brass turners, by the self-acting slide-lathe. Mr. Anthony Strutt, who conducts the mechanical department of the great cotton factories of Belper and Milford, has so thoroughly departed from the old routine of the schools, that he will employ no man who has learned his craft by regular apprenticeship; but in contempt, as it were, of the division of labour principle, he sets a ploughboy to turn a shaft of perhaps several tons weight, and never has reason to repent his preference, because he infuses into the turning apparatus a precision of action, equal, if not superior, to the skill of the most experienced journeyman.

An eminent mechanician in Manchester told me, that he does not choose to make any steam-engines at present, because with his existing means, he would need to resort to the old principle of the division of labour, so fruitful of jealousies and strikes among workmen; but he intends to prosecute that branch of business whenever he has prepared suitable arrangements on the equalization of labour, or automatic plan. On the graduation system, a man must serve an apprenticeship of many years before his hand and eye become skilled enough for certain mechanical feats; but on the system of decomposing a process into its constituents, and embodying each part in an automatic machine, a person of common care and capacity may be entrusted with any of the said elementary parts after a short probation, and may be transferred from one to another, on any emergency, at the discretion of the master. Such translations are utterly at variance with the old practice of the division of labour, which fixed one man to shaping the head of a pin, and another to sharpening its point, with most irksome and spirit-wasting uniformity, for a whole life.

It was indeed a subject of regret to observe how frequently the workman's eminence, in any craft, had to be purchased by the sacrifice of his health and comfort. To one unvaried operation, which required unremitting dexterity and diligence, his hand and eye were constantly on the strain, or if they were suffered to swerve from their task for a time, considerable loss ensued, either to the employer, or the operative, according as the work was done by the day or by the piece. But on the equalization plan of self-acting machines, the operative needs to call his faculties only into agreeable exercise; he is seldom harassed with anxiety or fatigue, and may find many leisure moments for either amusement or meditation, without detriment to his master's interests or his own. As his business consists in tending the work of a well regulated mechanism, he can learn it in a short period; and when he transfers his services from one machine to another, he varies his task, and enlarges his views, by thinking on those general combinations which result from his and his companions' labours. Thus, that cramping of the faculties, that narrowing of the mind, that stunting of the frame, which were ascribed, and not unjustly, by moral writers, to the division of labour, cannot, in common circumstances, occur under the equable distribution of industry. How superior in vigour and intelligence are the factory mechanics in Lancashire, where the latter system of labour prevails, to the handicraft artisans of London, who, to a great extent, continue slaves to the former! The one set is familiar with almost every physico-mechanical combination, while the other seldom knows anything beyond the pin-head sphere of his daily task.

It is, in fact, the constant aim and tendency of every improvement in machinery to supersede human labour altogether, or to diminish its cost, by substituting the industry of women and children for that of men; or that of ordinary labourers, for trained artisans. In most of the water-twist, or throstle cotton-mills, the spinning is entirely managed by females of sixteen years and upwards. The effect of substituting the self-acting mule for the common mule, is to discharge the greater part of the men spinners, and to retain adolescents and children. The proprietor of a factory near Stockport states, in evidence to the commissioners, that by such substitution, he would save 50l. a week in wages, in consequence of dispensing with nearly forty male spinners, at about 25s. of wages each. This tendency to employ merely children with watchful eyes and nimble fingers, instead of journeymen of long experience, shows how the scholastic dogma of the division of labour into degrees of skill has been exploded by our enlightened manufacturers.

They are, in truth, much better acquainted with the general economy of the arts, and better qualified to analyse them into their real principles, than the recluse academician can possibly be, who from a few obsolete data, traces out imaginary results, or conjures up difficulties seldom encountered in practice. He may fancy, for example, that in a great establishment, where several hundred people are employed in producing fine goods, much time and expense must be incurred in verifying the quality and quantity of the work done by each individual. But this verification forms an integral step in the train of operations, and therefore constitutes no appreciable part of the cost of the manufactured article. Thus, for example, the reeling of yarn into hanks measures its length; the weighing of a few miscellaneous hanks determines the grist of the whole; and the *taker-in of work* rapidly ascertains its soundness. For examining the quality of the very fine yarns used in lace-making, he is aided by machines which register rapidly the uniformity of its cohesive strength, and the exact volume which one hundred yards of it occupy. The lace-maker again, on his part, verifies the grist of all the thread he purchases, in the necessary act of filling the circular grooves of his tiny bobbins, preparatory to their entering into his machine.

The university man, pre-occupied with theoretical *formulae*, of little practical bearing, is too apt to undervalue the science of the factory, though, with candour and patience, he would find it replete with useful applications of the most beautiful dynamical and statical problems. In physics, too, he would there see many theorems bearing golden fruit, which had been long barren in college ground. The phenomena of heat, in particular, are investigated in their multifarious relations to matter, solid, liquid, and aeriform. The measure of temperature on every scale is familiar to the manufacturer, as well as the distribution of caloric, and its habitudes with different bodies. The production of vapours; the relation of their elastic force to their temperature; the modes of using them as instruments of power, and sources of heat; their most effective condensation; their hygrometric agency; may all be better studied in a week's residence in Lancashire, than in a session of any university in Europe. And as to exact mechanical science, no school can compete with a modern cotton-mill. . . .

24. Friedrich Engels on *The Condition of the Working Class in England*, 1845

Friedrich Engels (1820–95) is best known for his collaboration with Karl Marx (1818–83), which began in 1844. Engels' own contributions to the collaboration were his powers of observation, common sense, and his personal generosity. He was born the son of a German Rhineland manufacturer, and served part of his apprenticeship for business in his father's branch factory in Manchester, England. There he was able to study English industrial experience in the light of the Hegelian historical philosophy and the French revolutionary precepts that attracted many young men of his generation. Engels believed that material history, as distinguished from metaphysical speculation, was the key to understanding events and the guidebook to human progress, and he believed that the crucial historical phenomenon of the nineteenth century was industrial capitalism. In his *Condition of the Working Class in England*, compassion for the oppressed was conjoined with faith in progress and fascination with the course of industrial development—a combination characteristic of the forties and one that prophesied an imminent end to Metternich's Europe. [Friedrich Engels, *The Condition of the Working Class in England in 1844*, trans. F. K. Wischnewetzky (London, 1892), pp. 1–18.]

Introduction

THE HISTORY of the proletariat in England begins with the second half of the last century, with the invention of the steam-engine and of machinery for working cotton. These inventions gave rise, as is well known, to an industrial revolution, a revolution which altered the whole civil society; one, the historical importance of which is only now beginning to be recognised. England is the classic soil of this transformation, which was all the mightier, the more silently it proceeded; and England is, therefore, the classic land of its chief product also, the proletariat. Only in England can the proletariat be studied in all its relations and from all sides.

We have not, here and now, to deal with the history of this revolution, nor with its vast importance for the present and the future. Such a delineation must be reserved for a future, more comprehensive work. For the moment, we must limit ourselves to the little that is necessary for understanding the facts that follow, for comprehending the present state of the English proletariat.

Before the introduction of machinery, the spinning and weaving of raw materials was carried on in the working-man's home. Wife and daughter spun the yarn that the father wove or that they sold, if he did not work it up himself. These weaver families lived in the country in the neighbourhood of the towns, and could get on fairly well with their wages, because the home market was almost the only one, and the crushing power of competition that came later, with the conquest of foreign markets and the extension of trade, did not yet press upon wages. There was, further, a constant increase in the demand for the home market, keeping pace with the slow increase in population and employing all the workers; and there was also the impossibility of vigorous competition of the workers among themselves, consequent upon the rural dispersion of their homes. So it was that the weaver was usually in a position to lay by something, and rent a little piece of land, that he cultivated in his leisure hours, of which he had as many as he chose to take, since he could weave whenever and as long as he pleased. True, he was a bad farmer and managed his land inefficiently, often obtaining but poor crops; nevertheless, he was no proletarian, he had a stake in the country, he was permanently settled, and stood one step higher in society than the English workman of to-day.

So the workers vegetated throughout a passably comfortable existence, leading a righteous and peaceful life in all piety and probity; and their material position was far better than that of their successors. They did not need to overwork; they did no more than they chose to do, and yet earned what they needed. They had leisure for healthful work in garden or field, work which, in itself, was recreation for them, and they could take part besides in the recreations and games of their neighbours, and all these games—bowling, cricket, football, etc., contributed to their physical health and vigour. They were, for the most part, strong, well-built people, in whose physique little or no difference from that of their peasant neighbours was discoverable. Their children grew up in the fresh country air, and, if they could help their parents at work, it was only occasionally; while of eight or twelve hours work for them there was no question.

What the moral and intellectual character of this class was may be guessed. Shut off from the towns, which they never entered, their yarn and woven stuff being delivered to travelling agents for payment of wages—so shut off that old people who lived quite in the neighbourhood of the town never went thither until they were robbed of their trade by the introduction of machinery and obliged to look about them in the towns for work—the weavers stood upon the moral and intellectual plane of the yeomen with whom they were usually immediately connected through their little holdings. They regarded their squire, the greatest landholder of the region, as their natural superior; they asked advice of him, laid their small disputes before him for settlement, and gave him all honour, as this patriarchal relation involved. They were "respectable" people, good husbands and fathers, led moral lives because they had no temptation to be immoral, there being no groggeries or low houses in their vicinity, and because the host, at whose inn they now and then quenched their thirst, was also a respectable man, usually a large tenant farmer who took pride in his good order, good beer, and early hours. They had their children the whole day at home, and brought them up in obedience and the fear of God; the patriarchal relationship remained undisturbed so long as the children were unmarried. The young people grew up in idyllic simplicity and intimacy with their playmates until they married; and even though sexual intercourse before marriage almost unfailingly took place, this happened only when the moral obligation of marriage was recognised on both sides, and a subsequent wedding made everything good. In short, the English industrial workers of those days lived and thought after the fashion still to be found here and there in Germany, in retirement and seclusion, without mental activity and without violent fluctuations in their position in life. They could rarely read and far more rarely write; went regularly to church, never talked politics, never conspired, never thought, delighted in physical exercises, listened with inherited reverence when the Bible was read, and were, in their unquestioning humility, exceedingly well-disposed towards the "superior" classes. But intellectually, they were dead; lived only for their petty, private interest, for their looms and gardens, and knew nothing of the mighty movement which, beyond their horizon, was sweeping through mankind. They were comfortable in their silent vegetation, and but for the industrial revolution they would never have emerged from this existence, which, cosily romantic as it was, was nevertheless not worthy of human beings. In truth, they were not human beings; they were merely toiling machines in the service of the few aristocrats who had guided history down to that time. The industrial revolution has simply carried this out to its logical end by making the workers machines pure and simple, taking from them the last trace of independent activity, and so forcing them to think and demand a position worthy of men. As in France politics, so in England manufacture, and the movement of civil society in general drew into the whirl of history the last classes which had remained sunk in apathetic indifference to the universal interests of mankind.

The first invention which gave rise to a radical change in the state of the English workers was the jenny, invented in the year 1764 by a weaver, James Hargreaves, of Standhill, near Blackburn, in North Lancashire. This machine was the rough beginning of the later invented mule, and was moved by hand. Instead of one spindle like the ordinary spinning-wheel, it carried sixteen or eighteen manipulated by a single workman. This invention made it possible to deliver more yarn than heretofore. Whereas, though one weaver had employed three spinners, there had never been enough yarn, and the weaver had often been obliged to wait for it, there was now more yarn to be had than could be woven by the available workers. The demand for woven goods, already increasing, rose yet more in consequence of the cheapness of these goods, which cheapness, in turn, was the outcome of the diminished cost of producing the yarn. More weavers were needed, and weavers' wages rose. Now that the weaver could earn more at his loom, he gradually abandoned his farming, and gave his whole time to weaving. At that time a family of four grown persons and two children (who were set to spooling) could earn, with eight hours' daily work, four pounds sterling in a week, and often more if trade was good and work pressed. It happened often enough that a single weaver earned two pounds a week at his loom. By degrees the class of farming weavers wholly disappeared, and was merged in the newly arising class of weavers who lived wholly upon wages, had no property whatever, not even the pretended property of a holding, and so became working-men, proletarians. Moreover, the old relation between spinner and weaver was destroyed. Hitherto, so far as this had been possible, yarn had been spun and woven under one roof. Now that the jenny as well as the loom required a strong hand, men began to spin, and whole families lived by spinning, while others laid the antiquated, superseded spinning-wheel aside; and, if they had not means of purchasing a jenny, were forced to live upon the wages of the father alone. Thus began with spinning and weaving that division of labour which has since been so infinitely perfected.

While the industrial proletariat was thus developing with the first still very imperfect machine, the same machine gave rise to the agricultural proletariat. There had, hitherto, been a vast number of small landowners, yeomen, who had vegetated in the same unthinking quiet as their neighbours, the farming weavers. They cultivated their scraps of land quite after the ancient and inefficient fashion of their ancestors, and opposed every change with the obstinacy peculiar to such creatures of habit, after remaining stationary from generation to generation. Among them were many small holders also, not tenants in the present sense of the word, but people who had their land handed down from their fathers, either by hereditary lease, or by force of ancient custom, and had hitherto held it as securely as if it had actually been their own property. When the industrial workers withdrew from agriculture, a great number of small holdings fell idle, and upon these the new class of large tenants established themselves, tenants-at-will, holding fifty, one hundred, two hundred or more acres, liable to be turned out at the end of the year, but able by improved tillage and larger farming to increase the yield of the land. They could sell their produce more cheaply than the yeoman, for whom nothing remained when his farm no longer supported him but to sell it, procure a jenny or a loom, or take service as an agricultural labourer in the employ of a large farmer. His inherited slowness and the inefficient methods of cultivation bequeathed by his ancestors, and above which he could not rise, left him no alternative when forced to compete with men who managed their holdings on sounder principles and with all the advantages bestowed by farming on a large scale and the investment of capital for the improvement of the soil.

Meanwhile, the industrial movement did not stop here. Single capitalists began to set up spinning jennies in great buildings and to use water-power for driving them, so placing themselves in a position to diminish the number of workers, and sell their yarn more cheaply than single spinners could do who moved their own machines by hand. There were constant improvements in the jenny, so that machines continually became antiquated, and must be altered or even laid aside; and though the capitalists could hold out by the application of water-power even with the old machinery, for the single spinner this was impossible. And the factory system, the beginning of which was thus made, received a fresh extension in 1767, through the spinning throstle invented by Richard Arkwright, a barber, in Preston, in North Lancashire. After the steam-engine, this is the most important mechanical invention of the 18th century. It was calculated from the beginning for mechanical motive power, and was based upon wholly new principles. By the combination of the peculiarities of the jenny and throstle, Samuel Crompton, of Firwood, Lancashire, contrived the mule in 1785, and as Arkwright invented the carding engine, and preparatory ("slubbing and roving") frames about the same time, the factory system became the prevailing one for the spinning of cotton. By means of trifling modifications these machines were gradually adapted to the spinning of flax, and so to the superseding of hand-work here, too. But even then, the end was not yet. In the closing years of the last century, Dr. Cartwright, a country parson, had invented the power-loom, and about 1804 had so far perfected it, that it could successfully compete with the hand-weaver; and all this machinery was made doubly important by James Watt's steam-engine, invented in 1764, and used for supplying motive power for spinning since 1785.

With these inventions, since improved from year to year, the victory of machine-work over hand-work in the chief branches of English industry was won; and the history of the latter from that time forward simply relates how the hand-workers have been driven by machinery from one position after another. The consequences of this were, on the one hand, a rapid fall in price of all manufactured commodities, prosperity of commerce and manufacture, the conquest of nearly all the unprotected foreign markets, the sudden multiplication of capital and national wealth; on the other hand, a still more rapid multiplication of the proletariat, the destruction of all property-holding and of all security of employment for the working-class, demoralisation, political excitement, and all those facts so highly repugnant to Englishmen in comfortable circumstances, which we shall have to consider in the following pages. Having already seen what a transformation in the social condition of the lower classes a single such clumsy machine as the jenny had wrought, there is no cause for surprise as to that which a complete and interdependent system of finely adjusted machinery has brought about, machinery which receives raw material and turns out woven goods.

Meanwhile, let us trace the development of English manufacture somewhat more minutely, beginning with the cotton industry. In the years 1771–1775, there were annually imported into England rather less than 5,000,000 pounds of raw cotton; in the year 1841 there were imported 528,000,000 pounds, and the import for 1844 will reach at least 600,000,000 pounds. In 1834 England exported 556,000,000 yards of woven cotton goods, 76,500,000 pounds of cotton yarn, and cotton hosiery of the value of £1,200,000. In the same year over 8,000,000 mule spindles were at work, 110,000 power and 250,000 handlooms, throstle spindles not included, in the service of the cotton industry; and, according to MacCulloch's reckoning, nearly a million and a half human beings were supported by this branch, of whom but 220,000 worked in the mills; the power used in these mills was steam, equivalent to 33,000 horse-power, and water, equivalent to 11,000 horse-power. At present these figures are far from adequate, and it may be safely assumed that, in the year 1845, the power and number of the machines and the number of the workers is greater by one-half than it was in 1834. The chief centre of this industry is Lancashire, where it originated; it has thoroughly revolutionised this county, converting it from an obscure, ill-cultivated swamp into a busy, lively region, multiplying its population tenfold in eighty years, and causing giant cities such as Liverpool and Manchester, containing together 700,000 inhabitants, and their neighbouring towns, Bolton with 60,000, Rochdale with 75,000, Oldham with 50,000, Preston with 60,000, Ashton and Stalybridge with 40,000, and a whole list of other manufacturing towns to spring up as if by a magic touch. The history of South Lancashire contains some of the greatest marvels of modern times, yet no one ever mentions them, and all these miracles are the product of the cotton industry. Glasgow, too, the centre for the cotton district of Scotland, for Lanarkshire and Renfrewshire, has increased in population from 30,000 to 300,000 since the introduction of the industry. The hosiery manufacture of Nottingham and Derby also received one fresh impulse from the lower price of yarn, and a second one from an improvement of the stocking loom, by means of which two stockings could be woven at once. The manufacture of lace, too, became an important branch of industry after the invention of the lace machine in 1777; soon after that date Lindley invented the point-net machine, and in 1809 Heathcote invented the bobbin-net machine, in consequence of which the production of lace was greatly simplified, and the demand increased proportionately in consequence of the diminished cost, so that now, at least 200,000 persons are supported by this industry. Its chief centres are Nottingham, Leicester, and the West of England, Wiltshire, Devonshire, etc. A corresponding extension has taken place in the branches dependent upon the cotton industry, in dyeing, bleaching, and printing. Bleaching by the application of chlorine in place of the oxygen of the atmosphere; dyeing and printing by the rapid development of chemistry, and printing by a series of most brilliant mechanical inventions, a yet greater advance which, with the extension of these branches caused by the growth of the cotton industry, raised them to a previously unknown degree of prosperity.

The same activity manifested itself in the manufacture of wool. This had hitherto been the leading department of English industry, but the quantities formerly produced are as nothing in comparison with that which is now manufactured. In 1782 the whole wool crop of the preceding three years lay unused for want of workers, and would have continued so to lie if the newly invented machinery had not come to its assistance and spun it. The adaptation of this machinery to the spinning of wool was most successfully accomplished. Then began the same sudden development in the wool district, which we have already seen in the cotton districts. In 1738 there were 75,000 pieces of woollen cloth produced in the West Riding of Yorkshire; in 1817 there were 490,000 pieces, and so rapid was the extension of the industry that in 1834, 450,000 more pieces were produced than in 1825. In 1801, 101,000,000 pounds of wool (7,000,000 pounds of it imported) were worked up; in 1835, 180,000,000 pounds were worked up; of which 42,-000,000 pounds were imported. The principal centre of this industry is the West Riding of Yorkshire, where, especially at Bradford, long English wool is converted into worsted yarns, etc.; while in the other cities, Leeds, Halifax, Huddersfield, etc., short wool is converted into hard-spun yarn and cloth. Then come the adjacent part of Lancashire, the region of Rochdale, where in addition to the cotton industry much flannel is produced, and the West of England which supplies the finest cloths. Here also the growth of population is worthy of observation:

Bradford contained in 1801	29,000	and in 1831	77,000	inhabitants
Halifax	"	"	63,000	"	"	110,000	"
Huddersfield	"	"	15,000	"	"	34,000	"
Leeds	"	"	53,000	"	"	123,000	"
And the whole West Riding	564,000	"	"	980,000	"

A population which, since 1831, must have increased at least 20 to 25 per cent further. In 1835 the spinning of wool employed in the United Kingdom 1,313 mills, with 71,300 workers, these last being but a small portion of the multitude who are supported directly or indirectly by the manufacture of wool, and excluding nearly all weavers.

Progress in the linen trade developed later, because the nature of the raw material made the application of spinning machinery very difficult. Attempts had been made in the last years of the last century in Scotland, but the Frenchman, Girard, who introduced flax spinning in 1810, was the first who succeeded practically, and

even Girard's machines first attained on British soil the importance
they deserved by means of improvements which they underwent
in England, and of their universal application in Leeds, Dundee,
and Belfast. From this time the British linen trade rapidly extended.
In 1814, 3,000 tons of flax were imported; in 1833, nearly 19,000
tons of flax and 3,400 tons of hemp. The export of Irish linen to
Great Britain rose from 32,000,000 yards in 1800 to 53,000,000 in
1825, of which a large part was re-exported. The export of English
and Scotch woven linen goods rose from 24,000,000 yards in 1820
to 51,000,000 yards in 1833. The number of flax spinning establishments in 1835 was 347, employing 33,000 workers, of which one-
half were in the South of Scotland, more than 60 in the West
Riding of Yorkshire, Leeds, and its environs, 25 in Belfast, Ireland,
and the rest in Dorset and Lancashire. Weaving is carried on in
the South of Scotland, here and there in England, but principally
in Ireland.

With like success did the English turn their attention to the
manufacture of silk. Raw material was imported from Southern
Europe and Asia ready spun, and the chief labour lay in the twisting of fine threads. Until 1824 the heavy import duty, four shillings
per pound on raw material, greatly retarded the development of
the English silk industry, while only the markets of England and
the Colonies were protected for it. In that year the duty was
reduced to one penny, and the number of mills at once largely increased. In a single year the number of throwing spindles rose
from 780,000 to 1,180,000; and, although the commercial crisis of
1825 crippled this branch of industry for the moment, yet in 1827
more was produced than ever, the mechanical skill and experience
of the English having secured their twisting machinery the supremacy over the awkward devices of their competitors. In 1835 the
British Empire possessed 263 twisting mills, employing 30,000
workers, located chiefly in Cheshire, in Macclesfield, Congleton,
and the surrounding districts, and in Manchester and Somersetshire.
Besides these, there are numerous mills for working up waste, from
which a peculiar article known as spun silk is manufactured, with
which the English supply even the Paris and Lyons weavers. The
weaving of the silk so twisted and spun is carried on in Paisley
and elsewhere in Scotland, and in Spitalfields, London, but also in
Manchester and elsewhere. Nor is the gigantic advance achieved
in English manufacture since 1760 restricted to the production of

clothing materials. The impulse, once given, was communicated to all branches of industrial activity, and a multitude of inventions wholly unrelated to those here cited, received double importance from the fact that they were made in the midst of the universal movement. But as soon as the immeasurable importance of mechanical power was practically demonstrated, every energy was concentrated in the effort to exploit this power in all directions, and to exploit it in the interest of individual inventors and manufacturers; and the demand for machinery, fuel, and materials called a mass of workers and a number of trades into redoubled activity. The steam-engine first gave importance to the broad coal-fields of England; the production of machinery began now for the first time, and with it arose a new interest in the iron mines which supplied raw material for it. The increased consumption of wool stimulated English sheep breeding, and the growing importation of wool, flax, and silk called forth an extension of the British ocean carrying trade. Greatest of all was the growth of production of iron. The rich iron deposits of the English hills had hitherto been little developed; iron had always been smelted by means of charcoal, which became gradually more expensive as agriculture improved and forests were cut away. The beginning of the use of coke in iron smelting had been made in the last century, and in 1780 a new method was invented of converting into available wrought-iron coke-smelted iron, which up to that time had been convertible into cast-iron only. This process, known as "puddling," consists in withdrawing the carbon which had mixed with the iron during the process of smelting, and opened a wholly new field for the production of English iron. Smelting furnaces were built fifty times larger than before, the process of smelting was simplified by the introduction of hot blasts, and iron could thus be produced so cheaply that a multitude of objects which had before been made of stone or wood were now made of iron.

In 1788, Thomas Paine, the famous democrat, built in Yorkshire the first iron bridge, which was followed by a great number of others, so that now nearly all bridges, especially for railroad traffic, are built of cast-iron, while in London itself a bridge across the Thames, the Southwark bridge, has been built of this material. Iron pillars, supports for machinery, etc., are universally used, and since the introduction of gas-lighting and railroads, new outlets for English iron products are opened. Nails and screws gradually came to be made by machinery. Huntsman, a Sheffielder, discovered in 1790 a method for casting steel, by which much labour was saved, and the production of wholly new cheap goods rendered practicable; and through the greater purity of the material placed at its disposal, and the more perfect tools, new machinery and minute division of labour, the metal trade of England now first attained importance. The population of Birmingham grew from 73,000 in 1801 to 200,000 in 1844; that of Sheffield from 46,000 in 1801 to 110,000 in 1844, and the consumption of coal in the latter city alone reached in 1836, 515,000 tons. In 1805 there were exported 4,300 tons of iron products and 4,600 tons of pig-iron; in 1834, 16,200 tons of iron products and 107,000 tons of pig-iron, while the whole iron product reaching in 1740 but 17,000 tons, had risen in 1834 to nearly 700,000 tons. The smelting of pig-iron alone consumes yearly more than 3,000,000 tons of coal, and the importance which coal mining has attained in the course of the last sixty years can scarcely be conceived. All the English and Scotch deposits are now worked, and the mines of Northumberland and Durham alone yield annually more than 5,000,000 tons for shipping, and employ from 40 to 50,000 men. According to the Durham *Chronicle*, there were worked in these two counties: In 1753, 14 mines; in 1800, 40 mines; in 1836, 76 mines; in 1843, 130 mines. Moreover, all mines are now much more energetically worked than formerly. A similarly increased activity was applied to the working of tin, copper, and lead, and alongside of the extension of glass manufacture arose a new branch of industry in the production of pottery, rendered important by the efforts of Josiah Wedgewood, about 1763. This inventor placed the whole manufacture of stoneware on a scientific basis, introduced better taste, and founded the potteries of North Staffordshire, a district of eight English miles square, which, formerly a desert waste, is now sown with works and dwellings, and supports more than 60,000 people.

Into this universal whirl of activity everything was drawn. Agriculture made a corresponding advance. Not only did landed property pass, as we have already seen, into the hands of new owners and cultivators, agriculture was affected in still another way. The great holders applied capital to the improvement of the soil, tore down needless fences, drained, manured, employed better tools, and applied a rotation of crops. The progress of science came to their assistance also; Sir Humphrey Davy applied chemistry to agriculture with success, and the development of mechanical science bestowed a multitude of advantages upon the large farmer. Further, in consequence of the increase of population, the demand for agricultural products increased in such measure that from 1760 to 1834, 6,840,540 acres of waste land were reclaimed; and, in spite of this, England was transformed from a grain exporting to a grain importing country.

The same activity was developed in the establishment of communication. From 1818 to 1829, there were built in England and Wales, 1,000 English miles of roadway of the width prescribed by law, 60 feet, and nearly all the old roads were reconstructed on the new system of M'Adam. In Scotland, the Department of Public Works built since 1803 nearly 900 miles of roadway and more than 1,000 bridges, by which the population of the Highlands was suddenly placed within reach of civilisation. The Highlanders had hitherto been chiefly poachers and smugglers; they now became farmers and hand-workers. And, though Gaelic schools were organised for the purpose of maintaining the Gaelic language, yet Gaelic-Celtic customs and speech are rapidly vanishing before the approach of English civilisation. So, too, in Ireland; between the counties of Cork, Limerick, and Kerry, lay hitherto a wilderness wholly without passable roads, and serving, by reason of its inaccessibility, as the refuge of all criminals and the chief protection of the Celtic Irish nationality in the South of Ireland. It has now been cut through by public roads, and civilisation has thus gained admission even to this savage region. The whole British Empire, and especially England, which, sixty years ago, had as bad roads as Germany or France then had, is now covered by a network of the finest roadways; and these, too, like almost everything else in England, are the work of private enterprise, the State having done very little in this direction.

Before 1755 England possessed almost no canals. In that year a canal was built in Lancashire from Sankey Brook to St. Helen's; and in 1759, James Brindley built the first important one, the Duke of Bridgewater's canal from Manchester, and the coal mines of the district to the mouth of the Mersey passing, near Barton, by aqueduct, over the river Irwell. From this achievement dates the canal building of England, to which Brindley first gave importance. Canals were now built, and rivers made navigable in all directions. In England alone, there are 2,200 miles of canals and 1,800 miles of navigable river. In Scotland, the Caledonian Canal was cut directly across the country, and in Ireland several canals were built. These improvements, too, like the railroads and roadways, are nearly all the work of private individuals and companies.

The railroads have been only recently built. The first great one was opened from Liverpool to Manchester in 1830, since which all the great cities have been connected by rail. London with Southampton, Brighton, Dover, Colchester, Exeter, and Birmingham; Birmingham with Gloucester, Liverpool, Lancaster (via Newton and Wigan, and via Manchester and Bolton); also with Leeds (via Manchester and Halifax, and via Leicester, Derby, and Sheffield); Leeds with Hull and Newcastle (via York). There are also many minor lines building or projected, which will soon make it possible to travel from Edinburgh to London in one day.

As it had transformed the means of communication by land, so did the introduction of steam revolutionise travel by sea. The first steamboat was launched in 1807, in the Hudson, in North America; the first in the British Empire, in 1811, on the Clyde. Since then, more than 600 have been built in England; and in 1836 more than 500 were plying to and from British ports.

Such, in brief, is the history of English industrial development in the past sixty years, a history which has no counterpart in the annals of humanity. Sixty, eighty years ago, England was a country like every other, with small towns, few and simple industries, and a thin but *proportionally* large agricultural population. To-day it is a country like *no* other, with a capital of two and a half million inhabitants; with vast manufacturing cities; with an industry that supplies the world, and produces almost everything by means of the most complex machinery; with an industrious, intelligent, dense population, of which two-thirds are employed in trade and commerce, and composed of classes wholly different; forming, in fact, with other customs and other needs, a different nation from the England of those days. The industrial revolution is of the same importance for England as the political revolution for France, and the philosophical revolution for Germany; and the difference between England in 1760 and in 1844 is at least as great as that between France, under the *ancien régime* and during the revolution of July. But the mightiest result of this industrial transformation is the English proletariat.

We have already seen how the proletariat was called into ex-

istence by the introduction of machinery. The rapid extension of
manufacture demanded hands, wages rose, and troops of workmen
migrated from the agricultural districts to the towns. Population
multiplied enormously, and nearly all the increase took place in
the proletariat. Further, Ireland had entered upon an orderly
development only since the beginning of the eighteenth century.
There, too, the population, more than decimated by English cruelty
in earlier disturbances, now rapidly multiplied, especially after the
advance in manufacture began to draw masses of Irishmen towards
England. Thus arose the great manufacturing and commercial cities
of the British Empire, in which at least three-fourths of the population belong to the working-class, while the lower middle-class
consists only of small shop-keepers, and very very few handicrafts-
men. For, though the rising manufacture first attained importance
by transforming tools into machines, workrooms into factories,
and consequently, the toiling lower middle-class into the toiling
proletariat, and the former large merchants into manufacturers,
though the lower middle-class was thus early crushed out, and the
population reduced to the two opposing elements, workers and
capitalists, this happened outside of the domain of manufacture
proper, in the province of handicraft and retail trade as well. In the
place of the former masters and apprentices, came great capitalists
and working-men who had no prospect of rising above their class.
Hand-work was carried on after the fashion of factory work, the
division of labour was strictly applied, and small employers who
could not compete with great establishments were forced down
into the proletariat. At the same time the destruction of the former
organisation of hand-work, and the disappearance of the lower
middle-class deprived the working-man of all possibility of rising
into the middle-class himself. Hitherto he had always had the
prospect of establishing himself somewhere as master artificer,
perhaps employing journeymen and apprentices; but now, when
master artificers were crowded out by manufacturers, when large
capital had become necessary for carrying on work independently,
the working-class became, for the first time, an integral, permanent
class of the population, whereas it had formerly often been merely
a transition leading to the bourgeoisie. Now, he who was born to
toil had no other prospect than that of remaining a toiler all his life.
Now, for the first time, therefore, the proletariat was in a position
to undertake an independent movement.

In this way were brought together those vast masses of working-men who now fill the whole British Empire, whose social condition forces itself every day more and more upon the attention of the civilised world. The condition of the working class is the condition of the vast majority of the English people. The question: What is to become of those destitute millions, who consume to-day what they earned yesterday; who have created the greatness of England by their inventions and their toil; who become with every passing day more conscious of their might, and demand, with daily increasing urgency, their share of the advantages of society? —This, since the Reform Bill, has become the national question. All Parliamentary debates, of any importance, may be reduced to this; and, though the English middle-class will not as yet admit it, though they try to evade this great question, and to represent their own particular interests as the truly national ones, their action is utterly useless. With every session of Parliament the working-class gains ground, the interests of the middle-class diminish in importance; and, in spite of the fact that the middle-class is the chief, in fact, the only power in Parliament, the last session of 1844 was a continuous debate upon subjects affecting the working-class, the Poor Relief Bill, the Factory Act, the Masters' and Servants' Act; and Thomas Duncombe, the representative of the working-men in the House of Commons, was the great man of the session; while the Liberal middle-class with its motion for repealing the Corn Laws, and the Radical middle-class with its resolution for refusing the taxes, played pitiable roles. Even the debates about Ireland were at bottom debates about the Irish proletariat, and the means of coming to its assistance. It is high time, too, for the English middle-class to make some concessions to the working-men who no longer plead but threaten; for in a short time it may be too late.

In spite of all this, the English middle-class, especially the manufacturing class, which is enriched directly by means of the poverty of the workers, persists in ignoring this poverty. This class, feeling itself the mighty representative class of the nation, is ashamed to lay the sore spot of England bare before the eyes of the world; will not confess, even to itself, that the workers are in distress, because it, the property-holding, manufacturing class, must bear the moral responsibility for this distress. Hence the scornful smile which intelligent Englishmen (and they, the middle-class, alone are known on the Continent) assume when any one begins to speak of the condition of the working-class; hence the utter ignorance on the part of the whole middle-class of everything which concerns the workers; hence the ridiculous blunders which men of this class, in and out of Parliament, make when the position of the proletariat comes under discussion; hence the absurd freedom from anxiety, with which the middle-class dwells upon a soil that is honeycombed, and may any day collapse, the speedy collapse of which is as certain as a mathematical or mechanical demonstration; hence the miracle that the English have as yet no single book upon the condition of their workers, although they have been examining and mending the old state of things no one knows how many years. Hence also the deep wrath of the whole working-class, from Glasgow to London, against the rich, by whom they are systematically plundered and mercilessly left to their fate, a wrath which before too long a time goes by, a time almost within the power of man to predict, must break out into a Revolution in comparison with which the French Revolution, and the year 1794, will prove to have been child's play.

25. Amédée Pommier on "Progress," 1844

Amédée Pommier (1804–77), a minor French poet with a didactic turn of mind, took seriously the French literary community's interest in a new poetry, a poetry that would adopt the imagery and the vocabulary of the industrial age. In the 1844 poem "Progress" he turned them against the industrial age itself; but in 1848 he won a competition sponsored by the French Academy for poems on the discovery of steam power, with a poem in which he celebrated progress and modern technology. His biographer in the *Nouvelle Biographie Générale*, published in 1866, remarks: "M. Pommier is notable for his extreme verve, combined with a remarkable facility in versification, and by a craving for originality that sometimes leads him into inappropriate use of neologisms and to certain crudities of expression that offend good taste." In the translation below no effort was made to retain the rhyme scheme of Pommier's couplets, but the meter approximates his own. [Amédée Pommier, *Colères* (Paris, 1844), pp. 79–87. Translation by the editor.]

Judge by the talk of certain optimists,
Enthusiasts for the age in which we live,
And man seems drawing near to a millennium;
Marching with great strides toward perfection;

Everything improves; the human race improves,
And soon will give no causes for complaint.
The world has come into the age of reason;
We'll all be happy: general agreement.

Precious bliss, which seems to coincide
With sinking hearts, a taste for suicide!
Crowds of folk are so pleased with the world
They take up pistols and blow out their brains,
Breathe in the gases that the coals give out,
Or use a slipknot, hung up on a nail.
Self-poisoning everywhere; and morn to night
They take their razors and they cut their throats,
They jump off towers, bridges, through the window,
In flight, apparently, from too much comfort.

I do not know what gloomy, dark anxiety
It is that's moving through the whole society.
The human soul's a field where insane pens
Have now for long been sowing poison seeds;
The crop has sprouted; from the earth there comes
A bitter reaping, a harvest-time of death.
Analyses of man and God Himself;
And in the furnace atheism blows hot,
All has vanished, vaporized and lost;
And disenchantment, this sad residue,
This *caput-mortuum* of philosophy,
Is what remains in the crucible of life.

Make no mistake; it does the future wrong
To make it promise what it cannot give.
So many fortunetellers to the nations;
So many marvels promised future men:
But of this fine scene, sweet and so seductive,
Nothing is certain but the present's evils.
They bring out utopians in swarms,
Crude echoes of the Platos and the Mores,
Dreaming, in our inferno, delights of heaven.
The ideal heightens distaste for the real.

Out of these follies, visionary spirits
Contrive, on paper, imaginary worlds.
Strange El Dorado, earthly Paradise,
Where we shall be benumbed with too much good.
Indeed: but till they make their dreams come true,
Ennui, that haunting specter, nags and gnaws us,
Ennui, which always outlives human passions,
Ennui, that pestilence of worn-out nations.
It follows us: thence comes our eager appetite
For anything to shock or scourge existence;
Worn down incessantly by our own selves,
We throw ourselves in fits like those possessed.
Our era, like the needle of a compass,
Tormented by erratic vertigo,
Behaving like a fever, building up,
And so it sets the human spirit spinning.

We have in our convulsions but one wish,
To redouble our pace, speed up our lives;
We civilize ourselves at a full run,
We want to hurry and to improvise,
To do away with time, abolish distance,
Leap over vaster spaces all at once.
Progress, in our time, is running wild.
Hola! Ho! Hold in your fiery horses,
Perfectibility, intoxicated dame
Who drives the coach in which humanity rides!
This race of the compulsive frightens me;
I think it would be better to go slow,
Unless we want to finish up our drive
By tumbling arsy-versy in the ditch.

In vain such wise advice. We love it all,
This hellish haste, this leveling of the hills;
We fill up every gorge, and like an octopus,
The *railway* seizes Cybele in its arms,
The locomotive with its hot black breath
Passes at a speed that stuns the sight,
Dragging the wagons fastened in its train,

And on the waters see the steamship now,
Swift in its engines and its smoking stack,
A new leviathan, smash down the foaming waves,
Contemptuous of the squalls and swells it breaks
With those repeated blows of iron fins.

So all is conquered: mountains, vales, and seas.
It's not enough; learn how to steer balloons.
Yet in all this — often do I miss
The porters' chair, the humble vehicle,
The only transport that our forebears knew,
Who did not go so fast and traveled better.
I am old-fashioned: said defiantly!
A sluggish spirit, slow, behind the times.
I've never loved ambition overmuch,
Nor thought good fortune lies in agitation.
Our busy era made itself a habit
Out of noise, of changes, and unrest,
And its activity, so preached to us,
Is like the feverish twitching of the sick.
With its fine progress, its commercialism,
It lives a spastic, irritable life.
All our brains, tuned to the highest pitch,
Are like steel springs that no one can unwind.
Knowledge expands till we are overwhelmed,
There are so many skills and powers now.
Our times are marked by a precocity:
The overheated minds of adolescents
Seem, responding to our own impatience,
To race through knowledge like a railroad train,
Poor little old men, wise before their time,
Better they were thoughtless, didn't care.

The progressists are truly priceless people:
They talk of happiness, while frightful ills,
The fruits of competition and congestion,
Grow steadily among the Christian peoples.
Yes, of course; they work, produce; one speculates
In cotton yarns, another one in starch;

Every day we see how some invention
Has changed the processes of manufacture;
Sidewalks made of wood, and asphalt roads,
Gas reflectors with their glaring flames,
Give ecstasies to fools of artifice;
A thousand gadgets ornament our markets;
Rubber is king: the enema supplants
Pewter syringe and old injection tube.
But what do these efforts matter, after all,
When the more that we produce the more we want,
When the conflict among individuals,
And that hideous sore called pauperism
Belie each day, in sad reality,
False claims that all is well and prosperous?
Sphinx, Chimera, and Minotaur are less to fear:
A scourge besets us; it is plethora,
It is this teeming of our human cattle,
These leagues of laborers who have no work,
These far too many arms, these starving mobs,
Who swell demands upon the public dole.

Go, talk about the wealth of modern states,
With their artisans, pitiful slaves,
Who work themselves to death for wretched pay!
For my part, I'd as soon be in the galleys
As in their place. For every manual trade,
When it means life or death, is a cruel load.
For such a fate, oh! thank you, no!
And I a thousand times prefer the inertia
Of peoples who choose immobility.
I'd sooner copy in tranquility
The fakir's contemplation of his navel,
The savage crouching silent in his hut,
The indolent Negroes, and the lazzaroni
Content with just some soup or macaroni.
To praise hard work! A farce! stupidity!
The greatest boon is surely idleness.
Can our fatigue of body ever match
The divine nonchalance known in the East?

I like indolence, calm, laziness;
And everybody, really, though not seeming,
Is of this mind; all aim at leisure,
And if they work at something, want the choice.

     Still, if in the sweat of this poor proletariat
Real blessings should be born on this old earth!
Industrialism, though, however active,
Puts up a mighty show but goes nowhere.
The feverish motion of productive peoples
Is grandly sterile for the good of man.
And all our claimed advance toward perfection
Is only braggadocio and fraud;
We act just like the squirrel in his cage,
Who runs his wheel and works up to a rage,
And makes himself an endless, mighty fuss,
A panting gallop, which brings no advance.

     Beauty, now, which matters most to me,
Makes mockery of knowledge, and never is perfected.
The heavens blue, the sun, the stars, the forests,
The sea, the hills, the flowers: they do not progress;
Art now is not more moving, woman not more lovely
Than in the time of Phidias, Zeuxis, Apelles.
Homer need not fear the modern poets,
And the verse of Virgil goes unrivaled.

     So progress only comes in useful objects,
Like tables, houses, clothing, pots and pans;
At that low level, even, with such wretched objects,
Our age's victories are but absurd.
Such things now are corrupted and perverted!
I offer an example: pressure cookers.
The pressure cooker, now, is an invention
Very good for making very bad broth;
With it you can cook up stews most horrid;
True, in return it offers one advantage:
Most of the time it blows itself to pieces
As if it were a bomb, and breaks your bones.

Thus the progress of our time of blessings.
We have a supreme urge that drives us onward,
To buy things cheap, find bargains. What we purchase
Is like houses made of mud and spit, where man
Is packaged like a body in its coffin,
In plated pots, and metal cans, and pasteboard boxes,
In cheapside costume, meanly fabricated,
In chairs that crumble when you sit in them,
Everything is jerry-built, false, and wretched;
No more are things made well, or made to last.

    And that is why the European spirit,
This maddened spirit, drives itself so hard,
Working endlessly, like the Danaïdes
Forever filling casks forever empty!
They excavate the earth in many places,
They cut into its flanks, the operation
That's called Caesarian; they dig it and they probe it;
All's hollow, undermined—For God's sake, easy!
At least leave God's good earth to breathe in peace!
Don't override it, like the drunk postilion
Who flogs and flogs the horse entrusted to him;
Use the horse without such brutal spurring;
This poor sphere now is gasping for its breath.
You have stirred all matter to such turmoil,
It cries, it groans, this poor tormented slave.
We even see it often in rebellion,
Steam visits you with dread retaliation.
And with your coal besides, with all this burning,
You squander horribly here in this century;
What will remain to those unfortunate ages
That follow you? For them you are preparing
A plundered world, abominable, sterile.
The planet soon will cease to be inhabitable.
What you call achievement of perfection
Is leveling, and uniformity.
You make everything even, yours is a genius
Of chill, of boredom, of monotony.
A globe planed smooth is nothing that I want,
And I am truly sorry for our children.

26. Camillo di Cavour on Railways in Italy, 1846

Count Camillo Benso di Cavour (1810–61), a rather cosmopolitan
native of the North Italian Kingdom of Piedmont, was the son of an
Italian nobleman and a Swiss Protestant mother. Youthful radicalism
lost him the favor of the Piedmontese royal court, where he served as
a page, and he gave up a brief effort at a military career when it seemed
to him that royal disfavor blocked him there as well. Yet he remained
convinced that the progress of Italian national unity and freedom required the leadership of the relatively advanced Italian North. After
the Italian revolutionary risings of the thirties had been suppressed,
Cavour came to believe that only a movement based on political moderation, in contrast with what he considered the radical extravagances
of a Mazzini, could do the work of Italian progress and unity. During
the 1830's and 1840's he traveled, and studied and wrote on economics;
he helped organize banks, industries, and societies for agricultural improvements. In 1847 and 1848 he returned to politics (see his statement
of principles in the first issue of *Il Risorgimento* below, pp. 336–41). He
became prime minister of Piedmont; and from this position, through
the exercise of superb political grasp and intense personal effort, he
became the main architect of the constitutional Kingdom of Italy in
1861. The article "On Railways in Italy" was a review of a book of
that title by Count Petitti, counselor of state to the government of
Piedmont; it appeared in the *Revue Nouvelle* of May, 1846. [*Gli scritti
del Conti di Cavour*, ed. D. Zanichelli (Bologna, 1892). Translation by
Professor Laurence Veysey.]

TODAY NO one possessed of an ordinary share of good sense contests
any longer the utility, we shall even say the necessity, of railways.
A few years have sufficed to bring about a complete revolution in
public opinion in their favor. The doubts they used to inspire in
statesmen, the uncertainties over their financial success aroused in
the minds of the boldest speculators, have given way to an unlimited confidence. The public mind has passed almost without
transition from mistrust to so great an enthusiasm that there is
perhaps no longer in Europe any locality so poor, nor any joint
undertaking so modest, that it does not hope directly to participate,
sooner or later, in the benefits of this marvelous triumph of the
nineteenth century.

To be sure, the impatience of the public is not free from exaggeration. Under the influence of the violent change in opinion,

illusive hopes have come into being about the immediate results railways can achieve. Nevertheless, if one looks at the future as a whole in this respect, if one seeks to develop the entire series of consequences their general adoption must necessarily bring about, one is forced to agree that the hopes they have raised may be premature as to the exact time of their realization, but that in absolute terms these hopes still fall far short of the truth.

The steam engine is a discovery which in its great effects can only be compared to that of printing, or indeed to that of the American continent. These immense discoveries, although they trace back four centuries already, are far from having unrolled before our eyes the whole series of effects they are destined to produce. It will be the same with the triumph the world has achieved in transforming steam into a motive force unlimited in its action and applicable to so many uses. Many generations will pass before one may calculate all its implications. Nor has anyone yet tried to determine, so far, the full extent of the changes this new form of power must create in the economies of civilized peoples.

The influence of railways will be felt all over the world. Within the countries that have arrived at a high degree of civilization, they will give a mighty thrust to industry; their economic results will be magnificent right from the beginning, and they will accelerate the progressive movement of society. But the moral effects that must follow, greater still to our eyes than their material effects, will be above all remarkable in those nations which, in the upward march of modern peoples, have remained backward. For such nations railways will be more than a means of self-enrichment; they will be a powerful weapon with the help of which they will succeed in triumphing over the retarding forces that keep them in a baneful state of industrial and political infancy. The locomotive, we have the firm conviction, has for its mission the reduction, if not the utter disappearance, of the humiliating inferiority to which numerous branches of the great Christian family are reduced. Seen in this light, it plays a role that is in a manner providential; that may be why we see it triumph so easily and so quickly over difficulties and obstacles that seemed destined to prevent its penetration into certain countries for a long time.

If what we have just said is true, if we are not under the spell of a complete illusion, no country is more justified than Italy in basing the greatest hopes on the railways' effects. The extent of the

political and social consequences that must follow in that fair country will bear witness, better than anywhere else, to the greatness
of the role these new pathways of communication are called upon
to play in the world's future. Thus persuaded, we believe that it
will not be without interest to the readers of this review if we
proceed to develop, just as we intend to do, the questions that relate to the establishment of railways in Italy.

Our task will be singularly facilitated by the work whose title is
placed at the head of this article. The learned author, Count Petitti,
after having powerfully contributed as a statesman to the success of
railways in his country, has sought, in his role as a distinguished
publicist, to make his fellow citizens share the understanding he
has acquired thanks to his long labors and fruitful researches. To
this end he has composed a book in which first he has assembled the
most accurate and the most detailed ideas upon all the railway
projects that have been carried out in Italy, upon those whose
building has begun, and even upon those which are still only in
the planning stage; and then he has gone on to treat, in a profound
and illuminating manner, the chief problems to which the application of railways gives rise. His study is a kind of complete manual
for the use of Italian readers. It is also destined to provide the
greatest service in a country where the grand questions of industrial
development are familiar to only a tiny number of readers.

Everyone, no matter what his country is, who approaches these
questions with a high degree of interest, will do well to read this
remarkable work from cover to cover. We shall confine ourselves,
in this article, to extracting from it the most salient facts, so as to
enable us to conceive of the whole future system of Italian railroads, and to drawing forth the necessary documentation of our
opinion concerning their great moral effects.

The fully active development of railways is still extremely restricted in Italy. Locomotives operate only on some short, isolated
stubs of trackage. Nevertheless, railway projects have occupied us
for a long time. In 1835 certain companies were already soliciting
the governments of the peninsula for franchises to operate several
important lines.

But these large-scale enterprises initially inspired a mistrust
among the capitalists, which the financial crisis that followed the
events of 1840 aggravated. The bad effect produced by the scant
success of several French railways likewise contributed to this mis-

trust, the result being that these first tentative efforts bore only feeble accomplishments. The line from Naples to Castellamare and that from Milan to Monza were the only ones that may be attributed to that period of almost sterile attempts.

Since then, the results—each year more remarkable and better known—of the British, German, Belgian, and French railways have enormously changed the Italian attitude. There, as everywhere else, the demand has arisen for the building of these marvelous paths that make child's play of time and space alike. Yielding to popular wishes, most of the Italian rulers have declared themselves in favor of railway construction. Several governments have taken direct charge of the building of major lines, without declining, however, the aid of private industry for the secondary routes; others limit themselves to encouraging the formation of powerful private companies charged with constructing all the lines within their borders.

At the present time, if one excepts the Roman States and some minor principalities, all the countries of Italy have actively put their hands to the task of railway building. Work has begun on several considerable routes, and a much greater number of plans are so far advanced that one cannot doubt but that construction will immediately proceed. At the point to which things have now arrived, it is possible to determine, if not with perfect precision then at least roughly, the future outlines of the great network of railways destined in some years' time to link every point in Italy, from the foot of the Alps to the far end of the Gulf of Taranto.

So that we may grasp the whole picture, let us trace a rapid sketch of the principal lines that will constitute the network. This picture will suffice to give an idea of its immense importance.

Geographically, Italy can be divided into two large sections. To the north, the valley of the Po, which joins itself to the Roman plains and the Marches towards Ancona and Loreto. To the south, all the regions that the Apennines divide and the Adriatic and Mediterranean Seas surround on three sides. The first section, the valley of the Po, to which industrious Liguria [the region of Genoa] is joined by political ties and commercial interests, offers an admirable field for railway development. So is it destined, in our view, to receive the greatest actual fruition. Aware of this truth, the Austrian government and the government of Piedmont, which together control the greatest part of the area, have formally manifested their intention of cooperating in every way in their power to bring into being the network the region deserves.

Toward this goal, the government at Turin, utilizing the considerable resources it has at its disposal, without mortgaging its future or imposing new burdens on its subjects, thanks to the wise economy of its administration, has decided that the lines combining a considerable economic interest with a political value will be built at state expense. For the building of secondary lines, it has appealed to private industry, which, we are happy to say, has not been deaf to the call.

The government lines that have been decreed and can be considered as in the course of construction are three in number. Having a common point of departure in the town of Alessandria [midway between Turin and Genoa], whose strategic importance is so great, these lines are directed toward Genoa, toward Turin, and toward Lake Maggiore. A simple glance at the map of Piedmont suffices to prove that these routes could be considered as forming the great arteries of the country. In fact, they join the capital with the sea, with Switzerland, and with the rest of northern Italy.

For the attaining of this last result, one weak gap exists, however, in the approved plans. As a result of some difficulties raised by the Austrian government, it has been impossible as yet to decide how to join the Piedmontese lines with those of Lombardy. Such a gap cannot long remain. Lombardy has too real and pressing an interest in establishing rapid and easy communication with the Mediterranean and with France for the Viennese government seriously to refuse to construct—on its own account or by granting permission to industry—the short and easy line that, going from Milan to the Ticino [River], will permit the steam engine to move without interruption throughout the whole length of the valley of the Po. The plans of the Sardinian government are not limited to those we have just indicated. It has declared its intention of executing a much more grandiose and important enterprise. It wishes to join Savoy to Piedmont by a railway that, piercing the Alps close to their base, would pass close to the pass of Mont Cenis, already notable for the road still considered one of the marvels of the Napoleonic regime.

This admirable project has been given study, and, if insurmountable difficulties do not raise themselves (which up to the present the most competent experts do not seem to foresee), we shall not be long in seeing the construction undertaken.

The railway from Turin to Chambéry [in Savoy, as just described], crossing the highest mountains in Europe, will be the masterpiece of modern industry; it will be the finest triumph of steam power, the crowning piece of its glory; after having tamed the most rapid rivers and the stormy waves of the ocean, it only remains for it to conquer the eternal snows and the glaciers that rise between diverse peoples like insuperable barriers. This railway will be one of the marvels of the world; it will render immortal the name of the king Charles-Albert, who will have had the courage to undertake its construction and the energy to see it completed. The incalculable benefits that must result from it will forever endear the memory of his reign, already marked by so many glorious works, not solely in the minds of his own subjects, but among all Italians.

[Ten paragraphs are omitted which deal with the possible routes of railroads on the Italian peninsula and end with a proposal for a line connecting Vienna with Trieste:]

Of all the railways we have discussed so far, this last is perhaps the only one whose usefulness to Italy can be contested. The argument would be that while it would offer obvious advantages from the economic point of view by facilitating the export to Germany of the abundant products of the Italian soil, it would at the same time enhance the influence of the House of Austria upon all Italy, and facilitate action by Austrian forces to hold Italy under its control. This objection is plausible, but unfounded.

If the future holds a happier fortune for Italy, if this fair land— so one may hope—is destined one day to regain its nationality, it can only be as the result of a major alteration in Europe, or as the result of one of those great upheavals, of one of those almost providential events in which the ability to move troops more or less rapidly by procuring control of the railway will exert no influence. The time of conspiracies has passed; the emancipation of peoples can come neither from a narrow plot nor from taking the enemy by surprise. It has become the necessary consequence of the progress of Christian civilization, of the growing enlightenment. The material forces governments have at their disposal will be powerless to maintain conquered nations in bondage, when the hour of their deliverance sounds; these governments will bow before the action of moral forces, which are growing daily and which sooner or later must cause in Europe, with the aid of Providence, a political up-heaval, from which Poland and Italy are destined to profit more than any other country.

The railway that will place Vienna and Milan only a few hours apart cannot impede such great events.

That being so, the railway line from Vienna to Trieste is one of those whose construction is the most to be desired; because it is im-mediately advantageous to Italian agriculture in assuring it plentiful outlets, and because in the future, when the relations established by conquest have given way to relations of equality and friendship, this line will render immense services to the country, in facilitating the intellectual and moral contacts that we, more than anyone, wish to see established between grave and profound Germany and intel-ligent Italy.

The railway question has been confronted rather less on the right bank of the Po, as compared with the left bank. The small ter-ritorial extent of the principalities into which that area is divided, the weakness of their financial resources, the imperfections of their administrative systems, and finally the existence of prejudices not yet eradicated, render problematical the execution of railway proj-ects within the southern part of the valley of the Po, beyond the area under Sardinian control. However, the uncertainty we are forced to record applies only to the matter of time. It cannot be doubted that within the not very distant future the rich plains of Parma and Milan will be supplied with a network of railways just like the other regions of northern Italy. A company made up of the most distinguished elements of Bologna and the towns of the Romagna has already for a year been seeking authorization to build at its own expense a line from Ancona to Bologna, with the inten-tion of extending it to Modena and Parma. The Papal government, by an excess of prudence, which it is easier to explain than to justify, has thus far refused its consent to the project. Nonetheless, it seems likely that the entreaties of the company and the repeated requests of the population, supported by the remonstrances of the distinguished prelate who administers the Legations, are on the point of triumphing over the resistance of the Court of Rome. One hopes to see appear shortly a decree from the Papal sovereign, granting a concession for the line from Ancona to Bologna to the company we have mentioned.

We appeal with all our heart for this happy change in Roman

policy; we do this not solely because of the importance of the line in question, but above all because the execution of great public works in the Romagna should provide immediate relief to the lower classes of that district, who have been so cruelly troubled for some time, and it should give the patriotism and activity of the upper and middle classes a nourishment that will make it easier for them to pursue the policy of patient waiting, which alone is suited to the present situation in Italy.

The line from Ancona to Bologna will inevitably lead to the building of one from Bologna to the Sardinian States by way of Modena and Parma. The company that will own the first line will have such an interest in seeing the second constructed that it will submit to all the conditions the controlling governments may wish to impose, and those governments will not long resist the ardent and legitimate desires of their subjects, aided by the efforts of a powerful company.

Thus one may hope that in the near future railway construction will take place with equal ardor on both banks of the Po. Without being considered a utopian, one can predict that within ten years the magnificent basin that the river forms will be traversed along its entire length by two great lines, which, having Turin as their point of common departure, will both lead to the Adriatic as their terminus—the one to Venice, after having traversed the fertile plains of Piedmont and Lombardy, the other to Ancona, after having linked the Sardinian States, the Duchies of Parma and Modena, the Legations and the Marches.

To these two principal lines will be joined a host of secondary lines, which will circulate populations and wealth in all directions. Finally, when this network is linked to the German lines through Trieste and to the French and Swiss lines by the connection through the Alps (that admirable proposal of King Charles-Albert), the north of Italy will be in a position to regain the high degree of prosperity and power to which her geographical position, the richness of her soil, and her natural resources of every kind give her the right. That will be, we like to think, the finest triumph of the railways.

[Seventeen paragraphs omitted.]

Tuscany . . . is the region of Italy where railway building is the most advanced. The adjoining region, the Papal State, is in exactly the opposite position. There nothing has been done; and, with the exception of the line from Bologna to Ancona, so energetically solicited by the Romagna, there is no thought of doing anything.

Such a fact is sad; however, one should not exaggerate the importance of the unfortunate antipathy railways inspire in the Roman government. Facts always triumph over erroneous opinions. The results of a single major line's operation will suffice, we are convinced, to modify the opinions of a goodly number of the Roman prelates. Six months after the line from Leghorn to Florence is opened to the public, most members of the Sacred College will change their minds; one may even hope that the case for the railways will be won at Rome sooner than this. We have beheld such rapid transformations of this sort, we have seen so many prejudices and antipathies that seemed invincible disappear so easily, that it seems probable to us that the Papal government will not much longer be the only one in Europe to prevent its people from also enjoying one of the greatest benefits of Providence.

When the present sentiments of the Roman Court are modified, Rome will soon become the center of a vast network of railways that will tie that august city with the two seas, Mediterranean and Adriatic, and also with Tuscany and the Kingdom of Naples. This system—whose execution, it is true, offers material difficulties, but not beyond the reach of modern industrial efforts—assures Rome a magnificent position. As the center of Italy, and in a sense of all the countries surrounding the Mediterranean, her power of attraction, already considerable, will receive an enormous boost. Rome being situated on the route from East to West, the peoples of every land will crowd within her walls to pay their respects to the ancient mistress of the world, the modern metropolis of Christianity, which, despite innumerable vicissitudes, is still the richest of cities in precious memories and magnificent hopes.

Thank heaven, after we cross the Roman frontier [to the south] we are no longer reduced to hypotheses and conjectures. In the Kingdom of Naples one finds some railroads already built, some in the course of construction, and a great number of wisely elaborated projects whose realization will not take long.

Naples was one of the first states of Italy to witness the inauguration of a railway line. Already two years ago locomotives were running from Naples to Castellamare and shortly afterward from Naples to Capua. These railways as yet have only small economic importance; their principal merit consists in the entertainment they provide for the populace of Naples and its numerous visitors. They are, above all, an admirable means of traveling past enchanting vistas; but they will not be long in playing a more important role, because they are destined to become the center of the principal routes of the kingdom. Their extension has been approved. The Capua line will be extended to the Roman frontier and thus will become an important portion of the line destined to link the two greatest cities of Italy, Rome and Naples. The southern line, from Nocera, should run eastward and reach the Adriatic at a point not yet determined. This second project, less advanced than the first, is nonetheless being studied, and its execution will not long be waiting.

The Neapolitan railways will not stop when they have reached the Adriatic. It is probable that, turning southward, they will cross the rich provinces washed by that sea, and that, extended to the bottom of the peninsula, they will form the farthest line of communication between the European continent and the eastern world.

It is scarcely possible to foresee the exact time when the Neapolitan network will be brought to completion; it will likely be outstripped by the network in the valley of the Po. Nevertheless, the advantages the railway is bound to offer to private enterprise in as populous a country as the Kingdom of Naples, and the well-known inclination of the king, permit us to hope that the south as well as the north of Italy will be well supplied with these new pathways, whose marvelous effects are destined powerfully to influence the fate of the beautiful Italian peninsula.

After the review we have just made of what is happening throughout Italy, we are ready to take measure of the great development that railways will achieve in this country. Within a few years the Po basin will be traversed in every direction by a vast system of rail routes, which will link all major points in the area, and, extending toward France by way of Savoy and toward Germany by way of Trieste, will put Italy in constant communication with the European continent. This system will be joined by one or two routes to the Tuscan network, destined, as we have seen, to be greatly extended. Finally, in the Kingdom of Naples a complete system radiating from the capital will enable steam engines to move from one sea to the other, and, extending to Tarento or Otranto, will stretch its hand toward the Orient.

Judging the future only by what has been done so far, one is forced to agree that the picture we are tracing is blurred by the gap the Roman States present. But this annoying blemish will also disappear. The Papal government will bow, like so many others, to factual evidence and to the incessant demands of its subjects. Then the railway lines will extend without interruption from the Alps to Sicily, making disappear the obstacles and the distances that separate the inhabitants of Italy and prevent them from forming a single and great nation.

Now that the general railway system Italy may expect has been described, it remains to seek out what effects it will probably produce, and to justify the hopes of more than one kind that we should like to bring our compatriots to share.

[Here follow ten paragraphs describing the material economic benefits railroads would bring to Italian industry and agriculture.]

In short . . . Italy will be called to a new and high commercial destiny. Its position at the center of the Mediterranean, where, like an immense projection, it seems destined to join Europe to Africa, will incontestably make it, when the steam engine traverses it throughout its whole length, the shortest and most convenient route from the East to the West. From the moment when one can embark at Taranto or at Brindisi, the present maritime distance between England, France, and Germany, on the one hand, and Africa or Asia on the other, will be halved. There is then no doubt that the great Italian lines will serve to transport most of the travelers and some of the more highly valued merchandise that move between these vast regions. Italy will furnish the most rapid means to proceed from England to the Indies and to China; this will be yet another abundant source of new profits. After all the preceding, it seems to us clearly demonstrated that the railways open up to Italy a magnificent economic perspective, and that they ought to furnish the means to recover the brilliant commercial position she occupied during the whole Middle Ages.

But, however great may be the material benefits railways are destined to spread throughout Italy, we do not hesitate to say that these will remain well below the moral effects they are bound to produce.

Some brief considerations will suffice to justify this assertion in the eyes of all whose opinions about our fatherland do not rest on erroneous foundations.

The misfortunes of Italy date from long ago. We do not seek to point out their numerous sources in our history. Such a labor would be misplaced here and would moreover be beyond our powers. But we believe we can state with certainty that the primary causes should be attributed to the political influence foreigners have exercised among us for centuries, and that the principal obstacles that prevent us from freeing ourselves from that baleful influence are in the first place the internal divisions, the rivalries, I will almost say the antipathies, that animate the different parts of the great Italian family against one another and, secondly, the mistrust that exists between the national rulers and the most energetic part of the population. This group is plainly the one whose often immoderate desire for progress, whose more vivid feeling of nationality, and whose more ardent love of country make it the indispensable aid, if not the principal instrument, in all attempts at emancipation.

If the influence of the railways diminishes these obstacles, and perhaps even makes them disappear, it naturally follows that this is one of the things that will do most to advance the spirit of Italian nationality. A system of communications that will provoke an unceasing movement of persons in all directions, and will forcibly place in contact peoples hitherto foreigners to each other, ought powerfully to contribute to the destruction of petty municipal passions, born of ignorance and prejudice, which already are undermined by the efforts of all the enlightened men of Italy. This induction is so evident that no one would dream of contesting it.

This first moral consequence of the establishment of railways in the Italian peninsula is so large in our eyes that it suffices to justify the enthusiasm railways excite among all the true friends of Italy.

The second moral effect we expect, although it may be less easy to grasp in its full impact at first approach, has still more importance.

The organization Italy received at the time of the Congress of Vienna was as arbitrary as it was defective. Supported by no principle, no more heedful of violated legitimacy in respect to Genoa and Venice than of national interests or the popular will, taking into account neither geographic circumstances nor general interests nor the particular interests that twenty years of revolution had created, this august assembly acted solely by virtue of the rights of the strongest, raising a political structure deprived of any moral foundation.

Such an act could only produce bitter fruit. Thus, in spite of the

paternal conduct of several of our national princes, the malcontent-
ment provoked by the new state of things grew rapidly during the
years which followed the Restoration, and storm clouds formed,
ready soon to burst forth. The ardent spirits, the fomenters of
innovation, utilizing the bellicose passions whose development had
been furthered under the Empire, and finding support in the generous feelings frustrated by the decrees of the Congress of Vienna,
succeeded in bringing about the sad protest movements of 1820
and 1821.

These revolutionary efforts, however easily they were suppressed (because the upper classes were divided and the masses
played only a weak part), nevertheless had deplorable consequences for Italy. Without rendering tyrannical the governments
of the country, these disastrous attempts aroused in them a strong
mistrust against all ideas of nationality, and halted the development
of progressive tendencies that were natural to them and of which
one could already see visible signs. A weakened, discouraged, and
profoundly divided Italy could for a long time thereafter not think
of making any effort to better its lot.

The passage of time began to efface the somber traces of the
events of 1821, when the July revolution [of 1830] arrived to stir
the European social structure to its foundations. The repercussions
of that great popular movement were considerable in Italy. The
thunder of the victory achieved by the people over a blame-
worthy but regularly constituted government excited democratic
passions to the highest degree, if not among the masses, at least
among the enterprising spirits who aspired to sway them. The
chance for a war of principles enveloping all Europe came to
awaken all the hopes of those who dreamed of the complete emancipation of the peninsula with the help of a social revolution. The
movements organized after 1830, with the exception of one in a
province where administrative conditions were peculiar, were easily
suppressed even before they had openly broken out. It had to be
so; for these movements, founded solely on republican ideas and
demagogic passions, could not have wide appeal. In Italy a democratic revolution has no chance of success. To convince oneself
of this, it is enough to analyze the elements that compose the faction favorable to political change. This party meets no great sympathy from the masses, who, except for some rare urban groups,
are in general too attached to the old institutions of the country.

Active power resides almost exclusively in the middle class and in one part of the upper class. Now, both of these have some very conservative interests to defend. In Italy property, thank heaven, is not the exclusive privilege of any class. Even where there exists the faded remains of a feudal nobility, it shares the landed property with the third estate.

Among the classes so strongly interested in maintaining social order, the subversive doctrines of Young Italy have taken little hold. Thus, with the exception of youthful spirits, among whom experience has not yet modified the doctrines imbibed in the exciting atmosphere of the schools, one may affirm that there exists in Italy only a very small number of persons seriously disposed to put into practice the fiery principles of a sect embittered by misfortune. If the social order were truly menaced, if the great principles on which it reposes were in real danger, one would see, we are persuaded, a good number of the most determined and violent partisans of the most extreme republicans turn up at once in the ranks of the conservative party.

The revolutionary agitations that followed from the events of 1830 had consequences as baleful as the military insurrections of 1820 and 1821. The governments, passionately attacked, pondered only how to defend themselves; putting aside all idea of progress and of Italian emancipation, they displayed an exclusive preoccupation with averting the dangers that menaced them and that were heightened in their eyes by the perfidious exaggerations of the reactionary party. Without wishing to justify all the repressive measures of which they made use in those sad circumstances, we believe that one could not justly reproach the motives these measures revealed. Because, for governments as well as for individuals, there exists a supreme right of self-conservation, to which the most rigorous moralist cannot set limits without letting himself fall into gross contradictions or ending up with absurd conclusions, contrary to the simplest notions of good sense.

Thank heaven, the stormy passions the July revolution aroused have calmed down, and their traces are nearly effaced. Things in Italy having returned to their natural course, the shaken confidence among the national princes has little by little been re-established; already the peoples feel the salutary effects of this happy change, and everything shows that we are moving toward a better future.

This future, which we call for with all our prayers, is the triumph of national independence, that highest good, which Italy can only attain by the combined efforts of all her children, the thing without which she can hope for no real or lasting improvements of her political condition, nor walk with confident step forward along the road to progress. What we have just advanced in joining our feeble voice to the eloquent one of our friend Signore Balbo,[1] is not an idle dream, the result of unreflecting feeling or of exalted imagination; it is a truth that to us seems susceptible of a rigorous demonstration.

The history of all ages proves that no people can attain a high degree of intelligence and morality unless the feeling of its nationality is strongly developed. This remarkable fact is a necessary consequence of the laws that govern human nature. The fact is that the intellectual life of the masses moves within a very limited range of ideas. Among those which they can acquire, the noblest and the most elevated are certainly, after religious ideas, the ideas of fatherland and of nationality. If, now, the political circumstances of the country prevent these ideas from manifesting themselves or give them a baneful direction, the masses will remain plunged in a state of deplorable inferiority. But this is not all: among a people who cannot be proud of their nationality, feelings of personal dignity will exist only in exceptional cases, among a few privileged individuals. The numerous classes who occupy the humblest positions in the social sphere have need of feeling themselves important from the national point of view, in order to acquire awareness of their own dignity. Now, this awareness, we do not hesitate to say, even at the risk of shocking some too rigid publicist, constitutes for peoples, as well as for individuals, an essential element in morality.

So then, if we so ardently desire the emancipation of Italy, if we declare that before this great question all the questions that can divide us must retreat and all private interests must keep still, it is not solely to see our fatherland made glorious and powerful, but above all so that she may raise herself on the ladder of intelligence and of moral development to the level of the most civilized nations.

Unless there is a European upheaval whose disastrous consequences are such as to make the hardiest recoil, but which, thanks to heaven, becomes less probable every day, it seems evident to us that the precious triumph of our nationality can only be realized on

---

[1] Count Cesare Balbo (1789–1853), a moderate Piedmontese patriot.—Ed.

the condition that the effort combines all the aroused forces of the country, that is to say by the national princes freely supported by all parties. The history of the last thirty years, as well as the analysis of the elements that compose Italian society, demonstrate clearly how small a scope military or democratic revolutions can have among us. Leaving aside, then, these impotent, useless methods, the sincere friends of the country should recognize that they can only cooperate for the true good of their fatherland by grouping themselves around those thrones that have deep roots in the national soil and by promoting, without impatience, the progressive inclinations the Italian governments manifest. This mode of conduct, conforming to the wise counsel of a man whose patriotism and enlightenment are beyond doubt, Signore Balbo, in his remarkable book *On the Hopes of Italy*, will restore the union that it is so necessary to see established among the different members of the Italian family, so as to put the country in a position to profit from the favorable political circumstances the future must bring by freeing itself from all foreign domination.

This union that we preach with so much ardor is not so difficult to attain as one could suppose, if he judges the society from its external appearances, or lets himself remain preoccupied by the memory of our sad divisions. The sentiment of nationality has become general, each year it augments itself, and already it is strong enough to hold all the parties of Italy together despite their sharp differences. It is no longer the exclusive possession of a sect or of men professing wild doctrines. Thus are we persuaded that the eloquent appeal Signore Balbo has lately addressed to all Italians will have thrilled more than one highly decorated breast from among the high dignitaries of state, and that it will have aroused more than one echo among those who, faithful to the tradition of their ancestors, make the principle of legitimacy the basis of their political beliefs.

All the classes of the society can, in some measure, cooperate in this important work. All those who have some education and some influence in Italy have, toward this goal, a partial mission to fulfill, following the distinguished writers who, like Signore Balbo and the Count Petitti, consecrate their efforts to instruct and to enlighten their fellow citizens, even down to the humble individuals who, in the narrow circle where they move, can raise the intelligence and the moral character of those who surround them.

All these individual efforts, it is true, will remain sterile without the accord of the national governments. But we shall not lack that accord. The mistrusts that 1830 had aroused, long kept alive by a faction weak in numbers but powerful in intrigue, are almost entirely dissipated. Our sovereigns, reassured, follow their natural tendencies, and each day we see them give new proofs of their paternal and progressive dispositions.

It will suffice us to cite in this regard what is happening in Piedmont. The development given to primary instruction, the establishment of several [academic] chairs dedicated to the teaching of moral and political science, the encouragement accorded to the spirit of association in the arts as well as in industry, and several other measures, without speaking of the railways, sufficiently attest that the illustrious monarch who reigns so brilliantly over that kingdom has decided to maintain that glorious policy which, in the past, has made his family the leading Italian dynasty, and which must in the future elevate it to still higher destinies.

But, more than by all other administrative reforms, as much perhaps as by large political concessions, the realization of the plans for railways will contribute to the consolidation of that state of mutual confidence between the government and the people on which our coming hopes are based. The governments, in endowing the nations whose destinies are confided to them with these powerful instruments of progress, give high testimony to the benevolent intentions that animate them and to the security they feel. On their side, the people, made gratefully aware by such a great benefit, will come to hold complete faith in their sovereigns; docile but full of ardor, they will let themselves be guided by them in the acquisition of national independence.

If the preceding reasonings have some foundation, no one will be able to dispute that we are correct in placing the moral effects of railways in Italy above their material effects, and in celebrating their introduction among us as the presage of a better future. This is why, borrowing the vigorous language of Signore Balbo, we like to point to them as one of the principal hopes of our fatherland.

VI

Toward 1848, and the End of
Metternich's Europe

The European revolutions of 1848 were characteristic of Metternich's Europe, and they put an end to it. They put an end to it, on the whole, not by their successes, not even by driving Metternich himself out of office and into exile, but rather by their failures. The thwarting of them ended the era begun by the great French Revolution of 1789, because it showed that the course of history was not spontaneous and all of a piece, for liberals to delight in and conservatives to retard. It showed the men of social order that they could live in the modern world after all, and manage it, and it showed liberals that history would not do their work for them, nor need progress and liberty happily emerge from the dissolution of governments and social discipline.

In these terms, the contrast with what came after 1848 helps define the European era that ended in that year. The story of how the contrast took form and was recognized is not part of the business of this volume. But to see how 1848 at once illuminated Metternich's Europe and announced its end, one need not enter upon the outbreaks of February and March at all.

The selections in this group all were written and spoken in the months preceding the 1848 revolutions; but they all foretold the revolutions, and tried to explain why they were bound to come. Sometimes it is puzzling why revolutions broke out in so many different places in that spring of 1848, and under so many different kinds of circumstances. Historians seeking causes in economic conditions or stages of social development or even political practices sometimes are hard put to explain European unanimity in 1848. But the revolutions, whatever their specific aims, happened everywhere together because Metternich's Europe was everywhere. The unanimity of Metternich's Europe lay in its *expectations*, its shared sense of how things happened, stemming from the great Revolution of 1789 and what followed. The near-unanimity of revolution in 1848, therefore, derived from a shared expectation that European revolution was about to come, and awaited only the signal. That is how 1848 was characteristic of Metternich's Europe. The ubiquity of revolution in that year should not be puzzling, because the reasons for it lay in the very nature of the Metternich era.

Politicians and observers were watching for signs of the changing of the era, and as the forties drew on they saw more and more of them, and became more and more persuaded that the time of change was near. The evidence snowballed as each incident stimulated others. In 1845 and 1846 there were harvest failures (especially in potatoes), leading to peasant unrest in many places, but also raising the more critical question of what the new "proletariat" of the cities would do with food so short (but note that serious shortages were past before the real revolutions of 1848). In 1846 and 1847 the movement of politics in a liberal direction gained momentum: a new, avowedly liberal pope (Pius IX); in Great Britain, repeal of tariff laws that protected agricultural producers at the cost of townsmen (Corn Law Repeal); liberal victories in elections to the Diet of Hungary, of all places; and Swiss liberals defeated conservatives in the constitutional crisis called the Sonderbund War. The king of Prussia called a United Diet of the kingdom, ostensibly to raise money to build a railroad, but it promptly became the arena for debate over constitutional reform, and the German liberals took heart and began to hold meetings to discuss the future of a new Germany. French liberal writers and politicians, bored with the July Monarchy, began to hold "reform banquets" at which to make speeches denouncing the government. Karl Marx and Friedrich Engels prepared their "Communist Manifesto," beginning with the pronouncement: "A specter is haunting Europe."

There were plenty of signs of impending change, then; how much violence it would entail nobody could be sure. In Metternich's Europe, events like these were not looked upon separately and dealt with separately. They fed and multiplied one another, as symptoms of the way history was going. These selections are meant to show why certain experienced observers of Metternich's Europe thought upheaval was imminent. They are deathbed diagnoses of an era. The sense of historical sequence and organic development that underlay the political thinking of the time implied that what destroyed the old would be the foundation of the new. Politicians behaved accordingly, and so the pronouncement of the end of Metternich's Europe is part of the history of the revolutions that followed. But here they serve to mark the termination of one era, rather than the beginning of another.

A CHRONOLOGY

1845–46	Harvest failures
1846	Disturbances in Austrian Galicia
	British Corn Law Repeal
	Election of Pius IX
1847	Prussian United Diet
	Food riots in Berlin
	Liberal victory in Hungarian elections

(1847)   Reform proposals for the German Bund
                Liberal victory in the Swiss Sonderbund crisis
1847–48   Reform banquets in France
January, 1848   Revolutionary outbreaks in Sicily and Tuscany
February, 1848 Revolution in Paris
March, 1848   Revolutions throughout Germany, Italy, and the
                Austrian Empire

BIBLIOGRAPHY

F. Fejtö, *The Opening of an Era, 1848* (London, 1948).
K. R. Greenfield, *Economics and Liberalism in the Risorgimento* (rev. edn. Baltimore, 1965).
K. Marx and F. Engels, *The Communist Manifesto* (many editions).
C. E. Maurice, *The Revolutionary Movement of 1848–49 in Italy, Austria-Hungary, and Germany* (New York, 1887).
P. Robertson, *Revolutions of 1848, a Social History* (New York, 1960).
A. Whitridge, *Men in Crisis; the Revolutions of 1848* (New York, 1949).

27. A Farewell to Metternich's Europe in the *Revue des deux Mondes*, 1846

Alexandre Thomas (1818–57), the author of this selection, was a professor of history at the University of Dijon. He wrote on international affairs, and especially on Germany, contributing regularly to the *Revue des deux Mondes* and other prominent European journals. In 1846 he began a long series for the *Revue des deux Mondes* on contemporary Germany, based on travels he had recently made. He framed the introduction to his series as an open letter to Prince Metternich, announcing the end of Metternich's régime in Germany, and hence in Europe. Perhaps Thomas, as a historian, was especially likely to see Metternich's Europe as a historic stage, now giving way to another stage; and perhaps as a Frenchman he was predisposed to use his own national past for analogies and evidence to support this view. But in both respects he shares patterns of thought typical of his time. [Alexandre Thomas, "L'Allemagne du présent: à M. le Prince de Metternich," *Revue des deux Mondes* n.s. XIII (1846), 488–493. Translation by the editor.]

A SENSE of conflict pervades the world; nor could all the skills of politicians suppress it, for it is you yourself, Prince, you who have failed. May God give you peace, then, for men want no more of it. France, quick to fatigue, had gone to sleep; but now Germany awakes, and you will gain nothing in the exchange, for she is awakening in earnest. As an unnoticed traveler, I have collected along my way the first signs of this new life; now I declare them to you. Make no mistake about it, these are no longer schoolboys or dreamers who declare war against you; you have had too much sport with those poetic conspiracies you pretend to fear. These are no longer the honest Teutons who meditated the death of kings and the ruin of thrones for the sake of restoring the primeval splendors of the Holy Roman Empire. The conspiracy is taking place no longer in the universities, in beer cellars, to the sound of ringing glasses and clashing swords; it is a daylight conspiracy, Prince, and you can do nothing about it. They conspire in frock coat and round hat, with no picturesque costumes and no romantic fantasies, each one in his place and at his business; here one at his counter, there another at his rostrum, one in his office, another at his plow. They say to themselves quite simply that it would not be so bad, finally, to learn how to get along on their own, and that now they are old enough and sensible enough to walk by themselves. They are devoutly grateful for the goodly princes the country has received, lords born magnanimous and mild; but they would not be sorry to have some guarantee of their own, in case their rulers should take a mind to turn worse. There is a feeling that in the matter of royal promises, the ones that have been written down are more reliable than those that have not; and charmed though they may be by the master orations of these fine crowned palaverers, they still would prefer to see the eloquence put in contract form and inscribed on paper. That is more vulgar, but it is more sure. In short, they are convinced that the governed are competent enough in their own affairs for the governors to take their advice at least sometimes, and they think they have the right advice. All this is said without much groping, and without much ceremony; it is said out loud, at any time, by anybody. That is what they think, and they never suppose anything else.

For these tireless conspirators are in fact the most peaceable people in the world, and precisely that is the bad sign for you; they are people of firm disposition, with tame habits, merchants and proprietors who never before cared about anything but running their businesses or their estates, or scholars who fed on footnotes, or jurists who never emerged from the digest—all the philistines of yore! But the philistines are no more, or at least the species has changed. Now here come the bourgeois, the true bourgeois of con-

FAREWELL TO METTERNICH'S EUROPE

stitutional society; defend yourself as best you can, for this is a race without pity. It is just this type that arrived with us at the time of the Empire, and now it is moving, after the fashion of the type, all the way to the foot of the Johannisberg [the site of Metternich's Rhineland castle]. To lead the blind masses, all it takes is a popular spellbinder who whips them up with the tip of his switch and puts them in whatever harness he likes. The trouble is, progress that way is very noisy and very difficult. But reasonable men, who are deliberately set on what is proper and possible, persevere and succeed without, so to speak, needing to do anything but live; for these high expectations, having become parts of their lives, are accomplished in the measure that their lives are long. That was the history of France in '89, and today it is Germany's. Today it is you who are confronted, Prince, as we were then, with an irresistible desire for enlightenment and freedom. You face an absolute confidence in the political and moral efficacy of grand assemblies to regenerate the fatherland. You face a universal expectation. Everybody is on his feet. Everywhere I found spirit, faith, enthusiasm— how shall I describe it to you?—the naïve virtues of revolutionaries, appearing, though, in the very heart of public life, so that they are already accompanied by tactical sense, cool heads, and the wise virtues that win parliamentary battles within established civic order.

Thus your skill has finally struck shallows, and your ship is wrecked. Still, when I think of how long you have guided it over the raging sea of modern ideas and passions, over the deep sea you wanted to turn into ice, I bow before your spirit, once so powerful. I hold the greatness of your name the higher when I see how much it takes to overcome it; as an observer of your decline, I cannot help feeling a kind of admiration for your successes. That is why I have ventured to dedicate these letters, which are like a report of a victory in full swing, to you. I have done so because I have realized everywhere that it is you who are vanquished. It is fitting to honor such mighty ruins.

Yes, Prince, you are one of those vanquished whom the future will remember. It is fashionable nowadays, among some of the newer diplomats, to belittle the services you rendered to your cause; and now that the cause is lost, as in fact it was bound to be, it is safe for them to complain of your past artfulness. The truth is that they are trying to begin again in their own way the dangerous game that is never won. They understand nothing of the game you have played; they are clumsy and presumptuous children. The century goes its way; it shall have its will. But they think they can fool it, and make it believe they are moving with it by pretending to move. Men intend from this time forward to act on their own and hold themselves responsible for their actions; but look how these weighty politicians have contrived to shout the great words reason and liberty even louder than the mob. You want reasonable institutions, they ask? Return to those that time has destroyed; we shall prove to you that they were wisdom's ideal. You yearn for equal freedoms? We shall offer you privileges and you will find them more attractive. Like everybody you have tasted the forbidden fruit of the tree of knowledge, and you perceive that you are naked? We'll take care of that. We'll dress you in the castoffs of the past; they have shiny buttons. Foolish men, who deceive only themselves, and who with their false pretensions will only stir up those legitimate desires they seek to ensnare! At least you, Prince, when you struggle against the impossible, do not deceive yourself, nor involve yourself in wasted efforts. You do not wear yourself out thinking up constitutions that are no constitutions, or change that is no change; you calmly say that all change is bad, and arrange your troops on a continuous front. You make no effort to outthink public opinion, you have enough to do suppressing it; you do not look for this expedient or that for it to feed upon, you do not encourage it at all. You stop it short. Against all the forces that have pressed upon you, you have opposed only the force of inertia. For thirty years past, you have stayed on the defensive; you have lost a yard every day, and you have recovered a yard every day. That has been your genius. For thirty years you have managed to do nothing. Your detractors indeed have said that this was the genius of mediocrity; but mediocrity is what acts at random and changes for change's sake. As ruling minister of a badly put together state, you were aware that any shock would break it to fragments; you have devoted your life to keeping out of the way. You are the first politician whose whole ambition has been to remove stones from the paths of others for fear they might throw you off balance as they fell. You have been neither emotional nor systematic; you have sought only the silence and the immobility of the *status quo*. Yours has in the end a sad kind of wisdom; it has been a most unjust scorn for the most ardent prayers of your own times! But let him condemn you without pity who has found some other means of survival for that shapeless empire whose destinies have weighed upon your shoulders! Let him curse you who would find the courage to sacrifice, to the general progress of ideas, the reputation and power associated for three centuries with your country's name, some noble patriot who could bravely accept such abasement of the national fortune for the common profit of humanity!

The fact is that you, Prince, are a patriot who has a country no longer; the times have passed when the victories of a kingdom were made with treaties and battles, ignoring the interests and the rights of subjects. With each advance of the modern spirit your forces shrink; what will you have left tomorrow? Your enemy is *the inevitable,* just as people used to say in the earliest ages of the world, speaking of fate. That is the style of thought of our times too. It is a new fatalism, but a reasoned fatalism; it is that invincible force that henceforth results from the conscious conjuncture of human wills and human intelligence, an immense force embodied forever in the men and the facts of your revolution. Thus you will be one of the last victims of the French Revolution, not a passionate and repelled victim like Pitt or Castlereagh, but a stubborn and patient victim, like a soldier who dies in his place with his weapon in his hands; you will fall with Austrian indifference. Perhaps you try sometimes to delude yourself, but you will not succeed. You close your eyes in vain; your conqueror shouts his name.

It came to me from a good source that on the day when His Prussian Majesty received you at his palace at Stolzenfels, you repaid his hospitality with a phrase after your fashion. "Would it be true, Sire," you are supposed to have said, "that finally you would like to give us a constitution? Take the 1830 one from our good neighbor. That has the freshest date; that's the latest thing." History does not report the answer; but your royal interlocutor was probably not flattered either in his vanity as an unpublished author, nor in his self-esteem as a Teuton of the old stamp. And yet you spoke with better sense than you may have intended; your advice was more serious than you thought. A French constitution for German subjects. That would not be so great a mockery as you meant it to be. We are more like one another than is good for you. There are not two ways of being sensible; that is what amazed me on my trip: the entry of the new spirit even within that network whose meshes you tighten in vain at your Diet at Frankfurt; the disappearance of the old Germany, abdicating and vanishing so as to revive and live as the whole world now lives; no more distracting visions now, nor dreams for dreaming's sake. The call is for action, and for realities instead of chimeras. Religion, philosophy, and politics all are moving in that same direction, and already at that brisk and confident rate that we here use for the right causes on the right occasions.

This is the transformation I should like to tell you about now. Perhaps it will seem here that it is still largely a matter of theologians and philosophers, more than of politicians and diplomats; but Prince! do not try to say, as did that pope of such spiritual memory, "These are monks' quarrels." Wait for the end of the metamorphosis. However simple the details whose humble historian I seek to be, and however commonplace my histories may seem to you, I conceive they still will interest you. I know of nobody else who has said these things to you with such candor, and why should you find it so bad to be freely informed for once? Thus I have put your name in the salutation of my modest reports, without conscious irony, and with the deference owed to illustrious careers in ruin. I did so from that spontaneous respect which the most obscure soldier in a victorious army instinctively pays to the most skillful general in the defeated army. We are told, Prince, that not all the kings together can spoil you now, they have spoiled you so much! For me to pay you tribute after them is either very naïve or very bold. It is true that my compliments are not the ones you hear every day; and I count a little on the novelty of the language to earn my pardon.

28. Heinrich von Gagern on Coming Developments in Germany, 1847

In 1818 the youthful Heinrich von Gagern had tried to describe to his father what the student national liberal movement in Germany was all about (above, pp. 44–48). Now his generation was in its prime years, and a mature Heinrich von Gagern, an influential liberal politician with great expectations, wrote his father again, in response to another anxious paternal letter, to explain himself, his colleagues, and their

beliefs and plans. Three months later he made an important speech in
the Hessen-Darmstadt Diet, of which he was a member. The occasion
was the impending meeting of representatives of all the Prussian provinces, called by the Prussian king. Remember, in reading Gagern's discussion of this event, how a conservative Prussia, amenable to Austria's
German and European policies, had been the cornerstone of Metternich's Europe from the beginning. Gagern became president of the
German national Constituent Assembly in 1848, and when that failed
was without political influence for the remaining thirty years of his
life. [*Deutscher Liberalismus im Vormärz. Heinrich von Gagern,
Briefe und Reden 1815–1848*, ed. Paul Wentzcke and Wolfgang
Klötzer (Göttingen, 1959), pp. 343–344, 353–356, 384–387. Translations by the editor.]

Hans von Gagern to his son, Heinrich von Gagern:

Hornau, January 1, 1847

[New Year's greetings; family affairs]

JUST A few words more. Don't get in over your head. I can
see from here many elements and wishes for the dissolution of all
civil society, ideas pressed especially by starving proletarians, and
littérateurs and journalists, infecting the whole nation with their
own particular discontents and hungers and exaggerated complaints.
I have very harsh words to say about that. Such complete dissolution without any ideas or plans or organization—to substitute something better and stronger, like Robespierre himself, in all his frightfulness, but yet conceived in state forms that clearly would be
lacking here—I can take no part in this, but must oppose it with all
the strength of my spirit and my understanding. Now you need not
fear that I don't think highly of you. After your fashion. I see you
trying to avoid evil things too. But when I think of the future I
can only see you coming to power and office—so it is in [your
brother] Fritz's eyes too—under favored circumstances. That was
my hope and my teaching. How far that will be set back by your
activities and your writing, destroyed, I cannot judge.

When you call my position a very *exclusive* one, of course I have
to interpret that first. Mediation is my avowed purpose. If this
purpose succeeds, it will be a very *in*clusive one. Of course that
will not reach the point of converting everybody and satisfying
everybody, but it can achieve a majority, and that can be the outcome. . . .

Heinrich von Gagern to his father, Hans von Gagern:

Monsheim, January 11, 1847

[Family affairs; revolt in India]

Fritz's small interest in going back to India could be more disturbing to you after he has taken a look at Europe. But I think he won't
feel like going, unless the conservative speeches you have in mind
to make have such an effect that the whole German development
stops in its tracks, so that boredom with our stereotyped circumstances drives him out. But joking aside, I have no doubt that what
you say will be considered and wise. But I am very doubtful that
it is exactly *your* role to lead attacks on the press. Now, you wrote
to me: *I can see from here many elements and wishes for the
dissolution of all civil society, ideas pressed especially by starving
proletarians, and littérateurs and journalists, infecting the whole
nation with their own particular discontents and hungers and exaggerated complaints. I have very harsh words to say about that.*
Now, I do not belong to the starving proletariat, and my attention
to literature is only too neglected because of lack of time, so that
I am not nearly so active a journalist as you are, dear Father—a
fact which in itself, apart from a fair judgment of the profession,
should keep you from talking about journalists, littérateurs, and
advocates in a contemptuous fashion that you cannot seriously intend, a fashion current only among German court nobility, and
which should remain their own particular style. So I am of the
opinion, and you really are too, that German affairs could not be
managed worse, and no complaints about it could be exaggerated.
Where there is such stuff for just dissatisfaction, so that even
inarticulate elements take it over and exploit it to their own
purposes, that is in the nature of things, always was, always will
be, does no harm, and you will not change it with your speeches.
And if this supremacy of the bad press, as I too am willing to call
it, were to become more complete in Germany and thus more
dangerous, then the guilt lies entirely with the German governments, which give neither room nor freedom for the good press—
that is, to people who know what they want, who want the better,
but stay independent and want to say it in an independent way. So
the latter withdraw and leave the field to the bad press. . . . But

I concede even more. The moderate, right-thinking people are gradually developing a taste for the bad press. Dissatisfied with the way of things, in the opposition, they are glad or at least amused at whatever annoys the governments and embitters their lives: *Tu l'as voulu, George Dandin!*

But then you go on to say: *Such complete dissolution without any ideas or plans or organization—to substitute something better and stronger, like Robespierre himself, in all his frightfulness, but yet conceived in state forms that clearly would be lacking here—I can take no part in this, but must oppose it with all the strength of my spirit and my understanding.* Now, the first part of this sentence is based on error, and in the second you are tilting at windmills. It is an error to believe that if it should come to dissolution, or rather to a loosening of certain connections, no thought has been given to this and there is no plan for a substitute. Indeed there is no existing organization. That would be dangerous and illegal; the time for that has not yet come. But do not believe that Germany will be short of men whom she could with satisfaction see coming to the front of public affairs at the decisive moment; and the German spirit is through and through too conservative and organizational for evil elements and anarchy to hold the field for very long. By this I certainly do not mean to say that it could not come to civil war in Germany; and that would indeed be a very sad thing, but not the worst that could happen. But in Germany you will find neither the spiritual poverty nor the cowardice of the French émigrés to such a degree, but rather a massive store of intelligence, patriotism, and energy.

In fact, you contradict yourself in this sentence. When we talked about the political unity of Germany, your objection was *it won't work; the Bavarians will want to stay Bavarian, the Württemberger will want to be Württemberger.* If that is the case, then you have nothing whatever to fear, and our political and social circumstances will remain in the *status quo* for a long time to come —when no German Robespierre can hope for a *tabula rasa* without any state form.

But now with regard to the thoughts and plans for a better future for Germany, which probably will for some time yet remain pious and impious wishes—here you cannot say out of your own knowledge and experience that there aren't any; and you must in some incomprehensible way have pulled in your own political feelers, which are usually so sensitive to the movements of the time, if you cannot see how exactly these thoughts of the future have gained ground, men, and prospects. You can still say *I do not agree with this; I do not believe in this solution,*—but unless you deceive yourself you can no longer say *These are less than empty fantasies; there is nothing here but planlessness and absurdity. . . .*

Hans von Gagern speaking before the Hessian Diet, April 9, 1847

A new spirit is now irresistibly asserting itself in Germany. It is a strengthened *public* spirit; and in our times the German people cannot be put off as they were put off in 1819, 1832, perhaps 1834. It is the unquestionable conviction of the whole people that only by the developing principle of a representative and constitutional monarchy throughout Germany can the unity of the fatherland be strengthened, freedom come forth, and the rule of law be secured for our future public life. This conviction, indeed, is not new; it has only entered upon a new phase. As long as the German states composing the Bund were divided in terms of constitutional principles into two camps, those standing in the camp of free constitutions were fully justified in their fear that the stronger, opposing party would put every obstacle in the way of the development of that civic and political freedom which a great, manly, law-abiding people has the right to demand.

This was not just empty anxiety, but a fact, to which the better intentions and better sentiments even of individual governments were obliged to submit. This anxiety has been reduced; it has been reduced by an event on whose eve we stand and which without doubt will stand as one of the most significant, perhaps most beneficent in the history of our century. Today is the ninth of April; and on the eleventh of April the largest German people [Prussia] will see its many representatives come together, to join with the King in directing the fate of that great land. This event changes Germany's political situation. The center of gravity in German politics no longer lies in the camp of unrestricted authority, but on the side of the constitutional states. I shall not here inquire, gentlemen, whether the Prussian constitution, or the provisions whereby the full representation of the various German elements in Prussia is coming about, can satisfy the wishes and demands of the people, whether they are appropriate, whether

Prussia will be content with them. Treatment of this question lies outside my proper sphere here. I have fullest confidence in the intelligence and the manliness of this German people, that it will take the right path to achieve the fulfillment of those guarantees of political freedom and guarantees of law that now it lacks. . . .

[After considering certain procedural alternatives, Gagern goes on:]

I have, then, certain and joyous confidence that the Prussian assembly will choose the right way. Whatever the form of the constitution, with or without that name, the nature of this law-giving effort will be to secure the rights of the people, provide freedom of person and property, and give voice and weight to public opinion, which is made easier by the mass of a numerous assembly. So we shall find our way together in the ranks of constitutional states and peoples, firmly united, and go on to even higher fulfillment of the conditions for the freedom as well as the unity of Germany.

It has been necessary for me to take note of this change in our political circumstances. There was a time, gentlemen—I believe it is past—when a friend of his people and fatherland was subject to an inner contradiction and was caught by it if he entered public life. He was required, if he worked for one value, to work against another that he held to be an equally high value. If he were to fight for Freedom, he had to fight against the one symbol and organ of German unity, that had come out of the battles and the labors of the nation for unity [the German Bund, created at Vienna in 1815]. He had to oppose it, certainly not because he was against unity, but so as to bring nearer the moment when a unity of greater strength and energy might emerge. And this moment is now upon us! But at that time, the best men in Germany gave up and turned aside, because of the essential contradiction between their duties. Many withdrew from a struggle that distressed them so, causing them genuine, severe agonies. I am thinking of the sturdy men of the Württemberg opposition, Pfizer, Schott, Römer, Uhland, and others. They preferred leaving public life to remaining there, after they realized that the freedom of their land could only be sustained by resisting any strengthening of the authority of the Bund, by virtue of which authority the federal edicts threatening these freedoms were made. This very authority, had it chosen to base itself on national sentiment and to promote true national interests, would have rallied the support of all parties, to uphold it gladly with everything they had. ¡Those men were criticized then. Many would have preferred to see them remain publicly active; good grounds can be found for any opinion. Dilemma seized those who held it their first duty to maintain whatever freedom was provided by our operating constitutions and, therefore, to resist whatever might threaten or even destroy those constitutions; and this dilemma resulted directly from the unnatural circumstance in which states with the most widely incompatible state constitutions were together in the Bund, with one group embracing the principle of absolute power beyond what the constitutions of the other states would allow, but with the others too weak, perhaps willingly too weak, to offer resistance.

Therefore, for those who believed that the preservation of guaranteed liberties required the upholding of monarchic-representative constitutions as the means and the way to further progress, the cardinal principle and first duty was to resist any extension of Bund authority, for so long as there was no uniformity of constitutions or constitutional principle or so long as the center of gravity in Bund politics had not shifted to the side of the constitutional states. It was a defensive resistance, in the interest of freedom. But the need for this resistance is now, I am firmly convinced, coming to an end. Soon the necessary preconditions will exist for us to move, with confident courage, to meet another era, so long awaited, to meet the moment from which the principle of national unity in the constitution of the German nation can develop with greater power, the moment from which the looser ties of a confederacy of states can progressively be replaced by the stronger forms of a federal state. This will not fail, though the hour of danger for the fatherland threaten; and the task of the future will then be to find the ways and means for the living actions of the Bund, both in representing the nation without and in developing its civic life within, to become the expression of national feeling and the national will. . . .

29. Cavour on the Rebirth of Italy: *Il Risorgimento*, 1847

In 1847, Camillo di Cavour (see above, p. 306) judged that the time was ripe for fundamental political changes in Italy. He had spent the preceding years making ready, studying British and French affairs and promoting the economic development of his native Piedmont. Now he joined with other Italian patriots in founding a newspaper at Turin with the significant title *Il Risorgimento*—The Resurgence—to prepare Piedmont for its role in the liberal unification of Italy. The article here, from the opening issue of the journal, considers the economic aspects of *risorgimento*. Recall that one of Cavour's chief anxieties was that social radicalism and violence in the spirit of Mazzini might spoil all his hopes and Italy's. [*Il Risorgimento*, December 15, 1847. Translation by the editor.]

THE NEW public spirit spreading so rapidly in every part of Italy cannot fail to have a very great influence on material conditions. The political rebirth of a nation can never be separated from its economic rebirth. When a people governed by a benevolent prince progresses in the ways of civility it must of necessity progress in wealth and material power. The conditions for the two kinds of progress are identical. Civic virtue, provident laws that safeguard all rights equally, and good political ordinances, indispensable for the improvement of the moral conditions of a nation, are also the principal causes of its economic progress.

Where there is no public life, where national sentiment is languid, there will never be vigorous industry. A nation kept in intellectual infancy, whose every political action is prohibited, whose every innovation is an object of suspicion and is blindly obstructed, cannot attain a high degree of wealth and power, even though its laws are good and its administration benevolent.

The history of the past three centuries and also the present state of the European nations offer many incontestable proofs of this great truth.

In every country where political progress did not come from the collapse of the feudal régime, either industry did not arise or it languished undeveloped; and not infrequently it declined. In those whose political circumstances improved, in which the nation was called to participate in the work of governing, industry grew steadily, in some places so gigantically that it filled the world with its marvels. Compare the cases of Spain and of England. At the beginning of the last century Spain, though in decline for about a hundred years, seemed still second in riches and in power. Though the English population was more energetic, the Spanish was larger and richer; and the colonies she had established in the four corners of the world were more numerous and blooming. Both, after the

Treaty of Utrecht, enjoyed uninterrupted internal peace; and
though they were disturbed by foreign wars, the treatment they
received in them was about the same. Though the Seven Years'
War was a glorious success for England, sustained by the fiery
might of Lord Chatham, the War of American Independence
turned out disastrously for her. And yet by the end of the
eighteenth century the relative economic conditions of the two
countries had been utterly changed. The British Empire, where
public life was broadly established, where the political system had
steadily progressed, found that its industry, wealth, and strength
had so increased that it was able almost alone to resist the fury
of the French Revolution and the overwhelming power of Napoleon. Spain, on the other hand, even though its empire had not yet
been diminished in size, despite the energetic character of its inhabitants, despite the natural riches of its own soil and those
copiously furnished it by its colonies, had, nevertheless, fallen so
low, through the fault of a government sharply opposed to anything new, that it could no longer exercise the slightest influence
on the affairs of Europe.

Further arguments for our proposition could be brought in from
the histories of other civil societies; but restricting ourselves to
Italy, we note that among the various states that compose it Piedmont has almost always been outstanding for its economic progress, which it owes chiefly to the wise and mild government of
its rulers, who knew enough to introduce into the State changes
appropriate to the spirit of the times. It owes it to having had
in the eighteenth century and in the nineteenth two reformist
rulers. It is because the great King Charles III prepared the path
of reform for the magnanimous Charles Albert.

The economic condition of a people is best improved when the
progressive movement operates in an orderly fashion. Yet for
industry to develop and prosper there must be such a degree of
liberty that we do not hesitate to affirm that progress will be more
general and more rapid in a state that is actually inquiet, but solidly
endowed with liberty, than in a more tranquil state that lives under
a system of compression and regression. Thus Spain, despite the
civil wars, political confusion, and administrative disorder that
have harassed her for almost twenty years, has made much more
economic progress during this period than during the quiet and
peaceful reigns of the successors of Philip II and of the Bourbon

kings. From this we see that violent change is a condition less harmful to Spanish industry than the calm of obscurantism. It grew amid civil tempests, but lay prostrate under the tranquil dominion of a despotism averse to any change.

Fully convinced of this truth, we frankly declare that the political rebirth of Italy, celebrated with fraternal enthusiasm in the Romagna, in Tuscany, and in Piedmont, is the unmistakable sign of a new era for the industry and commerce of our country.

We have complete faith in the future of Italian industry, not so much from the beneficial reforms instituted by our princes, not so much from the principles of the tariff league, nor from domestic and foreign conditions of Italy that will impel rapid improvements, but mainly because we confidently expect to see an awakening among our compatriots, animated by a generous and harmonious spirit, called to new political life. We expect to see aroused in them that vigor, that industriousness, that energy which made their fathers famous, powerful, and rich in the Middle Ages, when the manufactures of Florence and Lombardy and the fleets of Genoa and Venice had no rivals in Europe. Yes, we have faith in Italian vigor, energy, and industriousness; they are more apt to bring commercial and industrial progress than overprotection and unjust privilege.

This journal will endeavor with all its power to induce and to propagate this kind of economic rebirth. It will seek out facts that can be useful to commerce and production both in agriculture and manufacture. It will endeavor to spread good economic doctrines, combatting the false ones that are the offspring of ancient prejudices, or masks for special interests. It will endeavor to bring out all questions that bear directly or indirectly on the production and distribution of wealth.

The journal will not hesitate to declare itself openly in favor of freedom of exchange; but it will seek to move prudently along the path of liberty, so that the transition may take place gradually and without grave disturbances. Yet it will support the transition as effectively as it can, so that all internal Italian tariffs may be removed and the economic unity of the peninsula established; it will advise on the other hand a steady but moderate process of reform in the tolls imposed on foreign products.

Anticipating that little by little our markets must be opened to foreign competition, it will be this journal's task to seek out the most suitable means of meeting and overcoming it. Thus, it will endeavor to promote institutions of credit, professional schools, and industrial honors, means which if wisely used will aid the rapid development of the various branches of industry especially suited to Italian conditions, which may within a short time raise her to a place among the first economic powers of the world.

But the increase of national production will not be the only economic target the journal will aim at; it will pay as much or more attention to the factors that affect the betterment of that part of society which contributes most directly to the creation of public wealth, the worker class. For this reason all those who heartily undertake the publication of this journal unanimously declare that no increase in wealth would do good or be really useful to the country if those people who make up part of it, the greatest part, did not participate in the benefits—the workers. The industrial edifice arising everywhere has attained and will continue to attain such a height as to risk collapse and terrible catastrophes if its foundation is not reinforced, if one does not bind more closely to the other parts of the edifice the main base on which it rests, the working class, by rendering it more moral and more religious, by giving it a broader education and a more comfortable livelihood.

Though we are ready to combat anything that might destroy social order, we declare that we believe it our strict social duty to dedicate part of the wealth that will accumulate with the progress of time to the amelioration of the material and moral conditions of the lower classes.

England, that country of great teachings, ignored this sacred duty too long. While its great commercial centers and its immense industrial centers were growing to be giants, while Liverpool and Manchester were being transformed in little more than seventy years from humble market towns to colossal cities, while in the counties of Lancaster and York and elsewhere capital built up to the millions, nothing was done by the government and little by private persons to meet the intellectual and moral needs of the new populations that commerce and industry were concentrating in those parts of the kingdom. The effects of this culpable neglect, disastrous though it was, went long unnoticed. But when there were plain signs of rising public disorder, and threatening actions by the Chartists' associations, parliament and public were forced to seek out the causes and to clean up the conditions of the workers in the great commercial and industrial centers.

A terrible spectacle came out of these investigations. England discovered with horror that while at the peak of the social edifice there glittered an enlightened, energetic, and prosperous class, yet in the lower regions the majority lay deprived of light, of moral understanding, bereft of any religious sentiment, and some in so abject a condition as not even to know the name of God, or that of the divine Redeemer!

The government and the public, distressed by such social disorder, have undertaken to remedy it with that marvelous energy that distinguishes the mighty Anglo-Saxon race. Will these efforts be enough to cleanse the whole horrible sore? Let us hope so.

But let the example of England stand ever before our eyes. Let Italy learn from it, now that she stands preparing to travel the paths of industry; let her learn to hold the conditions of the popular classes in high respect, and to work eagerly and incessantly for their amelioration.

To escape the evils that harass Great Britain, let us take care to develop those benevolent instincts that honor our past history and our present, yet subjecting them to the scientific laws that must be observed if effective and really fruitful direct measures for the alleviation of human misery are to be achieved. Let us act in such a way that all our countrymen, rich and poor, the poor more than the rich, participate in the benefits of civic progress, and we shall have solved in peaceful and Christian fashion the great social problem that others pretend to solve by dreadful convulsions and frightful destruction.

30. Tocqueville on Impending Revolution, January 27, 1848

By 1848 Alexis de Tocqueville (1805–59) had already gained much of the reputation as a political and social analyst that his name still enjoys. Born of a family with a distinguished tradition as magistrates and soldiers, Tocqueville himself had studied law; and his journey to the United States to study penology there had provided the basis for his *Democracy in America* (1835), which won him an immediate European reputation. *Democracy in America* was a speculative study of the effects of democracy and social equality, and its importance and success came from the assumption that Europe too was moving inescapably toward the democracy and equality that already existed in the United States—a prospect Tocqueville disliked, fearing it would destroy individual liberty and dignity, but one he thought had to be faced. Tocqueville believed that as Europe became like America, with the passing of the old régimes of aristocracy and crown, the only remaining form of privilege would be money, and that would be the next to come under leveling attack. He made the speech quoted in part below as an Opposition member of the French Chamber of Deputies, in a debate on social conditions and social policies. [*Le Moniteur Universel*, January 28, 1848. Translation by the editor.]

M. DE TOCQUEVILLE: . . . Gentlemen, I might be mistaken, but it seems to me the present state of things, the present state of opinion, the mental state of France, is of a kind that should alarm and trouble us. Speaking for myself, I say sincerely to the Chamber that for the first time in fifteen years I feel a certain fear for the future; and what proves to me that I am right is that this impression is not mine alone. I think I could ask everyone who hears me now, and all would reply that there is a similar feeling in the districts they represent, that a certain uneasiness, a certain fear has spread through men's minds, that for the first time in perhaps sixteen years, the feeling or the instinct of instability, that feeling which precedes revolutions, which always proclaims them, which sometimes gives rise to them, that this feeling exists in the country to a very serious degree.

If, gentlemen, I correctly understood what the Minister of Finance said the other day when he was concluding, the cabinet itself in some measure admits the reality of the impression I speak of; but it attributes it to certain specific causes, to certain recent accidents in political life, to certain disturbing circumstances, to certain words that have excited emotions.

Gentlemen, I fear that those who attribute the kind of malaise of which I speak to such causes are seizing not on the malady, but only the symptoms. I myself am convinced that the malady is not there; it is more general and more profound. This malady, which must be cured at all costs, and which, you may be sure, will infect us all if we do not guard against it, is the existing state of the public mentality, of public morals. That is where the malady is; that is the point to which I wish to draw your attention. I believe that public morality, the public mentality, are in a dangerous state; I believe, moreover, that the Government has contributed and is contributing in the gravest way to increase the peril. That is why I have come to the rostrum.

If, gentlemen, I take a close look at the class that governs, the enfranchised class, I am alarmed and disturbed by what is happening there. And speaking first of what I have called the governing class—take careful note that I include in this class not only what has been inaccurately called in our times the middle class, but rather all those, whatever their situations, who have full legal rights and exercise them, taking these words in their most general accepted sense—I say, what exists in that class disturbs and alarms me. What I see there, gentlemen, I can express with a word: public morality is changing there. It has already changed profoundly there; it is changing more and more every day. More and more, the opinions, the sentiments, and the ideas of the whole are replaced by individual interests, individual designs, by points of view derived from private life and private interests.

Gentlemen, it is not my intention to force the Chamber to dwell upon these sad details more than necessary; I shall address myself only to my adversaries themselves, to my colleagues of the ministerial majority. I ask them to make for themselves a kind of statistical review of the constituencies that have sent them to this Chamber, that they set up, first, a category to include those who vote for them, not by reason of political opinion, but only from sentiments of personal friendship and neighborliness. In the second category let them place those who vote for them not from the viewpoint of the public interest or the general interest, but from the viewpoint of purely local interest. To this second category let them add a third, composed of those who vote for them from motives of purely individual interest. And I ask them whether those who vote from disinterested public sentiments, from public views or public feelings, whether these make the majority; I am confident they will readily discover the contrary. I further permit myself to ask them whether, to their knowledge, in the last five years, ten years, fifteen years, the number of those who vote for them by reason of political opinion has not steadily shrunk? Finally, let them tell me whether it is not true that around them, before their eyes, there has little by little been established in public opinion a remarkable degree of tolerance for the facts of which I speak, whether little by little a sort of low and vulgar morality has not come into being, according to which a man possessed of certain political rights owes it to himself, owes it to his children, his wife, and his relatives to make a personal use of these rights in the interests of all of them; whether this has not gradually come to be a kind of family obligation? Whether this new morality, unknown in the great moments of our history, unknown at the beginning of our revolution, is not developing more and more, and infecting more minds every day? I ask them this.

For what is all this if it is not a continuous and profound degradation, a more and more complete corruption of public morals?

And if I turn from public life to private life and consider what is happening, if I turn my eyes to all you have been witness to, especially in the past year, all the noisy scandals, all the crimes, all the errors, all the offenses, all the strange vices that every incident has seemed to bring to light in all places, and which every judicial proceeding reveals; if I take note of all that, have I not cause for alarm? Have I not reason to say that it is not only a matter of change in our public morals, but that private morals, too, are being corrupted? (*Denials from the Center*)

And bear in mind, I am not talking from a moralistic point of view, I am talking from a political point of view; do you know the general, essential, underlying cause for the corruption of private morals? It is the change in public morals. Because morality does not rule in the higher actions of the society, it cannot descend into lesser actions. Because self-interest has replaced disinterested sentiments in public life, self-interest is the law of private life.

It is said that there are two moralities, a political morality and a morality of private life. But, in fact, if what is happening among us is what I think it is, then never has the falsity of such a maxim been more clearly proven than in our time. Yes, I think so. I believe that something is happening to our private morality that must disturb and alarm good citizens; and I believe that what is happening in our private morals derives in large part from what is happening in our public morals. (*Denials from the Center*)

Very well, gentlemen, if you do not believe me on that point, believe at least that Europe has this impression. I think I am as well-informed as anybody in this Chamber on what is being printed and said about us in Europe.

Well, then, I assure you with heartfelt sincerity that I am not only saddened but wounded by what I read and what I hear every day. I am wounded when I hear the charges brought against us, which derive from the facts of which I speak, when I see the exaggerated conclusions drawn from these facts to discredit the whole nation, the whole national character. I am wounded when

I see the degree in which French power in the world shrinks little by little. I am wounded when I see how not only the moral power of France is growing weaker. . . .

M. JANVIER: May I have the floor? (*A stir*)

M. DE TOCQUEVILLE: . . . but also the power of her principles, her ideas, her attitudes.

It was France that first cast before the world, amid the noisy thunder of her first revolution, regenerating principles for all human societies. That was her glory; that is the most precious part of her. Now, gentlemen, those are the very principles we weaken now by our own example. The applications we ourselves now seem to make of them cause the world to doubt her. The Europe watching us begins to ask itself whether we are right or wrong; it asks whether we are, in fact, as we have repeated for so long, leading the societies of men toward a happier and more prosperous future, or whether we really are carrying them with us toward moral calamity and ruin. That, gentlemen, is what troubles me most about the spectacle we are presenting to the world. It injures not us alone; it injures our principles too, it injures our cause, it injures that intellectual fatherland which, for my part, as a Frenchman, means more to me than the physical, material fatherland that we can see. (*Diverse movements*)

Gentlemen, if the spectacle we present produces this effect at a distance on the European scene, what effect do you think it produces within France herself on those classes which have no rights, and which, out of the passivity to which our laws condemn them, see us acting alone on the great stage where we are? What effect do you think a spectacle like this has on them?

For my part, it frightens me. It is said that there is no danger, because there has been no unrest; it is said that because there is no physical disorder on the surface of society, revolutions are remote from us.

Gentlemen, let me say to you with complete sincerity that I think you deceive yourselves. To be sure, disorder does not exist in deeds; but it has entered deeply into minds. Consider what is happening among the working classes, which today, I concede, are peaceful. It is true that they are not goaded by political passions strictly speaking, to the degree they were goaded before; but do you not see that their passions from being political have become social? Do you not see spreading among them, little by little, opinions and ideas that aim not to overturn such and such a ministry, or such laws, or such a government, but society itself, to shake it to the foundations upon which it now rests? Do you not see how little by little it comes to be said among them that all those placed above them are incapable and unworthy of governing them, that the division of wealth as it has happened in the world up to now is unjust, that private property rests on bases that are unjust bases? And do you not believe that when such opinions take root, when they spread in almost a general way, when they penetrate deeply down into the masses, they bring sooner or later, I know not when, I know not how, but sooner or later they bring the most massive revolutions?

That, gentlemen, is my profound conviction. I believe that at this very hour we are sleeping on a volcano. (*Protests*) I am profoundly convinced of it. (*Diverse movements*)

Index

DOCUMENTARY HISTORY OF WESTERN CIVILIZATION
edited by Eugene C. Black and Leonard W. Levy

ANCIENT AND MEDIEVAL HISTORY OF THE WEST

Morton Smith: ANCIENT GREECE

A. H. M. Jones: A HISTORY OF ROME THROUGH THE FIFTH CENTURY
Vol. I: The Republic
Vol. II: The Empire

Deno Geanakopolos: BYZANTINE EMPIRE

Marshall W. Baldwin: CHRISTIANITY THROUGH THE CRUSADES

Bernard Lewis: ISLAM THROUGH SULEIMAN THE MAGNIFICENT

David Herlihy: HISTORY OF FEUDALISM

William M. Bowsky: RISE OF COMMERCE AND TOWNS

David Herlihy: MEDIEVAL CULTURE AND SOCIETY

EARLY MODERN HISTORY

Hannah Gray: CULTURAL HISTORY OF THE RENAISSANCE

Florence Edler De Roover: MONEY, BANKING & COMMERCE, 13TH-16TH CENTURIES

V. J. Parry: THE OTTOMAN EMPIRE

Ralph E. Giesey: EVOLUTION OF THE DYNASTIC STATE

J. H. Parry: THE EUROPEAN RECONNAISSANCE

Hans J. Hillerbrand: THE PROTESTANT REFORMATION

John C. Olin: THE CATHOLIC COUNTER-REFORMATION

Orest Ranum: THE CENTURY OF LOUIS XIV

Thomas Hegarty: RUSSIAN HISTORY THROUGH PETER THE GREAT

Marie Boas-Hall: THE SCIENTIFIC REVOLUTION

Barry E. Supple: HISTORY OF MERCANTILISM

————: IMPERIALISM, WAR & DIPLOMACY,1550-1763

Herbert H. Rowen: THE LOW COUNTRIES

C. A. Macartney: THE EVOLUTION OF THE HABSBURG & HOHENZOLLERN DYNASTIES

Lester G. Crocker: THE ENLIGHTENMENT

Robert Forster: EIGHTEENTH CENTURY EUROPEAN SOCIETY

REVOLUTIONARY EUROPE, 1789-1848

Paul H. Beik: THE FRENCH REVOLUTION

David L. Dowd: NAPOLEONIC ERA, 1799-1815

René Albrecht-Carrié: THE CONCERT OF EUROPE

John B. Halsted: ROMANTICISM

R. Max Hartwell: THE INDUSTRIAL REVOLUTION

Mack Walker: METTERNICH'S EUROPE

Douglas Johnson: THE ASCENDANT BOURGEOISIE

John A. Hawgood: THE REVOLUTIONS OF 1848

NATIONALISM, LIBERALISM, AND SOCIALISM, 1850-1914

Eugene C. Black: VICTORIAN CULTURE AND SOCIETY

Eugene C. Black: BRITISH POLITICS IN THE NINETEENTH CENTURY

Denis Mack Smith: THE MAKING OF ITALY, 1796-1866

David Thomson: FRANCE: *Empire and Republic*

Theodore S. Hamerow: BISMARCK'S MITTELEUROPA

Eugene O. Golob: THE AGE OF LAISSEZ FAIRE

Roland N. Stromberg: REALISM, NATURALISM, AND SYMBOLISM: *Modes of Thought and Expression in Europe, 1848-1914*

Melvin Kranzberg: SCIENCE AND TECHNOLOGY

Jesse D. Clarkson: TSARIST RUSSIA: *Catherine the Great to Nicholas II*

Philip D. Curtin & John R. W. Smail: IMPERIALISM

M. Salvadori: SOCIALISM, MARXISM AND SOCIAL THEORY

THE TWENTIETH CENTURY

Jere C. King: THE FIRST WORLD WAR

S. Clough & T. & C. Moodie: TWENTIETH CENTURY EUROPEAN ECONOMIC HISTORY

W. Warren Wagar: SCIENCE, FAITH AND MAN

Paul A. Gagnon: INTERNATIONALISM AND DIPLOMACY BETWEEN THE WARS, 1919-1939

Henry Cord Meyer: WEIMAR & NAZI GERMANY

Michal Vyvyan: RUSSIA FROM LENIN TO KHRUSHCHEV

Charles F. Delzell: MEDITERRANEAN TOTALITARIANISM, 1919-1945

_____: THE SECOND WORLD WAR